SERIES PREFACE

The United Nations' designation of 1979 as the International Year of the Child marked the first global effort undertaken to heighten awareness of the special needs of children. Activities initiated during this special year were designed to promote purposive and collaborative actions for the benefit of children throughout the world. Michigan State University's celebration of the International Year of the Child was held from September 1979 through June 1980. A variety of activities focused attention on the multiplicity of factors affecting the welfare of today's children as well as the children of the future. Many people involved with the university were concerned that benefits to children continue beyond the official time allocated to the celebration. The series *Child Nurturance* is one response to this concern. The first five volumes of *Child Nurturance* reflect directly the activities held on the Michigan State University campus and consist of original contributions from guest speakers and invited contributors. Subsequent biennial volumes will present original contributions from individuals representing such fields as anthropology, biology, education, human ecology, psychology, philosophy, sociology, and medicine. We hope the material presented in these volumes will promote greater understanding of children and encourage interdisciplinary inquiry into the individual, family, societal and cultural variables which influence their welfare and development.

We would like to express both our thanks and our admiration for Margaret Burritt who not only typed the camera-ready copy for each of the volumes, but also served as general manager of the entire project. Although her contribution to the production of these volumes will not be noted in any chapter headings or indexes, each page reflects her devotion, care, and hard work. We also thank Mary Ann Reinhart for her careful and scholarly preparation of the subject index. Finally, we thank the editors and authors for their cooperation and for their concern for children and their families.

Marjorie J. Kostelnik
Hiram E. Fitzgerald
East Lansing, MI

CHILD NURTURANCE

VOLUME 2
Patterns of
Supplementary Parenting

Edited by

Marjorie J. Kostelnik,
Albert I. Rabin,
Lillian A. Phenice, and
Anne K. Soderman

Michigan State University
East Lansing, Michigan

PLENUM PRESS • NEW YORK AND LONDON

Library of Congress Cataloging in Publication Data

Main entry under title:

Patterns of supplementary parenting.

  (Child nurturance; v. 2)
  Includes bibliographies and indexes.
  Contents: Child nurturance/A. K. Soderman...(et al.)—Parenting by related adults/V. Campbell and M. Bubolz—The contribution of siblings and peers to the parenting process/W. Furman and D. Buhrmester—(etc.).
  1. Child rearing—Addresses, essays, lectures. 2. Parenting—Addresses, essays, lectures. 3. Children—Institutional care—Addresses, essays, lectures. I. Kostelnik, Marjorie J. II. series.
HQ769.P445 1982   362.7   82-16530
ISBN 0-306-41175-X

CONTENTS

Child Nurturance: Patterns of Supplementary Parenting 3
A. K. Soderman, M. J. Kostelnik, B. D. Ames, and L. A. Phenice

Parenting by Related Adults 33
V. Campbell and M. Bubolz

The Contribution of Siblings and Peers to the Parenting Process . . . 69
W. Furman and D. Buhrmester

The Day Care Movement: Past, Present, and Future 101
D. L. Peters and J. Belsky

The Effectiveness of Foster Care as Supplementary Parenting 131
L. F. Guerney

Residential Homes and Institutions 181
H. Grossbard

Child Nurturance in Other Cultures: A Perspective 207
E. E. Werner

Families and Child Care: A Global Ecosystem Perspective 239
V. Hildebrand

Supplementary Parenting in the Kibbutz Childrearing System 265
A. I. Rabin

Parenting: Alternatives and Continuities 287
L. J. Kaplan

Author Index 305

Subject Index 315

PATTERNS OF SUPPLEMENTARY PARENTING

CHILD NURTURANCE: PATTERNS OF SUPPLEMENTARY PARENTING

Anne K. Soderman, Marjorie J. Kostelnik,
Barbara D. Ames, and Lillian A. Phenice

Department of Family and Child Ecology
Michigan State University
East Lansing, MI 48824

INTRODUCTION

Without consistent, long-term care, the human infant would not survive. In Western cultures, the family unit has traditionally been seen as the most advantageous and viable social context for meeting the biophysical and psychosocial needs of a young child. As a result, theorists and researchers have long been interested in the range of variability and consistency that may be found in both particular and universal family settings and the ultimate effect these characteristics have on human development. Moreover, there is growing interest, as well as growing concern, that there may be certain aspects of childrearing that are unique to, and dependent upon, the family as we have come to know it. Today, these are being more urgently examined in light of the rather dramatic social changes being experienced by families and other social institutions. It may be that resulting adaptations have mandated an increasing prominence in the supplementary parenting patterns described in the bulk of this volume.

In this chapter, we shall look at the social institution long considered the primary context for childrearing--the family. Considered will be the problem of its definition, its legitimately dynamic attributes as a living social system, and some of the more intimate tasks performed by family systems. We also shall examine briefly several of the outstanding social changes important to the family if it is to continue as a primary social context for the rearing of children in this society.

3

WHAT IS A FAMILY?

The "Family" is an evolving and adapting institution that, historically and universally, has provided a system of norms and a standard solution to the problems of collective life in societies (Martindale, 1962; Goldberg and Deutsch, 1977). The importance of the family as a solution to social problems and a control element in the social structure in getting individual members to contribute to the collective welfare of society has been observed throughout the history of the human race as may be seen in the earliest moral and ethical writings (Goode, 1971).

Efforts to define the family have become increasingly problematic among those who have a strong professional interest in families from an historical, anthropological, service, or policy-making perspective. The term family has been used to describe a multitude of groupings, some of which include: (1) father, mother, children, (2) people living together in the same house, (3) any group of people related by blood, marriage, or adoption, (4) a tribe, (5) one's ancestors, (6) two or more persons who share resources, responsibilities for decisions, values and goals, and have a commitment to one another over time (Adams, 1975; Blood, 1972; Winch, 1968).

Many consider the nuclear family, consisting of a married couple and their dependent children, as the dominant family form in our culture, but it is not the only form, nor is it universal in all societies. Birdwhistell (1974) suggests that this view of *the* family has been idealized by the press, over-valued by both moralists and social scientists, and, in reality, is considered by some to be a relatively recent development. Moreover, there is considerable evidence that this idealized form of the family may be represented today by only a small percentage of all families in the United States. Variations of this form abound; furthermore, there is considerable variation within these structures. Appropriately, Skolnick (1981) maintains that defining the family goes beyond being merely an academic exercise. Instead, these definitions frequently determine which kinds of families "will be considered normal and which deviant" (p. 43).

Allen (1979) provides the following critical summary of present-day conceptions of the family:

1. Legal definition--A group consisting of married heterosexuals and their legitimate children.

    Criticism: Definition is conservative, even regressive and has little ability to enlighten us about the present or future.

2. Structural definition--That utilized by the U.S. Census where family is defined as two or more persons residing together who are related by blood, marriage, or adoption.

> Criticism: Does not account for actual experiences of large groups of American society, nor capture the true essence of family life. Model often generates biased measurement, analysis, and legislation, and subjects those who do not conform to sanctions and penalties.

3. Normative or moral definition--Sees the nuclear family as an ideal model; assumes the moral rightness of biological links, legal recognition, and patriarchal hierarchy within the family.

> Criticism: Model reflects a lag between ideal and actual lifestyles; labels non-conforming family units as dysfunctional, aberrant, or unhealthy.

4. Social-psychological definition--Emphasizes interactions between persons who live in the same residence and/or have significant and frequent contact.

> Criticism: Is not descriptive enough to develop needed policy.

5. Functional definition--Focuses on fundamental functions played by the family for society or the individual, i.e., reproduction, physical protection, nurturance, socialization, control of sexual expression, and economic cooperation.

> Criticism: Requires comprehensive social policy, which is difficult to implement in reality.

> (In Paolucci and Bubolz, 1980, p. 16.)

Allen (1979) concludes that it is the "necessity to cooperate through the family for survival and mutual benefit that appears to offer the best connection between individuals and their families and individuals in their society" (p. 35), i.e., survival through production and consumption. She offers a "new definition": family is defined as "a group of people who are bound by their common work efforts, from which their common consumption derives" (p. 35).

Paolucci and Bubolz (1980) suggest that enlargement and increased specification of such a definition be considered:

> Such a conception can take all forms of family life into account, would make the "head of the household" concept passe, would recognize unpaid work in the home, and would emphasize families' connections with the rest of society. Policies deriving from such a model could be more emancipative, less limited and controlling (p. 16).

Our inability to perceive the family as dynamic in the face of advancing technology and change has spawned growing attacks on nontraditional family forms. While we have watched a society being transformed before our very eyes during the past century, and have looked on technological advances as progress, the corresponding adaptive changes that have occurred in the structure of the American family have been looked on as rather frightening.

Friedman (1981) suggests that the most valuable "umbrella" under which the various theoretical perspectives of the family may be considered is that of a systems approach. It is under that rubric that one may study how the family unit, no matter how it is defined, relates to and interacts with both larger and smaller units. Providing a brief discussion of the family as a system may dispel some of the anxiety about the plurality in current family forms and the continued diversification that is certain to occur in the decades ahead.

THE FAMILY AS A SYSTEM

In speaking of the family as a system, we must keep in mind that the family, as considered in this chapter, constitutes a *human* system. Human systems, as opposed to purely inorganic systems, are uniquely individual and subject to differing interpretations of stimuli and varying patterns of implementation. However, there also are certain characteristics of families that are cybernetic in nature and extremely useful in understanding family behavior when it is viewed holistically from a systems perspective. Kantor and Lehr (1975) describe four characteristics indicative of the family system and useful in looking inside that system. These characteristics include organizational complexity, adaptation, information-processing, and openness. We will review each briefly.

Organizational Complexity

The term, organizational complexity, implies that the family consists of subsystems and elements that continually interact among themselves and with the larger suprasystem. The family system may be described as embedded within the larger suprasystem and consisting of two or more subsystems, any one of which may be considered a system within itself.

Examples of subsystems commonly identified within the nuclear family include the spouse subsystem, parent-child subsystem, and sibling subsystems; examples of extended family subsystems include such combinations as grandparent-child or uncle-nephew (Friedman, 1981). These subsystems contribute to family structure, and it is through them and the process of their interaction with one another that the system strives to fulfill its functions. Each family member belongs to different subsystems simultaneously. Moreover, each family member interacts to a greater or lesser degree with *particular* components of the suprasystem that may be relatively unfamiliar to other members of the family. Therefore, any one person at any one time is functioning within multiple roles in which s/he exercises varying degrees of power (Friedman, 1981) or has available differentiated resources (Newman and Newman, 1978). For example, an adult male simultaneously may be a husband, father, son, nephew, worker and/or community member. His interaction within the family system is affected by his unique access to particular resources determined by his interface with the suprasystem, i.e., work, education, social status in the community, and bonds with extended family members.

This interaction among family members is reciprocal, rather than linear in nature (Kantor and Lehr, 1975). Broderick and Smith (1979) note:

> Family scholars tend to concentrate mostly on causal models that are linear, recursive, and without too many interaction effects or contingency variables. But life is nonlinear, nonrecursive, and full of interaction effects and contingencies (p. 126).

This reciprocity has been the focus of many recent investigations looking at the nature of the parent-child relationship, particularly during infancy (Bowlby, 1958; Ainsworth, 1973). Most recently, Hartup (1978) has documented renewed interest in the mutual regulation that occurs between parents and children as opposed to social mold theories of the past which have indicated unidirectional interaction. As a case in point, Lamb (1978) describes a theory of child abuse founded on the notion of parent-child reciprocity by examining the relationship between temperamental characteristics of the child and parental role strain. He hypothesizes that children may contribute to their own abuse. For instance, a difficult baby as described by Thomas, Chess, and Birch (1970) may cry often and with little predictability. In time, crying may become an aversive stimulus, which elicits aggressive behavior from parents. This negative adult behavior can lead to more crying by the child and continued destructive behavior by adults. Conditions favoring abuse may be compounded by factors such as lack of parenting skills, an unwanted pregnancy, or unexpected stress.

Reciprocity is characteristic not only of interactions within the system but of those which occur between the family system and the environmental suprasystem. Changes in economic, political, bio-medical, and social systems impact in a complex manner upon family systems and enhance or impede their ability to meet their goals. The result may be a strengthening of the family system or a weakening to such an extent that increased dependence on the suprasystem is necessitated.

Certainly the present inflationary and economic situation, coupled with high unemployment, reflect the extreme importance of the economic system to families. A great deal of economic behavior happens within the context of families, and there is a strong positive correlation between socio-economic status and various facets of family behavior, such as marital stability and instability. Economic status also can affect basic development and nurturance. For example, siblings in very poor families often are expected to take on parenting roles before they are developmentally ready.

Similar to economics, the political system has an all-encompassing impact on families. This impact may be overt, such as day-care or welfare policies, or it may be covert, such as defense appropriations which take funding from other programs. Clearly, it is very difficult to identify whether a policy is pro-family or anti-family because many policies have elements of both, and family systems are extremely diverse. Likewise, changes in the bio-medical or social systems present both opportunities and difficult dilemmas for families. For example, the recent bio-medical advances in reproduction have created opportunities for parenthood where formerly it was not possible, but they also have created some very serious ethical dilemmas for families.

As previously stated, interdependence implies reciprocity; therefore, a discussion of the impact of the suprasystem upon the family system must include recognition that the family system in turn impacts upon the suprasystem. For example, dual-worker families have exerted pressure upon the formulators of public policy and have become an impetus for change within the marketing system. Families also may impact on the larger systems in more subtle but equally profound ways, such as teaching children that people of a certain race are inferior or that government officials are to be mistrusted.

The extreme complexity of the larger system also greatly affects the family system in that the proliferation of goods, services and technologies available to families are often vast and confusing. In an earlier era, most families educated their children, provided medical care, served as vocational models, produced the necessary food, clothing, and shelter, and imparted basic religious or values training. In contrast, Keniston (1978) speaks of today's parent as serving in an "executive" role, or taking on a very complex managerial function in regard to choosing communities, schools, medical care, consumer goods and other programs in order to leave their children in the best possible hands.

Paolucci, Hall, and Axin (1977) have theorized that this intimate interaction between the family and the suprasystem should be looked on from a family *ecology* perspective; this view:

> ...allows one to better understand problems and arrive at solutions because it forces one to look at each part of the ecosystem and the relationships among them. Thus, families can learn to be efficient stewards, not just manipulators of their environments, understanding that a reverence for life is dependent upon a concomitant reverence for its conditions (p. 25).

Adaptation

The extreme interdependence of the suprasystem and the family system just described obviously calls for a combination of all forces working synergistically. When this happens, the result is often disequilibrium, necessitating adaptation. A second supposition projected by Kantor and Lehr (1975) is that family systems are adaptive, reacting to their internal as well as external environments. Families adhering to this notion would behave very differently from families who interpret their function as maintaining established or familiar patterns of interaction. For example, families whose male breadwinners have lost their jobs may react in two significantly different ways. Those who interpret adaptation as a legitimate function of the family may encourage a female bread-winner or make radical changes in spending patterns; those who interpret maintenance of the status quo as a primary function of the family would be left with fewer options. Differing interpretations of the function of the family would seriously affect the overall functioning of the system.

Adaptation in one part of the system that may be aimed at restoring equilibrium may, in turn, cause disequilibrium in other parts of the system or in the larger system. For example, an employed mother may receive input from her own mother that, because of her employment, she is harming the satisfactory development of her three-year-old child. In processing that information from the extended family, several outputs are possible. The woman may feel guilty enough to quit her job, thereby having more time to spend with her child but fewer economic resources to contribute to the family coffers. On the other hand, she may see an alternative, such as inviting a relative to come and live in her home in order to provide nurturance to her child in a familiar environment. This action, while relieving some job-related stress, may increase the strain on the spouse subsystem, as new ways of interacting with a relative present in the family must be learned. Clearly, there are infinite variations or adaptations, depending upon input, integration of the information, and resources and the resulting behavior, or output.

Whatever decision is made, it will have an obvious impact on the relationships between the subsystems and the system as a whole. One of the most prevailing trends in American society is the participation of women in the work force. This trend at least partially resulted from a combination of input from the economic system (i.e., greater opportunities for women). Women reacted by going to work, and this action resulted in such intrafamilial phenomena as the blurring of traditional male-female roles and the increased need for extrafamilial child care. Those who adhere to a very traditional family model may interpret this chain of events as a failure of the family system. Rather, it may indicate a healthy and normal adaptative attempt by the family system to maintain equilibrium. The nature of the adaptation will, of course, depend heavily upon the quality and quantity of information processed in the system.

Information Processing

Families must assimilate unrelenting volumes of information. In a discussion of the tremendous increase in information, Toffler (1980) contrasts the number of images or amount of information available to pre-industrial and industrial persons with the amount available to "Third Wave" or post-industrial persons. He notes that we must speed up image-processing and take action based on current information or become progressively less competent. The ability of family members to take in and assimilate new information will seriously affect the functioning of the family system, including their childrearing activity. When the autonomous nature of individuals within families, and families in general, is considered, it is easy to see how resulting behavior may be viewed differentially as negative or positive, depending upon the match in integration between components in the subsystem or between the subsystem and the larger system. For example, the working mother described in the previous section, based on her knowledge of child development and her knowledge about the suitability of a nearby day care center, may decide that no change is necessary in the current arrangement; however, the decision may continue to be viewed very negatively by her mother, who has none of the information her daughter has. If the working mother can share that information, and if the new pieces of information can then be assimilated positively into her mother's current value system about the care of children, both women may then view the outcome positively.

Coupled with factors inherent within the family system are the different external messages and perception of external messages received by family systems. Factors such as education and economic level influence the interpretation of these messages. For example, a family with very low socio-economic status may see as its primary function the feeding and clothing of a child rather than education, psychological development, or other more abstract functions. A more global example of this phenomenon surfaced at a recent international conference(1) during which delegates from affluent nations debated the finer points of social and psychological development of children while delegates from less affluent countries insisted their priority was simply in keeping their children alive. Conversely, a relatively affluent parent may interpret the nurturing function as exposing a child to music and other fine arts while ignoring good nutrition or basic love and affection.

This constant flow of informational input and output between subsystems and the larger system takes place because of permeable boundaries in these systems. These boundaries serve a gatekeeping function for the family, screening and interpreting the information flow.

Openness

The attribute of openness indicates that the family receives input (in the form of material, energy, and information) from the environment, transforms it in some way, and then returns output to the suprasystems. Interchange between the system, subsystems, and suprasystem is the "*essential* factor underlying the system's viability, its continuity, and its ability to change" (Buckley, 1967, p. 50).

In an effort to be more precise, family theorists recently have redefined the family as a semi-open system that has permeable boundaries that open and close selectively, thus regulating input received and output transmitted (Goldberg and Deutsch, 1977; Friedman, 1981; Paolucci, Hall, and Axin, 1977). Numerous authors have discussed the problems that may exist when boundaries are either too rigid or too open. Rigidity results in deprivation to the system in terms of necessary information and support (Kantor and Lehr, 1975). Keniston (1978), for example, speaks of the myth of the self-sufficient family. This myth has its roots in the American ideal of independence and rugged individualism and implies that families are autonomous units, relatively free from outside pressures. According to the myth, to depend on others is a certain sign of weakness and dysfunction in the family system. This myth has many carry-overs and implications for today's families. Family members who adhere to this myth may unnecessarily restrict themselves from services designed to help families adapt to an ever-changing environment. Their boundaries are neither permeable nor flexible. For example, child abuse may occur in a family because a parent feels it is his/her duty to care for the child twenty-four hours a day rather than to seek respite care. Compounding the effect of the myth is the likelihood that policy-makers and other persons who work with families may expect them to be self-sufficient or closed systems.

Located at the opposite end of the continuum is the family system that is open to the point of total disorganization or entropy. A system which is incapable of defining its boundaries may be infringed upon by other systems. For example, government may intervene in families which are so loosely defined that they do not provide basic care for their children. Optimal conditions exist when a family has clear, yet permeable and flexible boundaries. In this case, a family is aware of its functions, takes action to perform them, but is free to seek outside support to provide adaptability and maintain equilibrium.

Families decide the degree to which they will open or close their boundaries based on the nature of the feedback they receive from the environment. Feedback involves the process by which the system provides information to subsystems about how to relate to one another and to the suprasystem in order to enhance achievement of desired system functions (Kantor and Lehr, 1975). Buckley (1967) identifies two specific types of feedback: positive, or deviation amplifying feedback, and negative feedback, which is deviation counteracting. More simply stated, positive feedback involves the family system receiving input, which then stimulates change in family behavior to more closely match standards accepted by the family. Negative feedback occurs when families resist changing their behavior in response to input. This response is aimed toward maintaining sameness or the status quo of the system.

A healthy balance in responding to internal and external input is necessary if the family system is able to grow, mature, and develop over time. Viewed in this light, change in the family is seen as normal and desirable. Friedman (1981) suggests that a continual exchange of inputs and outputs across family boundaries is desirable. However, the family's ability to mediate effectively depends upon its ability to recognize the effect a particular stressor is having on the overall unit, that is, the unit's ability to enact simultaneously its other functions. Inability or unwillingness by the family unit to recognize anxiety-inducing stress or to employ available stategies for reduction of that stress may lead to disorganization of the unit, e.g., spouse or child abuse, marital disruption, mental or physiological illness, unhealthy member alliances, or dysfunction and increased dependence on the suprasystem.

It has been suggested that families who adjust to stressors do so by employing one of three strategies: 1) using defense mechanisms to avoid the stressor; 2) using coping tactics in attempting to solve or reduce the problem; 3) mastery or resolution of the stressful event (Friedman, 1981). According to Friedman (1981), adaptation may be either negative or positive, resulting in the increase or decrease of a family's state of wellness (homeostasis). If, in the family's attempt to adjust to change or restore homeostasis to the unit, it develops a long-range dependency upon external support systems and does not develop intrafamilial strategies for mastering the problem, the adaptation would be considered negative. Stressor events that cannot be effectively reduced by adaptative strategies result, then, in what may be termed family crises. It is difficult to predict which stressors may become crises for any particular family unit in that disorganization or dysfunction results not from the stressful event itself but from a family's ineffectiveness in coping with the event.

To this point, we have considered the nature, structure, and operable characteristics of "the family" as a socially dynamic unit that is organizationally complex, adaptive, responsible for mediating a constant flow of information, and open. As a highly viable system, it also is capable and tolerant of internal change, flexible, and internally determinant (Friedman, 1981).

Since the problems of society are bound to alter with changes occurring within that society, the functions of a structure devised as a primary problem-solving unit must necessarily undergo change. When viewed from a systems perspective, and considering advances in industrialization and technology, recent changes in the American family's structure or function should not seem threatening, but a natural and legitimate evolution. It may be beneficial for critics of current modes of family functioning who focus their solutions solely on a revitalization or restructuring of the family unit to consider the complexity of the larger picture. While a systems approach is not intended to serve as an excuse for inadequate family functioning, it does remind us that families do not exist within a vacuum. Instead, they are embedded within a larger system whose calmness or turbulance is always reflected in the functioning of the subsystem.

Bronfenbrenner (1979) hypothesizes that the changes that affect family functioning and to which families must continually adjust are more often based on unseen forces than on deliberated choice. It is (perhaps) the family's rebalancing act when it is thrown out of sync by the larger system or by changes in its own growth and development that causes continual distress among its critics. More realistically, this movement toward homeostasis is comforting proof that the family remains a viable, living system. It remains partially open to the environment, sometimes at the expense of the environment (or the family), expanding materially, psychologically, or functionally in order to become more efficient in dealing with that environment.

The interrelated characteristics of family systems elaborated upon here interact both internally (within the family) and externally (with the environment) to effect the fulfillment of family and societal needs. It has been noted that family systems are ultimately evaluated by how well families function to meet the goals viewed as necessary to their members and society, or, in other words, by their *output*. In the next section, we shall look more selectively at several functions particularly relevant to childbearing, i.e., those of procreation, nurturance, socialization, and mediation between the child and extra-familial systems.

FAMILY FUNCTIONS RELATED TO CHILDREARING

It is generally assumed that one of the primary reasons for the existence of the family, no matter what its structure, is the fulfillment of certain functions that promote survival of the human species. When functional theory is applied to the real world where families work everyday to maintain themselves, it becomes clear that the functions that will be described are neither mutually exclusive nor easy to prioritize as to their importance. Most germane to our task of looking at the family as a context for child nurturance would be at least a cursory look at such general functions as procreation, nurturance, socialization and child care, and mediation (both inside the family and in the family's interaction with the suprasystem).

Procreation

Undoubtedly, the most basic of all family functions is the bearing of children for the continuance of society. Related to this particular function, many questions are currently surfacing about the regulation of reproduction and sexual behavior (both inside and outside of the family), population control, family planning, and increasingly popular decisions to delay childrearing or remain childless altogether. Bane and Masnick (1980), in a study of fertility attitudes among three generations, report:

> About 20 percent of the women in the younger generation expect to have only one child or none at all. The speed with which the generation is moving toward small families indicates that 40 percent or more of (the) women born in the 1950's may end up childless or with only one child. This figure compares with 20 percent or less for the high fertility mothers of the middle generation; and 43 percent for women born 1906-1910 who represent the older generation's low fertility....Every indication is that women born in the late 50's will surpass the oldest generation in delaying motherhood. Such a delay in childbearing is bound to have a considerable and continuing impact on the living arrangements, labor force experiences, and life style of the younger generation (p. 40).

Martinson (1970) noted that, overall, the population of the United States has been increasing at a decreasing rate with a decline in the birth rate since the peak of 4,308,000 births in 1957. Though contraceptive methods were introduced in the 1930's, they have received widespread acceptance only the last 10 or 15 years. Though there has been growing concern and hard evidence that the birth rate has remained high in low-income populations and low in upper- and middle-income families, Martinson (1970) reports that recent studies of working-class families find they want as few, or fewer, children than higher-status families. However,

> ....the wish is not the deed, and, in 1962, 34 percent of the families with five children and 44 percent of those with six children had incomes below four thousand dollars. By comparison, 22 percent of the families with three children were in the same income bracket.

> The 1950 GAP (Growth of American Families) report indicated that one out of five couples with children have excess fertility--excess fertility being defined as the last child being unwanted by either husband or wife. The problem of unwanted prognosis is most severe in the low income and low education groups. Some of them have more children because they do not use contraceptives regularly and effectively. If the wife has a grade-school education and if the husband has an income of less than three thousand dollars a year, 39 percent have excess fertility as judged by their own opinions (p. 135).

Tien (1974) hypothesizes that particular characteristics of family systems impact predictably on fertility as follows:

> 1. The more closed the family is as a boundary-maintaining system in a society, the higher the fertility (p. 334).

This is due, according to Tien, because of increasingly divergent *types* of families, increased transductive behavior with the suprasystem, and "the erosion of the insularity of the family as a boundary-maintaining system rather than urbanization" (p. 334).

> 2. The less distinct the stages of the family life cycle in a society, the higher the fertility...suffice it to say that fertility is likely to be high in a society where the life stream flows on evenly, and that fertility is likely to be low in a society where life unfolds like a kaleidoscope with varied patterns at every turn.

> 3. The lower the diversity in role clusters of adult family members in a society, the higher the fertility (pp. 335-337).

This latter point is relevant in that there is increasing role diversity among both men and women in this society because of the dramatic shift of women from the home to the marketplace. Tien (1974) suggests that American families may be characterized by components that are presumed determinants, then, of low fertility: "low insularity from external agencies, marked discontinuities in role patterns over time, and diversified role components of specific positions" (p. 337).

Procreation and the resulting transition to parenthood and subsequent increased complexity within the family structure requires considerable adjustment within the family system and may be problematic because parenthood is not always voluntary, is relatively irrevocable, and is often carried out with little or no preparation (Rossi, 1977). It is a common and mistaken notion that one function performed in a family will automatically lead to another (e.g., procreation to affective functioning) or that the level of performance or interest in one will be present in the other.

Nurturance

Research data on family nurturance have indicated that it is highly correlated with children's moral development, prosocial behavior, and ultimate sense of independence (Smart and Smart, 1977). Children's language development and problem-solving skills also are affected by the nurturant behavior of family members (Newman and Newman, 1978). Moreover, there is considerable evidence to indicate that the manner and degree in which families nurture their children have lasting repercussions throughout adolescence and adulthood.

Nurturance, according to Ainsworth (1973) and Bowlby (1958), may be defined as a function of love, or attachment. Both postulate that there is a reciprocal relationship between caregiver and child that progresses through a normative sequence of stages until a positive emotional tie is formed. Parents and others demonstrate nurturant behavior when they express affection and interest in children by providing food, clothing, shelter, stimulation, comfort and help (Smart and Smart, 1977). Certain behavior in infants, such as sucking, grasping, cuddling, vocalizing, and rooting, as well as such behaviors in young children as crawling, snuggling, sucking, and touching, evoke care-giving responses from others (Lamb, 1976). Thus, emotional bonds are developed and maintained (Bowlby, 1958).

The extreme variation in environments in which infants find them- selves has been examined by Segal and Yahares (1979).

> A newborn may be plunged into a household warmed by an abiding love between parents, or torn from the beginning by strife and hate; burdened by the mental illness of mother or father--or both--or blessedly free of the grinding strains that anxiety, depression, and paranoia bring; without competition from other children, or already filled with siblings who have long since begun to leave their mark on the household; supported by an extended family available to help meet the child's needs, or isolated and bereft of outside human contact.
>
> It is in this complex system of constantly interacting family members that the child is embedded. The quality of that system leaves its mark--for better or worse-- from the very beginning (p. 135).

Friedman (1981) suggests that affective maintenance, or the family's perception and care of the socioemotional needs of all its members, is primarily a parental role. It is in the family that children experience their first attachment to other human beings. Erikson (1950) has labeled this as a basic sense of trust and deems it critical in the future health and well being of children. There is strong evidence to indicate that this supposition is true (Klaus and Kennel, 1976; Bowlby, 1958). Fraiberg (1977) also underscores the importance of the first three years of life as laying the cornerstone for an individual's later mental health. While few families are completely free of illness, trouble, or crisis during the early unfolding of a child's development, serious, long- standing disruption in the family's affective functioning may be very costly to the developing individual.

Selma Fraiberg (1977) concludes from available data on children who have been unable to form a human bond in the first two years of their life that the degree of impairment is roughly equivalent to the degree of deprivation.   According to Fraiberg, children who suffer more severe ruptures in the formation of human bonds in the first two years of life may manifest permanent impairment in their capacity to make human attachments in later childhood, even when substitute families are provided for them.   She further suggests that deprivation during this particularily vulnerable period may result also in impairment in intellectual functioning (specifically conceptual thinking) and in disorders of impulse control, especially in the areas of aggression.

Other researchers, however, and primarily Schaeffer and Emerson (1964), Kotelchuck (1976), and Wortis (1977) have challenged the primacy of the mother-infant bond, suggesting that there is no evidence to assume that primary attachments must be confined to the mother or even the child's father. Schaeffer and Emerson (1964) conclude:

> Whom an infant chooses as his attachment object and how many objects he selects depends, we believe, primarily on the nature of the social setting in which he is reared and not on some intrinsic characteristic of the attachment function itself (p. 71).

These findings need to be looked at further and examined closely in light of their implications for the number of American mothers who have young infants and children and find labor force participation necessary for a variety of economic or psychological reasons.   Recent demographic figures on employed mothers suggest that the fastest growing groups of women entering the labor force are those with children under six years of age.

While the family, then, is not the only unit that *can* function to provide a setting for attachment and affectional development in the young child, it is more often than not, the center for the development of affective human expression, providing the child with knowledge about loving and caring (Frankena, 1970; Rice, 1977). As a result, children learn to value themselves and other human beings. It is through this confirmation of their own self-worth and that of others that their humanness is established (Watzawick, 1967).

Continuous attention by the family unit to the affective needs of its members is perhaps the most critical factor in predicting how well the overall unit will function. The growing importance of the nurturing function within the family, and particularly among American middle- and upper-class families, recently has been given much attention. It is in these more affluent populations that affective functioning has swollen to include additional family member responsibility for increased sexual satisfaction, quality leisure-time activity, and meaningful companionship.

Conversely, in families experiencing undue strain in providing for their basic necessities, nurturance may be reduced to the point where breakdown of a unit may be imminent. This may be seen most clearly in families who are forced to shift great portions of their psychic and physical energy toward simply providing for the biological maintenance of their members. The ability of a family to acquire sufficient resources and allocate them effectively within the family correlates highly with how well and how autonomously it can then carry out its other functions and has particular relevance for the family's ability to nurture.

Moreover, as can be seen, family functions are both numerous and varied. Therefore, while child nurturance as a family function is of primary importance to both family members *and* society, it is not the only function the family must perform; nor is it ever performed in isolation. When individual families are evaluated on their ability to carry out adequately the functions most critical to child nurturance (or when families are collectively assessed), performance must always be seen in light of: 1) the configuration of particular family units, 2) the total responsibilities being met by those units, 3) the human and non-human resources available to any particular family unit, and 4) the virtual and *virtuous* efficiency with which the family utilizes those resources in carrying out its functions.

CHILD CARE AND SOCIALIZATION

A closely related task of the family system is that of child care and socialization. Gecas (1976) maintains that the socialization of children remains the "irreducible element of the structure known as a family" and, indeed, that child care and socialization "may be considered the definitive elements of the family" (p. 33). He separates the overlapping functions of child care and socialization, noting that while a good deal of socialization is dependent upon the child being physically cared for, i.e., the provision of such physical necessities as food, clothing, shelter, and protection against danger, socialization refers to the development of the child's social and psychological capacities. Family members provide guidance and emotional support to children as they learn how to adapt their behavior to adult expectations. This is accomplished when cues are provided to children about which behaviors to maintain and which to avoid (Kostelnik, 1978). While this is not an exclusive role of the family and is often shared with other social institutions, it is within the home that the process first begins. As a result of this training, children develop their first set of values, beliefs, and attitudes toward others (Leichter, 1975).

It seems obvious by the strength of sanctions on non-performance that there remains a high value on basic care of family members and particularly that of young children. Nye (1976) reports that child care was considered as important as the socialization function by an overwhelming majority of parents he studied and that, among those lower on the socioeconomic scale, *more* important than socialization. Both aspects of the function are carried out primarily by parents in the family system, and there appear to be wide social variation in how parents fulfill this function.

Kohn (1969) has proposed that a compelling link exists between parent occupation and education, resulting social class, and the socialization strategies within families. He concludes that children of blue-collar parents are socialized with respect to consequences of their behavior; white-collar families are more geared in their socialization strategies (goals) toward interpretation of intent or motive for behavior. Thus, generally, an internal locus-of-control more frequently results for children of the middle class.

Moreover, there are concerns related to the care of children who are born into families who find themselves experiencing alternatives to more traditional family living styles. Do the increasing arrangements of non-resident or surrogate parents and more fluid household changes enhance or detract from, or make little difference at all in a child's ultimate socialization? Clarke-Stewart (1979) seems to take the stance that the outcomes of these alternatives are not significant and that we have been too critical of parental variations in fulfilling this function. She charges that we have had, to date, rather constrained, limited, and middle-class views of the origins of well-socialized individuals:

> Since we know that many different people emerge from vastly different child-care environments, all apparently equally prepared for adult life, we suspect there is more than one route to competence, and possibly more than one expression of competence in childhood (p. 124-125).

Kagan (1977) asserts that any one set of socialization expectations for all children in all cultures would be inappropriate and that, in order to rear well-socialized children, it is necessary to know the specific demands that will be made by the particular community as the child grows to adulthood. He presumes that American child's psychological growth and ultimate socialization are positively promoted when:

1. The child believes he is valued by significant others in his environment.

2. The child builds a sense of worth or personal competence (usually through the sculpting of a particular talent or talents--for example, in an academic subject).

3. The child develops autonomy, i.e., the ability and desire to make independent decisions with regard to his own conduct and future.

4. The child must develop appropriate sexual identity and sex role behaviors (pp. 403-404).

It is important to note the child's role in the socialization process, and this may be understood by again looking at the above: The child believes...the child builds...the child develops....; in other words, socializational is not something that is done *to* a child or *for* him, despite the traditional view that it is a one-way process. Appropriately, Skolnik (1981) recently has challenged the viewpoint that parental behavior is cause and child behavior effect. She supports her stand by noting the many models of socialization coming out of cognitive psychology that view as important, the child's temperament as well as his other inherent tendencies to explore, adapt to, and modify his own environment. Thus, a child is seen to have a rather strong influence in the shaping of his own ultimate physical and social reality. When one views the family in a systems sense, it becomes apparent also that the socialization process is not something that happens only in childhood to children. It is an ongoing process within every family system that is affected greatly by a multitude of environmental variables in the systems surrounding the family. Again, the dynamic qualities of family member interaction would suggest a continual two-way socialization between parents and children, resulting in constant modification of the other's socialization.

Lerner and Spanier (1978), noting the embeddedness of the family in the social system and the family's primary charge to transform "social maintenance and perpetuation of goals into directives for the new individual" also acknowledge the common disregard for reciprocal dependency of familial change on intra-individual ontogeny as well as causal reciprocities between individuals, their families, and history. As more and more exchanges are made between family members and the environment, a backlog of both negative and positive experiences is developed for family members to draw upon as a guide for future activity. In this process of mediation and exchange, which will be examined in more detail in the following section, the family experiences some modification and, in turn, modifies the environment in which it functions. Seen in this light, the family may be viewed as a primary socializing and stabilizing force for the larger society.

Mediation

Williams and Leaman (1973) and Sussman (1971) describe the importance of the family role in terms of mediation with the environment. The degree of skill with which the family performs this role is directly correlated to the social success of family members. The way in which individuals experience maximum social rewards and minimize social costs is to take action which leads to compromise without undue loss of prestige, integrity, or control by family members. This mediation, therefore, is a process involving the ability to achieve one's own goals while adapting successfully to the goals of others. The more bureaucratic the society, the more crucial is this mediating process. It is Sussman's (1971) hypothesis that when mediation is poorly done, the family will be forced to rely more heavily on the suprasystem. Because other systems have their own goals, which may or may not meld well with any family's particular needs, the family unit that becomes increasingly dependent on the larger system may or may not find the support it needs.

Bell and Vogel (1968) elaborate on the mediation function by describing trade-offs that may occur between families and the institutions in the surrounding environment (Rice, 1977). Families who conform to the expectations of society are rewarded by that society by receiving approval. Families who do not conform, however, accrue costs, which may be delivered by the formal system, e.g., children being placed in foster homes.

The family's ability to mediate effectively depends upon its ability to recognize the effect a particular stressor is having on the overall unit, that is, the unit's ability to enact simultaneously its other functions. Inability or unwillingness by the family unit to recognize anxiety-inducing stress or to employ available strategies for reduction of that stress may lead to disorganization of the unit, e.g., spouse or child abuse, marital disruption, mental or physiological illness, unhealthy member alliances, or dysfunction and increased dependence on the suprasystem.

When we look at family mediation with respect to childrearing, we can see that it is a particularly important activity when there are young children in the family who do not, themselves, have mediation skills (Bagarozzi, 1977). As children develop, they move from their sheltered position at the heart of the family to one of greater interface with extra-familial systems. In our society, this often takes place as children have their first preprimary experience outside the home (for example, day care, nursery school, head start, and so forth). At this point, children have direct access to information which they must interpret and to which they must respond (Bagarozzi, 1977). They must begin to function somewhat more autonomously with the suprasystem. While the family maintains considerable direct control over the information flow during this period and continues to serve as a mediator between the child and the extra-familial systems, its role expands to help children learn how to select and interpret information they receive from others.

As children move into and through adolescence, family control decreases, the influence of the suprasystem increases (Bagarozzi, 1977) and the adolescent is expected to become more expert in his own mediation efforts. In our society, we recognize this movement from total dependency on caregivers toward autonomous selection of inputs as normal. However, problems may arise when families or family critics interpret the child's movement from the center of the family toward greater interface with the suprasystem as taking place too rapidly or inappropriately.

Wilbert E. Moore (1974) concludes that agencies that substitute for the family will never *replace* the family as the main source of child-bearing and childrearing:

> Since the family may be regarded as the primordial social
> structure in the social evolution of the human species, the
> fact that it is the first group for almost every member of
> the species means that each generation in a sense re-
> capitulates that evolution (p. 3).

The usefulness of well-functioning families in the maintenance of society
is at once obvious. No other institution can do so well, or would be willing
to do, what the family has done so long. Despite its changing structure
and dynamic characteristics, the family continues to function to meet the
needs of its members and those of the larger society.

IMPACT OF SOCIAL CHANGE ON THE FAMILY

In the past few decades, American families have been required to
make significant adaptations in the face of social change. Many of these
changes have occurred with absolutely no historic precedents that would
serve as guidelines in the critical decisions families have had to make
about present day and future living. Only recently have we begun to
gather the kind of data that helps us understand what effects these
changes are having on individual and family functioning. Also, highly
problematic in this recent evolution is our fervent clinging to a rather
idealistic concept of what the family *was* and should continue to be, the
speed at which social change is occurring, and the tremendous growth of
individualism within and outside the family unit. All subsystems within
the family unit are affected in unique ways by these events; moreover,
the major intrafamily activity of childrearing has been significantly
affected.

The Myth and Reality of Social Change

The interpretation we hold about what a system used to be greatly
influences our expectations about the current status of that system. The
apparent upheaval in current family life has led some to yearn for the
"good old days." Nostalgic views of the family suggest a past golden age
when family ties were closer, relationships were more stable, and family
life was less complex. The extended family thought to be in close
proximity, always ready to lend a helping hand or "pull together in a
crisis." Role allocation in the family was clear cut: fathers were breadwinners; mothers were present to provide nurturance and protection from
the outside world; children were obedient, respectful, and responsible.
Overall, the family was seen to be self-sustaining, independent, and
contributing significantly to the positive moral fiber of society.

However, historians find that our romantic picture of the family
may not be entirely accurate. For example, there is evidence to indicate
that the extended family never really existed on a widespread scale (Bane,
1976). Keniston (1977) writes that most Americans always have lived in
homes consisting of parents and children. Even in colonial times, it was a

common practice for children to marry and move far away from their families of origin. It was not unusual for children and parents never to see one another or communicate rarely once the move had been made. Thus, present-day mobility, often cited as a new destructive force, has, in fact, been a fairly common phenomenon over the past two hundred years. Neither was it possible to compensate for mobility through the technological advances of telephone, airplane, highways, and reliable mail service, as it is today.

There also is evidence to suggest that the voice of concern about families has been raised periodically through time. For example, Lasch (1977) notes that, at the end of the 19th century, Americans were becoming alarmed at the rising divorce rate and the declining birth rate among so-called "better," more affluent people. The changing position of women and the perceived revolution in individual moral behavior also were factors seen as leading to the disintegration of the family as it was then known. These same concerns continue to echo today and were cited earlier in this chapter. The growing numbers of children living in single parent homes is notable today; however, a closer look at earlier periods in American society reminds us that similar numbers of children also grew up in one-parent families due to high rates of parental death or desertion.

Another memory of the family included the mother as ever-present in the home. In time, this became an ideal toward which families strived and which reached its height in the 1950's. According to Keniston (1978), a woman at home "was a sign of the father's success and also a protection for her children from sin and temptation." However:

> Only a privileged few upper middle-class American families could afford the insulation of women and children that the myth decreed. Most families lived a very different life (p. 11).

A mother pictured at the hearth may, in reality, have been in the factory, the field, or in someone else's home scrubbing and cleaning in order to contribute to the economic well-being of her own family. Bane (1976) also notes that there is no evidence that yesterday's mothers, laboring from dawn to dusk in the home, devoted more time to their children than do today's employed mothers.

Speed at which Social Change is Occurring

Toffler (1980), in his comprehensive look at the changes that have occurred recently in the nation and elsewhere, shocks his reader by emphasizing the velocity with which these changes are currently taking place. The first, well-documented historical period, (i.e., the Agricultural "wave") took thousands of years to play itself out, lasting from approximately 8000 B.C. to 1700 A.D. Notably, the second wave, or industrialization, predominated for only 300 years and, though not completely diminished, is now being replaced by another major period. Toffler predicts that this third, current major social (r)evolution will be complete in only a few decades, causing critical and fast-moving changes in the technosphere, sociosphere, info-sphere, and powersphere. For example, we have witnessed at least a 30 percent increase in the divorce rate in the past three decades (with the most rapid increase occurring in those couples married 15 or more years), a 30 percent increase in employed mothers with children under five in the past two decades, considerable decrease in the fertility rate, and equally considerable changes in the average population age from 19 in 1969 to 40 in 1990. It has been stated that as much new information will be developed in the next ten years as has already been developed to this point in history.

The speed of change today is important primarily because it leaves wide and serious gaps between family member's behavioral repertories and their recognition that they *must* react now to the changes that are occurring in their lives, particularly if stress that is induced because of the change is to be alleviated. Though a family's initial reaction is sometimes frozen because of confusion, it dare not remain in that state long. On the other hand, alienation and frustration commonly accompany both the inability to act and the critical push to change. A case in point would be the push toward androgynous behavior in our society. Increasingly, women are demanding that men fill the void in the family created by the wife-mother's labor-force participation; though studies have reported a noted change in at least the middle-class male's attitudes and cooperative *spirit* in helping with child care and housework, his behavior continues to reflect pre-change patterns (Walker, 1976). It is difficult to know what effect these rapidly changing prototypes will have on the socialization patterns of children, particularly with respect to sex-role orientation, ability to make serious commitments over time, their ability to delay gratification, and their sense of history.

The Growth of Individualism

There can be little doubt that, as a society, we have been immersed in the heady growth of individualism in the past several decades that is markedly different from the popular and positive American "ideal of rugged individualism" engineered by Herbert Hoover. The theory that individual freedom is *as* important as the welfare of a community has possibly been superceded in the last several decades by the theory that it may be *more* important, at least for as long as it takes to realize some of the goals of the less powerful in our society. What we have witnessed are unprecedented movements by minorities, women, and other subgroups and individuals in our population to equalize their positions with respect to power. Phrases such as 'self-fulfillment', 'meaningful existence', 'meaningful relationship', and 'self-understanding' have become social by-words. The results of these attempts toward parity have been manifested in heated debates and the choosing of sides: one view is the perception that equality seekers are perhaps pathological in purpose, always looking out for number one, and part of the 'me' cult; the other perspective is that these changes in human interaction, however painful, are necessary if individuals and groups of individuals are to be successful in gaining what they consider a respectable identity and control of their own destinies.

Hitchcock (1981) has been critical of this latter group, charging that the "frank selfishness" of so many modern people is, in part, due to the sustained material prosperity we have for the past 30 years:

> People who have for a long time taken for granted that most of their material wants will be satisfied finally come to assume that their psychological wants will be similarly gratified...much of this narcissism is advertised under the rubric of growth. People are said to be growing when they are kicking over the traces, rejecting all limits, repudiating their responsibilities, violating conventions. Only a moment's thought is required to realize that this is not a formula for growth but for its opposite (p. 14).

He applies his theory of the pathology of secular liberalism to the women's liberation movement, the breakdown of contemporary marriages, adolescent rejection of parents, and parental rejection of children. According to Hitchcock (1981), these are due to such "soft reasons" as incompatibility, boredom, 'failure to grow', 'drifting apart', and 'lack of fulfillment', rather than the oft-cited "harder" sources of desertion, violence, non-support, or alcoholism.

Particularly with regard to the breakdown of contemporary marriage, Toffler (1980) would disagree:

> As millions of men and women climb out of the strewn wreckage of their marriages they, too, suffer agonies of self-blame. And once more, much of the guilt is misplaced.

> When a tiny minority is involved, the crack-up of their families may reflect individual failures. But when divorce, separation, and other forms of familial disasters overtake millions at once in many countries, it is absurd to think the causes are purely personal (p. 224).

Thus, it is difficult to figure out how much an impact individualism has had on the larger society or whether, in fact, the growth of individualism is a defensive reaction to changes in the macroenvironment.

McWhirter (1981), in a recent newspaper column looking at the numbers of taxpayers who are turning their backs on support of public schools, suggests that what we have been talking about here might, in fact, be depersonalized alienation. She maintains that, growing non-support for schools, may be due to community non-involvement in the schools, coupled with burgeoning inflation-recession. The picture grows more complex:

> ...school enrollments are declining; more and more people are living together without the commitment of marriage, and without children. They move around a lot. Why should they support the schools their non-existent children won't attend or their future children probably won't attend? No reason.
>
> It also means that fewer and fewer persons beyond childbearing years have connection with schools. When 25-year-olds, married or not, eschew procreation, the parents of the 25-year-olds do not become grandparents. The same theoretical interest in schools may persist, but the personal stake is missing. And the elderly who may who may have seen two generations of their own complete the school process may, rightly or wrongly, decide that their involvement in school concerns is long past.
>
> Beyond all this, we are members of the fabled nuclear family, which means that some kids go to five or six or more schools before they graduate from high school. There is little feeling of belonging. There is almost none of the old school spirit. Two sets of grandparents live in separate towns, and their kids and grandkids live all over the free world. In what schools should anyone of any age take a personal propriety, abiding interest? None. (McWhirter, 1981, p. B-1).

As can be seen, individualism always extends beyond the individual. The result of individualism often becomes widespread isolationalism of families and family members. Kreinin (1981), in describing the need for added touchpoints for human interchange, notes such indications as:

> increased reports of child abuse, battered wives, parents who can't 'talk' to their children, children who can't 'talk' to parents, (all in need of a counselor or intermediary), increased incidents of runaway children, runaway wives, abandoned wives, juvenile suicide, widespread depression, and emphasis on a type of actualization that supersedes a sense of responsibility for someone else. All of these say that some nurturing force is absent or scarce (p. 41).

Moreover, she cites Scitovsky's (1974) study of actual, observed differences between Americans and Europeans in their interactions with others:

> The average time Americans spend alone while awake (6.6
> hours a day) exceeds by 2.5 hours or more than 50 percent
> of the western European's time (4.1 hours a day) so spent,
> and our tendency to keep to ourselves seems to cut across
> more of our activities... People in other countries stay put
> in retirement because they want to be near friends and
> relatives; we move. The implication is that our human
> contacts are either not too numerous or not very strong or
> not very precious (p. 195).

Bronfenbrenner (1981), in his discussion of the effects of socio-political and technological developments and increased social stratification, sees as the end result the further erosion of the power of the family and the childrearing system as well as the transfer of childrearing functions to other institutions. He predicts this will happen unless we come to terms with:

> ...some hard realities--and increased support for the
> family systems such as tax incentives for flextime and
> other family oriented employment policies, developmental
> day care, strong linkages between home and school, and
> closer ties between families both at the kinship and the
> neighborhood level (p. 41).

Toffler and Toffler (1981) have noted that it seems reasonable that we cannot experience these major revolutions in the fields of energy, technology, work, economics, and communication without expecting a revolution in family life as well. It cannot be predicted whether the pace families are experiencing, or the diversification to which they everyday muster their most adaptive capabilities will slacken. We can be sure, however, that tomorrow's family will never be the family we knew yesterday, even given our faulty memories. Only when we look candidly at this changing phenomenon can we begin to understand what shape it may eventually take and the kinds of morally responsible behavior that will be required, both inside and outside the family system, to meet the needs of that new society. Our overreactive protectiveness toward the state of the family--our concern that it may become less than the vital force it has always been--underscores its continual critical importance, at least for today.

CONCLUSION

In a discussion of social change and family renewal, William J. Goode (1973) emphasizes that the family is related to all other institutions, and what we really need to know to accurately predict the future of families is how the larger social structure will be altered. In essence, Goode is reflecting on the family as a system within a suprasystem. The preceding chapter discussed the nature of family, family functions, and the impact of societal change on families. Perhaps recapitulating these three segments in an inverse manner will provide insight and closure.

Major social changes will necessarily alter the functions of families which, in turn, will modify the nature of family itself. For example, Toffler (1980) illustrates how industrialization separated the functions of production and consumption, thereby changing the nature of those family functions as well as separating the functions by rigidly defined sex roles. Examples of this hierarchal change which begins in the larger society or suprasystem, alters family functions, and eventually changes the nature of family itself. This phenomenon is critical to recognize because many of the arguments concerning the health or viability of the family center around change or loss of family function.

The preceding chapter has identified nurturance as a major family function. Previous discussion indicated that parents and others demonstrate nurturant behavior when they express an interest in children by providing food, clothing, shelter, comfort, stimulation, and help (Smart and Smart, 1977). Although the family is the primary context for nurturance, it is significant that the preceding statement recognizes that nurturing behavior may be demonstrated by parents *and others*. The remainder of this volume discusses those other potential nurturers. Does this imply that the family is less effective as a nurturer or that it is losing a critical function? The authors do not believe this to be the case. Non-family forms of nurturing are a complex reflection of conditions and changes in the suprasystem which impact upon families and their functions.

We have to assume that someone must care for children. In a discussion of the United Nations' Declaration of Rights of the Child, O'Neill and Ruddick (1979) point to the lack of specificity regarding who shall care for children. They state, "'*Mankind*', after all, is ill equipped to bathe a particular baby or to teach a particular group of children to read" (p. 111). As a result of the tremendous pressures placed on families by change in the suprasystem, nurturance within families is not always the optimal solution. It is in these cases that families, acting as adaptive systems, change their function from primary provider of nurturing behavior to procurer of some supplemental nurturance for their children. Although the family function has changed somewhat, the systems work together synergistically to provide optimum childcare. The suprasystem alters the function of families which, in turn, modifies the nature of families. The nature and viability of this continually adapting family can be evaluated only after lengthy retrospective study of human beings--the products of the nurturing process.

REFERENCES

Adams, B. W. *The family: A sociological interpretation.* New York: Rand McNally, 1975.

Ainsworth, M. D. S. The development of infant-mother interaction. In B. Caldwell and H. Ricutti (Eds.), *Review of child development research*, Vol. 3. Chicago: University of Chicago Press, 1973.

Allen, C. M. Defining the family for post-industrial public-policy. In *The family in post-industrial America*. Colorado: Westwind Press, 1979.

Bagarozzi, D. A. Family mediation between the larger culture and children. In S. R. Goldburg and F. Deutsch (Eds.), *Life span individual and family development*. Monterey, CA: Brooks/Cole Publishing Company, 1977.

Bane, M. J. *Here to stay: American families in the 20th century*. New York: Basic Books, 1976.

Bane, M. J., and Masnick, G. *The nation's families: 1960-1990*. Boston: Auburn House Publishing, 1980.

Bell, N. W., and Vogel, E. F. (Eds.) *A modern introduction to the family* (Revised Ed.). New York: The Free Press, 1968.

Birdwhistell, R. L. The idealized model of the American family. In M. B. Sussman (Ed.), *Sourcebook in marriage and the family*. Boston: Houghton Mifflin Company, 1974.

Blood, R. O. *The family*. New York: Free Press, 1972.

Bowlby, J. The nature of the child's ties to his mother. *International Journal of Psychoanalysis*, 1958, *39*, 350-373.

Broderick, C., and Smith, J. The general systems approach to the family. In W. R. Burr, R. Hill, F. I. Nye, and I. L. Reiss (Eds.), *Contemporary theories about the family*, Vol. II. New York: Free Press, 1979.

Bronfenbrenner, U. *The ecology of human development*. Cambridge, MA: Harvard University Press, 1979.

Bronfenbrenner, U. Children and families: 1984? *Society*, 1981, January/February, 38-41.

Buckley, W. *Sociology and modern systems theory*. Englewood Cliffs, NJ: Prentice-Hall, 1967.

Clarke-Stewart, A. *Child care in the family: A review of resources and some propositions for policy*. New York: Academic Press, 1979.

Erikson, E. *Childhood and society*. New York: Norton, 1950.

Fraiberg, S. *Every child's birthright*. Toronto: Bantam Books, 1977.

Frankena, W. Toward a philosophy of the family. Paper presented at the Clara Brown Symposium on Family Values, School of Home Economics, University of Minnesota, Minneapolis, MN, March, 1970, pp. 10-14.

Freidman, M. M. *Family nursing*. New York: Appleton-Century-Crofts, 1981.

Gecas, V. This socialization and child care roles. In F. I. Nye (Ed.), *Role structure and analysis of the family*. Beverly Hills, CA: Sage Publishing, 1976.

Goldberg, S. R., and Deutsch, F. *Life-span individual and family development*. Monterey, CA: Brooks/Cole Publishing Company, 1977.

Goode, W. J. Social and family renewal. *Families of the future*. Ames, IA: Iowa State University Press, 1973.

Hartup, W. W. Perspectives on child and family interaction: Past, present, and future. In R. L. Lerner and G. B. Spanier (Eds.), *Child influences on marital and family interaction*. New York: Academic Press, 1978.

Hitchcock, J. In defense of the traditional family. *New Oxford Review,* September, 1981, p. 14.

Kagan, J. The psychological requirements for human development. In A. S. Skolnick and J. H. Skolnick (Eds.), *Family in transition.* Boston: Little, Brown and Company, 1977.

Kantor, D., and Lehr, W. *Inside the family.* New York: Harper and Row, 1975.

Keniston, K. *All our children.* New York: Harcourt-Brace-Jovanovich, 1978.

Klaus, M. H., and Kennel, J. H. *Maternal-infant bonding.* St. Louis: Mosby, 1976.

Kohn, M. *Class and conformity.* Homewood, IL: The Dorsey Press, 1969.

Kostelnik, M. *Evaluation of communication and group management skills training program for child development personnel.* Doctoral Dissertation, The Pennsylvania State University, 1978.

Kotelchuck, M. The infant's relationship to the father: Experimental evidence. In M. E. Lamb (Ed.), *The role of the father in child development.* New York: Wiley, 1976.

Kreinen, M. M. Touchpoints for human interchange. *Journal of Home Economics,* 1981, 73(2), 40-42.

Lamb, M. E. (Ed.) *The role of the father in child development.* New York: Wiley, 1976.

Lamb, M. E. Influence of the child on marital quality and family interaction during the prenatal, perinatal, and infancy periods. In R. I. Lerner and G. B. Spanier (Eds.), *Child influences on marital and family interaction.* New York: Academic Press, 1978.

Lasch, C. *Haven in a heartless world.* New York: Basic Books, 1977.

Leichter, H. J. *The family as educator.* New York: Teachers College Press, 1975.

Lerner, R. I., and Spanier, G. B. (Eds.) *Child influences on marital and family interaction.* New York: Academic Press, 1978.

Martindale, C. *Social life and cultural change.* Princeton: Van Nostran, 1962.

Martinson, F. M. *Family in society.* New York: Dodd, Mead, and Company, 1970.

McWhirter, N. Reading between the lines as schools are written off. *Detroit Free Press,* 1981, October 23, B-1.

Moore, W. E. The family. In M. B. Sussman (Ed.), *Sourcebook in marriage and the family.* Boston: Houghton Mifflin Company, 1974.

Newman, D. M., and Newman, P. R. *Infancy and childhood.* New York: John Wiley and Sons, 1978.

Nye, F. I. *Role structure and analysis of the family.* Beverly Hills, CA: Sage Publications, 1976.

O'Neill, O., and Ruddick, W. *Having children.* New York: Oxford University Press, 1979.

Paolucci, B., and Bubolz, M. Toward a critical theory of the family: Analysis and synthesis of three perspectives, with suggestions for a critical theory of quality of family life. Paper presented at Research and Theory Workshop, National Council on Family Relations Annual Meeting, Portland, OR, October 21, 1980.

Paolucci, B., Hall, O. A., and Axinn, N. *Family decision making: An ecosystem approach.* New York: John Wiley and Sons, 1977.

Rice, R. *American family policy.* New York: Family Service Association of America, 1977.

Rossi, A. S. Transition to parenthood. In A. S. Skolnick and J. H. Skolnick (Eds.), *Family in transition.* Boston: Little, Brown and Company, 1977.

Schaffer, H. R., and Emerson, P. E. The development of social attachments in infancy. *Monographs of the Society for Research in Child Development,* 1964, *29,* (3 serial No. 94).

Scitovsky, T. *The joyless economy.* New York: Oxford University Press, 1976.

Segal, J., and Yahares, H. *A child's journey: Forces that shape the lives of our young.* New York: McGraw Hill, 1979.

Skolnick, A. The family and its discontents. *Society,* 1981, *18*(2), 42-47.

Smart, R. C., and Smart, M. S. *Children: Development and relationships.* New York: Macmillan, 1977.

Sussman, M. B. Family systems in the 1970's: Analysis, policies, and programs. *The Annals of the American Academy of Political and Social Science,* July, 1971.

Thomas, A., Chess, S., and Birch, H. The origin of personality. *Scientific American,* 1970, *223,* 102-109.

Tien, H. Y. Cooperative analysis of fertility change in developmental perspective. In M. B. Sussman (Ed.), *Sourcebook of marriage and the family.* Boston: Houghton Mifflin Company, 1974.

Toffler, A. *The third wave.* New York: Bantam Books, 1980.

Toffler, A., and Toffler, H. The changing American family. *Family Weekly,* 1981, March 22, 8-13.

Walker, K. E. *Time use: A measure of household production of family goods and services.* Washington, D.C.: Center for the Family of the American Home Economics Association, 1976.

Watzlawick, P., Beavin, J., and Jackson, D. *Pragmatics of human communication.* New York: Norton, 1967.

White, B. L. Critical influences in the origin of competence. *Merrill-Palmer Quarterly,* 1975, *21,* 243-266.

Williams, J., and Leaman, T. Family structure and function. In H. Conn and R. Rakel (Eds.), *Family practice.* Philadelphia: Saunders, 1973.

Winch, R. F. *Selected studies in marriage and the family.* New York: Holt, Rinehart, and Winston, 1968.

Wortis, R. P. The acceptance of the concept of the maternal role by behavioral scientists: Its effects on women. In A. S. Skolnick and J. H. Skolnick (Eds.), *Family in transition.* Boston: Little, Brown and Company, 1977.

FOOTNOTES

(1) International Consortium in Human Rights and Development, Tokyo, Japan, March, 1980.

PARENTING BY RELATED ADULTS

Vivian Campbell and Margaret Bubolz

Department of Family and Child Ecology
Michigan State University
East Lansing, MI 48824

INTRODUCTION

The extended family household consisting of many people of all ages and at least three generations living together in a large rural home, depicted in such popular television programs of the 1970's and 80's as *The Waltons* represents what Goode (1971) has labeled "the classical family of western nostalgia." This myth, and it is that, symbolizes for many people something of the past that was good and that we have lost. With alleged loss of the extended household and kin network, families are said to be isolated, lacking a sense of their own history, and without the supportive help of grandmothers, aunts and uncles for child care, housework and family emergencies. Children are said to lack contact with older persons, to have few role models for their own future, to have negative views about older persons, and to be deprived of valuable learning experiences that come from close relationships with a loved grandparent from whom they can gain a sense of continuity and of what life was like in past days.

New historical studies of the American family have revealed the extended family household as the dominant form of family structure in the past to be an idealized folk image. Families of parents and their own children have been the most common family form since colonial days; households of older persons and married children and grandchildren were not the norm, both because of personal preferences for independent households and because of shorter life expectancies (Gordon, 1978). As in the past, the most common residential form of the American family today is the nuclear family. Estimates of the proportion of families that are extended families range from that of Troll, Miller and Atchley (1979) who report that less than eight percent of American households are three generation households to that of Winch (1977) who estimates that only two

33

percent of American families are extended families. Just four percent of persons residing in families are non-nuclear kin, that is relatives other than the family head, spouse of head and their children (Winch, 1977). About 18 percent of persons over 65 live with one of their children, a decline from 36 percent in 1957 (Shanas, 1979).

However, the prevalence of the nuclear household does not mitigate against extensive kin contact.   In spite of mobility and urbanization, factors often advanced as contributing to the decline of the extended family as a structural and social unit, the majority of American families live near some relatives, have frequent contact, and exchange services and resources across generations.   For example, Gibson (1972) found in a study of older persons that only one-fourth did not have any kin living in the same community.   Over half of all older persons live either with a child or within ten minutes from at least one child, and three-fourths live either with a child or within a half hour's distance from a child (Shanas, 1979).   Distance from kin has been found to be one of the most important factors influencing amount of kin contact (Klatzky, 1972).   Many studies of the past two decades have documented that contact between kin is extensive (Hill, Foote, Aldous and MacDonald, 1970; Adams, 1970; Lee, 1980).   In a 1975 national study, half of all old people with children said they had seen one of their children the day they were interviewed or the day before, and three-fourths of them had seen one child during the week they were interviewed (Shanas, 1979).   In addition to contact, help and services across the generations are continuing features of American family life.   For instance, in 1975 seven of every ten older persons said they gave help to their children; the same proportion gave help to grandchildren; and 50% gave help to great-grandchildren (Shanas, 1980).

Thus, while the myths of the extended family of the past and the isolated nuclear family of today have some elements of truth, we can conclude that kinship continues to be an important component of American social life and that relatives are still significant elements of family structure and interaction.   What can we say, however, about the role and involvement of related persons, other than parents and siblings, in the parenting and nurturance of children?   Do they play a significant role?   If so, are there effects on child personality and behavior?   What is the role of particular relatives, that is, grandparents?   Are there variations among ethnic and racial groups in parenting by related adults?   Do contemporary changes in the family influence parenting by relatives?

The overall purpose of this chapter is an attempt to provide some answers to these questions through an examination of relevant literature of the past several years.   The chapter is not developed from the standpoint of a single discipline; the stance is primarily sociological, but not exclusively so.   Major sources utilized represented a range of disciplines and fields including child development, gerontology, psychology, anthropology, sociology, home economics/human ecology, and interdisciplinary studies.   The theoretical perspective which will be mainly employed is that of role theory, utilizing both a structural-functional and interactional stance. From a structural-functional perspective, various expectations are associated with the positions in a system of social relations. These expectations define the roles for the positions. Carrying out the role expectations fulfills functions for the system. The position of parent, for example, has societal expectations, governed by social norms, which are necessary for child nurturance and socialization. From an interactionist perspective, roles have meanings for the persons occupying the various positions. These meanings arise both from socialization for the role which one has learned through interaction and from forces within the individual which meet personal needs. Analytically, the two concepts, position and role, can be differentiated, but in everyday usage the two are often used interchangeably and, in this chapter, the concept of role will be used to refer to both position and role.

The role of parenting will be used to include behaviors and activities carried out in behalf of or in relation to children by persons related to them by blood, marriage, or adoption who do not occupy the position of biological or social parent or sibling. Parenting behaviors and activities are defined very broadly to include child care and nurturance; socialization; child rearing; and meeting social-emotional as well as economic and material needs of children. These behaviors and activities are included in commonly held social expectations for the parent role. Obviously, such an inclusive definition is problematic and implies that any and all ways in which related adults play a part in the parenting role shall be included. Given the nature of the literature in the area and the state of conceptualization and research, this broad conceptualization seems warranted at this time.

The chapter is divided into four main parts, followed by a brief statement of conclusions. Grandparenthood will be dealt with first and most extensively because it is this role with which parenting expectations are most often associated, and because more is known about grandparents than any other relatives. Other involvement in parenting by related adults, parenting and child care by relatives in selected minority groups, and the consequences of contemporary family changes on parenting by related adults comprise the other sections.

THE ROLE OF GRANDPARENTS

About three-fourths of all Americans age 65 and over have living grandchildren, and 40 percent have living great-grandchildren (Harris and Associates, 1975). Earlier marriage, earlier childbirth and longer life expectancy of the past few decades have resulted in grandparenthood becoming also a middle-age phenomenon. Contact between grandparents and grandchildren is frequent, nearly one-half of grandparents reported seeing a grandchild within the last day or so, and another 28 percent within the last week or two (Harris and Associates, 1975). Clearly, the position of grandparent is ubiquitous, and, based on frequency of occurrence and contact, the probability of parenting by grandparents might be a rather common occurrence. Indeed, by virtue of its name, grandparenthood implies that there is some expectation that the role should include aspects of or an extension of the parenting role. But, in fact, is this the case? What are expectations for the grandparenting role? To what extent are these carried out? Has the role of grandparents in American families changed in the past few decades? In what ways?

This section will be devoted to a review of the literature of the last several decades(1) related to roles and behaviors of grandparents, meanings of grandparenthood, and the nature of grandparent-grandchild interactions. Taking this brief, historical perspective helps to give some insight into how the role has changed and some sense of the direction and state of knowledge in the field.

Grandparenthood in the Past

In the 19th century and in the early part of this century, when America was primarily an agricultural nation with large numbers of the population immigrants and second generation Americans, grandparents played a more instrumental function in family life. While the generations did not live together in common households as frequently as our folk myths would have us believe, economic interdependence through ownership of farms, property and family businesses linked the generations more closely. In addition, strong religious and ethnic ties and a greater acceptance of the authority of older persons contributed to grandparents playing a more central function in the lives of their grown children and grandchildren.

Consistent with our proclivity to build idealized images of family life of past days have arisen conceptions of grandparents of earlier days. Grandmother is seen as a jolly, often plump, bespectacled old woman making cookies or teaching children to make them, indulging grandchildren, but also reprimanding them when necessary. Grandfather is envisioned as a source of wisdom and authority, with homely knowledge about making useful things, telling stories about the past history of the family to which children respectfully listened. Just as in myths, there are kernels of truth in our images, and many grandparents did do these things; they served as teachers and disciplinarians, as well as providing a sense of continuity of the family line. Margaret Mead (1974) emphasized the importance of the presence or absence of grandparenthood in the ease with which immigrants to America related to those around them, and in how children were reared with a strong sense of place. The presence of grandparents nearby often delayed or cushioned the process of acculturation through their reliance on the "mother tongue" and other customs and rituals they brought with them. In the older, earlier settled regions of the United States, grandparents remained custodians of family style, especially among the upper classes where knowledge of lineage was important.   Among the poor, grandmothers provided child care for mothers who had to work in fields or factories. Mead (1974) asserts that the absence of grandparents among the upwardly and residentially mobile middle and working classes contributed to a shallowness of family life and a tendency to conform to outer forms of current residential locations. For some, grandparents became a source of embarrassment and, in efforts to become Americanized, learning language and customs of immigrant grandparents was not continued in succeeding generations.

Several interrelated social and economic changes resulted in the role of grandparents becoming less central in most American families in the 20th century.   The nation's population shifted from being primarily rural farm residents to urban dwellers engaged in industrial, white-collar and professional occupations.   Many functions previously carried on within the home such as home production of food, clothing and other necessities, religious training, education, and recreation were transferred to systems outside the family.   These changes resulted in fewer functional roles for older persons within the family. Increasing emphasis on the autonomy of the individual and on decision-making by the nuclear family contributed further to a diminished role for grandparents.

The 1930's and 1940's

The literature of the 30's and 40's is limited in quantity and perspective, with sources primarily writings of psychiatrists and psychoanalysts; thus, a rather negative picture of grandparental influence is presented.   Vollmer (1937) and Borden (1946) characterized problem grandparents as usurpers and dominators of the mother's role; Fox (1937) saw them as excessive users of parental time and interfering with parent-child relations.   Strauss (1943) saw grandparents as precipitators of antisocial behavior in adolescents because they carried excessive hostility which was transmitted to children.   Fried and Stern (1948) viewed grandparents as overindulgers of grandchildren. These less than benign or helpful depictions are probably due to the fact that the data come from case materials on families and individuals with problems and pathologies. The cases may also represent families who were in historical time transitions in which the earlier more valued role of older persons and grandparents was shifting, becoming what has been called a "roleless" role.   Interfering grandparents may have been struggling to retain a position of authority and self-esteem.

Later in this period, and in succeeding decades, the literature in the field comes more often from studies conducted by sociologists, developmental psychologists, home economists and anthropologists. While most of the studies used small localized samples, they do begin to provide a somewhat more complete picture of the role of grandparents in the lives of grandchildren.

In the mid-40's, von Hentig (1946) suggested that grandparents, especially the grandmother, can replace the position of a missing member and assume a sociological function in the family. This was frequently seen during the immediate post World War II period when divorce, desertion, housing shortages, and unemployment were not uncommon. Grandmothers came to the rescue of younger generations and assumed a vital role of providing parent support and surrogate parenting in the survival of the family. They were crucial figures in the stability and mental health of other family members.

The 1950's

The question of parental roles and responsibilities of grandparents began to be addressed more fully in this decade. A representative sample of 100 persons over 65 years old in a midwestern community, of whom 90 percent were grandparents and 30 percent great-grandparents, was studied in the late 1940's by Albrecht (1954). Only five percent of grandparents and none of the great-grandparents in the study regularly took care of children while parents worked. An additional 25 percent took on child caring jobs occasionally, with grandmothers more frequently than grandfathers carrying out this role. Those who did care for children expressed a feeling of pride and satisfaction, but the majority agreed that it was not a role they wanted to do continuously or take over completely from parents. Role expectations of grandparents toward grandchildren were explored and offer a valuable bit of evidence of the expectations emerging in the mid-20th century, against which we may examine current roles of grandparents. Albrecht concluded that parents were expected to take care of their own children, and grandparents and great-grandparents were supposed to let them do this without interference except in cases of illness or other crises when they were expected to help if they could. The extent of help depended on the youth, health, strength and resources of the elderly person. Direct aid or full responsibility for grandchildren was expected only if absolutely necessary, for example, if children were orphaned. A "hands off" policy prevailed and, while love, pride, and interest were expected on the part of grandparents, responsibility and authority were not desired.

An anthropological study by Apple (1956) on the social structure of grandparenthood revealed the significance of the social norms in governing the nature of the relationships between grandparents and grandchildren. Evidence came from ethnological reports on 75 societies, 54 of which were in the Yale Human Relations Area Files. Analysis supported the hypothesis that informality and more friendly equality and closeness in relationships between grandparents and grandchildren were associated with lack of family authority by grandparents. When grandparents continued to exercise parental authority over their children, grandchildren were more submissive, respectful and not on easy and friendly terms with their grandparents.

The 1960's

A study by Neugarten and Weinstein (1964) of changes in American grandparenthood resulted in development of a typology of grandparent roles which has been widely used and adapted in subsequent research and theory regarding the parenting role of grandparents. Data came from 70 grandmother-grandfather pairs in middle class families in metropolitan Chicago; ages ranged from the early 50's to the late 60's. A majority of grandparents expressed only satisfaction and pleasure with their role, but approximately one-third made open reference to their discomfort, disappointment, or lack of positive reward from the role. The most common source of significance and meaning for the role came from seeing it as a means of biological renewal, continuity, and emotional fulfillment that parenthood had not given them. Through inductive analysis, five major role-types of grandparenting emerged:

1. Formal Grandparents. This was the most common type (31% of grandmothers and 33% of grandfathers); the majority were older, over 65. These grandparents maintained some reserve and followed what they felt to be the proper role. They enjoyed treating grandchildren but were careful not to offer advice or serve as surrogate parents. They occasionally served as baby sitters but maintained clear roles between parenting and grandparenting.

2. Fun Seekers. About 30 percent of grandmothers and one-fourth of grandfathers were in this group; they were generally younger. Informality and playfulness characterized their relationships with grandchildren. Major emphasis was on a companionable relationship and mutuality of satisfaction, with authority not important. Grandchildren were viewed as a source of enjoyment or self-indulgence.

3. Surrogate Parents. This type occurred only for grandmothers in the sample (14%) and usually was assumed only after young parents requested help when mothers were working.

4. Reservoir of Family Wisdom. Only grandfathers were found to fit this style and then only rarely (6%). It was characterized by clear maintenance of authority and subordination. Sometimes, but not in all cases, the grandfather's advice was resented.

5. Distant Figures. This type characterized about 20 percent of grandmothers and 30 percent of grandfathers; they were more likely to be younger. These grandparents were not involved in the daily lives of grandchildren; contact tended to be only on special occasions such as holidays and birthdays. These grandparents enjoyed providing gifts, but remained distant and remote.

Neugarten and Weinstein (1964) suggested that the Fun Seekers and Distant Figures, who represented one-half of all the cases, were new grandparent roles which were then emerging. They reflected secular changes in values, expectations and socialization, the younger ages at which grandparenthood was occurring, and more independent and healthy lives of older persons. Traditional roles of grandparents as authority figures, caregivers or sources of wisdom were becoming less common.

Updegraff (1968) reported on perceptions of their grandmothers' roles by three age groups: 69 seventh grade girls, 54 mothers, and 17 maternal grandmothers. Each person was asked to recall her relationship with her maternal grandmother. In all three generations, grandmothers were not perceived as authority figures in the family nor as assisting in time of crisis to any extent. Casual visits and family occasions were the most common forms of interaction across generations. Major differences were in increased perceptions of leniency and indulgence by the succeeding generations of grandchildren, with over 90 percent of seventh graders perceiving their grandmothers as lenient, compared to 53 percent of their mothers and 28 percent of their grandmothers. Contemporary grandmothers were also perceived as giving significantly more child care than in previous generations, reflecting the rise in the phenomenon of the baby sitter with more mothers involved in work, recreation, and community activities outside the home. This change also reflected the greater availability of grandmothers to provide child care because of increased longevity and better health. The frequency of providing child care, however, was not overwhelming; only one-fourth of seventh graders perceived that grandmothers often provided child care. In terms of generational continuity, about one-half of the grandmothers were seen to provide some family history, with no differences between the generations. A limitation of this study lies in the problem of accurate recall of events and relationships which, in the case of the older generations, had taken place many years previously. However, the data do provide some evidence of continuity and change in perceptions of the grandparent role; findings of increased leniency support Neugarten's and Weinstein's findings of the emergence of the fund-seeking role and decline of the authority role among grandparents.

Crase and Hendrickson (1968) also report perceptions of grandmothers as lenient and responsive to their needs on the part of 141 preteen boys and girls. Maternal grandmothers were seen as more lenient than mothers, differing from research of the previous decade (Staples and Smith, 1954) which had found mothers more permissive than grandmothers in attitudes toward childrearing. These findings reflect generational changes in childrearing attitudes and behaviors by grandparents and give further support to Neugarten's and Weinstein's work.

The 1970's

A study by Hill et al. (1970) of family development in three adult generations in 312 metropolitan Minneapolis-St. Paul area families that were linked intergenerationally revealed extensive kin contacts and mutual help, supporting the continued existence of modified extended family networks rather than isolated nuclear families. The most frequent kind of help given was child care, with 78 percent of the married child generation receiving this kind of help. Fifty percent of their parents provided child care help; 16 percent of the grandparent generation also gave help with child care. Economic help was frequently given, with half of the youngest generation receiving economic aid from parents or grandparents. Forty-one percent of the parent generation gave economic help. Help with household management and in times of illness was reported less frequently. All of these instances of aid, while not evidence of an intensive parental role, are illustrations of help given to the younger generation in carrying out parental roles.

Kahana and Kahana (1970) studied perceptions of grandparents by children of three age groups: 4 to 5; 8 to 9; and 10 to 11. With the exception of the youngest group's perceptions of contact with paternal grandfathers, over 50 percent of the children reported seeing their grandparents every few weeks or more. Older children tended to report more frequent contact with all four grandparents than did the youngest group. More frequent contact was reported by all age groups with maternal rather than with paternal grandparents; the maternal grandmother was the most frequently favored by all grandchildren. These findings support other research which indicated greater involvement of women in intergenerational relations (Adams, 1970) and the contention that, in contemporary families, the grandparent role is essentially a grandmothering role. The youngest children viewed preferred grandparents almost exclusively in egocentric and concrete terms, that is, on the basis of what grandparents give in love, food, and presents. Responses of eight- to nine-year-olds focused mainly on mutuality and shared activities. The oldest group gave more general responses, related to characteristics such as "He is nice," and fewer responses indicating mutual activities. The interactions with favored grandparents overlap, somewhat, with the grandparents' styles described by Neugarten and Weinstein (1964). Indulgent grandparents who bring gifts may represent the formal type. Grandparents who join in activities are the fun-seeking type, while the statements by older grandchildren may represent contact with a distant type of grandparent.

In another study, the Kahanas (1971) report that many of the direct and vicarious satisfactions from grandparenthood reported by grandparents referred to relationships with young children. The Kahanas' studies point out the importance of seeing grandparenthood from the perspectives of both generations, and of taking into account developmental stages of grandchildren and grandparents in analyzing their relationships. Children's views of and relationships with grandparents may change as they grow older because of maturational differences and cognitive shifts from concrete operations and thinking to higher developmental and cognitive levels. Differences may also result from changing characteristics of grandparents as they age, changing equilibrium between needs of grandparent and grandchild, and from differential contact with grandparents.

Wood and Robertson (1978) and Robertson (1977) report on behaviors of grandmothers and the significance of grandmotherhood to an area sample of 125 grandmothers in Madison, Wisconsin, interviewed in 1970. About 38 percent were 70 and over; nine percent were in their 40's. The average age at which they became grandmothers was 46. Grandmotherhood was a role enjoyed by 80 percent of the group. Thirty-seven percent preferred grandparenting to parenting because it gave them joy and pleasure without the responsibilities of child rearing. Thirty-two percent preferred the parenting role, but 25 percent enjoyed both roles equally. Only three of 14 behaviors were engaged in with high frequency --baby sitting, home recreation and drop-in visits. These were initiated more frequently by parents and children than by grandparents, suggesting that parents affect and may control the frequency of role interaction between grandparents and grandchildren. Providing gifts and taking grandchildren shopping or to the zoo were done by a majority of all grandparents but only frequently by about 20 percent. Teaching such skills as sewing, helping with family emergencies or relating family history, often suggested as meaningful roles for grandparents, were done relatively infrequently. Giving advice was the least frequently reported activity, only five percent saying they did this frequently, and less than 30 percent saying they did this at all. The "hands off" policy reported by Albrecht (1954) two decades earlier was still very much in evidence.

The meaning of grandparenthood was examined by Wood and Robertson within the contexts of two independent but not mutually exclusive dimensions: A personal dimension and social dimension. The former stems from personal forces within the individual and meets his or her personal needs. The latter is determined by social and normative forces and meets expectations of society. Four role-types were identified based on high or low scores on each of the two dimensions. Persons scoring high on both dimensions were assigned to the *apportioned* type; those low on both to the *remote*; those high on personal but low on social to the *individualized* type and those low on personal and high on social to the *symbolic* type. Table 1 presents the number of cases which fell into each grandparent role type.

The *individualized* group (17%) placed heavy emphasis on personal satisfactions from grandparenthood, with little regard for normative expectations of the role. This was the oldest group, had the least education, was least involved with community and friends, and had high involvement in behaviors with grandchildren. In contrast, the *symbolic* group (26%) was more concerned with what was morally good or right for grandchildren and placed little emphasis on personal satisfaction from relations with grandchildren. This group was the youngest, had the highest educational level, was highly involved with friends, had high community involvement, and was second lowest in behaviors engaged in

TABLE 1

Grandparent Role Types
(Adapted from Robertson, 1977)

		Personal	
		High	Low
Social	High	Apportioned (36)	Symbolic (33)
	Low	Individualized (21)	Remote (35)

N = 125

with grandchildren. The *apportioned* group (29%) was as likely to be concerned with doing what was normatively and morally right as with feeling free to indulge children and satisfy personal desires. This was the second youngest group, the second highest in education, was highly involved with community and friends, and also highly involved with grandchildren. The *remote* group (28%) placed little emphasis on either social or personal aspects of grandparenthood, was not very involved with or concerned about relationships with grandchildren, and scored lowest on behaviors with them. This was the second oldest group, lower than average in education, and relatively low in friendship and community involvement. Members of this group also scored considerably lower in life satisfaction than the other three groups. The authors conclude that grandparenting is a role which has different meanings for individuals. It is related to degree of involvement with their families and in community activities and to whether the meaning is normative, personal, both, or neither. It is influenced to some degree by age and education.

The Wood and Robertson (1978) studies update Neugarten's and Weinstein's (1964) findings of the previous decade; the types they described parallel and suggest some reconceptualizing of the earlier grandparent typology. Robertson's *symbolic* type is similar to the formal type described earlier, and represents the growing proportion of younger grandparents who are involved in their own lives at work or in the community and less personally involved in grandparenting. The *remote* type is somewhat similar to the distant figure described earlier, and is still a relatively common role type. The *individualized* type and the *apportioned* type, both of whom derived personal meaning from involvement with grandchildren may represent element of the fun seeker. While babysitting was a common activity in the Robertson (1977) study, the parent surrogate type was not identified. Older women as well as younger women were participating in the labor force in increasing numbers and appeared to be less available to be child caregivers on a continuing basis than they may have been in the past. Likewise, while grandparents may have wisdom, they were not playing the role of reservoir of family wisdom very often, either through advice giving or relating of family history.

Clavan (1978) has contributed a useful theoretical analysis of the role of grandparents which partially encompasses on a more general level conceptualizations of earlier researchers. She suggests that grand-parenting differs by degree of "functional centrality" in middle and lower socio-economic status families. For the middle class, the role can be characterized as more "ideological" than "real" in the sense that, while there is a kinship position of grandparent, there are no normative rights and obligations attached to the position, making grandparent essentially a "roleless role." Becoming a *valued* grandparent thus becomes an earned and acquired status, rather than an ascribed one. On the other hand, in poor families, the grandparent, especially the grandmother, is more integrated into family life and performs many valued and needed parent-ing activities. The grandparent is more often essential in family life and at times serves as a true surrogate for a parent. In this sense the role is more "real." The concept of functional centrality can also help explain the neglect of grandfathers in studies of family life and why the grandparent role is often called a grandmothering role. If grandparents are valued for the parenting help they give, a functional role for grandfathers may be difficult because of traditional sex role behaviors.

The increasing number of older persons has stimulated research on how attitudes toward aging are formed. Troll et al. (1979) concluded after summarizing the research in the area that young people who have grandparents tended to have less prejudice toward the aged than those who did not have grandparents. Phenice (1981) contributed further data in this regard. Perceptions of grandparents and elderly persons held by 44 preschool children enrolled in two day care centers in Lansing, Michigan, were studied. Only one child did not have a living grandparent. Eighty-six percent of the children saw one grandparent about once a week. On a semantic differential scale grandparents were viewed by the children somewhat more positively than were elderly persons in general, with grandparents being perceived as significantly more friendly than other elderly persons. Children who had the most frequent contact with grandparents had the most positive views of grandparents, but the least positive views of elderly persons in general. Children with less contact with grandparents had generally positive views of both grandparents and elderly persons. Children who had the most contact with grandparents mentioned more things they could do with and for elderly persons than children who had the least contact. Children in one of the day care centers had a foster grandparent program. Children in this center did not generally differ in their perceptions of elderly persons than children enrolled in the other center. Findings indicated that contact with "real" grandparents had more influence on children's perceptions of older persons than did involvement with foster grandparents or other elderly persons. Piaget's cognitive developmental theory may help to explain the results. That is, as children acquire more experience with particular older persons, such as grandparents, global interpretations and perceptions of older persons become more differentiated, specified, and integrated.

This same study investigated parental attitudes toward grandparents' and elderly persons' expectations of and behaviors toward preschool children. Parental attitudes toward grandparents were generally more positive than were their attitudes toward elderly persons in general. For instance, nearly all of them thought grandparents liked preschool children, but fewer thought elderly persons liked preschool children. Sixty percent of the parents did not think grandparents were too old fashioned in their views about childrearing but 63 percent thought elderly persons in general were too old fashioned in these views. Findings suggest that parental attitudes are important influences on grandparent-grandchild relationships and support other research which has revealed the significance of parents in this regard (Troll, et al., 1979). Where there is high involvement by older adults with their children, especially along the female line, there is more likely to be high involvement with grandchildren. Aldous (1978) emphasized the importance of successful completion of the developmental tasks of the grandparent generation in establishing harmonious relationships across the generations. If parents are not successful in letting their adult children go, but try to guide them and offer advice and counsel that is unwanted, strained relationships across generations result and interactions between grandparents and grandchildren are affected. But, where good relationships exist between the adult generations and where attitudes and values are consonant, interactions with grandparents generally serve as positive and stabilizing influences in grandchildren's development. Grandparents can supply a special love and warmth that promote self-esteem.

Another type of literature which began to appear with greater frequency during the 1970's bears mention, not because it reports research data or presents theoretical formulations but because it illustrates changing norms and expectations about roles of grandparents. This literature consists of "how-to" articles and books for grandparents which serve as guides to grandparents on such matters as how to stay in touch and visit, how to and how not to give advice, when and how to give presents and how to do things with grandchildren. Books by Shedd (1976) and Goode (1976) are examples of this genre and offer evidence that socialization for the role of grandparents can no longer be taken for granted, and that while some traditional expectations for the role may exist, how the role is played has become more complex and can no longer be assumed to be part of the common knowledge.

The 1980's

The literature reported thus far in this decade continues the theme of exploring the meaning and role of grandparenthood. Kivnick (1980) suggests that, currently, the meaning of grandparenthood is ill-defined and ill-understood but is integral to the lives of older people. On the basis of a study of 286 grandparents, using a Likert type scale, five factors each representing a dimension of the meaning of grandparenthood were identified. To some extent, these factors reflect the roles and types of grandparents, identified in research and theory of previous decades. Factors identified were conceptualized as: (1) *Centrality--*grandparenthood as central to grandparents' lives; (2) *Valued Elder--*passing on tradition and being valued; (3) *Immortality through Clan--*patriarchal responsibility, and family immortality; (4) *Re-involvement with Personal Past--*grandparents' re-living their lives; (5) *Spoil--*attitudes of lenience and indulgence toward grandchildren. The meaning of grandparenthood varies along these dimensions and is influenced by the degree and nature of grandparent-grandchild interaction.

Sprey (1980) sees grandparents as a peripheral part of family life with very little power in terms of normal family functioning. Because they have no legal rights or definition, and because social norms and expectations have changed, grandparents occupy a very tenuous position. He asserts that they could potentially have a more functional and significant role in family life.

Summary

A headline in a recent news story read: "Grandparents seem to be fading away" (*Detroit Free Press*, 1981). Is this a valid conclusion based on the evidence found in the literature reviewed above? The best answer seems to be, no, they're not fading away but, on the whole, they do not play a major role as surrogate parents in the majority of American families. There are exceptions, as will be discussed later in this chapter, but, in general, the role of grandparents in parenting is characterized by supplemental parenting.

Grandparents provide some child care; they give love, gifts, money, and other goods and services and have varying degrees of interaction through visits, recreation and other activities with grandchildren. The majority of grandparents are not consciously perceived as teachers or authority figures or as conveyors of family history, but they can serve as role models of older persons and can help socialize children about growing older. Interaction with grandparents probably helps to socialize children to become aware of family and kinship structure, that there are persons who have some relationship to them and their parents who are not neighbors or friends or teachers, etc., but who occupy roles which have some special expectations and behaviors. Relationships with grandparents also broaden the range of persons with whom children interact. These relationships can help different rules and expectations. Children, thus, learn to differentiate their behavior toward others. Interaction with a wider range of persons can also help a child to see that not everyone does things in the same way. However, such effects on children of involvement with grandparents have not been well documented.

Grandmothers are more often perceived as favorite grandparents and play a more dominant role than grandfathers in most grandchildren's lives.(2) Friendly, mutually satisfying interactions between grandparents and grandchildren are more common when grandchildren are young. Involvement is generally greater with maternal rather than paternal grandparents.

Parenting in most families is the responsibility of parents, and grandparents are neither expected nor allowed to assume this responsibility. Parents of children, thus, play a major mediating role in governing grandparent-grandchild relationships. Where relationships across generations are harmonious, results of grandparent-grandchild interactions are generally positive and can provide stability and continuity in children's lives.

Becoming a grandparent is for most persons a desired role which brings satisfaction and happiness. How grandchildren feel about their relationships with grandparents has been largely unexplored. The evidence indicates that they are viewed as being more lenient and indulgent than grandparents of the past.

Differing styles and role-types of grandparents have been revealed in several studies, ranging from those who are more intimately involved with grandchildren to formal or distant grandparents who have little direct relationships with grandchildren. Geographic proximity and ease of contact, the extent to which older persons are involved in the family life of their children, the degree of involvement in their own work or community or social life, their health and age as well as the age of grandchildren influence relationships with grandchildren. Changes in roles of women, changes in family structure and functioning, demographic changes and changes in normative expectations for the roles of children and parents as well as of grandparents contribute to variations in the extent and meaning of supplemental parenting by grandparents.

OTHER INVOLVEMENT IN PARENTING AND CHILD NURTURANCE BY RELATED ADULTS

Research, other than that related to roles and relationships of grandparents, on parenting and child care provided by relatives in the general population of families is very scarce. Most of the information found was that from child care studies of the mid 1970's which revealed that relatives do provide substantial amounts of child care in American households. The particular relatives providing care were not identified.

A study in the early 1970's conducted for the Office of Child Development for HEW (Unco, 1976) revealed that nearly nine-tenths of all households with children under 14 used supplementary child care of some kind once in a while.   Nearly 50 percent reported using relatives as caregivers on some occasion. Of those who used child care from one to nine hours per week, care by relatives in their home or the child's home was frequently used (33% and 27%). Of those who used at least ten hours of care a week, relatives provided about 45 percent of the care.   In another study of mothers in paid work who used child care at least ten hours a week, relatives, including siblings, accounted for a third of all caretakers (Duncan and Hill, 1975).   Shoffner (1979) reports that of 525 mothers of children twelve and under in the rural Carolinas, the most frequently used plan was child care by a relative.   In a study of 72 licensed family day care providers in four rural Michigan counties (Rawson, 1979), over half of whom provided day care more than 20 hours a week, one quarter of the providers were relatives of the children cared for.

Parenting and child care by relatives is also sometimes provided in cases where temporary child custody is needed.   The total extent and consequences of such placement are, however, unknown.   Hughes (1969) reports a study in Baltimore County, Maryland, and states that, where a child cannot remain with his or her own parents a home within the family constellation should always be and usually is considered before foster care.   However, her investigation revealed that in the majority of cases described the children had been placed in homes of relatives or guardians without a home study, and in several instances results were destructive for the child. Resentment toward the child's natural parents may be felt, and where a home is provided out of a sense of duty or obligation, the feeling may be conveyed toward the child, with impairment of self-identity and esteem.   Hughes suggests that temporary child placement with relatives, while it may be desirable, should be subject to the same criteria as any other placement.   Applying bureaucratic standards and practices to situations in which familial norms and customs usually apply may, however, create dilemmas and problems.

The effects of various kinds of child care, including that provided by relatives, is difficult to assess.   The evidence we have from studies of working parents and their satisfaction with child care arrangements suggests that children thrive best when parents are satisfied with their work lives and child care arrangements and when the caretaker is responsible and stable (Howell, 1973). Care by relatives appears to be the most reliable (Dickinson, 1975) and may be one reason why care at home with relatives is nearly universally reported to be the most satisfactory child care (Unco, 1976). Shared values and child caring methods and goals may also be more common among related persons and be contributing factors to satisfaction.

Some evidence of the importance of the values of the extended kinship system in child development comes from research on preschool intervention programs. Karnes (1969) compared five different approaches to preschool programming for low-income children. In analysis of data from this project to determine factors influencing intellectual development, Farber, Harvey, and Lewis (1969) found that variables extraneous to specific programs had more influence on children's performance than program variables. Farber et al. studied the kinship organization of the families enrolled in the preschool programs and found that kinship systems affected children's developing competence by socialization practices that were consistent with their norms. Farber (1971) concluded that the fit or lack of fit between a particular kinship pattern and the political, economic and educational systems of American society influence the functioning of families and the ability of their children to profit from educational programs. Kessen and Fein (1975) provided further support for this perspective. They found that families with extensive kin relations and expanded households were far more responsive to home visiting programs than were families with restricted social ties. These studies point out the necessity of taking into account the total ecological context in which the family lives, in which kin may play an important part, in understanding child development.

Summary

We can conclude that relatives do provide a substantial amount of child care and supplementary parenting in many American households, and that most people are well satisfied with the care and parenting provided. The effects on children have not been systematically assessed, but if relatives provide needed stability and continuity in children's lives, consequences are potentially positive. There is also evidence that the socialization practices and the norms of the kin group influence children's developing competences.

PARENTING AND CHILD CARE BY RELATIVES IN MINORITY GROUPS

Most of the research reported in the previous sections has not differentiated child care and parenting by ethnic, racial, or religious groups or by socio-economic status. There are, however, some important differences among groups, and cases where parenting and child care by relatives is highly significant.

Black Families

The kinship network is more extensive among blacks than among whites and the extended family has played a unique and important role in the nurturing and socialization of black children (Hill, 1977). The need for mutual aid and survival in a hostile environment, poverty, and the presence of female headed families needing assistance [36 percent of black families in 1975 (U.S. Dept. of Commerce, 1976)] are some of the reasons for stronger kinship ties among blacks. The continuation of the African heritage of functioning as members of a corporate extended family, with children seen as belonging to the community, has also been advanced as a factor influencing the strength of the extended family among blacks.

One of the key roles the black extended family has played is in informal adoption or foster care of children by grandparents and other relatives. Although the practice has declined somewhat in recent years, it is still common (Bianchi and Farley, 1979). Several reasons have accounted for this practice. Martin and Martin (1978) assert that it is important for black extended families to develop a sense of family and obligation to relatives. Persons who take in relatives' children are showing their concern for the family and receive respect and gratitude. Some feel an obligation because they were cared for by relatives; love and concern for children are other motives. Stack (1974) concluded on the basis of an ethnographic study of low income black families in the midwest that the natural mother is not expected to assume all the responsibility for parenting her child. This is especially the case for unwed mothers. In 1976, fifty percent of black births were to unmarried women, many of them teenagers (Bianchi and Farley, 1979). Black children born out of wedlock are much less likely than white children to be given up for adoption. In nine out of ten cases they are retained by the extended family (Hill, 1977). Children are also informally adopted in cases of divorce, separation, death or illness of one or both parents, or to allow parents to work or go to school.

Of the three million children in America in the mid 1970's who lived with relatives, over half were black. Of these children, one-half did not have either parent present; 39 percent had the mother present; eight percent both parents, and two percent the father present. Over half of the black children living with relatives without their parents present were being reared by persons who were without mates. In most cases these were grandmothers, but ten percent were maternal aunts. Nearly one-half of black families headed by elderly women had children living with them who were not their own. Three-fifths of all black children living in homes without either parent present were grandchildren or great-grandchildren of their caretakers; one-fourth were nieces or nephews. Younger children are more likely to be living with grandparents than with aunts and uncles (Hill, 1977).

In addition to the black children who are informally adopted, it is estimated that millions more live with relatives for shorter periods of time as a way of providing low cost child care services. Mutual aid networks comprised of relatives and close friends sociologically defined as kin are also significant sources of help to black families. Stack (1974) has described the "swapping" that goes on among low-income families as an important form of distribution and exchange of limited resources available to the families she studied. Doubling up of families for varying lengths of time because of economic and emotional need is also increasing among black families (Hill, 1977).

Kin who assume responsibility for children acquire many of the rights and duties associated with parenting, and we can thus conclude that in black families a substantial amount of parenting is carried on by relatives, most frequently grandmothers. Additional help to parents through providing goods and services is also a common phenomenon. These patterns are more likely to be present among economically disadvantaged families but are more likely to be present among economically disadvantaged families but are not limited to them. McAdoo (1978) found that kinship help patterns remained strong among middle-class blacks who had achieved mobility.

The consequences of care by the extended family are difficult to assess and to compare with care by nuclear families. Undoubtedly these informal means of providing support and mutual aid serve as sources of stability and survival in the lives of many black families and their children. Shared values, customs and child rearing patterns may be similar among family groups and facilitate and provide continuity in child socialization. Positive aspects of living in extended families are reported in two studies. Kramer and Redick (1974) found that children living with relatives were about one-half as likely as children living with both parents to be admitted to outpatient psychiatric clinics and one-fifth as likely as children living with mothers only. The degree of harmony and stability appear to be major factors. Billingsley (1973) reports that child abuse is more likely to occur in white families than in black families who live in similar or worse economic circumstances. The mutual aid of the extended family network can serve as a deterrent against abuse because an abused or neglected child can be moved to a more wholesome environment in the network. Additionally, when children are cared for because of deep affection and concern rather than because of legal obligation, less abuse may be expected.

Emphasis on the positive aspects of the extended family's role in parenting should not obscure the fact that there may be other consequences. Davis (1968) has suggested that role strain and conflict between grandmothers about rearing of children may occur and may be resolved by young mothers relinquishing their roles as mothers and behaving as older sisters. It has been suggested that, since the composition of some families shifts, the structure of authority for children may change considerably depending on the status of the incoming and outgoing relatives. Children may also be shifted between families and subjected to different family constellations and authorities. These shifts may create problems for some children, but for some may be functional in developing adaptability and skills necessary for surviving in a shifting environment. On the whole, the quality, as well as quantity, of child care provided by the black extended family is remarkable and can benefit several generations--grandparents have a "real" role, as Clavan (1978) pointed out, and parents and children can find stability and meaning as well as a way to survive.

Mexican American Families

Mexican Americans make up the second largest ethnic minority group in America. Two characteristics emphasized by Mexicans as typical features of the traditional Mexican American family which have particular relevance for child rearing by relatives are strong familistic values, with the family of deep importance to its members, and the subordination of younger to older persons. Familism and respect for the aged are reflected in the idealized role given to the extended family, with close relationships extending over a range of relatives, and to *compadres* (godparents) who may not be blood kin who traditionally functioned as parent substitutes. Care of aged parents in the household, living close to relatives and providing help to kin with child care and other services and goods, as well as emotional support, have been typical patterns in traditional Mexican-American families. In a study of children ages seven to thirteen in a Houston *barrio*, Goodman and Beman (1971) reported that grandparents were important in the lives of children. They were more likely to be seen as warm and affectionate rather than authority figures. In addition to being loved, grandparents were respected because they were considered older and wiser.

These family patterns still exist, especially in rural areas and in the more isolated *barrios*; however, as more Mexican families become participants in urban middle class life styles, family structure and functions change, and we may expect them to become more like mainstream families. For example, the absence of extended family living arrangements in Los Angeles and San Antonio (Grebler, Moore and Guzman, 1970) and in the midwest (Miller, 1975) is reported. However, an intensive study of four cases of three generations of Mexican-American families in the midwest revealed that the extended family system was still evident, with interdependency in personal services among and between generations taken for granted, both on a voluntary basis as well as from a sense of duty (Sena-Rivera, 1979). The authors predict that *familia* in the sense of the extended family system, will continue for at least one more full generation. Moreover, Mexican American families differ from the dominant American form in terms of having more children and being less likely to be divorced (Staples and Mirande, 1980). This evidence of strong familistic values portends continuance of the extended family in many aspects of family life, including child care and socialization.

Puerto Rican Families

Puerto Ricans now constitute one of the major minority groups in the eastern part of America. A deep sense of the network of primary personal relationships which are their family and a strong sense of family obligation and mutual help have characterized Puerto Ricans. On the island, the most common pattern of family life was the extended family system, but the nuclear family with weakened ties to the kin group is becoming more common. Families composed of a father, mother, their children, and those of another union or unions of the parents are also not uncommon. Mother headed families are also increasing, particularly on the mainland. In 1970, 19 percent of island families and 28 percent of mainland families were headed by females without a male present (Fitzpatrick, 1976). The experience of migration has tended to weaken family bonds, and the support of the extended family in child rearing and perpetuation of personal and family values and virtues may be lessening as migrants seek to adjust to the dominant patterns of American society in which old values and customs conflict with the new. Nevertheless, it has been concluded (Fitzpatrick, 1976) that, during this period of struggle in which the Puerto Rican family is often a broken family wrestling with poverty, unemployment and poor health, the family remains a major source of support for its members and provides help with many family problems and needs, including child care and nurturance.

Asian American Families

The traditional cultures of Asian Americans have stressed the importance of the family unit in contrast to individual persons; the extended family has been important in conveying family values, standards of behavior and acceptable norms. Respect for the authority of elders was generally expected. Earlier Asian migrant groups, the Japanese and Chinese, have typically become acculturated and assimilated into mainstream America, and have adopted values, roles and behaviors of the majority group. However, extended family patterns still exist to some extent. Kitano and Kikumura (1976) report that many Japanese Americans absorb grandparents into the household, and the in-law apartment is a popular feature in want ads aimed at Japanese Americans. Large family outings and gatherings, including doting grandparents and in-laws, are important for young families. Huang (1976) states that, in general, Chinese-American children grow up in the midst of adults, including grandparents, uncles and aunts and other kin; they are seldom left with babysitters or unrelated adults. The new Asian immigrants such as the Vietnamese and Cambodians bring similar family patterns with them. No research has yet been reported on their child rearing patterns, but personal observations give the impression that strong family ties and mutual support systems are significant elements in their social structure, and we can expect that, where available, kin play an important role in child socialization and care.

Native American Families

It is difficult to generalize about family lifestyles of Native Americans because they represent so much diversity. They are organized into 280 tribal groupings, and family structure and values differ from tribe to tribe. But, for many Native Americans the extended family is the basic functioning family unit. Children are raised by relatives who, even though they live in separate households, carry out family functions across multiple households. Redhorse, Lewis, Feit and Decker (1979) report on a community where 92 percent of the elderly lived in separate households but fulfilled traditional family roles on a daily basis for their children, grandchildren, and great grandchildren. Native American families are characterized by high rates of out-of-wedlock births, strong roles of women, high rates of female headed households, high rates of unemployment and poverty (Staples and Mirande, 1980). These factors, plus traditional patterns of family support, account for the extended family playing a significant role in child care and nurturance. Since many Native Americans have been opposed to assimilation and integration into the mainstream of America we may expect these family patterns to continue. Also, while many have left the reservations, Miller (1980) found that 40% of urban Native Americans had returned to the reservation where traditional patterns are more likely to be in force.

Other Ethnic or Religious Minority Families

Many other immigrant groups and ethnic and religious minorities have been characterized by strong familistic values and kinship ties. Among groups which are reported to have maintained these bonds with greater strength perhaps than others are Italian Americans and Jewish Americans. In a comprehensive ethnicity study, Greeley (1971) found that, of all the ethnic groups, Italian Americans most often tended to live in the same neighborhoods as their parents and siblings and saw them every week, thus maintaining a strong kin network. Greeley (1974) also found that third generation Italians found their same-sex parent their primary source of identification, and that Italian females, while less traditional than males in terms of sex roles, were more so than other ethnic groups. This strong sense of identification and adherence to traditional roles illustrates generational continuity in child rearing and socialization in which kin play an important part. Gambino (1974) has also reported on the importance of la famiglia, composed of all one's blood relatives, in the nurturing of the Italian American personality.

It is estimated that about ninety percent of America's Jewish population is from or descends from immigrants from Eastern Europe where most Jews lives in small towns--the shtetls. The shtetl was viewed as an extended family in which the Jews considered themselves related to the "Children of Israel" and in fact were often blood kin because of extensive intermarriage. Family obligations were strong and close kin ties expected. While the extent of familism among American Jews has declined with changing patterns of geographic mobility, marriage, and integration into the American culture, a number of studies have shown that kin ties and contacts have remained strong among the generation referred to as the Holocaust generation (Farber, Mindel and Lazerwitz, 1976) who spent their formative years during years of the Nazi regime. Leichter and Mitchell (1967) found that women exchanged considerable help with relatives, much of which was child care. In terms of frequency of help given or expected, relatives ranked first for both babysitting and care of children if children were orphaned; however, they ranked third compared to friends and others on the basis of the most used or desired source of child rearing advice. Parents said they preferred this kind of help from other sources because of the gap between themselves and their immigrant parents in child rearing values. Grandparents, on the other hand, coming from the more traditional family system where such advice was expected to be given, were often hurt if their childrearing advice was not accepted. The husband's kin was reported to attempt to dominate the family, and their interference was perceived to provoke greater conflict within the family than interference or involvement with the wife's kin (Leichter and Mitchell, 1967). The nurturance, protection and domineering of the *Yiddisheh Mahmeh* which characterize the stereo- typical "Jewish Mother", may be more easily dealt with by women when it is their mothers, rather than their husbands' mothers who are involved. It may also be less acceptable to criticize one's own mother.

Summary

On the basis of these examples of ethnic and religious minorities, we can conclude that where strong familistic values and traditional expecta- tions of kin interactions and mutual aid continue we may expect greater involvement by relatives in parenting roles and in providing assistance with child care and nurturance. Involvement with kin is a major means of providing continuity in socialization of values, beliefs, and life styles. Where traditional values and patterns conflict with "newer" values and patterns, or where migration and mobility preclude extensive kin contact, lesser involvement and influence in child care, nurturance and sociali- zation can be expected.

CURRENT FAMILY CHANGES INFLUENCING PARENTING AND CHILD CARE BY RELATED ADULTS

The 1970's saw the acceleration of several interrelated trends which affected family structure, roles, and relationships. The rising divorce rate with an increase in the numbers of children involved, growth in single parent families, increase in births to adolescent girls, and the changing roles of women, especially their increased participation in the paid labor force, have particular importance for relationships with kin.

Divorce and Related Changes

The U.S. divorce rate per 1,000 population increased from 3.5 in 1970 to a provisional rate of 5.3 in 1979 (Andrews and Boger, 1980). From 1953 to 1974, the number of children involved in divorce increased by 333 percent; over 60 percent of all divorces involve at least one child (U.S. Dept. of Commerce, 1976). Changes in living arrangements of children are a result of divorce and also of remarriage. About 30 percent of marriages in 1977 were remarriages (Andrews and Boger, 1980, p. 24). About three out of four persons who divorce eventually remarry (Furstenberg, Spanier and Crawford, 1980).

Glick reports that from 1960 to 1978 the number of children who lived with two parents declined from 87 percent to 77 percent. In this same period, the percent who lived with two natural parents also declined ten percent, from 78 percent to 68 percent (Glick, 1979). In 1978, nearly 19 percent of children lived with only one parent; 17 percent lived with mothers. Three percent lived with relatives other than parents.   Ten percent lived with one natural parent and one stepparent, representing children living in what have been called reconstituted or blended families resulting from remarriage.

Changes in the involvement of grandparents and other relatives in parenting and child care might be expected as a result of these new family forms and living arrangements.   The research evidence we have indicates that contact with some relatives, particularly the former affinal kin (former in-laws) of the custodial parent decreases, but in some families there may be more involvement of relatives in children's lives. Anspach (1976) reports that where mothers are awarded custody, which has been the traditional pattern, children may lose contact with paternal kin.   Whether or not children have the opportunity to see these relatives depends on the amount of contact with the noncustodial father.   Spicer and Hampe (1975) reported that, after divorce, consanguinal contact remained about the same for the majority of respondents, with an increase for one-fifth.   Almost three-fourths of the respondents said they interacted less or not at all with former affinal kin.   Females interacted more frequently than males with both consanguinal and affinal kin, with the highest rate of interaction for females with children.   Some divorced mothers may feel an obligation to maintain contact with former affines; their children are still related to them.   A longitudinal study by Furstenberg, Spanier and Crawford (1980) supports this contention and provides further information on intergenerational ties between grandparents and grandchildren following divorce and remarriage. The original study was conducted in 1977.   It included 210 persons in a central Pennsylvania county who had either filed for separation or obtained a divorce in the previous 26 months and who were still living in the county. In 1979, 181 persons, 86 percent of the original sample, were reinterviewed.   In addition, interviews were completed with 60 spouses or partners of the 87 original respondents who had remarried or were living with someone at the time of the 1979 study. Information on children's contacts with grandparents was obtained from 104 respondents who had a child under the age of 18 living with either the respondent or their former spouse.   Lengthy in-depth interviews were also conducted with 25 remarried couples all of whom had children from their previous marriages.

Children were reported to have more frequent and more regular contact with grandparents on the custodial parent's side than with those on the non-custodial parent's side. Nearly 40 percent of the former saw grandparents at least once a week while only four percent of the latter saw grandparents that often. However, most of the grandchildren did see the latter grandparents at least occasionally, and about a third of the children saw them once or twice a month. Some of these contacts were arranged by the custodial parent; others took place when children visited the custodial parent. Apparently, at least ritual contact is maintained between children and grandparents on the non-custodial parent's side. Findings suggest that the amount of contact between parents may influence the amount of contact the child has with the non-custodial parent appeared to influence the amount of contact with grandparents on that side, suggesting that the fate of grandparent-grandchild relations following divorce is directly linked to the parent-child relations which evolve. Physical proximity was also found to be an important condition affecting overall level of contact between grandparents and grandchildren, especially for grandparents on the non-custodial side.

Information obtained from respondents who had remarried or who were living with a partner revealed that in most cases relations with new in-laws had been quickly and easily established. Relationships between children and their new stepgrandparents were likewise readily established. One-fourth of the respondents said that stepchildren, who were living in the respondents household, saw their biological grandparents on the custodial parent's side at least once a week, but nearly as many (one-fifth) said stepchildren saw their new stepgrandparents just as often. There was a slight positive association between levels of visitation with the two sets of biological grandparents and visitation levels between step grandparents and biological grandparents. Findings suggest that remarriage following divorce results in augmentation and expansion of kin for children. Frequent contact is maintained with biological grandparents on the custodial parents side; at least ritualistic contact is maintained with biological grandparents of the non-custodial parents side, and relatively frequent contact is established with stepgrandparents.

Currently there are pressures and desires by some men to gain custody. There is also some increase in joint custody. In these cases we may expect that men may carry out more of the responsibilities for kin contact and relationships, which have heretofore been more often a female role. Furstenberg et al. (1980) found that non-custodial fathers relied heavily on parents for child care assistance. An Australian study by Katz (1979) reported similar findings. Nearly all (95 out of 102) of single parent fathers who tried to get help with child care went to either the child's grandparents or other relatives. The next largest sources of help were friends and neighbors. Thirty-seven percent rated the help received from relatives as helpful, while 49 percent rated help from friends and neighbors as helpful. Hetherington, Cox and Cox (1976) found that divorced mothers and fathers thought parents and relatives helped them to be better parents after the divorce, but to a lesser extent than friends.

Another kind of evidence for changes in kin relationships following divorce come from the political action that "Grandparents' Rights" groups have taken in recent years. For example, Michigan recently enacted legislation to provide for visitation rights by grandparents or other close relatives following divorce (Michigan P.A. 161, 1980). Webb (1981) reports that 32 states had some form of grandparent visitation rights legislation, with bills under consideration in four other states. Grandparents who believed they were denied opportunities to see their grandchildren were instrumental in getting this legislation passed and have established contact networks across the states to share information and strategies (Sumpter and Sumpter, 1981). It is interesting to note that when traditional social relationships are altered, legal means are sought in an attempt to maintain such relationships.

Births to Adolescents

One long term trend which has resulted in greater involvement of grandparents and other relatives in child care and nurturance is the increase in proportion of births to unmarried persons, particularly to adolescents. In 1940, one child in thirty was born to unmarried persons; in 1960 one in twenty; in 1970 one in ten and in 1974, one in eight (Nye, 1976). The rate has been declining for older women but increasing for teenagers. Between 1940 and 1975 the birth rate per 1,000 unmarried females age 15 through 19 tripled. The number of infants born to unmarried teenagers in 1975 was 233,500. For mothers under 17 between 1965 and 1975, the rate of out of wedlock births increased 60 percent (Chilman, 1980, p. 195). Out of wedlock birth rates for blacks are higher than for whites, 95.1 per 1,000 females 15 to 19 for the former, compared to 12.1 for the latter, in 1975. Higher abortion rates for teenage whites, 45 percent of conceptions compared to eight percent for blacks, account for much of the difference (Zelnik and Kantner, 1978). The out of wedlock birth rate for women 15 to 19 declined for blacks from 1971 to 1975, but rose for whites.

There has been a decline in the proportion of pregnant adolescents who marry prior to the birth, and an increase in numbers who keep their children (Chilman, 1980, pp. 197-198). Young adolescent mothers are in need of a supportive relationship and assistance with child care and often receive help or continue to live with their parents (McCall, 1975; Smith, 1975). Where teenage sexuality, pregnancy, and out of wedlock births are more accepted, and there is a tradition of family support, provision of child care by the family is more common, and outcomes probably quite positive. But, where this is a newer phenomenon as in white middle-class families, provision of child care is more problematic and care outside of the home is more frequently sought. In a longitudinal study of low income, predominantly black adolescent females, Furstenberg (1976) found that about half of the mothers shared parenthood with another adult, most often a relative. The family was crucial in providing help to make it possible for young mothers to continue in school or be employed.

In this same study the cognitive development of three- to four-year-old children of unmarried adolescents was assessed using the Preschool Inventory.   Children of lower socio-economic mothers tended to have higher scores if they were cared for by more than one adult, either the father of the child or other caregivers, such as a relative.

While families of many young mothers do provide economic, emotional and other support to their adolescent child-parents and grandchildren, there are other consequences.   Smith (1975) and Bryan-Logan and Dancy (1974) found that the pregnancy of a school-age daughter can be a severe crisis for the girl's mother.   The mother of a pregnant adolescent may be a relatively young woman herself with her own family responsibilities.   She may be working, or in school, or just beginning a period in her own life when she expects to be free of major childrearing responsibilities.   Becoming a grandmother and having to assume responsibility for a grandchild is unexpected and unwelcome.   Conflict over the roles of the young mother and her family can result.   Who is the mother in the family?   Can the system function with two mothers?   What is the role of the grandmother?   The single parent may find it difficult to exercise authority in child rearing decisions or may be blamed for not accepting responsibility.   Dell (1977) has used the term "trigenerational enmeshment" to ascribe the conflicts which can result as single parents play overlapping roles of parent and child.   The child of the young parent may have difficulty in differentiating between parent and grandparent (Bemis, Diers and Sharpe, 1976).

There are no satisfactory studies on the long term consequences on children of unmarried adolescents; hence it is not possible to draw any definitive conclusions about the effects of child care by grandparents or other relatives.   We can surmise that socio-economic status is a major contributing variable to any differences which might be found.

Women's Employment

The increase in participation of women in paid work outside the home has been called one of the major revolutions of our time.   During the past decade married women with children have shown the sharpest increase in labor force participation of any population group.   During 1978, nearly 50 percent of all married women with children under three, and 54 percent of those with children three to five had some paid work experience away from home.   Of those with children from six to seventeen, 64 percent were in the labor force in 1975.   The labor force participation rate of female heads of families with children has kept pace with that of married women. In 1975, 62 percent of these females were in the labor force (Masnick and Bane, 1980).

The high rate of labor force participation of women is one of the dominant factors in the increased need for child care services.   Data reported earlier on child care by relatives indicated that relatives do supply a considerable amount of child care in American families. Indeed, such care has been an expected pattern, and the norms regarding such care were embodied in our policies about tax deduction. Until recently, when the so-called "anti-grandmother" provision in the income tax deduction for child care was eliminated in the Tax Reform Bill of the mid 1970's, families who employed a relative closer than a cousin to provide child care were disallowed child care costs (Johnson, 1976). Presumably grandmothers and other close relatives were supposed to give child care for nothing. The fact that the policy changed indicates changing norms about family responsibilities and some recognition that, when relatives provide child care, it is a job for which they are entitled to be paid. It should also be noted that while relatives do provide child care, and it is often judged the most satisfactory, non-relatives are also a major source of child care for American families. Along with mothers, many grandmothers and other female relatives are in the labor force, and, for this as well as other reasons, cannot or do not provide child care for working parents. The women's movement with its emphasis on creating alternatives for women beyond traditional family and parental roles as sources of self-fulfillment has resulted in some women becoming less willing to assume surrogate or supplemental parenting roles.

Summary

The current high divorce rate and its consequences such as the new family constellations resulting from re-marriage and the increasing numbers of single parents, especially female-headed families, have impacts on kin relationships. The evidence that is beginning to come in suggests that contacts between children and kin on the custodial parent's side generally remain high. Contacts with kin on the non-custodial parent's side are diminished but some contact is usually maintained. Contacts with step kin acquired when the custodial parent marries appear to be relatively easily established. The current high rate of births to unmarried adolescents has resulted in an increased need for surrogate parenting. Care by the extended family has been a long term pattern for blacks, but is less frequently practiced among middle-class whites. If the trend continues, increased need for child care services will result. Changing roles of women with their continued high labor force participation have also increased the demands for child care services.

CONCLUSION

Changes in the patterns of supplemental parenting and child nurturance by related adults may be viewed from the perspective of interacting forces which, on the one hand, tend to decrease the extensity and intensity of such involvement and, on the other hand, those which tend to sustain or increase involvement. Some forces work toward both a decrease and increase. Forces influencing parenting by relatives are societal as well as individual in nature.

One of the forces which has lessened the role and authority of grandparents and other kin in child care and nurturance has been emphasis on the decision-making autonomy of each individual family unit. Americanization, urbanization, and social and geographic mobility have contributed to this trend and have tended to lessen direct involvement of kin in day-to-day child rearing. Shifting of such family functions as education, recreation, home production and religious training to systems outside the family has diminished the need for a meaningful role for relatives within the family. Grandparents and other kin have few normative or legal roles in relation to children.

Demographic changes such as the smaller number of children in each family, completion of child bearing at earlier ages, and increased longevity have resulted in a relatively long period of time in the family cycle when there are no children in the home, the so-called empty nest. To some extent, this may have resulted in women being more available for care of grandchildren or other relatives, but this is no longer as common. Greater stress on individual development and self-fulfillment on the part of women and their increased involvement in work and social and community life beyond the home and family have affected their willingness as well as availability to provide child care, which at present is still viewed primarily as a female role. Additionally, expectations that close relatives should provide child care, especially on a continuing basis without pay, are no longer strongly held. Changes in policy, practice and the social norms related to work and child care could make it possible for men as well as women to be more directly involved in child care. Part-time work for either or both, child care leaves, flexible work schedules and the like, would enable fathers and mothers to provide child care without outside support systems or the help of relatives. These same changes could also make it possible for related adults of both sexes to provide more child care.

There are other forces which tend to sustain or which may increase involvement of kin in parenting or child nurturance. The modified extended family is still very much alive, and becoming a grandparent continues to be an expected and highly anticipated role by many parents of young adults. Indulging children, providing love, gifts, and aid, and interacting with grandchildren (or nieces or nephews) bring happiness and pleasure to many persons. In groups which have strong familistic traditions and expectations of mutual help and support, and in which values and family patterns are expected to be transmitted across generations, the kin network is more extensively involved in child care and nurturance. The increase in births to unmarried adolescents has required more surrogate and supplemental parenting; the extended family has often provided this, especially in black and other minority groups. The increase in numbers of divorces involving children and resulting increase in single parent families has tended to increase the need for supportive help from relatives, at least on a short term basis. However, lesser involvement with former affinal kin also often follows divorce. The norms and expectations for relationships with "ex-kin" and "new-kin" are just being established and what the long term effects on parenting by related adults will be are uncertain.

In the past, in times of economic crisis and shortages of resources, families were usually the major support systems. During recent decades, however, public support systems have grown and have been both cause and effect of the family changes described here. Given the current (1981) economic situation and the politically conservative views extant toward less public funding of social supports, we may expect that, in the future, the extended family could become more significant in child care and nurturance. There will be some doubling up of families; perhaps greater numbers of elderly relatives will live with their children and be available for child care. There may be more exchange of child care services among the extended family. The role of grandparents and other related adults may become more central and functional in American family life. Outcomes will depend on the balancing of forces in the total ecological context which impinges upon individual families.

ACKNOWLEDGEMENTS

The authors wish to thank Cheryl Taylor, Virginia Soddy and Janice Steindler for their assistance with this chapter.

REFERENCES

Adams, B. N. Isolation, function, and beyond: American kinship in the 1960's. *Journal of Marriage and the Family*, 1970, *32*(4), 575-597.

Albrecht, R. The parental responsibilities of grandparents. *Marriage and Family Living*, 1954, *16*, 201-204.

Aldous, J. *Family careers.* New York: John Wiley, 1978.

Andrews, M., and Boger, R. (Eds.) *Michigan family sourcebook.* East Lansing: Michigan State University, Institute for Family and Child Study, College of Human Ecology, 1980.

Anspach, D. F. Kinship and divorce. *Journal of marriage and the family*, 1976, *38*(2), 323-330.

Apple, D. The social structure of grandparenthood. *American Anthropologist*, 1956, *58*(4), 656-663.

Bemis, J., Diers, E., and Sharpe, R. The teenage single mother. *Child Welfare*, 1976, *55*(5), 309-318.

Bianchi, S., and Farley, R. Racial differences in family living arrangements and economic well-being: An analysis of recent trends. *Journal of Marriage and the Family*, 1979, *41*(3), 537-551.

Billingsley, A. Black family structure: Myths and realities. Testimony presented to the Subcommittee of Fiscal Policy, Joint Economic Committee, U.S. Congress, *Studies in Public Welfare*, Paper No. 12 (Part II), December 3, 1973, pp. 306-319.

Bordon, B. The role of the grandparents in children's behavior problems. *Smith College Studies in Social Work*, 1946, *17*, 115.

Bryan-Logan, B. B., and Dancy, B. L. Unwed pregnant adolescents: Their mothers' dilemmas. *Nurses Clinics of North America*, 1974, *9*(1), 57-68.

Chilman, C. *Adolescent sexuality in a changing American society*. U.S. Department of Health, Education and Welfare, 1980.

Clavan, S. The impact of social class and social trends on the role of grandparent. *The family coordinator*, 1978, *27*(4), 351-258.

Crase, D. R., and Hendrickson, N. Maternal grandmothers and others as perceived by pre-teen children. *Journal of Home Economics*, 1968, *60*(3), 181-185.

Davis, E. The American Negro: From family membership to personal and social identity. *Journal of the National Medical Association*, 1968, *60*(2), 92-99.

Dell, P. F. Trigenerational enmeshment--unresolved ties of single parents to family of origin. *American Journal of Orthopsychiatry*, 1977, *47*(1), 52-59.

Detroit Free Press. Grandparents seem to be fading away. January 1, 1981, Section C, pp. 1, 5.

Dickinson, K. Child care. In G. J. Duncan and J. W. Morgan (Eds.), *Five thousand American families*, Vol. III. Ann Arbor: Institute for Survey Research, University of Michigan, 1975.

Duncan, G., and Hill, C. R. Modal choice in child-care arrangements. In J. Duncan and J. W. Morgan (Eds.), *Five thousand American families*, Vol. III. Ann Arbor: Institute for Survey Research, University of Michigan, 1975.

Farber, B. *Kinship and class: A midwestern study*. New York: Basic Books, 1971.

Farber, B., Harvey, D. L., and Lewis, M. *Research and development program on preschool disadvantaged children: Community, kinship and competence: Final report*. Washington, D.C.: U.S. Office of Education, 1969.

Farber, B., Mindel C., and Lazerwitz, B. The Jewish American family. In C. Mindel and R. Habenstein (Eds.), *Ethnic families in America*. New York: Elsevier, 1976.

Fitzpatrick, J. R. The Puerto Rican family. Reprinted in C. Mindel and R. Habenstein (Eds.), *Ethnic families in America*. New York: Elsevier, 1976.

Fox, F. Family life and relationships as affected by the presence of the aged. *Mental hygiene and old age*. New York: State Charities Aid Association, 1937.

Fried, E. G., and Stern, K. The situation of the aged within the family. *American Journal of Orthopsychiatry*, 1948, *18*, 31-54.

Furstenberg, F. *Unplanned parenthood: The social consequences of teenage childbearing*. New York: The Free Press, 1976.

Furstenberg, F., Spanier, G., and Crawford, A. Marital dissolution and generational ties. Paper presented at the 33rd Annual Meeting of the Gerontological Society, San Diego, November 1980.

Gambino, R. The Italian-American family system. *Blood of my blood: The dilemma of the Italian-Americans*. New York: Doubleday and Company, Inc., 1974.

Gibson, G. Kin family network: Overheralded structure in past conceptualizations of family functioning. *Journal of Marriage and the Family*, 1972, 34(1), 13-23.

Glick, P. Children of divorced parents in demographic perspective. *Journal of Social Issues*, 1979, 35(4), 170-182.

Goode, R. *A book for grandmothers.* New York: McGraw-Hill Book Company, 1976.

Goode, W. J. World revolution and family patterns. *Journal of Marriage and the Family*, 1971, Nov., 624-635.

Goodman, M. E., and Beman, A. Child's-eye-views of life in an urban barrio. In N. Wagner and M. Haug (Eds.), *Chicanos: Social and psychological perspectives.* St. Louis: V. Mosby Company, 1971.

Gordon, M. *The American family, past, present and future*, 1st Edition. New York: Random House, 1978.

Grebler, L., Moore, J. W., and Guzman, R. C. *The Mexican American people.* New York: The Free Press, 1970.

Greeley, A. M. *Why can't they be like us?* New York: John Wiley Company, 1971.

Greeley, A. M. *Ethnicity in the United States.* New York: John Wiley Company, 1974.

Harris, L., and Associates. *The myth and reality of aging in America.* Washington, D.C.: National Council on Aging, 1975.

Hetherington, E. M., Cox, M., and Cox, R. Divorced fathers. *Family Coordinator*, 1976, 25, 417-428.

Hill, R., Foote, N., Aldous, J., and MacDonald, R. *Family development in three generations.* Cambridge, MA: Schenkman, 1970.

Hill, R. B. *Informal adoption among Black families.* National Urban League, 1977.

Howell, M. C. Effects of maternal employment on the child--II. *Pediatrics*, 1973, 52(3), 327-343.

Huang, L. J. The Chinese American family. In C. Mindel and R. Habenstein (Eds.), *Ethnic families in America.* New York: Elsevier, 1976.

Hughes, S. L. Services to children living with relatives or guardians. *Children*, 1969, 16(3), 109-113.

Johnson, A. S. Toward family impact analyses: Some first steps. Paper prepared as a background paper for the *Smithsonian's Family Forum*, June 15, 1976.

Kahana, B., and Kahana, E. Grandparenthood from the perspective of the developing child. *Developmental Psychology*, 1970, 3, 98-105.

Kahana, E., and Kahana, B. Theoretical and research perspectives on grandparenthood. *Journal of Aging and Human Development*, 1971, 2, 261-268.

Karnes, M. C. *Research and development program on preschool disadvantaged children: Investigations of classroom and at-home interventions: Final Report.* Washington, D.C.: U.S. Office of Education, 1969.

Katz, A. Lone fathers: Perspectives and implications for family policy. *The Family Coordinator*, 1979, 28(4), 521-528.

Kessen, W., and Fein, G. *Variations in home-based infant education: Language, play and social development: Final Report.* Washington, D.C.: U. S. Office of Child Development, 1975.

Kitano, H. H., and Kikumura, A. The Japanese American family. In C. Mindel and R. Habenstein (Eds.), *Ethnic families in America.* New York: Elsevier, 1976.

Kivnick, H. Q. Grandparenthood: What it means to grandparents. Paper delivered at the 33rd annual meeting of the National Gerontology Society, San Diego, CA, 1980.

Klatzky, S. R. *Patterns of contact with kin.* Washington, D.C.: American Sociological Association, 1972.

Kramer, M., and Redick, R. Family environment of children and adolescents and the risks of mental illness and related social problems. Paper presented at the 8th International Congress of the International Association for Child Psychiatry Allied Professions, Philadelphia, PA, July, 1974.

LaBarre, M. B., Jessner, L., Ussery, L. The significance of grandmothers in the psychopathology of children. *American Journal of Orthopsychiatry,* 1960, *30,* 175-185.

Lee, G. R. Kinship in the seventies: A decade review of research and theory. *Journal of Marriage and the Family,* 1980, *42*(4), 923-934.

Leichter, H., and Mitchell, W. *Kinship and casework.* New York: Russell Sage Foundation, 1967.

Martin, E. P., and Martin, J. M. *The Black extended family.* Chicago: The University of Chicago Press, 1978.

Masnick, G., and Bane, M. J. *The nation's families: 1960-1990.* Cambridge, MA: Joint Center for Urban Studies of MIT and Harvard University, 1980.

McAdoo, H. P. Factors related to stability in upwardly mobile Black families. *Journal of Marriage and the Family,* 1978, *40*(4), 761-776.

McCall, A. M. *A follow-up study of students who attended the Hillsdale County Alternative School for Pregnant Girls 1968-1973.* M.A. Thesis, Michigan State University, East Lansing, MI, 1975.

Mead, M. Grandparents as educators. *Teachers College Record,* 1974, *76*(2), 240-249.

Michigan Public Act, No. 161, 1980.

Miller, D. The Native American family: The urban way. In E. Corfman (Ed.), *Families today.* Washington, D.C.: U. S. Government Printing Office, 1980, pp. 441-484.

Miller, M. V. Variations in Mexican-American family life: A review synthesis. Paper presented at the Rural Sociological Society Annual Meetings, San Francisco, CA, August, 1975.

Neugarten, B. L., and Weinstein, K. K. The changing American grandparent. *Journal of Marriage and the Family,* 1964, *26,* 199-204.

Nye, F. I. *School age parenthood.* Extension Bulletin 667. Pullman, WA: Washington State University, Cooperative Extension Service, 1976.

Phenice, L. A. *Children's perceptions of elderly persons.* Saratoga, CA: Century Twenty-one Publishing, 1981.

Rawson, J. A. *A descriptive analysis of the communication patterns between family day care providers and the parents of the children in their care.* M.A. Thesis, Michigan State University, Department of Family and Child Sciences, East Lansing, MI, 1979.

Redhorse, J. G., Lewis, R., Feit, M., and Decker, J. American Indian elders: Needs and aspirations in institutional and home health care. Unpublished manuscript, Arizona State University, 1979.

Robertson, J. F. Grandmotherhood: A study of role conceptions. *Journal of Marriage and the Family,* 1977, *39*(1), 165-174.

Sena-Rivera, J. Extended kinship in the United States: Competing models and the case of la familia Chicana. *Journal of Marriage and the Family,* 1979, *41*(1), 121-129.

Shanas, E. Social myth as hypothesis: The case of the family relations of old people. *The Gerontologist,* 1979, *19*(1), 3-9.

Shanas, E. Older people and their families: The new pioneers. *Journal of Marriage and the Family,* 1980, *42*(1), 9-15.

Shedd, C. *Grandparents.* New York: Doubleday and Company, Inc., 1976.

Shoffner, S. M. Child care in rural areas: Needs, attitudes and preferences. U.S. Department of Agriculture, Science and Education Administration. *Family Economics Review,* Fall, 1979, pp. 10-12.

Smith, E. W. The role of the grandmother in adolescent pregnancy and parenting. *Journal of School Health,* 1975, *45*(5), 57-68.

Spicer, W. J., and Hampe, G. D. Kinship interaction after divorce. *Journal of Marriage and the Family,* 1975, *37*(1), 113-119.

Sprey, J. The role of grandparents in the current American family system. Paper presented at the Third Annual National Symposium on Building Family Strengths, University of Nebraska, Lincoln, NE, May 13-15, 1980.

Stack, C. B. *All our kin.* New York: Harper and Row, Publishers, 1974.

Staples, R. Toward a sociology of the the Black family: A theoretical and methodological assessment. *Journal of Marriage and the Family,* 1971, 119-138.

Staples, R., and Mirande, A. Racial and cultural variations among American families: A decennial review of the literature on minority families. *Journal of Marriage and the Family,* 1980, *42*(4), 887-903.

Staples, R., and Smith, J. W. Attitudes of grandmothers and mothers toward child-rearing practices. *Child Development,* 1954, *25*, 91-97.

Strauss, C. A. Grandma made Johnny delinquent. *American Journal of Orthopsychiatry,* 1943, *13*, 343-346.

Sumpter, L., and Sumpter, L. Personal correspondence. East Lansing, MI, 1981. (The Sumpters have been instrumental in Michigan in getting legislation allowing grandparent visitation enacted and revised.)

Troll, L. E., Miller, S. J., and Atchley, R. C. *Families in later life.* Belmont, CA: Wadsworth Publishing Company, Inc., 1979.

Unco. *National childcare consumer study: 1975, Vols. I-II: Basic tabulations, current patterns of child care use in the United States, American consumer attitudes and opinions on child care,* (T. W. Rodes, Principal Author). Washington, D.C.: Prepared under Contract #HEW 105-74-1107 for the Office of Child Development, H.E.W., 1976.

Updegraff, S. G.   Changing role of the grandmother. *Journal of Home Economics*, 1968, *60*(3), 177-180.

United States Department of Commerce. *Social Indicators, 1976.* Washington, D.C.: U.S. Government Printing Office, Dept. of Documents, 1977.

Verway, D. I. (Ed.). *Michigan statistical abstract* (Fifteenth Edition). East Lansing: Michigan State University, Division of Research, Graduate School of Business Administration, 1980.

Vollmer, H.   The grandmother: A problem in childrearing. *American Journal of Orthopsychiatry*, 1937, *7*, 378-382.

Von Hentig, H. V. The sociological function of the grandmother. *Social Forces*, 1946, *24*, 389-392.

Webb, M. When grandparents must fight back. *Parade Magazine*, March 29, 1981, p. 22.

Winch, R. *Familial organization: A quest for determinants.* New York: The Free Press, 1977.

Wood, V., and Robertson, J.   Friendship and kinship interaction: Differential effect on the morale of the elderly. *Journal of Marriage and the Family*, 1978, *40*(2), 367-374.

Zelnik, M., and Kantner, J. F. First pregnancies to women aged 15-19: 1976 and 1971. *Family Planning Perspectives*, 1978, *10*(1), 11-20.

FOOTNOTES

(1) Research will be reported by decade of publication, although it may have been conducted in an earlier period.

(2) A nine-year-old girl in defining a grandmother said: "A grandfather is a man grandmother."

THE CONTRIBUTION OF SIBLINGS AND PEERS

TO THE PARENTING PROCESS

Wyndol Furman and Duane Buhrmester

Department of Psychology
University of Denver
Denver, CO 80210

INTRODUCTION

All social scientists would agree that the parent-child relationship is central in shaping development. Mother and father are simply the most important people in the growing child's life. More than anyone else, they are responsible for determining whether the child becomes a mature, healthy adult.

At the same time, the influence of other people in the social environment should not be overlooked. Not only do teachers and other adults have a significant impact, but siblings and peers play an important role as well. Until recently, social scientists have given little attention to the role children have in molding one another's growth. This oversight is ironic in light of the fact that half of a child's social interactions are with other children (Barker and Wright, 1955). Siblings and peers are not just playmates and classmates either; they have been shown to provide essential and often unique contributions to many facets of development (Hartup, 1976).

The purpose of this chapter is to describe the ways in which siblings and peers participate in the parenting process. Often children directly assume a parent-like role. In most households, they assist in the care of the young, serve as babysitters, or do household chores. In single parent families, the oldest sibling's responsibilities may be considerable. In some unusual cases children have even served as surrogate parents.

The contribution of siblings and peers can be seen as even greater when parenting is conceptualized in a broader light. Generally speaking, the function of a parent is to serve as a source of guidance and active stimulation which shapes the child's developmental course. Some of the tasks involved are caretaking, providing affection, promoting cognitive growth and learning, and serving as a socializing agent. When viewed in this perspective, the process of parenting is not the exclusive domain of parents, but instead is contributed to by all persons--adults and children --who shape the child's developmental course. This paper will explore how children participate in each of the different facets of parenting.

The influence of siblings and peers on development is by no means identical to that of parents. Sometimes their impact is very similar to parents, while other times it is markedly different or even in opposition. The influences are not equivalent because the various relationships take different forms. For example, interactions among agemates are egalitarian in nature, while parent-child interactions are not. Because of these qualitative differences, one can never truly replace the other. Rather, their influences are usually synergistic--i.e., their effects are concordant but not interchangeable. Together parents, siblings, and peers create effects that none alone is capable of producing.

Nor do all child-child interactions have identical effects. Interactions with agemates serve different functions than do mixed-age interactions (Hartup, 1978; Lougee and Graziano, 1980). Similarly, a sibling is more than just another peer. Brothers and sisters have a special impact because of their family ties and intimate knowledge of one another. Thus, while the major goal of this chapter is to explore how siblings and peers contribute to parenting, we will also consider how these influences differ from each other.

PROVISION OF CARETAKING

If an observer's only source of information about childrearing was the psychological literature, he would probably conclude that the only one who feeds, clothes, and looks after the welfare of the developing child is the mother, and in some cases a daycare worker. This picture is incomplete. Not only do fathers help (Lamb, 1976), but young children are also cared for by older siblings, babysitters, and even conscientious neighborhood children. In an ethnographic survey of 186 societies, Barry and Paxson (1971) found that, in the majority of cultures, children and peers helped in caretaking; moreover, in approximately 25 percent of the societies older children were the *principal* companions and caretakers. In the United States a 1969 survey showed that 22 percent of the children of working mothers were cared for by other children or adolescents (Low and Spindler, 1969). Thus, child caretaking is very common, although its effects have not been extensively examined.

Older female siblings most commonly take on the caretaking role, both within American families (Bossard and Boll, 1956) and cross-culturally (Weisner and Gallimare, 1977; Whiting and Whiting, 1975). By virtue of her age, the older daughter is more responsible and adult-like; by virtue of her sex, this role adoption is an opportunity to prepare for a future maternal role (Rosenberg, 1965). Generally, females do display more interest and ability in caretaking than males. Jane Goodall (1975) reports that young female primates are eager to hold infants, although their efforts are initially clumsy. Both sexes of preadolescent rhesus monkeys display affection toward young infants but the females' behavior is more social in nature while the males' is more aggressive and rough (Brandt and Mitchell, 1973). In humans, adolescent females are more interested in infants than males, particularly during high school (Feldman and Nash, 1979). While it is uncertain whether the predominance of female caretakers is rooted in genetic or cultural factors, it is clear that the norm is for child caretakers to be girls.

Although most child caretaking is done by older siblings, children outside the nuclear family can contribute. Babysitters and interested neighborhood children often assist in various tasks, although little is known about their effect. Cross culturally, older peers and agemates contribute to the daily caretaking of children in various collective societies, such as the Israeli Kibbutzim (Spiro, 1975) or Russian collectives (Bronfenbrenner, 1970). While less influential than care by siblings, caretaking by children outside the family is nevertheless a common occurrence.

The amount of child caretaking varies from family to family and from culture to culture. One may expect that it occurs more often in large families where there are more children to care for and more children to serve as caretakers. In fact, older siblings do participate in the management of the younger ones in over 90 percent of families with five or more children (Bossard and Boll, 1956). Other conditions commonly leading to increased child caretaking include: a) divorce or the illness, death, or incarceration of a parent, b) both parents being employed fulltime, or c) the presence of a sibling who is mentally ill or retarded (Myers and Roberts, 1959). With the increasing number of working mothers and the rising cost of daycare, we may see an even greater reliance on child caretakers.

The complexity of the culture also seems to be associated with the use of child caretakers. In their study of six cultures, Whiting and Whiting (1975) reported that less complex societies relied more heavily on children as caretakers. In the simplest culture studied (Nyansongo, Kenya), 69 percent of the mothers reported that some child had aided in the care of their infant. In the most complex society (Orchard Town, U.S.A.), only 12 percent had used children as caretakers. Similarly, in the simple cultures mothers were around the home less frequently than were siblings and peers, while the reverse was true in the most complex one. Apparently, in less complex cultures the mother is more involved in obtaining sustenance for the family, thus leaving older children at home to take over the caretaking duties.

Although similar in function, child caretaking is by no means identical to that of adults. Unlike adults, children have to balance two sources of pressure--one being the often times tyrannical behavior of their small charge, and the other the watchful eye of parents (Weisner and Gallimore, 1977). As a consequence, the styles of discipline differ. For example, Mead (1978) reports that Samoan children are more indulgent of their siblings than are parents. In the Kibbutz schools, peers use as many positive sanctions as teachers do, but fewer negative ones (Spiro, 1975). In large American families siblings depend upon leadership, goodwill, counseling, group pressure, and appeals for cooperation to maintain order, while parents are more apt to rely on physical punishment. In fact, the discipline of older siblings is often seen by the younger as more meaningful and appropriate than that of parents (Bossard and Boll, 1960). It seems that siblings have a greater awareness of the younger child's problems and can more fairly judge what is actually misbehavior. Some of the differences between adult and child caretaking may also be due to the greater equity in the power status of siblings.

Child caretaking has direct and indirect effects on the development of both the child who is cared for and the child who serves as the caretaker. One certain positive effect for the child caretaker is the role training it provides for parenthood. Helping rear a sibling may even make children more competent parents of their own offspring (Essman, 1977). In effect, societies which rely heavily on child caretaking are providing earlier and stronger sex-role training for girls than those that don't (Weisner and Gallimore, 1977). Finally, the caretaking experience has been hypothesized to promote the development of pro-social, responsible and nuturant behaviors (Whiting and Whiting, 1975).

On the negative side, Bossard and Boll (1956) report that being saddled with the responsibility of tending a younger sibling may have a detrimental effect on the older child's own social life and growth. The responsibility of parenting at an early age can prove to be a frustrating burden for some children. Another child has neither the preparation nor the authority that an adult does.

Being cared for by another child also has mixed effects on the development of the recipient. Several indirect positive effects have been hypothesized. Gallimore, Boggs and Jordan (1974) suggest that sibling caretaking lightens the mother's responsibility, thus allowing her more time to play and interact positively with her children. Further, when an older sibling is substantially involved in the caretaking, an infant may develop an attachment to both the mother and the sibling. Multiple attachments have the effect of reducing separation distress from mother (Bowlby, 1969). On the other hand, child caretaking may weaken the socializing influence of parents (Levy, 1968; Mead, 1968). Ritchie (1956) argued that older siblings provide only a weak approximation of adult values, and thus their socializing influence is not as desirable. Similarly, Mead (1968) suggested that sibling caretaking perpetuates a lower level of social individuality because the siblings themselves do not have well defined personalities. Child caretakers may lack the maturity and experience necessary for the responsibility of caring for another.

In sum, child caretaking is common in modern America and most other societies. There is little question that it affects the provider, recipient and even the parents, but substantial controversy exists concerning the relative advantages and disadvantages of caretaking by children. Unfortunately, little evidence can be garnered in support of any position. The existing data are simply too sparse and scattered. An accurate account of the overall effect of child caretaking on development will require substantially more research.

PROVISION OF AFFECTION

Children have a deep need for affection; they require much more than just nutritional and protective care to develop normally. In their classic studies of primates, Harlow and his colleagues have repeatedly documented that early social and affectional deprivation has long-lasting debilitating effects (Harlow, Dodsworth, and Harlow, 1965). Monkeys deprived of early affection and social contact engage in bizarre stereotyped rituals and typically never develop appropriate social, sexual, and parenting behaviors. Similarly, in his review of the effects of early derpivation, Bowlby (1952) reported that institutionalized infants were often developmentally arrested, withdrawn, depressed, and limited in their capacity for social relationships. Although recent data indicate that the effects of early deprivation may have been overstated (c.f. Cairns, 1979), it is clear that the provision of affection is essential to children's growth.

The infant's first affectional tie is to the primary caregiver, typically mother (Bowlby, 1969). In the latter half of the first year of life, the infant develops a specific preference for her and perceives her to be a source of security and affection. Children protest upon separation from mother and are comforted on her return. Attachments to father also begin to develop at this time (Cohen and Campos, 1974; Lamb, 1977). These early ties between infant and parents appear to be critical determinants of subsequent social and cognitive growth (Sroufe, 1979). Although their form changes with development, parent-child relations remain central throughout life.

Important as they may be, parents are not the only providers of affection to the child. Siblings and children outside the home play a critical role in meeting affectional needs, particularly as the child grows older. Children may have older siblings who give them both guidance and love. Brother and sisters close in age often are constant companions and sources of warmth and security to each other. Outside the home, bonds of friendship are made and provide a strong sense of being cared for and accepted. Looking back on our own childhood experiences, it would be hard to deny how powerful these sources of affection are to the growing child.

As the infant enters the social world, some of the earliest affectional ties are likely to be with siblings. Although they still prefer the presence of their parents, young infants do attend to their siblings and often imitate their behavior (Lamb, 1978a, 1978b). During the second year of life, infants increasingly direct social behaviors toward their siblings. Most of these behaviors are pro-social or positive in nature (Abramovitch, Corter and Lando, 1979). Older siblings tend to reciprocate in kind, although older males direct commands and verbal aggression toward their siblings as well. These early forms of pro-social behavior can be seen as overt manifestations of the emotional attachment growing between siblings.

As siblings grow older, they are likely to spend much time playing together and consequently, acquire an intimate knowledge of each other's lives. While this high degree of intimacy may contribute to sibling rivalry, it also creates a strong sense of loyalty and comradeship (Bossard and Boll, 1956). Siblings commonly stick up for one another and make every effort to protect each other. The large majority are strongly attached to each other. In an extensive study involving 8,000 junior and senior high school students, Bowerman and Dobash (1974) found that 65 percent of the subjects reported feeling close to their siblings; a third of these said "extremely close" and the others were "quite close." At the other extreme, only 13 percent said they were "not close" or "not particularly close." Girls felt more affection toward their siblings than boys did. Also, on the average, children are closer to same-sex and older siblings. Many of the affectional ties between siblings last long into adulthood. Bossard and Boll (1956) found that as adults, two-thirds of the siblings from their sample of large families reported still feeling close to at least one of their brothers or sisters. Certainly, siblings serve as important sources of affection for one another.

As they move into the outside social world, children begin to establish friendships. Like other attachments, friendships involve companionship, intimacy and affection. The attachment of friendship, however, differs from that of family members in several ways (Furman, in press; Hartup, 1978). Friends are usually similar in age and status. Throughout this paper such egalitarianism will be shown to have a decided effect on the nature and impact of the relationship. Friendships are also voluntary. Children have no choice about who is a member of their family, but they do select with whom they want to be friends. Affection can be given or withheld by either person. Friendships can be short-lived, but the affection from friends is special because it comes from someone who is under no obligation to give it.

Affectional ties with peers undergo several developmental transformations. During the toddler phase, many children begin to establish relationships with children outside the home. By twenty-four months of age, children begin to display mutual preferences for each other (Vandell and Mueller, 1980). Proximity seeking, sharing, positive affect and play all occur more commonly in interactions with familiar peers than in those with unfamiliar ones (Lewis, Young, Brooks, and Michalson, 1975). Very young children seem to derive a sense of security from other children. For example, infants and nursery school children show less distress when separated from parents if peers are present (Howe and Mueller, in press; Ipsa, 1977).

Peers are a significant part of preschool-aged children's lives. Much of the day is spent interacting with neighborhood playmates or preschool classmates. The majority of these peer encounters are of a positive nature (Charlesworth and Hartup, 1967; Furman and Masters, 1980). Affection, support, and other pro-social behaviors are all common. During this developmental period children first begin to establish friendships with specific peers. These relations are usually centered around play activities, but affection is also recognized as an important component of the relationship (Furman and Bierman, 1980b).

During the school years, children develop "chumships" or long lasting relationships with same-sex peers (Sullivan, 1953). Earlier friendships were somewhat unstable and transitory, but "chumships" often continue for years. Children feel genuine affection and love for their chums; they develop a real sensitivity to what matters to the other. According to Sullivan, a "chumship" is a major developmental milestone. It gives children the opportunity to express interpersonal intimacy, teaches them a sense of humanity, and promotes positive self-esteem. With the appearance of these relationships children's conceptions of their friendships undergo an important transformation. Their conceptions change from an emphasis on superficial concrete behaviors to more intimate and personal characteristics. Empathy, trust, self-disclosure, and admiration all become central features of friendships (Bigelow and La Gaipa, 1980; Furman and Bierman, 1980a). In adolescence, concerns over peer acceptance greatly intensify as children move from a family orientation to a peer orientation (Bowerman and Kinch, 1959). Many of their peer relationships are very deep, intimate and stable in nature, some lasting long into adulthood. Thus, as children mature and break away from their dependency on parents they turn to their agemates for affection and support.

Although peers, siblings, and parents all serve as important sources of affection, the different relationships should not be equated. Even in infancy, affection is expressed differently in the various relationships. Physical contact is more common between mother and infant, while eye contact and sharing are more frequent among peers (Lewis et al., 1975; Vandell, 1980). Parents, rather than peers, are also more likely to be the first source of security and comfort for young children. For instance, when frightened, young primates seek proximity to mother rather than to peers (Patterson, Bonvillian, Reynolds, and Maccoby, 1975).

As children grow older, the degree of differentiation increases. Heathers (1955) observed marked differences in preschool children's affectional behavior toward peers and adults. Children sought affection from adults by physical contact and clinging, while with peers they sought attention and approval. Apparently, throughout childhood, physical affection is principally limited to parent-child relations.

Although the two systems are distinct, the quality of the peer-peer and parent-child relationships affect each other. Vandell (1980) found significant correlations between an infant's pattern of interaction with another infant and that with his/her mother. Similarly, significant relationships have been observed between attachment status and behavior toward peers (Easterbrooks and Lamb, 1979). Infants who were more sociable and sophisticated with peers were more independent around their mother. Apparently, peers foster the separation from adult caretakers. Finally, both the security of attachment to mother and early peer experience predicted subsequent social competence in the preschool (Lieberman, 1977).

At one time the prevailing theoretical conception stated that the parent-child relationship served as a precursor to and prototype for later peer-peer relations (Bowlby, 1969). In more recent conceptualizations, however, the peer-peer and parent-child affectional systems have been hypothesized to reciprocally influence one another (Easterbrooks and Lamb, 1979; Vandell, 1980). This framework seems more promising in light of recent work documenting the influence of peers on the parent-child relationship. After being exposed to a series of play experiences, toddlers were found to interact differently toward parents (Vandell, 1979). They displayed greater proximity seeking and more object-related social acitivities. Apparently, the peer experience led the children to become more equal participants in their interactions with parents. Thus, the different relationships markedly influence each other, but none are replaceable or interchangeable. Affection and acceptance by parents, siblings and agemates are all essential to the developing child.

PROMOTION OF COGNITIVE GROWTH AND LEARNING

Parents are an important part of the child's learning environment. They introduce them to words, concepts, and new parts of the world. Their input stimulates the processes of asimilation and accommodation essential to cognitive growth. Stories of far-off lands, trips to the zoo, and walks in the park all serve as opportunities for new learning. After the child enters school, parents continue to foster intellectual development. A good parent encourages academic efforts, recognizes achievements, and may provide tutoring when needed.

Siblings and peers are also important parts of the child's learning environment. An older brother or sister can serve as an invaluable guide to experiences yet to be encountered. A large part of every day is spent with peers in school, on the neighborhood playground, and at home. During these encounters information is shared, knowledge is transmitted, and intellectual abilities are challenged. One learns about a variety of topics ranging from science to sports. In fact, information about some subjects such as sex is almost exclusively acquired from other children (Hartup, 1976). Even with today's liberal values, sex is rarely discussed between parents and children.

While all serve to stimulate cognitive growth, the influence of peers and siblings is expressed through different mechanisms than that of parents. The following sections describe: a) how the egalitarian structure of child-child interactions promote the resolution of conflicting perspectives, b) how social play fosters role-taking and creative skills, and c) how children have been used to tutor one another.

Resolution of conflicting perspectives. Young children view the world in an egocentric fashion. They perceive things from their viewpoint alone and have little knowledge that other viewpoints may exist. As they grow older, they become increasingly aware that alternative perspectives and representations of the world exist. Piaget (1932) proposed that peer interactions play a fundamental role in this decrease of egocentrism. In the course of interacting with peers, children often are confronted with different ideas and opinions. Such confrontations serve as sources of disequilibrium and more specifically, as opportunities to take the perspective of another. Often the resolution of divergent opinions requires the adaptation of a nonegocentric perspective, thus fostering cognitive restructuring.

If it is true that peer interactions do foster cognitive growth, children's cognitive abilities should be related to the quantity and quality of such interchanges. Several correlational studies support this hypothesis. For example, Deutsch (1974) found a significant relationship between preschool children's rates of positive peer interaction and their communicative role-taking ability. Similarly, the role-taking ability of third and fifth graders has been found to be correlated with measures of leadership and sociability (Rothenberg, 1970). Role-taking ability and popularity may also be related, although the data are rather mixed (Rubin and Pepler, 1980).

While the preceding findings are only correlational, the effects of confrontations with peers have also been demonstrated through experimental manipulation. Several investigators have examined the effects of having conservers and nonconservers discuss their solutions to Piagetian conservation tasks (Miller and Brownell, 1975; Murray, 1972; Silverman and Geiringer, 1973). As a result of these confrontations, the nonconservers typically change to conserving solutions, while the conservers remain the same or report even more advanced ideas. Children do not have to be at different levels of understanding to benefit from these exchanges. When both have only a partial understanding of a perspective-taking task, they can discuss a problem together and often achieve a more complete understanding than either had before (Mugny and Doise, 1978).

Interactions with other children may even facilitate greater gains than adult-child interchanges. Older peers can sometimes explain a conservation task better than an adult (Rothenberg and Orost, 1969). Weinheimer (1972) found greater reconciliation of perspectives when alters were peers than when an adult was involved. He suggested that peers may be more able to serve as models and that adults may inhibit children from reconsidering their views. Thus, the research to date provides support for Piaget's thesis that peer interactions foster a decline in egocentrism by serving as a source of disequilibrium.

Play. Siblings and peers serve as the primary playmates for the growing child. Countless hours are spent playing "make-believe", making art projects, building blocks, and playing sports and games. While once overlooked, play is now recognized as serving numerous functions (Bruner, Jolly and Sylva, 1976). Children acquire substantial cognitive and social knowledge through the medium of play. Play also stimulates the assimilatory and accommodatory processes of development. In play, children have the opportunity to suspend reality and exercise their innovative and creative capacities. Similarly, achievement pressure is reduced in certain types of play, thus allowing potentially beneficial risk-taking behavior which might normally be inhibited.

Sociodramatic or fantasy play, in particular, is thought to be instrumental in cognitive development (Rubin and Pepler, 1980; Smilansky, 1968). The experience of developing and acting out social fantasies is believed to improve numerous cognitive, creative, and social skills. It serves to liberate the child from concrete situational thinking, promotes imagination, and strengthens verbal mediation (Singer, 1973; Vygotsky, 1962). Finally, sociodramatic play provides children with frequent opportunities for role-taking--an activity central to cognitive growth.

Although limited, empirical research on the effects of social play has been promising. In several studies, Rubin and his colleagues have found a significant relationships between role-taking ability and the amount of associative and dramatic play engaged in by preschool children (Rubin and Pepler, 1980). Efforts have also been made to enrich underprivileged preschool children's experiences in sociodramatic play. In these training studies children act out a series of imaginary dramas, such as giving aid to a person in distress. Although effects are not completely consistent, changes have been observed in communication skills (Smilansky, 1968), social-role conservation (Fink, 1976), and role-taking ability (Burns and Brainerd, 1979; Saltz, Dixon, and Johnson, 1977). Many of these studies, however, have methodological limitations which temper the significance of the findings. As Rubin and Pepler (1980) concluded, the theoretical reasons for believing that social play contributes to cognitive growth are stronger than the existing empirical data.

Tutoring. Children often need and seek out information and assistance in their schoolwork. While parents and teachers are obvious sources of knowledge, siblings and peers can also be tutors. Classmates and siblings often help each other with their school assignments. Other children may be even better teachers than parents when they have direct knowledge of the subject (e.g., childhood norms or school assignments) or when the topic is taboo (e.g., sex or death) (Irish, 1964). Cicirelli (1976) has further argued that at times siblings make better teachers than either parents or non-siblings; siblings have an intimate understanding of each other and can be very frank in their comments.

Educators have also used children as formal tutors for younger peers. The idea of peer tutoring was first suggested in the early 1900's by Lancaster and Bell, but was not widely adopted until the last decade (Allen, 1976). Such tutoring can provide individualized instruction to those needing help and yet is not prohibitively expensive. Anecdotal reports of the effects of peer tutoring have been promising (cf. Feldman, Devin-Sheehan and Allen, 1976). Children seem to profit from the individualized attention and role-modeling by older tutors. More impressively, the tutors themselves benefit. Many show increases in self-confidence, responsibility, interest in school, and academic ability. Peer tutoring seems to be particularly valuable for children who are low achievers.

Unfortunately, empirical studies of the effects of peer tutoring have yielded only mixed results. Several critical reviews of the literature have come to similar conclusions (Cloward, 1967; Erickson and Cormack, 1972; Feldman, Devin-Sheehan, and Allen, 1976). Children acting as tutors often show positive gains in both achievement and attitudes toward school, but several studies also report no such effects. A few studies have shown academic gains by tutees, most have not. Generally tutors are more likely to show positive benefits from acting as a teacher than the tutees are as learners (Strodtbeck, Rouchi and Hansell, 1977).

Future research may, however, yield more positive effects of peer tutoring. Currently, numerous types of programs are all described as peer tutoring. Some are likely to be effective, some not. Finally, more effective programs can be developed once it is determined what processes are responsible for the effects of tutoring (Bierman and Furman, in press). One crucial factor seems to be the relative competence of the tutor and tutee. If the tutor is clearly superior to the tutee--because of either training or a large difference in age--then the tutee is much more likely to gain from the experience (Feldman, Devin-Sheehan and Allen, 1976).

Thus, peer tutoring shows promise, but much work needs to be done in designing the programs. It should be noted that these comments are equally applicable to the tutoring efforts of parents. Moreover, while the effectiveness of peers as tutors in the formal school setting is somewhat unclear, it is difficult to doubt the importance of the informal teaching and learning that goes on between siblings and friends. Children learn much from each other in the course of their daily interchanges.

Limitations of the peer environment. Thus far, the positive contribution that siblings and peers make to cognitive development has been emphasized. In some areas of intellectual growth, however, age-mates are unable to provide the same quality of stimulation as parents do. Siblings and peers are themselves intellectually immature, and thus lack some of the skills and knowledge necessary to promote optimal cognitive growth.

Consider the research on language development. In many cultures, children depend on agemates or older peers for linguistic experience (Slobin, 1975). In her review of the literature, Bates (1975) found little evidence that language development was enhanced by either being a twin or by having extensive interactions with peers. If the primary source of input is peers, development may even be retarded. Apparently, relative agemates serve as poor linguistic models and teachers.

Zajonc and Markus (1975) have also argued that having a large number of brothers and sisters may have negative effects on intellectual development. As the family size increases, the overall level of intellectual maturity of a family is lowered because of the greater number of immature thinkers. Thus, later born children in large families may develop in an environment which is intellectually less sophisticated and stimulating. Some support of this view is garnered from research demonstrating an inverse relationship between IQ scores and both numbers of siblings and birth order (Belmont and Marolla 1973; Berbaum and Moreland, 1980; Breland, 1974). Verbal ability particularly seems to be affected by increased family size (Breland, 1974).

While in some ways the quality of intellectual input from siblings and peers may not equal that of parents, it nevertheless is clear that they make a significant and unique contribution to cognitive growth. The egalitarian give-and-take which characterize peer interactions fosters the working through of conflicting perspectives and promotes cognitive development. Playing together provides children with opportunities to practice role-taking skills. Finally, much information is transmitted among children, through both formal and informal tutoring.

AGENTS OF SOCIALIZATION

In the course of development, children must learn appropriate social behaviors, acquire numerous social competencies and master the rules, mores, and values of their culture. Parents, siblings, and peers all have key roles in this socialization process. The contribution of each has been documented in a variety of areas, including sex-role identification, modulation of aggression, transmission of norms and values, moral development, self-concept formation, and general adjustment. As will become evident, the impact of children on one another is probably its greatest in the area of social development.

Sex and sex-role development. Children must learn how males and females differ and what behavioral patterns are deemed appropriate for each sex. While parents contribute to this process, other children are key sources of information and act as influential role models. As mentioned previously, most information about sexual functioning is obtained from siblings and peers (Hartup, 1976). Furthermore, sexual experimentation occurs almost exclusively in interactions among peers (Kinsey, Pomeroy and Martin, 1948). Apparently, the incest taboo is so pervasive that almost any attention to sexuality is prohibited in the parent-child relationship.

The development of sex-roles involves more than just learning about sexual functioning. Children must also acquire sex-typed behaviors and attitudes. Research has shown that siblings and peers serve as important models and reinforcers of sex-role behavior. In a study by Kobasigawa (1968), kindergarten children were exposed to a peer model who either: a) played with opposite-sex-typed toys, b) resisted playing with the "inappropriate" toys, or c) played with neutral toys. Peer modeling markedly influenced the children's subsequent behavior. Those who observed the resistant model played with the cross-gender toys less. The effect of the cross-gender modeling varied depending upon the sex of the subject and model. For girls, both male and female models increased the amount of imitation. For boys, the amount increased only if the model was also a boy. Wolf (1973) also found that modeling of opposite-sex-typed behavior was influential only if the model was of the same gender.

Children not only model, but reinforce gender-appropriate behavior. In a series of investigations, Fagot and her colleagues have observed preschool children's responses to gender appropriate or inappropriate behavior (Fagot, 1977; Fagot and Patterson, 1969). Children of both sexes were found to reinforce gender-correct behavior and punish cross-gender behavior. Cross-gender behavior by boys was particularly likely to be disapproved of, suggesting that the norms for boys are more rigid. A similar pattern of results was observed by Lamb and Roopnarino (1979). They reported that positive reinforcement for masculine activities affected boys more than girls, while reinforcement for feminine activities affected girls more than boys.

While most of the research has focused on the preschool years, peers may even be more influential in subsequent years. In fact, in one study children's perceptions of their same-sexed friends and the media's attitudes towards cross-gender behavior were the two major determinants of sex-role attitudes. Perceptions of their parents' attitudes were also related but not as strongly (Katz, 1979). Thus, other children, particularly those of the same sex, have an influential role in modeling and shaping sex-role development.

Since siblings spend large amounts of time interacting, their impact on one another's sex-role identity is potentially great. Controversy exists, however, as to the nature of this influence. Two basic positions are taken. The first states that siblings reinforce and model sex-typed behaviors for each other, and thus siblings should be similar in their sex-role identity. The second position states that siblings tend to differentiate themselves from each other rather than becoming alike (c.f. Adler, 1959). Thus, boys with sisters may be more masculine than is typical; girls with brothers, more feminine. Both positions have received some empirical support (contrast Brim, 1958; Sutton-Smith, Roberts and Rosenberg, 1965, with Grotevant, 1978). Thus, further research is needed to determine when modeling and contrast effects each prevail. It is quite evident, however, that siblings are major influences on sex-role development.

Expression and control of aggression. A major developmental task for children is to learn how to modulate their aggressive impulses. On the one hand, children must learn to control inappropriate impulses; on the other hand, they must learn to be appropriately assertive in affirming their rights and desires. Hartup (1976) has argued that children gain an appropriate balance of control and expression by interaction with children who are approximately the same age as they are. Unlike parent-child interactions which contain an imbalance of power, child-child interactions provide the egalitarian give-and-take essential for learning appropriate aggressiveness. When interacting with equals, a child's attempts to dominate another are sometimes successful and sometimes unsuccessful. This mixture of outcomes promotes the desired modulation of aggressive impulses. Thus, children are able to practice initiating and responding to various forms of aggression, such as rough-and-tumble play, directive commands, verbal insults, and physical attack.

Hartup's (1976) thesis has received empirical support. The results of research with primates suggests that practice in aggression is necessary for normal development to occur. When rhesus monkeys are reared by their mother alone and have no contact with agemates, they do not develop appropriate aggression control. Instead, they fluctuate between bouts of hyperaggressiveness and a general fearfulness and timidity (Suomi and Harlow, 1975).

Children are also responsible for shaping, modifying, and reinforcing one another's aggressive behaviors. In a classic study, Patterson, Littman and Bricker (1967) observed incidents of aggression and their outcome in a preschool setting. They found that teachers were rarely involved in aggressive episodes. Instead, peers were the major agents determining the outcome of aggressive behavior. The majority of the time children reinforced aggressive acts by complying with or submitting to the aggressor's wish. Not surprisingly, children who were successfully aggressive continued to be aggressive in the same manner; if unsuccessful, children were not as likely to repeat that type of aggressive act or be aggressive towards that person again.

These findings illustrate how children close in age (either peers or siblings) are major agents in the socialization of aggressive impulses. Mixed-aged interactions also play a role, but in another manner. Different power tactics are required for influencing younger and older children. Often children master these techniques in their interactions with their siblings. Because of the intimacy and frankness of sibling relations, brothers and sisters commonly have conflicts of will accompanied by anger and quarreling. When these occur, older siblings tend to use direct dominance techniques, such as bossing, using status, being offensive, bribing, ignoring, and physically attacking (Sutton-Smith and Rosenberg, 1970). On the other hand, because of their relative physical and cognitive immaturity, younger siblings are forced to rely on counter-reaction techniques such as appeals to parents, pleading, reasoning, and attacking the other's property. Thus, through interacting with peers and siblings of various ages, children both develop a variety of effective power tactics and learn to control inappropriate impulses.

Acquisition of norms and values. In the course of development, a child acquires a set of values, norms, and attitudes. Like parents, siblings and peers are important parts of the social environment which shape the growth of these values. In the home, sibling interactions come to be governed by agreements about what constitutes fair and responsible behavior. Younger children often look up to and attempt to emulate the values and goals of older brothers or sisters (Bossard and Boll, 1956). Outside the home, school and neighborhood peer groups form their own systems of norms and values. Children learn age-appropriate attitudes and codes of behavior from these peer and sibling interactions.

Even young children's interactions are governed by group norms and values. Nursery school children establish numerous group traditions, such as a seating order, play rituals, collective ownership of certain toys, and a group jargon (Merei, 1949). Although the data are primarily anecdotal, it appears that these groups are organized around shared interests and common play preferences (Hartup, 1970).

During the early elementary school years, group norms become more evident. Groups become more cohesive and structured (Smith, 1960) and the opinions and values of one's peers are more formal and influential (Hartup, 1970). Several investigators have provided detailed descriptions of the growth and structure of group norms (Crane, 1952; Fine, 1980; Sherif, Harvey, White, Hood and Sherif, 1961). Although the specific groups studied have ranged from Little League teams (Fine, 1980) to Australian gangs (Crane, 1952), some remarkable commonalities have been observed. First, the initial formation of a group requires that members begin with certain shared values and objectives. As the group is formed, specific norms quickly develop. Sherif et al. (1961) found that summer camp groups had developed nicknames, identifying colors, and rules of conduct within the first few days of their existence. In typical neighborhood and school groups, children develop secret signals, scatological jargon, codes for communicating (e.g., Pig Latin) and initiation rites for admission. The group will prohibit or sanction numerous activities. Often members of a group engage in illicit activities such as smoking or petty crimes together. In a positive vein, some groups will organize pro-social activities, such as charity drives or volunteer work. Thus, peer values and norms come to pervade all aspects of group functioning.

The influence of peer norms is greatest during adolescence (Bowerman and Kinch, 1959). Adolescents are very concerned about their peers' opinions of them and are strongly influenced by the peer culture's values, customs, and fads (Conger, 1973). In general, conformity to peer norms increases during the late preadolescent and early adolescent years and then decreases during the later part of adolescence (Blos, 1941; Costanzo and Shaw, 1966; Iscoe, Williams and Harvey, 1963). The precise age of the peak in conformity does vary from study to study and seems dependent upon the specific situation involved.

Typically, the popular media has portrayed peer and parental norms as being in great conflict. If we believe the media, parents' efforts to raise well-behaved and aspiring children are to no avail because their offspring become corrupted by peers. Such a view is both simplistic and misleading. Adult and peer values are typically concordant (Douvan and Adelson, 1966; Langworthy, 1959). Children also tend to select friends who meet their parents' approval, thus increasing the amount of concordance between parental and peer values (Lesser and Kandel, 1969; Offer and Offer, 1976).

At times, however, parental and peer values come in conflict. When these cross-pressures do occur, children do not necessarily adhere to the peer norm. Instead, their response depends upon the specific circumstances. Adolescents tend to rely on their parents' opinion when the situation involves a moral issue, while they are more influenced by peer opinions when a social issue is involved (Brittain, 1963; Young and Ferguson, 1979). In most cases, children are affected by *both* parents and peers (Siman, 1977). The influences of these two systems are strongest when they are concordant with each other. Such effects have been found on a variety of topics including educational goals (Lesser and Kandel, 1969), social aspirations (Simpson, 1962), use of marijuana (Kandel, 1973) and kosher practices (Rosen, 1955). Finally, it should be noted that the degree of cross-pressures varies considerably from culture to culture. In Russia, the peer group serves as a direct extension of adult socialization (Bronfenbrenner, 1967). Similarly, in the peer-oriented Kibbutz, differences in values are uncommon (Spiro, 1975). In all cultures, however, children help transmit the norms and values of their parents and society.

Moral development. Siblings and peers are not only involved in the acquisition of cultural norms and attitudes but also contribute to the development of personal values and moral codes. Like parents, they often model and reinforce appropriate conduct and shape the child's conception of right and wrong. Children look to one another to learn age-appropriate forms of morality. Siblings and peers also actively impose moral rules and regulations on each other. Even preschool children will comply with peer-imposed rules. Some children, in fact, adhere to peer-endorsed restrictions more than to teacher-endorsed rules (Furman and Masters, 1980). By early elementary school, children seem to be capable of generating their own rules and imposing a self-governed system for enforcement. Turner (1957) describes an instance in which a group of kindergarten children was asked to develop rules for resolving social problems. After some time, the children established a body of rules and procedures which closely resembled conventional adult actions.

During the school years, the influence of peer group values increases. The group becomes more able to elicit conformity to moral standards and when deviations do occur, peers and siblings have the power to induce guilt.

Peer interactions also contribute to the development of the child's moral reasoning ability. Piaget (1932) hypothesized that such experiences are a major factor responsible for the developmental change from moral realism to the morality of reciprocity. In the earlier stage of moral realism young children perceive rules to be sacred and immutable. As they grow older, children begin to recognize that rules are not absolute, but instead are determined by group consensus. This recognition of the subjective nature of rules is more likely to be fostered by interactions with peers than by interactions with parents. Parents' rules are likely to be perceived as absolute, and be imposed on the child by the parent. In contrast, peer rules are more likely to be seen as arbitrary. When disagreements about a rule arise, neither child is likely to acquiesce automatically; instead, they argue until a mutually acceptable decision is reached. Thus, it is the egalitarian nature of peer interactions which promotes a recognition of the subjective basis of rules.

Although somewhat limited, the existing data support Piaget's hypothesis. Keasey (1971) found significant correlations between moral judgment level and amount of social participation, ratings of popularity, and ratings of leadership. In other studies, peer acceptance has been found to be related with level of moral judgment (Kohlberg, 1958), peers' perceptions of good moral judgment (Porteus and Johnson, 1965) and sensitivity to others' feelings (Loban, 1953).

Experimental evidence of the effects of peer interactions is provided in studies by LeFurgy and Woloshin (1969) and Turiel (1966). In both studies, young adolescents were confronted with peers making moral judgments at higher or lower levels than their own. In each case, the most stable change in moral judgment level was shown by children who interacted with peers of a higher level of moral reasoning. Since level of moral reasoning is highly related to age, interactions with older peers may foster moral development (Lougee and Graziano, 1980). The mixed-age interactions inherent in sibling relations may be a particularly salient source of growth-promoting confrontations. Overall, while the evidence is still sparse, it seems reasonable to conclude that children of both the same and different ages (e.g., siblings) are major influences in stimulating the growth of moral reasoning and shaping moral conduct.

Self-concept and self-esteem. Siblings and peers not only contribute to the acquisition of specific norms and values, but are major determinants of a child's general self-concept. Mead (1934) proposed that self-concepts arise in social interactions where children perceive themselves in ways that others perceive them. That is, a person's self-concept is "the generalized other." Harry Stack Sullivan (1953) also stressed the importance of peer perceptions in self-concept formation. In particular, he proposed that "chumships" provide consensual validation for pre-adolescents' conceptions of themselves. Research by Mannarino (1978) lends support to Sullivan's hypothesis. Sixth-grade boys who had close chums were found to have higher self-esteem than boys with no chums. More generally, self-esteem has been found to be related to peer acceptance (Horowitz, 1962; Reese, 1961). Similarly, a negative evaluation from the peer group causes a decrease in a child's self-acceptance (Marshall, 1958).

Peers also serve as a major reference group for describing and evaluating oneself. For example, when asked to tell about themselves, children refer to their friends more frequently than anyone else including family members (McGuire and Padawer-Singer, 1976). Children also compare themselves with their peers when evaluating their cognitive, social, and physical competence (Minton, 1979). Such social comparison processes increase as children get older (Ruble, Feldman, and Baggiano, 1976; Veroff, 1969).

Siblings play a dual role in the establishment of self-concept. On the one hand, children identify with their siblings and come to think of themselves in similar ways (cf., Bigner, 1971). They adopt many of each others values, norms, and interests. At the same time, each child makes an effort to be unique within the family group by striving to be different from their siblings. Such deidentification is hypothesized to arise out of sibling rivalry and the child's efforts to establish areas of superiority (Adler, 1959). Generally, siblings describe themselves on personality inventories as similar to one another (Cattell, Eber, and Tatsuoka, 1970; Schachter, Gilutz, Shore, and Adler, 1978). More direct comparisons of siblings' self-concepts have, however, not been made.

Social and emotional adjustment. Since peers and siblings are involved in many facets of social development, it is not surprising that they have an enormous impact on social and emotional adjustment. In the course of interacting with peers and siblings, children acquire numerous social competencies essential for a healthy adjustment. Intimate relationships with peers serve as a unique context for acquiring skills such as appropriate self disclosure, conflict resolution techniques, and appropriate expression of affection. Consequently, one can expect there to be a strong reciprocal relationship between positive peer relations and social skills. In fact, peer acceptance has been found to be correlated with acquaintanceship skills (Gottman, Gonso, and Rasmussen, 1975), appropriate helping skills (Ladd and Oden, 1979), communication ability (Gottman, et al., 1975) and social sensitivity (Rothenberg, 1970).

Many studies have documented that children with few or no friends are not well adjusted. In his review of the literature, Hartup (1970) reported numerous correlates of low sociometric status including general unhappiness, poor school adjustment, anxiety, and other neurotic symptoms. Children who are reserved are also described as submissive, anxious, unstable, and vulnerable (Bronson, 1966).

Early peer relations have a long term impact on adjustment. Children who are rejected by their peers are at high risk for numerous problems including juvenile delinquency (Roff, Sells, and Golden, 1972), emotional difficulties in early adulthood (Cowen, Pederson, Babijian, Izzo and Trost, 1973), psychiatric problems (Roff, 1963) and suicide (Stengle, 1964). The adequacy of peer relations is actually one of the strongest childhood predictors of adult mental health. The strength of this relationship may reflect the fact that both peer interactions and adult social relationships involve interchanges among equals.

Little research has been done on the effects of siblings on the adjustment of children. Available evidence, however, suggests that they too have a strong influence. Infant monkeys who are reared with a twin are more social and affiliative than those reared by mother alone (Deets, 1974). Similarly, toddlers with siblings are more sociable than only children (Howe, 1978). If a parent is absent or overburdened, a brother or sister may provide essential emotional support (Bossard and Boll, 1956). In father-absent homes, girls with older brothers and boys with brothers (younger or older) show the least amount of maladjustment (Sutton-Smith, Rosenberg, and Landy, 1968). On the other hand, strong rivalries and jealousies between siblings may have a negative impact on adjustment (Irish, 1964). Moreover, the form of maladjustment is affected by the family constellation. Children from small families are more frequently bothered by personality and emotional problems such as anxiety and childhood neuroses (Sutton-Smith and Rosenberg, 1964), while larger families yield more acting out problems such as juvenile delinquency, antisocial behavior and poor school performance (Tuckman and Regan, 1967).

Not only do peers and siblings naturally influence emotional adjustment, but they can be used as therapeutic agents. They have served in this capacity in a variety of structured and unstructured programs (Furman, Binger, and Rosen, 1979). Several clinical investigators have been successful in teaching peers to attend selectively to appropriate behaviors, thus, causing decreases in deviant behavior (Nelson, Worrell, and Polsgrove, 1973; Solomon and Wahler, 1973). In other instances, peers have been taught to initiate interactions with withdrawn children (Strain, Shores, and Timm, 1977). As a consequence of this intervention, isolate children became more social. Additionally, peers have been employed as confederate partners for targeted children to practice social skills taught to them by an adult (Kelly, Furman, Phillips, Hathorn, and Wilson, 1979; Oden and Asher, 1977).

Siblings have also been trained to be change agents in behavior modification programs (Miller and Cantwell, 1976). Although the results were somewhat mixed, the authors observed increased rates of positive sibling interactions and reported that both the child and sibling therapist had benefitted. Sibling relations can also be capitalized on in individual child therapy (Bank and Kahn, 1975). Siblings can be used as consultants on family interaction problems; they can help clients and their parents rehearse new patterns of interactions; finally, sibling "rallies" can be called to foster encouragement, support and honestly within the sibling group.

In the preceding types of programs, peers and siblings were given careful guidance and structure about how to serve as a therapist. In other programs, the therapeutic effects are obtained by creating situations where the desired interactions occur in the natural course of events. For example, having children engage in cooperative projects promotes pro-social behaviors and interpersonal attraction (Chennault, 1967; Heber and Heber, 1957; Stendler, Damrin, and Haines, 1951). Chandler (1973) was successful in reducing rates of crime and improving role-taking ability by having juvenile delinquents make a movie about themselves--a task which required frequent role-taking and cooperation. In our own work, we were able to increase the sociability of withdrawn preschoolers by having them participate in a series of unstructured play sessions with younger peers (Furman, Rahe, and Hartup, 1979). This experience seemed to have given the isolates opportunities for successful peer interactions. Thus, peers and siblings have a significant impact on the emotional adjustment of the child, both in the normal course of events and in planned therapeutic interventions.

SURROGATE PARENTING

In the previous sections we have seen how siblings and peers complement the efforts of parents. In some unusual circumstances, children have even served as surrogate parents. Interestingly, children can largely compensate for absent parents. In a classic study Freud and Dann (1951) observed a group of six children who had been separated from their parents as infants in a World War II concentration camp. They had been shifted from camp to camp and had had little contact with adults. As a consequence, their behavior towards adults was abnormal. They were either completely indifferent or actively hostile. On the other hand, the group members had developed strong attachments to each other. They provided emotional support to one another and resisted any effort to be separated. All in all, they were remarkably healthy. According to Freud and Dann, they were "neither deficient, delinquent, or psychotic. They had found an alternative placement for their libido and on the strength of this, had mastered some of their anxieties, and developed social attitudes" (p. 168).

Experimental research also suggests that children can serve as substitute parents. Suomi and Harlow (1975) compared the effects of rearing monkeys in either total social isolation, with only their mother, with only peers, or with both mother and peers. Those reared alone displayed serious social deficits. When returned to the natural social environment, they engaged in little social behavior and, instead, exhibited marked stereotypic behaviors, such as rocking or clasping. As adults, these monkeys proved to be poor sexual partners and parents. Those monkeys reared with either mother or peers displayed significantly fewer deficits than those reared in total isolation. Monkeys reared with mother alone appeared normal except that they failed to develop adequate peer interaction competencies. They were contact-shy, avoided play and were hyperactive when touched. Monkeys reared with peers alone displayed normal peer behavior except that they were hyperattached to each other. The peers had done a remarkable job of compensating for the mothers' absence.

These studies describe unusual instances of surrogate parenting. Children almost never have such minimal contact with adults. It is rather common, however, for the oldest sibling to assume many of the parental roles if a parent should die (Bossard and Boll, 1956). Similarly, after a divorce, the older children often have many new responsibilities thrust upon them. While anecdotal reports suggest that the sibling usually fulfills the new role adequately, further work is needed to determine the effects of such substitute parenting on both the growing child and the surrogate parent. If the Suomi and Harlow (1965) and Freud and Dann (1951) studies provide us a clue, it would seem that we may expect that children can provide a partial, but not complete compensation for the loss of a parent.

CONCLUSION

The goal of this chapter has been to explore how peers and siblings contribute to the parenting process. Our conception of parenting has viewed parents as active sources of stimulation and guidance which shape the child's developmental course. When viewed in this broad perspective, siblings and peers can be seen as deeply involved in the parenting process. In this review we have clearly shown that siblings and peers actively affect all aspects of the child's cognitive, social and emotional growth and adjustment.

Taken together, the contributions made by parents, siblings, and peers can best be characterized as *synergistic*. Such synergism can be seen in all spheres of development. Although their methods differ, parents, siblings, and peer babysitters all assist in the care of the young. Parents, brothers, sisters, and friends each serve as essential sources of affection to the growing child. Each also makes a unique contribution to the child's cognitive growth. Finally, all are important agents of socialization, although their contributions are not interchangeable. For instance, in the area of moral development, peers and siblings act as partners in democracy, while parents are guiding authorities of right and wrong.

Although the significance of peers and siblings to the parenting process has been demonstrated, much research remains to be done. As mentioned previously, numerous topics have received little attention. Often strong theoretical arguments can be made for the influence of children, but empirical tests have not been conducted. In general, the literature on the influence of siblings is sparse. Research has been done on birth order effects (Wagner, Schubert and Schubert, 1979), but these data tell us little about whether the observed correlates of sibship rank are due to differential treatment by parents or intersibling influences. Moreover, little work has been done on the pattern of interactions among siblings or how the qualitative features of their relationships affect development. Certainly, the study of sibling relations deserves greater theoretical and empirical attention.

More generally, there is a need for a unified perspective in studying the influences on children's development. Researchers interested in parents, siblings, and peers have remained relatively isolated from one another. They have their own particular questions of interest, methodological approaches and theoretical perspectives. As a consequence, it is difficult to integrate the various findings or determine how the various social relationships are interrelated. A few studies suggest that positive family relationships and peer adjustment are correlated (Elkins, 1958; Rose, 1956; Stone, 1960; Warnath, 1955), but further work is needed to delineate the specific ties among the systems. Particularly absent is research on the effects of siblings and peers on the parent-child relationship. Recent exceptions are Vandell's (1979) study of the effects of playgroups on the attachment bond, Cicirelli's (1978) work on the effects of siblings presence on mother's teaching style, and Kendrick's (1980) study of the effects of second-born children on mothers' interactions with the first-born child. These point out promising directions for subsequent research.

We need to recognize that our subject matter is a *single* child who is involved in a network of interrelationships involving parents, siblings, peers, and others. All of the different influences combine to create the child's social environment (Rheingold and Eckerman, 1975). In the course of development, the child is confronted with numerous developmental tasks which demand various types of social input. Sometimes several, or even all, persons in the child's social network can interchangeably fulfill a functional role; other times, what is needed can only come through a particular type of interaction (e.g., egalitarian interactions with age-mates). In this conceptual framework parents, siblings, and peers are no longer considered isolated units of influence. Instead, the theoretical unit of interest is the social input and its functional properties. The goal of research is not to obtain a serial listing of the influences of parents, siblings, and peers. Rather, the goal is to determine which characteristics of the social interchanges are responsible for specific effects. Then, one can determine whether this input is provided in a certain relationship. Thus, "parenting" no longer need be viewed as the unique influence of the biological parents. Instead, it is a set of processes and inputs which any member of the social environment can contribute to is their interaction with the child contains the requisite properties. Hopefully, the value of such a perspective can be seen in the current review of how siblings and peers contribute to the parenting process.

REFERENCES

Abramovitch, R., Corter, C., and Lando, B. Sibling interactions in the home. *Child Development*, 1979, *50*, 997-1003.

Adler, A. *Understanding human nature.* New York: Premier Books, 1959.

Allen, V. L. The helping relationship and socialization of children: Some perspectives on tutoring. In V. L. Allen (Ed.), *Children as teachers: Theory and research on tutoring.* New York: Academic Press, 1976.

Bank, S., and Kahn, M. Sisterhood-brotherhood is powerful: Sibling sub-systems and family therapy. *Family Process*, 1975, *14*, 311-337.

Barker, R. G., and Wright, H. F. *Midwest and its children.* New York: Harper and Row, 1955.

Barry, H., III, and Paxson, L. M. Infancy and early childhood: Cross-cultural codes 2. *Ethnology*, 1971, *10*, 466-508.

Bates, E. Peer relations and the acquisition of language. In M. Lewis and L. A. Rosenblum (Eds.), *Friendship and peer relations.* New York: Wiley, 1975.

Belmont, L., and Marolla, F. A. Birth order, family size, and intelligence. *Science*, 1973, *182*, 1096-1101.

Berbaum, M. L., and Moreland, R. C. Intellectual development within the family: A new application of the confluence model. *Developmental Psychology*, 1980, *16*, 506-515.

Bierman, K. L., and Furman, W. Effects of role and assignment rationale on attitudes formed during peer tutoring. *Journal of Educational Psychology*, in press.

Bigelow, B. J., and La Gaipa, J. J. The development of friendship values and choice. In H. C. Foot, A. J. Chapman, and J. R. Smith (Eds.), *Friendship and social relations in children.* Chichester, England: Wiley, 1980.

Bigner, J. Sibling position and definition of self. *Journal of Social Psychology*, 1971, *84*, 307-308.

Blos, P. *The adolescent personality: A study of individual behavior.* New York: Appleton, 1941.

Bossard, J., and Boll, E. *The sociology of child development.* New York: Harper, 1960.

Bossard, J., and Boll, E. *The large family system.* Philadelphia: University of Pennsylvania Press, 1956.

Bowerman, C. E., and Dobash, R. M. Structural variations in inter-sibling affect. *Journal of Marriage and Family,* 1974, *36,* 48-54.

Bowerman, C. E., and Kinch, J. W. Changes in family and peer orientation of children between the fourth and tenth grades. *Social Forces,* 1959, *37,* 206-211.

Bowlby, J. *Attachment and loss* (Vol. 1, *Attachment*). New York: Basic Books, 1969.

Bowlby, J. *Maternal care and mental health* (2nd ed.), Monograph Series, no. 2. Geneva: World Health Organization, 1952.

Breland, H. M. Birth order, family configuration, and verbal achievement. *Child Development,* 1974, *45,* 1011-1019.

Brandt, E. M., and Mitchell, G. Pairing preadolescents with infants *(Macaca mulatta). Developmental Psychology,* 1973, *8,* 222-228.

Brim, O. G., Jr. Family structure and sex-role learning in children. *Sociometry,* 1958, *21,* 1-16.

Brittain, C. V. Adolescent choices and parent-peer cross-pressures. *American Sociological Review,* 1963, *28,* 385-391.

Bronfenbrenner, U. *Two worlds of childhood: U.S. and U.S.S.R.* New York: Basic Books, 1970.

Bronfenbrenner, U. Response to pressure from peers versus adults in Soviet and American school children. *International Journal of Psychology,* 1967, *2,* 199-207.

Bronson, W. C. Central orientations: A study of behavior organization from childhood to adolescence. *Child Development,* 1966, *37,* 125-155.

Bruner, J. S., Jolly, A., and Sylva, K. *Play--its role in development and evolution.* New York: Basic Books, 1976.

Burns, S. M., and Brainerd, C. J. Effects of constructive and dramatic play on perspective taking in very young children. *Developmental Psychology,* 1979, *15,* 512-521.

Cairns, R. B. *Social development: The origins and plasticity of interchanges.* San Francisco: W. H. Freeman, 1979.

Cattell, R. B., Eber, H. W., and Tatsuoka, M. M. *Handbook for the sixteen personality factor questionnaire (16 PF).* Champaign, IL: Institute for Personality and Ability Testing, 1970.

Chandler, M. J. Egocentrism and antisocial behavior: The assessment and training of social perspective-taking skills. *Developmental Psychology,* 1973, *9,* 326-332.

Charlesworth, R., and Hartup, W. W. Positive social reinforcement in the nursery school peer group. *Child Development,* 1967, *38,* 993-1002.

Chennault, M. Improving the social acceptance of unpopular educable mentally retarded pupils in special classes. *American Journal of Mental Deficiency,* 1967, *72,* 455-458.

Cicirelli, V. G. Sibling teaching siblings. In V. L. Allen (Ed.), *Children as teachers: Theory and research on tutoring.* New York: Academic Press, 1976.

Cloward, R. D. Studies in tutoring. *Journal of Experimental Education,* 1967, *36,* 14-26.

Cohen, L. J., and Campos, J. J. Father, mother, and stranger as elicitors of attachment behavior in infancy. *Developmental Psychology,* 1974, *10,* 146-154.

Conger, J. J. *Adolescence and youth.* New York: Harper and Row, 1973.

Costanzo, D. R., and Shaw, M. E. Conformity as a function of age level. *Child Development,* 1966, *37,* 967-975.

Cowen, E. L., Pederson, A., Babijian, H., Izzo, L. D., and Trost, M. A. Long-term follow-up of early detected vulnerable children. *Journal of Consulting and Clinical Psychology,* 1952, *81,* 113-124.

Deets, A. C. Age-mate or twin sibling: Effects on monkey age-mate interactions during infancy. *Developmental Psychology,* 1974, *10,* 913-928.

Deutsch, F. Observational and sociometric measures of peer popularity and their relationship to egocentric communication in female preschoolers. *Developmental Psychology,* 1974, *10,* 745-747.

Douvan, E., and Adelson, J. *The adolescent experience.* New York: Wiley, 1966.

Easterbrooks, M. A., and Lamb, M. E. The relationship between quality of infant-mother attachment and infant competence in initial encounters with peers. *Child Development,* 1979, *50,* 380-387.

Elkins, D. Some factors related to the choice status on ninety eighth-grade children in a school society. *Genetic Psychology Monographs,* 1958, *58,* 207-272.

Erikson, M. R., and Cormack, T. Evaluating a tutoring program. *Journal of Experimental Education,* 1972, *41,* 27-31.

Essman, C. S. Sibling relations as socialization for parenthood. *Family Coordinator,* 1977, *26,* 159-162.

Fagot, B. I. Consequences of moderate cross-gender behavior in preschool children. *Child Development,* 1977, *48,* 902-907.

Fagot, B. I., and Patterson, G. R. An *in vivo* analysis of reinforcing contingencies for sex-role behaviors in the preschool child. *Developmental Psychology,* 1969, *1,* 563-568.

Feldman, R. S., Devin-Sheehan, L., and Allen, V. L. Children tutoring children: A critical review of research. In V. L. Allen (Ed.), *Children as teachers: Theory and research on tutoring.* New York: Academic Press, 1976.

Feldman, S. S., and Nash, S. C. Changes in responsiveness to babies during adolescence. *Child Development,* 1979, *50,* 942-949.

Fine, G. A. The natural history of preadolescent male friendship groups. In H. Foot, A. Chapman, and J. Smith (Eds.), *Friendship and social relations in children.* Chichester, England: Wiley, 1980.

Fink, R. S. Role of imaginative play in cognitive development. *Psychological Reports,* 1976, *39,* 895-906.

Freud, A., and Dann, S. An experiment in group upbringing. In R. Eisler et al. (Eds.), *The psychoanalytic study of the child* (Vol. 6). New York: International Universities Press, 1951.

Furman, W. Children's friendships. In T. Field (Ed.), *Review of human development*. New York: Wiley, in press.

Furman, W., and Bierman, K. L. *Children's conceptions of friendship: A multidimensional study of developmental changes.* Unpublished manuscript, University of Denver, 1980. (a)

Furman, W., and Bierman, K. L. *Children's conceptions of friendship: Developmental changes in the preschool years.* Unpublished manuscript, University of Denver, 1980. (b)

Furman, W., Binger, C. G., and Rosen, L. A. *Peers as therapeutic agents.* Paper presented at Society for Research in Child Development, San Francisco, March 1979.

Furman, W., and Masters, J. C. Affective consequences of social reinforcement, punishment, and neutral behavior. *Developmental Psychology*, 1980, *16*, 100-104.

Furman, W., and Masters, J. C. Peer interactions, sociometric status, and resistance to deviation in young children. *Developmental Psychology*, 1980, *16*, 229-236.

Furman, W., Rahe, D. F., and Hartup, W. W. Rehabilitation of socially-withdrawn preschool children through mixed-age and same-age socialization. *Child Development*, 1979, *50*, 915-922.

Gallimore, R., Boggs, J. W., and Jordon, C. *Culture, behavior, and education: A study of Hawaiian-Americans.* Beverly Hills: Sage, 1974.

Goodall, J. Chimpanzees at the Gombe Stream Reserve. In I. De Vore (Ed.), *Primate behavior.* New York: Holt, Rinehart, and Winston, 1965.

Gottman, J., Gonso, J., and Rasmussen, B. Social interaction, social competence, and friendship in children. *Child Development*, 1975, *45*, 709-718.

Grotevant, H. Sibling constellations and sex typing of interests in adolescence. *Child Development*, 1978, *49*, 540-542.

Harlow, H. T., Dodsworth, R. O., and Harlow, M. K. Total social isolation in monkeys. *Proceedings of the National Academy of Science*, 1965, *54*, 90-97.

Hartup, W. W. Peer interaction and social organization. In P. H. Mussen (Ed.), *Carmichael's manual of child psychology* (3rd ed., Vol. 2). New York: Wiley, 1970.

Hartup, W. W. Children and their friends. In H. McGurk (Ed.), *Child social development.* London: Methuen, 1978.

Hartup, W. W. Peer relations and behavioral development of the individual child. In E. Schopler and R. J. Reichler (Eds.), *Psychopathology and child development.* New York: Plenum, 1976.

Heathers, G. Emotional dependence and independence in nursery school play. *Journal of Genetic Psychology*, 1955, *87*, 37-57.

Heber, R. F., and Heber, M. E. The effects of group failure and success on social status. *Journal of Educational Psychology*, 1957, *48*, 129-134.

Horowitz, F. D. The relationship of anxiety, self-concept, and socio-metric status among fourth, fifth, and sixth grade children. *Journal of Abnormal and Social Psychology*, 1962, *65*, 212-214.

Howes, C. *Toddler social competence in family and center daycare.* Unpublished doctoral dissertation, Boston University, 1978.

Howes, C., and Mueller, E. Early peer friendships: Their significance for development. In W. Spiel (Ed.), *The psychology of the Twentieth Century.* Zurich: Kindler, in press.

Ipsa, J. *Familiar and unfamiliar peers as "havens of security" for Soviet nursery children.* Paper presented at the biennial meeting of the society for Research in Child Development, New Orleans, 1977.

Irish, D. P. Sibling interaction: A neglected aspect in family life research. *Social Forces*, 1964, *42*, 279-288.

Iscoe, I., Williams, M., and Harvey, J. Modifications of children's judgements by a simulated group technique: A normative developmental study. *Child Development*, 1963, *34*, 963-978.

Kandel, D. Adolescent marihuana use: Role of parents and peers. *Science*, 1973, *181*, 1067-1070.

Katz, P. A. *Determinants of sex-role flexibility in children.* Paper presented at Society for Research in Child Development, San Francisco, March 1979.

Keasey, C. B. Social participation as a factor in the moral development of preadolescents. *Developmental Psychology*, 1971, *5*, 216-220.

Kelly, J. A., Furman, W., Phillips, J., Hathorn, S., and Wilson, S. Teaching conversational skills to retarded adolescents. *Child Behavior Therapy*, 1979, *1*, 36-113.

Kendrick, C., and Dunn, J. Caring for a second baby: Effects on interaction between mother and firstborn. *Developmental Psychology*, 1980, *16*, 303-311.

Kinsey, A. C., Pomeroy, W. B., and Martin, C. E. *Sexual behavior in the human male.* Philadelphia: W. B. Saunders, 1948.

Kobasigawa, A. Inhibitory and disinhibitory effects of models on sex-inappropriate behavior in children. *Psychologia*, 1968, *11*, 86-96.

Kohlberg, L. *The development of modes of moral thinking and choice in the years ten to sixteen.* Unpublished doctoral dissertation, University of Chicago, 1958.

Ladd, G. W., and Oden, S. L. The relationship between peer acceptance and children's ideas about helpfulness. *Child Development*, 1979, *50*, 402-408.

Lamb, M. E. (Ed.) *The role of the father in child development.* New York: Wiley, 1976.

Lamb, M. E. Father-infant and mother-infant interaction in the first year of life. *Child Development*, 1977, *48*, 167-181.

Lamb, M. E. The development of sibling relationships in infancy: A short-term longitudinal study. *Child Development*, 1978, *49*, 1189-1196. (a)

Lamb, M. E. Interactions between eighteen-month-olds and their pre-school-aged siblings. *Child Development*, 1978, *49*, 51-59. (b)

Lamb, M. E., and Roopnarino, J. L. Peer influences on sex-role development in preschoolers. *Child Development*, 1979, *50*, 1219-1222.

Langworthy, R. L.   Community status and influence in a high school. *American Sociological Review*, 1959, *24*, 537-539.

Lefurge, W. G., and Woloshin, G. W.   Immediate and long-term effects of experimentally induced social influence in the modification of adolescents' moral judgments.   *Journal of Personality and Social Psychology*, 1969, *12*, 104-110.

Lesser, G. S., and Kandel, D. B.   Parental and peer influences on educational plans of adolescence.   *American Sociological Review*, 1969, *34*, 213-223.

Levy, R. I. Child management structure and its implications in a Tahitian family. In E. Vogel and N. Bell (Eds.), *A modern introduction to the family.* New York: Free Press, 1968.

Lewis, M., Young, G., Brooks, J., and Michalson, L.   The beginning of friendship. In M. Lewis and L. A. Rosenblum (Eds.), *Friendship and peer relations.* New York: Wiley, 1975.

Lieberman, A. F. Preschoolers' social competence with a peer: Relations with attachment and peer experience. *Child Development*, 1977, *48*, 1277-1287.

Loban, W.   A study of social sensitivity (sympathy) among adolescents. *Journal of Educational Psychology*, 1953, *44*, 102-112.

Lougee, M. E., and Graziano, W. G. *Age relationships in children's groups.* Unpublished manuscript, Wheaton College, 1980.

Low, S., and Spindler, P. *Child care arrangements of working mothers in the United States* (Children's Bureau of Publications #461-1968). Washington, D.C.: United States Government Printing Office, 1969.

Mannarino, A. P.   Friendship patterns and altruistic behavior in preadolescent males. *Developmental Psychology*, 1976, *12*, 555-556.

Marshall, R. J. *Variations in self-attitudes and attitudes toward others as a function of peer group appraisals.*   Unpublished doctoral dissertation, University of Buffalo, 1958.

McGuire, W. J., and Padawer-Singer, A.   Trait salience in the spontaneous self-concept. *Journal of Personality and Social Psychology*, 1976, *33*, 743-754.

Mead, G. H. *Mind, self, and society.*   Chicago: University of Chicago Press, 1934.

Mead, M. *Coming of age in Samoa.* New York: Morrow, 1928.

Merei, F.   Group leadership and institutionalization. *Human Relations*, 1949, *2*, 23-29.

Miller, N. B., and Cantwell, D. P.   Siblings as therapists: A behavioral approach. *American Journal of Psychiatry*, 1976, *133*, 447-450.

Miller, S. A., and Brownell, C. A.   Peers, persuasion, and Piaget: Dyadic interaction between conservers and nonconservers. *Child Development*, 1975, *46*, 992-997.

Minton, B. A. *Dimensions of information underlying children's judgements of competence.* Paper presented at the Society for Research in Child Development, San Francisco, March 1979.

Mugny, G., and Doise, W.   Socio-cognitive conflict and structure of individual and collective performances. *European Journal of Social Psychology*, 1978, *8*, 181-192.

Murray, F. B. Acquisition of conservation through social interaction. *Developmental Psychology*, 1972, *6*, 1-6.

Myers, J., and Roberts, B. *Family and class dynamics in mental illness.* New York: Wiley, 1959.

Nelson, C., Worrell, J., and Polsgrove, L. Behaviorally disordered peers as contingency managers. *Behavior Therapy*, 1973, *4*, 270-276.

Oden, S., and Asher, S. R. Coaching children in social skills for friendship making. *Child Development*, 1977, *48*, 495-506.

Offer, D., and Offer, J. *From teenage to young manhood.* New York: Basic Books, 1976.

Patterson, F. G., Bonvillian, J. D., Reynolds, P. G., and Maccoby, E. E. Mother and peer attachment under conditions of fear in rhesus monkeys *(Macaca mulatta)*. *Primates*, 1975, *16*, 75-81.

Patterson, G. R., Littman, R. A., and Bricker, W. Assertive behavior in children: A step toward a theory of aggression. *Monographs of the Society for Research in Child Development*, 1967, *32*, (Whole No. 113).

Piaget, J. *The moral judgment of the child.* Glencoe, IL: The Free Press, 1932.

Porteus, B. D., and Johnson, R. C. Children's responses to two measures of conscience development and their relation to sociometric nomination. *Child Development*, 1965, *36*, 703-711.

Reese, H. W. Relationship between self-acceptance and sociometric choice. *Journal of Abnormal and Social Psychology*, 1961, *62*, 472-474.

Rheingold, H. L., and Eckerman, C. O. Some proposals for unifying the study of social development. In M. Lewis and L. A. Rosenblum (Eds.), *Friendship and peer relations.* New York: Wiley, 1975.

Ritchie, J. E. *Basic personality in Rakau.* Wellington: Victoria University Press, 1956.

Roff, M. Childhood social interaction and young adult psychosis. *Journal of Clinical Psychology*, 1963, *19*, 152-157.

Roff, M., Sells, S. B., and Golden, M. M. *Social adjustment and personality development in children.* Minneapolis: University of Minnesota Press, 1972.

Rose, A. M. Reference groups of rural high school youth. *Child Development*, 1956, *27*, 351-363.

Rosen, B. C. Conflicting group membership: A study of parent-peer group cross-pressures. *American Sociological Review*, 1955, *20*, 155-161.

Rothenberg, B. Children's social sensitivity and the relationship to interpersonal competence, intrapersonal comfort, and intellectual level. *Developmental Psychology*, 1970, *2*, 335-350.

Rothenberg, B. B., and Orost, J. H. The training of conservation of number in young children. *Child Development*, 1969, *40*, 707-726.

Rubin, K. H., and Pepler, D. J. The relationship of child's play to social-cognitive growth and development. In H. C. Foot, A. J. Chapman, and J. R. Smith (Eds.), *Friendship and social relations in children.* Chichester, England: Wiley, 1980.

Ruble, D. N., Feldman, N. S., and Boggiano, A. K. Social Comparison between young children in achievement situations. *Developmental Psychology*, 1976, *12*, 192-197.

Saltz, E., Dixon, D., and Johnson, J. Training disadvantaged preschoolers on various fantasy activities: Effects on cognitive functioning and impulse control. *Child Development*, 1977, *48*, 367-380.

Schachter, F. F., Gilutz, G., Shore, F., and Adler, M. Sibling deidentification judged by mothers: Cross-validation and developmental studies. *Child Development*, 1978, *49*, 543-546.

Sherif, M., Harvey, O. J., White, B. J., Hood, W. R., and Sherif, C. W. *Intergroup conflict and cooperation: The Robbers' Cave Experiment.* Norman: University of Oklahoma Press, 1961.

Silverman, I. W., and Geiringer, E. Dyadic interaction and conservation induction: A test of Piaget's equilibration model. *Child Development*, 1973, *44*, 815-820.

Siman, M. L. Application of a new model of peer group influence to naturally existing adolescent friendship groups. *Child Development*, 1977, *48*, 270-274.

Simpson, R. L. Parental influence, anticipatory socialization, and social mobility. *American Sociological Review*, 1962, *27*, 517-522.

Singer, J. L. (Ed.) *The child's world of make believe.* New York: Academic Press, 1973.

Slobin, D. On the nature of talk to children. In E. Lenneberg, and E. Lenneberg (Eds.), *Foundations of language development: A multidisciplinary approach.* New York: Academic Press, 1975.

Smilansky, S. *The effects of sociodramatic play on disadvantaged children: Preschool children.* New York: Wiley, 1968.

Smith, A. J. A developmental study of group processes. *Journal of Genetic Psychology*, 1960, *97*, 29-30.

Solomon, R. W., and Wahler, R. G. Peer reinforcement of classroom problem behavior. *Journal of Applied Behavior Analysis*, 1973, *6*, 49-55.

Spiro, M. E. *Children of the kibbutz.* Cambridge: Harvard University, 1975.

Sroufe, L. A. The coherence of individual development. *American Psychologist*, 1979, *34*, 834-841.

Stendler, C. B., Damrin, D., and Haines, A. C. Studies in cooperation and competition: I. the effects of working for group and individual rewards on the social climate of children's groups. *Journal of Genetic Psychology*, 1951, *79*, 173-193.

Stengel, E. *Suicide and attempted suicide.* Baltimore: Penguin, 1964.

Stone, C. L. Some family characteristics of socially active and inactive teenagers. *Coordinator*, 1960, *8*, 53-57.

Strain, P., Shores, R., and Timm, D. Effects of peer social initiations on the behavior of withdrawn preschool children. *Journal of Applied Behavior Analysis*, 1977, *10*, 289-298.

Strodtbeck, F. L., Ronchi, D., and Hansell, S. Tutoring and psychological growth. In V. L. Allen (Ed.), *Children as teachers: Theory and research on tutoring.* New York: Academic Press, 1976.

Sullivan, H. S. *The interpersonal theory of psychiatry.* New York: Norton, 1953.

Suomi, S. J., and Harlow, H. F. Effects of differential removal from group on social development of rhesus monkeys. *Journal of Child Psychology and Psychiatry,* 1975, *16,* 149-164.

Sutton-Smith, B., and Rosenberg, B. G. *The sibling.* New York: Holt, Rinehart and Winston, 1970.

Sutton-Smith, B., Rosenberg, B. G., and Landy, F. Father-absence effects on families of different sibling compositions. *Child Development,* 1968, *39,* 1213-1221.

Tuckman, J., and Regan, R. A. Ordinal position and behavior problems in children. *Journal of Health and Social Behavior,* 1967, *8,* 32-39.

Turner, M. E. *The child within the group: An experiment in self-government.* Stanford: Stanford University, 1957.

Turiel, E. An experimental test of the sequentiality of developmental stages in the child's moral judgments. *Journal of Personality and Social Psychology,* 1966, *3,* 611-618.

Vandell, D. L. Effects of a play-group experience on mother-son and father-son interaction. *Developmental Psychology,* 1979, *15,* 379-385.

Vandell, D. L. Sociability with peer and mother during the first year. *Developmental Psychology,* 1980, *16,* 355-361.

Vandell, D. L., and Mueller, E. C. Peer play and friendships during the first two years. In H. C. Foot, A. J. Chapman, and J. R. Smith (Eds.), *Friendship and social relations in children.* Chichester, England: Wiley, 1980.

Veroff, J. Social comparison and the development of achievement motivation. In C. P. Smith (Ed.), *Achievement related motives in children.* New York: Russell Sage Foundation, 1969.

Vygotsky, L. S. *Thought and language.* Cambridge, MA: The M.I.T. Press, 1962.

Wagner, M. E., Schubert, H. J. D., and Schubert, D. S. P. Sibship-constellation effects on psychosocial development, creativity, and health. In H. W. Reese and L. P. Lipsitt (Eds.), *Advances in child development and behavior,* (Vol. 14). New York: Academic Press, 1979.

Warnath, C. F. The relation of family cohesiveness and adolescent independence to social effectiveness. *Marriage and Family Living,* 1955, *17,* 346-348.

Weinheimer, S. Egocentrism and social influence in children. *Child Development,* 1972, *43,* 567-578.

Weisner, T. S., and Gallimore, R. My brother's keeper: Child and sibling caretaking. *Current Anthropology,* 1977, *18,* 169-170.

Whiting, B., and Whiting, J. W. M. *Children of six cultures.* Cambridge: Harvard University Press, 1975.

Wolf, T. M. Effects of live modeled sex-inappropriate play behavior in a naturalistic setting. *Developmental Psychology,* 1973, *9,* 120-123.

Young, J. W., and Ferguson, L. R. Developmental changes through adolescence in the spontaneous nomination of reference groups as a function of decision content. *Journal of Youth and Adolescence,* 1979, *8,* 239-245.

Zajonc, R. B., and Markus, C. B. Birth order and intellectual development. *Psychological Review,* 1975, *82,* 74-88.

THE DAY CARE MOVEMENT: PAST, PRESENT, AND FUTURE

Donald L. Peters and Jay Belsky

Individual and Family Studies
The Pennsylvania State University
University Park, PA 16802

INTRODUCTION

Although the day care movement has received much attention from policymakers, researchers, and the general public during the past decade, great ambiguity remains concerning the nature and purposes of supplementary child care--particularly as day care relates to the family unit and parenting (cf. Belsky and Steinberg, 1978; Belsky, Steinberg, and Walker, in press; Peters, 1975, 1980). This ambivalence toward day care in the United States stems, in part, from historical traditions that stress individualism and the sanctity of the family, as well as from current societal circumstances that have led to a "dual" day care system. The intent of this paper is to briefly trace the evolution of the present day state of affairs, to describe the current day care world, and to project some visions of its future place in American society.

HISTORICAL CONCEPTS: THE FOUNDATIONS OF A DUAL SYSTEM

The history of day care in America, which dates back to the mid 1880's, indicates that when government sponsored or supported out-of-home child care, its policy derived from concerns regarding family inadequacy or welfare dependence, and non-child related national needs. Indeed, throughout its early history, day care was viewed primarily as a child welfare service to provide care and protection for "children of destitute widows and those with sick husbands" (Fein and Clarke-Stewart, 1973, p. 26). Thus, it was conceived in the settlement house tradition, and initially intended to relieve women "bent under the double burden" of earning money to support their children while at the same time trying to care for and rear their offspring.

This early beginning, in which day care was judged to be a legitimate form of child care only under conditions of dire necessity and family deviance, cast an image which became well embedded in the public consciousness. In fact, Ruderman (1968) argues that because social workers were the first professionals to involve themselves in day care, supplementary child care came to be seen as a response to family inadequacy, that is, as a problem service for problem families. Vestiges of this perspective are still evident today: most contemporary federal day care legislation is directed at the poor, often with the expressed purpose of reducing the welfare roles by providing child care so that impoverished parents can work.

This initial conceptualization of day care as a service for problem families has undoubtedly impeded widespread public acceptance of federal sponsorship of day care. In support of this claim, we can cite figures indicating that while only 29 percent of mothers have been found to reject the use of day care for other people's children under normal circumstances, 44 percent of these same women reject this option for their own children (Sibbison, 1972). Similarly, many women report that "working women miss the best years of their children's lives," and one in five believes that working women neglect their children (Rodes and Moore, 1975). Capitalizing on such attitudes, those in the public arena often have found it politically expedient to condemn the "family weakening" implications of a broad-based and presumably expensive day care system (Peters, 1980). President Nixon's 1972 veto message which accompanied his rejection of the Mondale-Brademas comprehensive child development act, which would have made publicly supported day care widely available, is the most notorious instance of such politicizing of the day care issue. Contrary to President Nixon's statement, the United States government has supported day care for persons other than the indigent. In times of national emergency, day care has been viewed to be an acceptable alternative or supplement for home-based care. As a case in point, the establishment of day care centers during the depression (beginning in 1932) provided a means of employing out-of-work school personnel. Given this motivation, it should come as no surprise that it was administered by the Works Project Administration, but dismantled with the start of World War II, when mobilization for war made the WPA unnecessary (Kamerman and Kahn, 1976); this despite the fact that by 1937, 1,900 nurseries had been established and more than 40,000 children were being served.

After a brief hiatus, national defense women power needs required the reinstatement of a government day care policy. Thus, with the passage of the Community Facilities Act (also called the Lanham Act) in 1942, the federal government made available 50 percent matching funds to private industries to establish and operate child care centers in war impacted areas. Once again, however, the creators of this program never intended for the legislation to extend beyond government sponsorship of child care within the defense-emergency framework (Emlen and Perry, 1974). Thus, this program, which served 105,000 children and cost 51 million dollars, was, in Steiner's (1976) words, "a win-the-war program, not a save-the-child program" (p. 16). And, consequently, by 1946 and the war's end, funds were withdrawn and programs dismantled--despite the fact that many mothers continued to work. Public sentiment not only supported the idea that mothers belonged at home, but governmental involvement in family life continued to be viewed with suspicion (Kamerman and Kahn, 1976).

The federal government did not involve itself again in day care until the 1960's with the passage of amendments to the Social Security Act authorizing grants-in-aid to states for child care services (Emlen and Perry, 1974; Peters, 1980; Steiner, 1976). For the second time in its brief history, but unlike the Depression and World War II experience, day care was conceived and established as a program for the poor during the war-on-poverty years. Out-of-home child care had thus come full circle, returning to its nineteenth century conception as a service for inadequate families with problems.

This conception of day care remains a cornerstone of federal day care policy. In 1962, for example, amendments to the initial Social Security Act of 1935, which authorized grants-in-aids for child welfare services, substantially enlarged federal authorization to pay for child welfare services. And, under the Title IV-A, which was intended to encourage state departments of public welfare to develop day care facilities, federal reimbursement to states was substantially increased to a 75:25 matching-funds formula. By 1974, this law, which targeted programs for the economically impoverished, was responsible for the provision of child care to over one-half million children at a cost of 464 million dollars (Kamerman and Kahn, 1976).

In 1975, states were given greater freedom to spend monies earmarked for social services, since the Title XX amendment to the Social Security Act made available block grants to states (i.e., revenue sharing). And, while social services (including day care) were still primarily targeted for the poor, eligibility became more universal--at least in theory. For families with incomes below 80 percent of the state median income, day care services were to be available for free; graduated fees were mandated for those with income ranging from 80 percent to 115 percent of the median. But since total expenditure under Title XX were and still are limited by a ceiling level, and since half of all services must be reserved for welfare recipients, Title XX services are not always available to all those who are eligible for them (Kamerman and Kahn, 1976).

In addition to these revisions of the Social Security Act, there is additional evidence that federal programs have been developed primarily to provide day care services for poverty families. In 1962, for example, Title II of the Manpower Training Act mandated the provision of child care for children of the hard-core unemployed who were provided jobs or vocational training. Similarly, a 1972 amendment (Title IV-C) of the 1967 Work Incentive Program (WIP) required states to provide child care for children whose welfare-recipient parents were required to obtain work or undergo job training. Although WIP specifically excluded parents with children under six from this work requirement, in 1975, 78,000 such children were receiving child care under WIP's auspices (Kamerman and Kahn, 1976).

This brief summary of the history of federal involvement in day care clearly demonstrates the degree to which supplementary child care is rooted in a welfare tradition in America, one which emphasizes the dysfunction or deviant nature of families relying on such a supportive service. Complimenting this history, and possibly even a result of it, is the slowness with which contemporary American society has come to distinguish between what is "traditional" and what is "typical"--this despite an ever-growing dependence of all sorts of families on supplementary child care services. Thus, underlyi..g many popular attitudes toward day care, which impede its widespread acceptance, are several critical assumptions about both the nature of the American family and day care. With respect to the family these assumptions include the following: (a) most families include a father, nonworking mother and children; (b) this type of family is the one against which all other family forms should be judged; (c) a principal function of the family is child-rearing; (d) most families provide the ideal learning and development environment for children; and (e) the family of the past is the family of the future. The day care assumptions include: (a) day care is closely akin to institutional child care; (b) thus, it is harmful to children; (c) primarily because it involves the daily separation of parent and child, while providing only minimal custodial services.

Despite the fact that evidence contradicting these basic assumptions has been in existence for over a decade (cf. Bronfenbrenner, 1976; Caldwell, 1967; National Research Council, 1976), and that millions of families have broken with tradition by relying on day care services, the utilization of supplementary child care arrangements is still regarded by many as non-traditional and, consequently, is viewed with suspicion. Moreover, confusion between idealized concepts of the "traditional" family and the reality of the typical American family has led to a dual system of day care in the United States (Peters, 1975), which is typified in the goals of the 1962 amendments to the Social Security Act. Those goals were to: (a) meet social needs of children and families stemming from the increased number of working women, and (b) provide necessary supportive services for adults seeking to escape the cycle of poverty.

From the perspective of the former goal, and on the basis of the rapidly changing demographics of the American scene, day care is viewed as a major component of an emerging "personal service" system (Kamerman and Kahn, 1976). This segment of the field has evolved into a middle-class childrearing alternative--purchasable convenience for the two-worker family and a rapidly growing industry (Lake, 1980). From the perspective of the latter goal, and on the basis of traditional ideas of the family, day care is viewed as a current extension of 120 years of social intervention into the lives of low income families.

CURRENT REALITIES

To fully understand the place of day care in the United States today and to grasp the process through which it functions, it is necessary to consider the social, economic, and political context of the nation, and the forms that day care has taken.

Demographic Analysis: The Changing American Family

Between 1940 and 1975, the number of women participating in the American labor force doubled, and the number of working mothers increased eight-fold (Hill, 1977, 1978). Whereas only 18 percent of mothers with children under six years of age were employed outside the home in 1955 (Office of the Assistant for Planning and Evaluation, DHEW, 1978), 10 years later the figure was 20 percent and in 1977, 41 percent (Hofferth, 1979). Thus, by 1980, over 14 million women with children were working--a tripling of the 1970 figure. Projections reveal that this rate of growth will continue to escalate to an *expected six million working mothers with children under six by 1985*--a 32 percent increase over a brief 10-year period (Hill, 1978). Indeed, it is estimated that by 1990 three out of every four mothers will work and that there will be 10.5 million very young children in need of day care (Urban Institute, 1980).

Further evidence of the changing nature of the American family can be found in census bureau data on single-parent families compiled by Bronfenbrenner (1975). From 1948 to 1975, the proportion of households with only one parent increased dramatically, with the largest increase taking place during the period from 1964 to 1974. In fact, as of 1974, one of every six American children under the age of 11 lived in a single-parent family--almost double the 1948 rate. Most importantly in the context of this chapter, this rise was most rapid among families with children under six. By 1974, one of every eight children under three was living in a single-parent household. And, across all ages, 80 percent of these single parents who were household heads were employed full time.

Recent census bureau projections, which estimate an average 2.1 children per family, suggest that demographic pressures like those just described, and which affect demand for supplementary child care, will increase still further during the next 10 years (Hofferth, 1979). This is because the children of the "baby-boom" era (1946-1964) will, as parents, produce a sizeable increase in the number of preschoolers in the American population. Specifically, the population of 0-5 year olds is expected to rise from a low 17.1 million in 1977 to a high of 23.3 million in 1990; and about one-half of the mothers of these preschoolers, projections indicate, will return to work before their offspring reach their sixth birthday.

Day Care Today

According to the most recent data gathered by the United States Department of Health, Education and Welfare, as of June 1978, 11 million children under 14 years of age spend a substantial part of their week in supplementary child care arrangements. When broken down by age, these data indicate that 2.5 million infants and toddlers, 3.7 million pre-schoolers, and 4.9 million school-age children spend a sizeable amount of their waking day being cared for by someone rather than their parents (Office of the Assistant for Planning and Evaluation, 1978).

The programs serving all these children are noteworthy for both their diversity and their rapid growth. While popular assumptions suggest otherwise, it happens to be the case that not all day care is alike, nor is it all federally funded. The method by which public and private resources are allocated to provide day care services is generally determined by the type of agency actually providing the services. The clientele using the center, the range of services provided, and decisions regarding the operation of the center are all closely related to the agency type and the auspices under which it operates. Generally speaking there are two distinct types of day care programs (center care, family day care homes, extended family day care systems) and four different categories of day care auspices: (a) private for-profits; (b) private not-for-profit; (c) public; and (d) industrial. We consider first administrative approaches to day care management and then, in more detail, the strengths and weaknesses of center- and family-based programs.

> *Day care centers*--any facility including an occupied residence which regularly provides day care for 13 or more children including children living in the home and children received for day care who are related or un-related to the resident caregiver.

> *Family day care home*--an occupied residence in which day care is regularly provided for not more than six children from more than one unrelated family including those of the caregiver.

> *Extended family day care home* (minicenter)--any facility including an occupied residence in which day care is regularly provided for more than six but fewer than thirteen children from more than one unrelated family.

> *Day care system*--an organization of individual day care facilities in which each facility is related to a licensed or approved central operator by an exclusive contractual arrangement or administrative structure.

In actuality, day care systems may be administrative super-structures which coordinate various combinations of all three types of day care programs in a given community. Their expressed purpose is often to provide coordinated service delivery, administrative efficiency, and professional support to assume the maintenance of quality care.

Private for-profit day care. The purpose of private proprietary day care is to offer a service to families in the provision of child care while at the same time making a reasonable profit for the owner/operator. Such programs, while usually requiring licensure and inspection by a state or local regulatory body, operate relatively independently and receive their income from fees paid directly by the parents of the children enrolled. Fees are established by the competitive open market and usually exceed those that could be paid by low-income families. As such, the majority of the clientele tend to be middle class and relatively affluent.

Proprietary programs vary widely in the range and quality of services they provide and the degree to which parents have input into the decision-making process concerning program, staffing, and the like. In general, such programs tend to be primarily child focused, providing few if any supplementary family health or social services. Many actually represent extended nursery school programs.

The majority of day care programs in the United States are proprietary (Fleming, 1976, p. 71), and this service area is growing most rapidly, particularly in the form of day care chains or franchise services. For example, the ten leading day care corporations in the United States now manage more than 1,000 centers serving some 120,000 children (Lake, 1980). The largest of the chains, Kinder Care, currently owns over 400 day care centers. Perry Mendel, the president of Kinder Care, aspires to own 2,000 centers by 1986 and perhaps 4,000 eventually (Lake, 1980).

Private not-for-profit. Private nonprofit day care providers are generally organizations of citizens incorporated under the nonprofit corporation laws of the particular state or governing unit. Many are affiliated with churches, educational institutions, or humanitarian service organizations. Such organizations are usually dependent for their funds on some combinaton of private contributions and state or federal funds. They may be single-purpose agencies whose sole purpose is to provide child care and related services to selected categories of clientele, or they may be a component of a larger multiservice organization that provides a rich, coordinated array of health, welfare, and education services (as for example, full-day Head Start programs that are a part of a broad service Community Action Agency).

Private nonprofit agencies are usually governed and administrated by a voluntary board of directors. When such agencies receive federal money or other resources toward their operation, they are subject to federal regulation.

Public. Public day care programs are generally under the auspices of state, county, or municipal governmental bodies. They receive their support almost exclusively from public funds, and their services are delivered at no or reduced cost to the clientele. Eligibility requirements for the receipt of such services are set by regulation and result in an economically homogeneous clientele. Program requirements and service provisions are more closely monitored than are those of the prior two categories of day care services.

Private industry. A small minority of day care programs in the United States operate under the auspices of private industry or labor unions. These programs are financed either through union funds or directly by management. The clientele is drawn almost entirely from the company's employees or the union's membership. Such programs are provided as a convenience or fringe benefit to employees and as a means of attracting and enhancing the productivity of female workers. Decision-making in this type of program is usually accomplished by paid professional staff who are responsible to a committee of union and/or management officials.

Center-based day care has received the most systematic attention of investigators. The greatest strength of center programs is their stability and predictable hours of operation. Such strengths can also be weaknesses as centers tend to have fixed hours of operation that often limit their ability to respond to the individual and special needs of working parents. As additional advantages, center-based programs tend to offer a wider variety of formal learning experiences, are usually licensed, and are most likely to employ at least some trained professionals and staff. On the negative side, centers rarely provide care for children under two years of age and, because of the professionalism of the staff, can create an undesirable distance between parents and caregivers since these persons may not always share childrearing or other values. Indeed, today, with so many caregivers themselves nonparents, the possiblity for communication gaps appears sizable.

Variation within center programs can be great. Center/group size and child-caregiver ratio are the characteristics of centers that have received the most empirical attention in efforts to understand how variation in programs affects children's experience. In an early observational study of 69 California preschool/day care programs, Prescott, Jones, and Kritchevsky (1967) found that when center population exceeded 60, more emphasis was placed upon rules and routine guidance then when size ranged from 30 to 60 children. Teachers, in fact, placed twice as much emphasis on control in the large groups, possibly accounting for the observation that in small centers children displayed more pleasure, wonder, and delight. Additional evidence from this study revealed that large centers were less flexible in their scheduling, offered children fewer opportunities to initiate and control activities, and had teachers who displayed less sensitivity to the individual needs of the children (Heinicke, Friedman, Prescott, Puncel, and Sale, 1973).

Most of these results have been replicated recently in a large-scale national study of 57 day care centers in Atlanta, Detroit, and Seattle (hereafter referred to as The National Day Care Study or NDC Study). Travers and Ruopp (1978) reported that for children three-to five-years of age, group size was the single most important determinant of the quality of children's experience.   In groups of less than 15 to 18 children, caregivers were involved in more embellished caregiving (e.g., questioning, responding, praising, comforting), less straight monitoring of children, and less interaction with other adults. In these smaller groups, children were more actively involved in classroom activities (i.e., considering and contemplating, contributing ideas, cooperating, persisting at tasks).   Undoubtedly, such caregiving styles and childhood experiences determine the effect of day care on social and intellectual functioning.

Interestingly, the NDC Study found that child-to-caregiver ratio had little effect upon the quality of *preschoolers'* experience in day care, though it was an important determinant of *infants'* experience.   More overt distress was observed among children under three as the number of children per caregiver increased.   Additionally, in such high-ratio infant and toddler programs, staff spent more time in management and control interactions and engaged less in informal teaching (Connell, Layzer, and Goodson, 1979; Travers and Ruopp, 1978). Biemiller and his colleagues (1976) reported similar findings in a small study comparing two infant day care programs.

Day care centers also vary in their "curricula," and such variation appears to be of particular concern to parents when selecting a child care program.   In fact, Joffee (1977) discerned racial preferences in her sociological study of the relationship between parents and school-administered programs in Berkeley, California. Blacks preferred a formal school atmosphere with special attention paid to discipline, the structuring of activities, and an academic curriculum, whereas whites desired less structured programs emphasizing socio-emotional concerns.   In an independent study, Prescott (1973) compared the experiences of 112 children in just such "closed-" and "open-structured" day care programs. Observations revealed that, consonant with their philosophy, closed programs, such as the ones black parents preferred, set clear limits, lacked opportunity for the exercise of autonomy and initiative, and afforded little positively affective, adult-child interaction. Open structure, on the other hand, encouraged autonomy and warm relations with caregivers, but offered less frequent intellectually stimulating activities. On the basis of these comparisons, it should be evident that all day care centers are not alike (see also Sheehan and Abbott, 1979).

Another characteristic on which programs differ is the opportunity for contact with mixed age peers. In most centers, children are grouped in narrow age bands.   Beller, Litwok, and Sullivan (no date) found, however, in their observational study of 22 classrooms providing care for 80 lower income two- to three-year-olds, that age integration can have positive effects. Specifically, children in mixed-age groups spent more time engaged in complex social interaction such as that demanded by imaginative play, and teachers were more nurturant and complied more often to the demands of the children in such classrooms. The fact that Fein and Clarke-Stewart (1973) concluded, upon reviewing the literature on age integration in nursery school populations, that conflicts are more common and long lasting in age-segregated groups and that there is less affection, teaching, and more competition displayed in such groupings suggests one possible strength of family day care programs since age integration is the norm rather than the exception in this type of care (Howes and Rubenstein, 1980).

Family day care constitutes the most used system of out-of-home care in this country, both in terms of the number of families using care and the number of children served. An estimated 1.3 million family day care homes serve an estimated 2.4 million full-time children (over 30 hours per week), 2.8 million part-time children (10-29 hours per week), and 16.7 million children in occasional care (less than 10 hours per week). Over 50 percent of the full-time children in family day care are less than six years of age, with the greatest proportion of these children under three. Family day care also represents the most prevalent mode of care for the five million school children between six and thirteen whose parents work (Fosberg, 1980).

It is important to note that three different types of family day care homes can be identified. *Unregulated homes* are those that are not licensed or registered by a public agency. Unregulated care, although illegal in many cases, is the most prevalent form of family day care. Indeed, a 1971 survey estimated that unlicensed care constituted 90 percent of all day care arrangements (Westinghouse-Westat, 1971). In *regulated or licensed care*, the provider has been licensed by the state, county, or local government agency (e.g., department of human resources, county board of health). Across the nation, there is considerable variation in licensing standards, but most deal with group composition (i.e., staff-child ratio) and basic health and safety measures. Licensed homes are visited (often irregularly) by local officials who review the health and safety of the environment. Finally, *sponsored or supervised homes* (either family day care homes or extended family day care homes) are part of day care systems. These are groups of licensed caregivers whose organization provides them with referrals and training or other chld support services (e.g., play material). As noted earlier, such networks frequently work on the assumption that provision of training and assistance to caregivers improves the quality of care provided.

Two generally cited strengths of family day care are the daily and close contact it affords children with mixed-age peers, and its limited isolation from the non-caregiving world. Other advantages include more flexible hours, convenient location, and the freedom parents possess in selecting caregivers with values similar to their own. For children without fathers, family day care frequently provides children with the man of the household to serve as a model. Of course, family day care has its own unique disadvantages. As Steinberg and Green (1979) and Saunders and Keister (1972) suggest, family day care is, in some cases, unstable. Others have found that this is not always the case (Peters, 1972). Additionally, there is often little assurance that the provider has any formal training in child care, though most are experienced parents. More often than not, however, these caregivers lack the licensing *and* super-vision that may help to assure quality care.

Nevertheless, the findings of the National Consumer Study (Rodes and Moore, 1975) showed that 72 percent of parents whose children were in family day care homes were very satisfied with such care and 19 percent of parents whose children were in day centers would have preferred to have their children in day care homes. It seems reasonable to assume that the preferences represent a match between the parent's image of desirable child care and its actual availability.

Parent Involvement

When federal money is used to provide day care programs, parental involvement is usually mandated. Many states have also encouraged such involvement even when public funds are not involved. The nature of parent involvement ranges from direct, voluntary participation in the day care program through parents holding major governance responsibilities in the agency (Fein, 1976; Gordon, 1969; Myers, 1972).

Rationale. There have been several rationales offered, both by the federal government and by private sources, for the involvement of parents in the planning, implementation, and governance of day care programs. Basically, three arguments are made: (1) those focused upon the family unit, (2) those focused upon democratic principles, and (3) those focused on the child's own developmental needs.

1. *The family unit.* The family unit rationale for parent involve-ment stresses the need for a family service focus, particularly when programs are designed to serve minority groups and the poor. The argument points to the extreme stress under which many families exist in our society and the serious inadequacies in the services that are available to them. An early Department of Health, Education and Welfare report, for example, emphasized that many child and youth services work to detach the child from the family and act as parent substitutes rather than parent supplements. Such services fail to recognize the rights and responsibilities of the family as the principal childrearing institution. As such, they tend to make parents feel incompetent and lower their self-esteem--forcing the parents to further relinquish their responsibility toward their children and undermining the functioning of the family as an emotional, social and economic unit (DHEW, 1968).

Parent involvement is seen as a means of preventing this separation and destruction of the family unit. Both by providing supplementary counseling, education, and social supports and by providing opportunities for parents to make a difference in the program and in the lives of their children, the parental role and the family unit can be strengthened (Auerbach, 1975; Peters, 1980; Yawkey and Bakawa-Evenson, 1975).

2. *The democratic principles.* The principle of participation is entirely consistent with the value system of a democratic society and has been used throughout United States history to prevent the exclusion of persons from political, economic, and educational activities. Its application in day care is construed as one mechanism by which the poor, minorities, and the otherwise disenfranchised may protect their children against value imposition of the existent power structure while at the same time gaining experience in and appreciation for the democratic process (Fein, 1976). The principle is predicated upon the assumption that every citizen has something to contribute to his community and has a basic right to representation in matters affecting his life and family.

Consumer participation is construed as making the social service delivery system responsive and accountable to those it serves (Lowry, 1970). Only when such accountability exists do the recipients of service retain control of their own present and future. The accompanying sense of control and commitment replaces apathy and alienation. Parents who are involved in their children's day care will encourage their children to participate more, to attend regularly, and to gain as much as they can from it (Myers, 1972, p. 23).

3. *Child development.* If the benefits for child development and learning attained in well-organized day care are to be retained over the long term, opportunities offered to the child must be consistent with and be sustained by the home environment (Fowler, 1978). Our cumulative experience with projects such as Head Start, Home Start, and the like also provides clear evidence of the value of participation. Bronfenbrenner (1975), summarizing the findings of a number of longitudinal studies, concludes:

> The evidence indicates that the family is the most effective and economical system of fostering and sustaining the development of the child....without family involvement any effects of intervention, at least in the cognitive sphere, appear to erode rapidly once the program ends. In contrast, the involvement of parents as partners in the enterprise provides an on-going system which can reinforce the effects of the program while it is in operation, and help to sustain them after the program ends (p. 55).

Similarly, as a result of more recent longitudinal research, Fowler concludes:

> Much of the strength of the intervention program was
> traceable to parent guidance, and, conversely, the later
> development declines are partly attributable to a leveling
> off in quality of day-care parenting at a period when
> children's cognitive needs are expanding (Fowler, 1978, p.
> 57).

Practice. The various federal mandates and incentives for parental
involvement have had as their goals both horizontal and vertical collaboration of the family and the institutions of society (Fein, 1976; Lippitt,
1968). Vertical collaboration is that which occurs within an institution
(i.e., day care); it is represented by communication and planning across
relationships between governing board, executive director, staff, and
children). Horizontal collaboration refers to coordination and communication between institutions (e.g., family and school). Several
national and statewide surveys suggest that these goals are being only
partially met. One national survey of quality day care programs concludes:

> Parents were involved in child care in many different
> ways. Some centers have parents making all major policy
> decisions; in others, parents operate in advisory capaci-
> ties. In still others, parent groups are basically social.
> Parents participate as volunteers, as recruiters, and
> donors of support and resources. All centers system-
> atically report children's progress to parents (Fitzsimmons
> and Rowe, 1971, p. 7).

Another national survey conducted during the same period but which
was not limited to quality programs found only a minority of programs to
have any degree of parental participation (Hoffman, 1971). Other studies
confirm that, as measured by positions on boards and committees and
attendance at meetings, parent participation is more extensive in federally funded programs than in other types (Westinghouse/Westat, 1971). The
Kirschner survey (1970) suggests a relation between parent participation
in Head Start and parent interest in other community activities. Similar
results are reported by Myers (1972) and Keiter (1972). However, in all
cases, the reported levels of participation are relatively low.

Although current data on parent involvement in day care are
limited, the relationships among the day care provider (home or center
staff), the natural parent(s), and the children are coming to be seen as
dynamic, multidimensional, and developmental ones that have the potential for serving many of the functions formerly provided by the
extended family (Peters and Benn, 1980). These functions include those
that bear directly on child development--nurturance, affection, instruction, and socialization--and those that influence the child indirectly
through their impact on the family as a whole. The latter include the
family's functions as an economic unit, as a basis for the self-

actualization of its adult members, and as an advocate for or mediator of interactions with other units of society.   Central to the sharing of functions is an ongoing communication process (Powell, 1977). It seems appropriate to conclude, then, that day care represents a family support system.

Research on Day Care

Because researchers are part of their culture and reflect the general values held by their society, including the basic assumptions about families and day care previously cited, the research on day care has had a unique quality about it (Peters, 1980). Specifically, the great majority of research studies have focused on determining whether day care is "harmful" to children.   Thus, available evidence tends to address five basic questions:

(1)   Does day care *damage* the attachment between the infant and the mother?

(2)   Does day care *retard* cognitive development?

(3)   Does day care produce children that *lack* self control, who are *overly* aggressive or *overly* passive?

(4)   Does day care lead to *too great* a reliance on peers or to later *unsatisfactory* peer relationships?

(5)   Does day care *usurp* the mother's responsibility for the child?

(Adapted from Kagan, 1977)

The results of this research, while subject to major limitations (Belsky, Steinberg, and Walker, in press), may be summarized as follows.

Intellectual development.   The overall picture of evidence, duly qualified, suggests that the day care experience has neither salutary nor adverse effects on the intellectual development of most children. For economically disadvantaged children, however, rearing in day care centers appears to attenuate declines in test scores typically associated with high-risk populations after 18 months of age (Belsky and Steinberg, 1978; Belsky, Steinberg, and Walker, in press). It must be emphasized that the available evidence does not indicate that day care enhances cognitive functioning, only that day care (with the exception of children from impoverished homes who had extensive, quality day care center experience [Fowler, 1978]) seems to prevent children from intellectual deterioration so long as they remain in the day care programs. The long term effects of such rearing will be undoubtedly determined by what the child takes from his day care experience and what he encounters in the world beyond day care.

Emotional development.   Historically, the mother-child bond has been of prime concern to those interested in the influences of early experience upon emotional development. Psychoanalytic theory and early research on institutionalized chidlren (e.g., Bowlby, 1951; Goldfarb, 1943; Spitz, 1945) suggested that any arrangement that deprived the child of continuous access to the mother would impair the development of a strong maternal attachment and thereby adversely affect the child's emotional security. Since day care, by its very nature, entails the daily separation of mother from child, a good deal of attention has been devoted to discovering whether child care outside the home does indeed disrupt the child's emotional tie to his mother. The major strategy for making such an appraisal has been to observe young children's responses to separation from and reunion with their mothers (usually in an unfamiliar laboratory playroom) and to see whether children prefer to interact with their mothers, their caregivers, or a stranger in free play situations.

A thorough review of the literature in this area suggests that supplementary child care seems to exert little influence on the child's emotional ties to his/her mother except when children from high-risk environments are enrolled in unstable day care arrangements prior to their first birthday (Belsky, Steinberg, and Walker, in press). Under such conditions, infants appear more likely to develop a particular kind of disturbance in their relations with their primary attachment figure: They will be likely to avoid her (Vaugh et al., in press). Since this avoidance is presumed to result from mother's psychological unavailability, it is reasonable to speculate that even under the conditions described above avoidant attachment relations with mother are not inevitable if the quality of maternal care is not compromised during those periods of the day when she is with the infant (Belsky, Steinberg, and Walker, in press).

Social development.   In our earlier reviews (Belsky and Steinberg, 1978; Peters and Koppel, 1977), we defined social development in terms of relations with peers and nonparental adults and concluded, on the basis of the available evidence at that time, that day care children, when compared to age-mates reared at home, interact more with peers--in both positive and negative ways. Some evidence suggested, moreover, that children enrolled in day care for extended periods displayed increased aggression toward peers and adults, and decreased cooperation with adults and involvement in educational activities once they entered school (Belsky, Steinberg, and Walker, in press).

Lest these findings be taken as a sweeping indictment of day care rearing, it should be noted that like all social and educational efforts, day care programs are likely to reflect, and in some measure achieve, the values held explicitly or implicitly by their sponsors, and, through them, by the community at large. From this perspective, it is quite possible that the social outcomes noted were characteristic of socialization in age-segregated peer groups in America generally. Indeed, the possibility that these developmental outcomes may be culture bound is indicated by comparative studies of peer group socialization in the United States, the USSR, Israel, and other contemporary societies.   Available evidence reveals that, depending on the goals and methods involved, group up-bringing can lead to a variety of consequences, ranging from delinquency and violence at one extreme to unquestioning conformity at the other (Belsky and Steinberg, 1978). Ambron's (1980) recent suggestion that day care staff are more permissive, more tolerant of disobedience and aggression, and less inclined to set behavior standards than parents, may provide an explanation as to why American day care children look different from their peers reared in Chinese, Russian, and Israeli day care centers when it comes to relations with peers and nonparental adults.

   Physical development.   Little data is available concerning the physical development of children within day care. Where data do exist, the focus is primarily upon height and weight. The lack of evidence to the contrary probably suggests that there are no notable differences between home-reared and day care children.   Evidence does exist that the incidence of illness (infectious disease) is not significantly higher among children in group day care than it is among home-cared children (Loda, 1976).

   In summary, the current research findings, sparse though they are, suggest that children enrolled in day care are developing in a fashion similar to children at home with their parents.   In general, few differences are noted between day care children and their home-reared counterparts. It does seem that day care children are more assertive and aggressive, though there is little to establish day care, per se, as the causal factor. In total, it seems that day care, at least that which has been studied, is not the negative childrearing environment that many initially believed it to be.

Effects Beyond the Child

   The availability and quality of child care arrangements can have a major impact upon the family unit that goes beyond immediate effects on the child. Indeed, much of the public justification for the provision of day care services has to do with family (particularly the mother), not the child (Peters, 1975), 1980).   Unfortunately, there is little research about such familial effects (Belsky, Steinberg, and Walker, in press).

   This absence of information represents only one limitation of our present understanding of the phenomenon of supplementary child care. Also lacking is systematic research on day care's influence on the community and American society, as well as on the reciprocal influence of these social units on day care itself. Absent, then, is an understanding of the linkages interconnecting the individual child in day care with the family, community, and cultural/historical contexts in which the child is embedded--that is, an ecology of day care.   Coordinated inquiry at several levels of analysis is required if progress is to be made in developing an ecology of day care.

To achieve such a goal, conceptual tools are needed that are capable of bridging disciplines and overcoming handicaps of professional specialization.   Bronfenbrenner's (1977, 1979) concentric-circle model of the ecology of human development represents one such conceptual device, as it conceives the individual to be embedded within several nested levels of context. Progressing outward from the center are the layers of micro-, meso-, exo-, and macrosystems.   According to Bronfenbrenner, the microsystem represents any immediate setting containing the developing individual; the mesosystem, the interrelation of these major settings; the exosystem, the formal and informal social structures that do not themselves contain the developing person but impinge upon or encompass the immediate settings, thereby influencing what goes on there; and the macrosystem, the over-arching patterns of ideology and organization that characterize a particular culture or subculture.

Although the discussion to follow is organized into separate subsections corresponding to the meso-, exo-, and macrosystems, respectively, the multiple levels of this ecological framework should not be viewed independently. Quite the contrary, factors at one level of analysis influence the shape of events at others.   In other words, in the ecology of day care, as in the ecology of human development more generally, levels of analysis are necessarily interconnected.

The mesosystem. Here the focus is on the interface of day care and the family.   Available research indicates that this interface has been examined in two general ways--by studying parent-caregiver communication and the effects of day care on the family. In neither case does the available work go far enough in exploring the mesosystem of day care.

Douglas Powell of the Merrill-Palmer Institute has conducted the most extensive examination of parent-caregiver communication (Powell, 1977, 1978b, 1979, 1980) and his in-depth interviews of 212 parents and 89 caregivers in 12 metropolitan day care centers in Detroit reveal that few efforts are made to coordinate children's socialization across contexts. In fact, Powell concludes, on the basis of his work, that "fragmentation and discontinuity" characterize the social world of day care children.

Powell's (1978b) detailed typology of parent-caregiver communication patterns indicates, however, that experiences across day care and home are not the same for all children. A small group of "interdependent" parents, Powell discovered, believe strongly that family information (on a wide variety of topics) should be shared with day care workers. And such parents practice what they preach, engaging in frequent communication with caregivers.   "Independent" parents, in contrast, maintain a significant social distance between themselves and their children's caregivers, most probably because they conceive of family and day care as two separate rearing environments. Finally, a third group of "dependent" parents were identified who view the family/day care relationship as a one-way street in which information flows only from day care to the home.

Inconsistent communication is not the only cause of discontinuous care between home and day care. General childrearing practice (e.g., regulatory strategies for dealing with curiosity, hostility, anxiety, etc.), physical environments (e.g., freedom of movement, opportunity for privacy), and value codes (e.g., delayed versus immediate gratification, justifiable aggression versus intolerance of aggression) represent other areas of potential home-care/day-care care discrepancies (Powell, 1980). Obviously, it is not entirely possible to maintain continuity across all these domains, nor is it necessarily advantageous to. However, in the case of young children, such continuity, which is enhanced by frequent parent-caregiver communication, undoubtedly serves to support optimal development by providing the child with a consistent and, thus, predictable social world (Lippitt, 1968). In the case of older children, it is possible that continuity is less important. Indeed, as Lightfoot (1975) suggests, dissonance between family and other rearing environments may make children more malleable and responsive to a changing world, whereas homogeneity across rearing contexts could discourage the development of adaptive functioning. Unfortunately, research that addresses this important issue is lacking.

In addition to influencing the parent-child relationship, day care can support family functioning in other ways. Most significant in this regard may be its impact on the marital relationship. Under two conditions day care may positively influence a marriage: when it frees a parent from the unsatisfying responsibilities of providing full-time child care and when it enables a second parent in an economically stressed family to seek gainful employment. Since a harmonious marital relationship provides support for parents in their caregiving roles (Belsky, in press), such effects of day care have the potential for positively (though indirectly) influencing the parent-child relationship.

Although fathers tend to be less enthusiastic, women claim that their marriages are happier with day care (Hoffman, 1971). In one quasi-experimental study, it was found that employed mothers whose children were cared for in day care centers had higher levels of marital satisfaction than either employed mothers with other forms of child care or unemployed (homemaker) mothers (Myers, 1972). The perceived quality of parent-child relations also has been found to be positively associated with work satisfaction in women, and work satisfaction has been found to relate positively to satisfaction with substitute child care (Harrell and Ridley, 1975). Since the child development literature also suggests that mother-child attachments do not differ for day care children as compared to home care children, it appears that, for some mothers at least, day care permits satisfaction in both the maternal role and the employment role while not having a detrimental effect on the child.

The exosystem. What transpires in day care is most certainly affected by forces and contexts with which the child is not directly involved. Moreover, the effects of day care most assuredly extend beyond the child and what transpires in his family.   Consideration of such influences on and effects of supplementary child care demands an examination of the exosystem of day care. In this exosystem analysis of day care, the interaction of the workplace and supervisory agencies with day care are considered.

Day care's influence on the world of work is most evident when parents' reasons for utilizing supplementary child care are considered. For most families, day care makes the employment of at least one parent (often the second parent) possible. But day care may influence the working world in ways other than through this general effect.   Specifically, the establishment of a *stable* caregiving arrangement is likely to reduce, if not eliminate entirely, the time and effort that go into making child care plans on a week-by-week or month-by-month basis.   To the extent that this is so, day care may effectively reduce absenteeism from the workplace and, thereby, enhance employee productivity. If a day care program has the resources to care for a sick child, such effects are likely to be especially pronounced.   In this regard, Steers and Rhodes (1978) note, in their recent review of the causes of employee absenteeism, that caring for a child who is ill is the major determinant of missed work days by female employees. Stable child care is thus likely to be a vehicle for advancing the career development of women in this society.

In addition to being influenced by day care, the world of work exerts an influence on it.   The general absence of flexible work hours, for example, makes supplementary child care a necessity in many families. Indeed, when parents are able to structure their working hours to accommodate the demands of child care, the very need for day care is reduced (Hofferth, 1979). Lein (1979) reports, for example, that in some families parents are able to work alternate shifts and avoid supplementary care entirely. Note that this effect of the workplace on day care has implications for child development. If parents are able to arrange their schedules so that supplementary care is not necessary or only minimally necessary, then the child will spend substantial time in the primary care of father as well as mother. By altering traditional sex roles, this indirect influence of the workplace should influence the child's sex role development.

The demands of the workplace, especially long hours, also place strains on day care programs and the families using them. All too often, employers are insensitive to family dependency on day care services. For example, required over-time, sometimes on short notice, can generate conflict between day care provider and parent as parents are late to pick up their children or want (and frequently expect) their caregivers to put in greater hours than are contracted.   Such conflict between parent and caregiver could negatively influence the child (Jones, 1980).   Even more distressing, though, is the possibility that such over-time demands on the caregiver could lead to the break-up of a stable caregiving arrangement. When industries make day care facilities available to employees, as some have already done (Kleinman, 1973), an important step is made in overcoming conflicts that may develop between the world of work, child care, and the family (Small, 1969).

Community organizations that supervise and provide support to day care networks also play an instrumental role in assuring that quality child care is provided and that families have access to it (Ristau, Gardner, and Hodges, 1976, 1977).

The macrosystem. As already discussed, United States culture has traditionally viewed supplementary child care arrangements as inherently inferior to home rearing. This is most clearly reflected in the rise of day care primarily during times of national emergency (when, presumably, an inferior mode of childrearing could be tolerated) and in our acceptance of governmental support for day care only among disadvantaged and/or minority families (for whom we could presumably conscience an inferior type of childrearing). As Peters (1980) has pointed out, this differential availability of government-sponsored day care programs is partly a function of our cultural heritage of free enterprise which emphasizes the individual's, and thus the individual family's responsibility for its own self-maintenance. From a broader vantage point, Keniston (1977) observed that this idealized view of the American family as a self-sufficient, autonomous social unit has impeded the development of a coherent family policy in the United States. In countries with more socialized economies, this has not been the case, and, not surprisingly, day care as well as other welfare programs are more universally available (Kamerman and Kahn, 1976). This relationship between political/economic philosophy and service provision underscores the role that the macrosystem plays in determining the quantity and quality of supplementary child care services available to families (Peters and Klein, 1980).

The development of the Women's Movement, with its ever-increasing influence on political, economic, and family life, demonstrates that prevailing ideologies are amenable to change. Most important, from the vantage point of this macrosystem analysis of day care, is the fact that such ideological change has direct consequences for the day-to-day experiences of children growing up in society. Indeed, the changes in the American family were stimulated largely by the emergent, nontraditional attitudes toward women's roles that have received wide acceptance in recent years.

Once the prevailing conception of woman as mother and housewife was amended, the kind of care provided children was bound to change. Initial fears that such changes would adversely affect the well-being of children have proved to be largely unfounded. Such social changes are far from over (Toffler, 1980). Peters and Klein (in press) suggest that changing cultural attitudes will greatly affect day care as well as vice versa. Today, day care is more widely accepted as a viable childrearing alternative or adjunct among middle-class families than it was 20 years ago. The role that increased day care utilization and availability may play in the future for sparking (or, at least, abetting) ideological change is formidable. Day care provides families with alternatives, and those alternatives include women in the labor force and single parenthood. Indeed, it is the availability of day care, no doubt, which has influenced more fathers to take custody of their children following divorce. Such nontraditional families are today possible because day care is available as a family support, enabling fathers to work as well as to rear their children.

THE FUTURE

Futurists make it clear that, because it has yet to come about, the future can bring with it any of an infinite number of possible tomorrows (Shane, 1971). They warn that the discontinuities of history--the innovations, breakpoints, the quantum jumps--are more important than the continuites (Toffler, 1980). The future cannot be extrapolated in linear fashion from the trends of the past. The specifics simply cannot be foretold even in the relatively short range. Yet, it is evident that society and the American family are changing rapidly and will continue to do so. Today, seven percent of the total population of the United States currently lives in the idealized nuclear family consisting of a working husband, a housekeeping wife, and two children (Toffler, 1980). Moreover, all the evidence suggests that nuclear households (even where both spouses are employed) are shrinking in number as other family forms multiply (e.g., child-free marriages, cohabiting couples with or without children, single-parent families, solos, etc.).

One useful way of looking at the changes that are occurring is in terms of the functions that families serve in society. Ogburn's (1938) classic work delineated seven family functions: (a) the production of economic goods and services, (b) status giving, (c) education of the young, (d) religious training of the young, (e) recreation, (f) protection, and (g) affection. All of these functions have undergone and continue to undergo rapid changes. Most family theorists are in agreement that all of the functions Ogburn specified are now either radically different, lost entirely, or shared with other institutions of society (Mott, 1977). New functions have arisen to supplant the old, such as self-actualization of family members, advocacy, and the like (Peters and Benn, 1980). One increasingly important function is that of coordinator and manager of interactions with other components of the social system (Powell, 1977). These new family functions may be best served by new family forms.

Projections for the future suggest no one single family form will replace the rapidly diminishing nuclear family. Rather, there will be an increasing proliferation of alternative "aggregates" that permit a wide range of personal options. The anticipated diversity will well serve the demassification process in the economic, social, and political spheres, as brought about by the advent of new technologies (Toffler, 1980). To meet the needs of these new family units, new forms of early education, child care, and family services will need to emerge. Indeed, the pressures are already present, and the changes in day care are already under way (Hofferth, 1979). The rapid expansion of the day care service industry is just one reflection of this pattern.

Toffler (1980) argues convincingly that we are moving rapidly away from one era and on toward the next. The era of standardization, specialization, and centralization in economics, politics, and society is over. The era of diversity, decentration, and roundedness is upon us.

Macrosystem changes of this sort have major implications for the new "ideal" person--the shared cultural norm for personality and behavior. For one thing, the ideal person of the future will be noted for his or her individuality and complexity. Accompanying the pursuit of one's own individuality is a respect for and encouragement of the individuality of others. Roles will be less rigidly held, permitting more flexibility in the development of individual skills and talents, and more fluidity in the way people come together to acomplish their goals. At a behavioral level, this encouragement of individuality and flexibility suggests the emphasis will be on the development of cooperation rather than competition, empathy rather than egoism, altruism rather than selfishness, balance rather than narrowness, and flexibility rather than rigidity. In short, the expectation is that it will be very hard to pigeon-hole the person of the future.

Two characteristics of the individual that are likely to be universally valued are technological sophistication and ecological awareness. As computers and other "electronic hardware" become more and more of an accepted part of most life styles (Toffler, 1980), facility with a certain level of technological skill will become almost mandatory. At the same time, the current and predicted severe limitation of natural resources will of necessity force these technological skills in the direction of developing new means of preservation and conservation, rather than the exploitation of the past century. The person of the future will be required to maintain a balance between these urgent macrosystem demands.

The projected views of the society, the family, and the person of the future dictate certain trends in the rearing of young children. A decade ago, Shane and Nelson (1971) predicted that early childhood education programs for two- to five-year-olds would be a universal reality by 1985. If one includes experience with educational programing offered through television, it appears a virtual certainty that all children will enter the public schools having some preschool experience by mid-decade. Today, approximately 50 percent of all three- to five-year-olds are enrolled in nursery school, kindergarten, Head Start, or day care programs (Hofferth, 1979). It seems evident that rapid expansion will continue in the day care system--including both commercial day care (Lake, 1980) and federal and state-funded day care systems of centers and homes (Hofferth, 1979;

Peters and Koppel, 1977)--and most notably in the area of programs for infants (Elardo and Pagan, 1976; Fowler, 1980).

Parents will thus have a growing set of alternatives to choose from in meeting their family needs. Many of these alternatives represent a change in the relationship between the family and society. They indicate the emergence of a "personal service system" that relates to but is not identical with the welfare system, the educational and health systems, and the like (Kamerman and Kahn, 1976). Day care programs are being increasingly seen as a "social utility" (Kadushin, 1978) and a new form of "expanded family" for sharing the child-oriented functions of the new and emerging family types. Much of the "welfare stigma" is fading from the day care scene. In all likelihood, it will vanish in the next decade. Paralleling this change in attitude is a growing acceptance of the day care provider as a recognized professional (VanderVen, 1979).

In the future, the range of day care alternatives available to families also is likely to increase rather than decrease. As changes in the macrosystem and in the microsystem, particularly those in the structure of family life, occur, the form of delivery systems will continuously reflect those changes. Further, although the dichotomy between services to the poor and those to the more affluent will continue, both systems will grow and diversify (Peters, 1975). After school care, night care, flexible-hour care, weekend care, and so on will flourish.

Whether such changes in American life prove to be in the interest of the nation, the community, the family, and the individual child will depend upon the quality of care provided children. If day care is adopted as a quick fix to enable women to work and to enhance the viability of single-parent families, then short-term gains may result in long-term costs. It must not be overlooked that the conclusion that day care experience is not harmful to children is based principally on studies of children reared in high-quality programs. If such quality is not provided, there is no reason to assume that negative consequences of day care will not emerge.

Most important to quality care are the care providers themselves. Formal education and training are of little importance if a caregiver is insensitive to the individual needs of a child, engages in few one-to-one contacts with his/her charges, and lacks the creativity to turn daily mundane events (e.g., folding the laundry, a trip to the store, cooking) into interesting learning experiences. Language is essential to the cognitive development of all children, so caregivers must be willing, and able, to engage in frequent and meaningful discourse with those in their care.

Ultimately, the people selected to rear the next generation must be concerned with the welfare of children and enjoy their involvement in caring for them. Rarely are day care workers well paid. Much of the return for their efforts must come in the form of intrinsic satisfaction. Even if the pay were better, money would not be sufficient. No society should entrust its most important responsibilities, the care of its children, to persons seeking just a job. Commitment and concern to children and their families are also necessary prerequisites, then, of the caregiver capable of providing quality care.

There is already a rapid growth in the education and specialized training available to all persons engaged in providing day care services (Peters and Kostelnik, 1980) and an increase in professional activity (VanderVen, 1979). The future will bring about continued advances in this area.

CONCLUSIONS

Day care with the United States, over its approximately one-hundred-year history, has grown in the number of children it serves, diversified both in the types of programs offered and the characteristics of its clientele, and matured in the quality and professionalism of its staff. Most of this change has occurred during the past 20 years in response to changes in the social, economic, and political fabric of the country. Current surveys and projections indicate the demand for day care services continues to exceed supply (and will do so through 1990) both because of an increase in the number of children and because of an increase in the number of working women. Research also indicates that day care as a supplemental childrearing approach has at least a benign effect on children and families and may serve as a beneficial environemtn for at least some children. Attitudes toward day care are clearly changing. Together, the many interacting forces strongly suggest that day care as a major social entity, as a major influence in the lives of children and families, and as a major employer will be a part of the contemporary scene of America through the turn of the century.

REFERENCES

Ambron, S. Causal models in early education research. In S. Kilmer (Ed.), *Advances in early education and day care* (Vol. 2). Greenwich, CT: JAI Press, 1980.

Auerbach, A. Parents' role in day care. In D. Peters and J. Beker (Eds.), *Day care: Problems, process, prospects.* New York: Human Sciences Press, 1975.

Beller, E., Litwok, E., and Sullivan, K. *An observational study of interaction in day care.* Unpublished manuscript, Temple University, no date.

Belsky, J. Early human experience: A family perspective. *Develomental Psychology*, in press.

Belsky, J., and Steinberg, L. The effects of day care: A critical review. *Child Development*, 1978, *49*, 929-949.

Belsky, J., Steinberg, L., and Walker, A. The ecology of day care. In M. Lamb (Ed.), *Childrearing in non-traditional families.* Hillsdale, NJ: Lawrence Erlbaum, in press.

Biemiller, A., Avis, C., and Lindsay, A. *Competence supporting aspects of day care environments--a preliminary study.* Paper presented at the Canadian Psychological Association Conventin, Toronto, June, 1976.

Bowlby, J. *Maternal care and mental health.* Geneva: World Health Organization, 1951.

Bronfenbrenner, U. *Is early intervention effective?* DHEW Publication No (OHD) 76-30025. Washington, D.C.: U.S. Department of Health, Education and Welfare, 1975.

Bronfenbrenner, U. Research on the effects of day care on child development. In *Toward a national policy for children and families.* Report of the Advisory Committee on Child Development. Washington, D.C.: National Academy of Sciences, 1976.

Bronfenbrenner, U. Toward an experimental ecology of human development. *American Psychologist,* 1977, *32,* 513-531.

Bronfenbrenner, U. *The ecology of human development.* Cambridge, MA: Harvard University Press, 1979.

Caldwell, G. What is the optimal learning environment for the young child? *American Journal of Orthopsychiatry,* 1967, *37*(1), 8-21.

Connell, D. B., Layzer, J. I., and Goodson, B. *National study of day care centers for infants: Findings and implications.* Unpublished manuscript, ABT Associates, Inc., Cambridge, MA, 1979.

Department of Health, Education and Welfare. *Parents as partners in department programs for children and youth.* Washington, D.C.: U.S. Government Printing Office, 1968.

Elardo, R., and Pagan, B. *Perspectives on infant day care.* Little Rock, AK: Southern Association for Children Under Six, 1976.

Emlen, A., and Perry, J. Child-care arrangements. In L. Hoffman and F. I. Nye (Eds.), *Working mothers.* Washington, D.C.: Jossey-Bass, 1974.

Fein, G. *Infant day care and the family: Regulatory strategies to ensure parent participation.* Washington, D.C.: U.S. Department of Health, Education and Welfare, Office of the Assistant Secretary for Planning and Evaluation, 1976.

Fein, G., and Clarke-Stewart, A. *Day care in context.* New York: John Wiley and Sons, 1973.

Fitzsimmons, S., and Rowe, M. *A study of child care 1970-71.* Cambridge, MA: ABT Associates, 1971.

Fleming, V. *America's children 1976: A bicentennial assessment.* Washington, D.C.: The National Council of Organizations for Children and Youth, 1976.

Fosburg, S. *Design of the National Day Care Home Study.* Paper presented at the annual meeting of the American Educational Research Association, Boston, April, 1980.

Fowler, W. *Day care and its effects on early development.* Toronto: The Ontario Institute for Studies of Education, 1978.

Fowler, W. *Infant and child care.* Boston: Allyn and Bacon, 1980.

Goldfarb, W. The effects of early institutional care on adolescent personality. *Journal of Experimental Education,* 1943, *12,* 106-129.

Gordon, I. Developing parent power. In E. Grotberg (Ed.), *Critical issues in research related to disadvantaged children.* Princeton, NJ: Educational Testing Service, 1969.

Harrell, J., and Ridley, C. Substitute child care, maternal employment and the quality of mother-child interaction. *Journal of Marriage and the Family,* 1975, *37,* 556-564.

Heinicke, C., Friedman, D., Prescott, E., Puncel, C., and Sale, J. The organization of day care: Considerations relating to the mental health of child and family. *American Journal of Orthopsychiatry,* 1973, *43,* 8-22.

Hill, C. R. The child care market: A review of evidence and implications for federal policy. In *Policy issues in day care: Summaries of 21 papers.* Washington, D.C.: U.S. Department of Health, Education and Welfare, 1977.

Hill, D. R. Private demand for child care: Implications for public policy. *Evaluation Quarterly,* 1978, *2,* 523-545.

Hofferth, S. Day care in the next decade: 1980-1990. *Journal of Marriage and the Family,* 1979, 644-658.

Hoffman, D. *Parent participation in preschool day care.* Atlanta, GA: Southeastern Education Laboratory, 1971.

Howes, C., and Rubenstein, J. *Influences on toddler peer behavior in two types of day care.* Unpublished manuscript, Harvard University, 1980.

Joffee, C. *Friendly intruders: Child care professionals and family life.* Berkeley, CA: University of California Press, 1977.

Jones, L. *Family day care: A full time job.* Pittsburgh, PA: Health and Welfare Planning Association, 1980.

Kadushin, A. Child welfare strategies for the coming years: An overview. In *Child welfare strategy for the coming years* (OHDS 78-30158). Washington, D.C.: U.S. Department of Health, Education and Welfare, 1978.

Kagan, J. The effect of day care on the infant. In *Policy issues in day care: Summaries of 21 papers.* Washington, D.C.: U.S. Department of Health, Education and Welfare, Office of the Assistant Secretary for Planning and Evaluation, 1977.

Kamerman, S., and Kahn, A. *Social services in the United States.* Philadelphia: Temple University Press, 1976.

Keiter, L. The effects of day care parent participation on community involvement. In L. Myers (Ed.), *The family and community impact of day care* (CHSD Report No. 17). University Park, PA: The Pennsylvania State University, Institute for the Study of Human Development, 1972.

Keniston, K. *All our children.* New York: Harcourt, Brace, and Jovanovich, 1977.

Kirschner Associates, Inc. (Ed.) *A national survey of the impacts of head start centers on community institutions.* Washington, D.C.: Kirschner Associates, Inc., 1970.

Kleinman, C. Industry steps up its day care output. *Day Care and Early Education*, 1973, *1*, 27-30.

Lake, A. The day care business. *Working Mother*, September 1980, pp. 31-37.

Lein, L. Male participation in home life: Impact of social supports and breadwinner responsibility on the allocation of tasks. *The Family Coordinator*, 1979, 489-495.

Lightfoot, S. Families and schools: Creative conflict or negative dissonance. *Journal of Research and Development in Education*, 1975, *9*, 34-44.

Lippitt, R. Improving the socialization process. In J. Clausen (Ed.), *Socialization and society*. Boston: Little, Brown and Company, 1968.

Loda, F. The health of children in group day care. In R. Elardo and B. Pagan (Eds.), *Perspectives in day care*. Little Rock, AK: Southern Association on Children Under Six, 1976.

Lowery, R. Power to the people: Political evolution or revolution? *The Urban Social Change Review*, 1970, *2*, 25-28.

Mott, P. *American families in transition: Approaches to family policy.* Washington, D.C.: Social Workers' Association of America, 1977.

Myers, L. *The family and community impact of day care.* University Park, PA: The Pennsylvania State University, Center for Human Services Development, 1972.

National Research Council. *Toward a national policy for children and families.* Washington, D.C.: National Academy of Sciences, 1976.

Office of Assistant for Planning and Evaluation. *The appropriateness of the federal interagency day care requirements (FIDCR): Report on findings and recommendations.* Washington, D.C.: U.S. Department of Health, Education, and Welfare, June, 1978.

Ogburn, W. The changing family. *The Family*, 1938, *19*(4), 139-143.

Peters, D. L. *Day care homes: A Pennsylvania profile* (CHSD Report No. 18). University Park, PA: The Pennsylvania State University, 1972.

Peters, D. L. Editorial. In D. L. Peters and J. Beker, (Eds.), *Day care: Problems, process, prospects.* New York: Human Sciences Press, 1975.

Peters, D. L. Social science, social policy and the care of young children: Head Start and after. *Journal of Applied Developmental Psychology*, 1980, *1*, 7-27.

Peters, D. L., and Benn, J. Day care and parenting: Some thoughts on research and practice. In B. Klein and J. Stevens (Eds.), *The lives of families*. Little Rock, AK: SACUS, 1980.

Peters, D. L., and Klein, E. The education of young children: Perspectives on possible futures. *Theory Into Practice*, in press.

Peters, D. L., and Koppel, F. Day care: An overview. *Child and Youth Services*, 1977, *1*(4), 1-11.

Peters, D. L., and Kostelnik, M. Current research in day care personnel preparation. In S. Kilmer (Ed.), *Advances in early education and day care* (Vol. 2). Greenwich, CT: JAI Press, 1980.

Powell, D. R. *The interface between families and child care programs.* Detroit: The Merrill-Palmer Institute, 1977.

Powell, D. R. Correlates of parent-teacher communication frequency and diversity. *The Journal of Educational Research*, 1978, *71*, 333-341. (a)

Powell, D. R. The interpersonal relationship between parents and caregivers in day care settings. *American Journal of Ortho-psychiatry*, 1978, *48*, 680-689. (b)

Powell, D. R. Family-environment relations and early childrearing: The role of social networks and neighborhoods. *Journal of Research and Development in Education*, 1979, *13*, 1-11.

Powell, D. R. Toward a socio-ecological perspective of relations between parents and childcare programs. In S. Kilmer (Ed.), *Advances in early education and day care* (Vol. 1). Greenwich, CT: JAI Press, 1980.

Prescott, E. *A comparison of three types of day care and nursery school-home care.* Paper presented at the biennial meeting of the Society for Research in Child Development, Philadelphia, March, 1973.

Prescott, E., Jones, E., and Kritchevsky, S. *Group day care as a childrearing environment.* Final report to Children's Bureau. Pasadena, CA: Pacific Oaks College, 1967.

Ristau, C., Gardner, A., and Hodges, W. *West Virginia paraprofessional child care system.* Atlanta, GA: Family Training Centers, Inc, 1976.

Ristau, C., Gardner, A., and Hodges, W. *West Virginia paraprofessional child care system: Supplementary report.* Atlanta, GA: Family Training Centers, Inc., 1977.

Rodes, T., and Moore, J. *National child care consumer study: American consumer attitudes and opinions on child care.* Arlington, VA: Kappa Systems, Inc., 1975.

Ruderman, F. *Child care and working mothers.* New York: Child Welfare League, 1968.

Saunders, M., and Keister, M. *Family day care: Some observations.* Unpublished manuscript, University of North Carolina, Greensboro, 1972.

Shane, H. Future planning as a means of shaping educational change. In R. M. McClure (Ed.), *The curriculum: Retrospect and prospect* (NSSE Yearbook No. 70). Chicago: University of Chicago Press, 1971.

Shane, H., and Nelson, O. What will the school become? *Phi Delta Kappan*, 1971, *52*, 596-598.

Sheehan, A. M., and Abbott, M. S. A descriptive study of day care characteristics. *Child Care Quarterly*, 1979, *8*, 206-219.

Sibbison, V. *The influence of maternal role perception on attitudes toward and utilization of early child care services.* University Park, PA: The Pennsylvania State University, The Center for Human Services Development, 1972.

Small, W. *Evaluation of employer sponsored child day care center.* Washington, D.C.: Nellum Associates, 1969.

Spitz, R. A. Hospitalism: An inquiry into the genesis of psychiatric conditions in early childhood. *Psychoanalytic Study of the Child*, 1945, *1*, 53-74.

Steers, R., and Rhodes, S. Major influences on employee attendance: A process model. *Journal of Applied Psychology*, 1978, *63*, 391-407.

Steinberg, L., and Green, C. *How parents may mediate the effect of day care.* Paper presented at the biennial meeting of the Society for Research in Child Development, San Francisco, March 1979.

Steiner, G. *The Children's Cause.* Washington, D.C.: The Brookings Institution, 1976.

Toffler, A. *The third wave.* New York: William Morrow and Company, Inc., 1980.

Travers, J., and Ruopp, R. *National day care study: Preliminary findings and their implications: 31 January, 1978.* Cambridge, MA: ABT Associates, 1978.

Urban Institute. *The subtle revolution: Women at work.* Washington, D.C.: Department of Housing and Urban Development, 1980.

VanderVen, K. Conference activity in child care: Signpost of a consolidating profession. *Child Care Quarterly*, 1979, *8*(2), 148-149.

Vaughn, B., Gove, F., and Egeland, B. The relationship between out-of-home care and the quality of infant-mother attachment in an economically disadvantaged population. *Child Development*, in press.

Westinghouse Learning Corporation and Westat Research, Inc. *Day care survey--1970.* Washington, D.C.: Office of Economic Opportunity, 1971.

Yawkey, T., and Bakawa-Evenson, L. The child care professional-parent-child: An emerging triad. In D. Peters and J. Beker (Eds.), *Day care: Problems, process, prospects.* New York: Human Sciences Press, 1975.

THE EFFECTIVENESS OF FOSTER CARE

AS SUPPLEMENTARY PARENTING

Louise F. Guerney

Department of Individual and Family Studies
College of Human Development
The Pennsylvania State University
University Park, PA 16802

INTRODUCTION

"Foster family care refers to twenty-four hour child care *within the context of a substitute or surrogate family*....as distinguished from other forms of substitute extrafamilial child care, e.g., residential treatment and institutional care" (Horejsi, 1979, p. 8). Foster care is generally the least restrictive and most normal type of extrafamilial substitute care.

The standards for foster family service set forth by the Child Welfare League of America (1975) describe foster care or, as is frequently preferred, foster family care, as the

> child welfare services that provide substitute family care for a planned period for a child when his own family cannot care for him for a temporary or extended period, and when adoption is either not yet possible or not desirable....Foster family care should provide for the child whose parents cannot do so, experiences and conditions that promote maturation, prevent further injury to the child, and correct specific problems that interfere with healthy personality development....Foster family care is one of society's ways of assuring the well being of children who would otherwise lack adequate parental care. Society assumes certain responsibilities for rearing and nurturing of children....It discharges these responsibilities through the services of social agencies and other social institutions....Foster family service should be designed in such a way as to maintain and enhance parental

131

functioning to the fullest extent....Provide the type of
care and services best suited to each child's needs and
development...bring about the child's ultimate return to
his natural family whenever desirable and feasible, or
when indicated, develop an alternative plan that provides
a child with continuity of care (pp. 8-9).

In the child welfare system, of the children placed outside their
natural homes, the highest proportion, approximately 75 percent, are
placed in foster homes (Horejsi, 1979). Four of every 1,000 children in the
population are placed in foster care, and the number is increasing. With
the movement toward deinstitutionalization, children are being placed in
foster care that in years past would have been in institutions for the
emotionally disturbed, delinquent, or handicapped.   Thus, the foster
family frequently takes on the function of a treatment facility, and the
foster parents then become an indispensible part of the overall treatment
plan (Kadushin, 1967).

On the other hand, there has been a growing concern about the
number of children placed in foster care who might be served better while
remaining with their own families through the use of day care, parent
aides, or other services. Even greater concern has been expressed about
the length of time that children remain in foster care once placed. As
noted in the definition, inherent in the notion of foster care is the idea of
it being a temporary arrangement.   Long-term placement outside the
family is generally meant to be on an adoption basis. While many children
remain in foster care until the time of their emancipation, it is infrequently planned that way. It is this sort of uncontrolled happening that is
commonly cited as the major failing of the foster care system and has
spawned the phrases "adrift in foster care" (Sherman, Neuman, and Shyne,
1973) or "foster care limbo" (Fanshel, 1978). Criticism of the foster care
system runs very high and is emotionally charged. Many accuse the foster
care system itself of allowing foster care drift as an unconscious effort to
assure its existence.   It is considered big business in the child welfare
human service system, supplying work for many which would be threatened if the system made foster care minimally temporary (U.S. News and
World Report, 1979). Those less cynical of personal and system motives
remain critical on other grounds. Kadushin (1967), as well as The Oregon
Project (Emlen, Lahti, Liedtke, Sullivan, Clarkson, Casciato, and Downs,
1976), have demonstrated that length of stay in foster care and placement
in it to begin with, are a function of the experience of the social worker
as well as the availability of other options.   There is a need for some
place for children to go when the natural home fails them, or more
specialized living arrangements outside of the community become impossible to find or prohibitive in cost.   In his study of foster care in
Massachusetts, Gruber (1977) indicates that in spite of what might be
heroic efforts to maintain children in families with many unresolvable
problems, (essentially problems based on lack of education and income
potential) there is probably going to remain a high use of foster care at
least for short-term placements.

Growing demand for use of foster care as a less restrictive environment for children who would have at one time been institutionalized creates assaults on the system from two different sources, one to reduce the number of placements in favor of home management, and the other to add to the number of placements in preference to institutional placement. In 1980, the latter averaged $35.00 per day in the non-urban areas and as high as $100.00 in the urban areas for placements in specialized care, whereas a typical monthly reimbursement for a child in specialized foster family care in 1980 is $7.00 per day to the foster family (Watson, 1980) (generally minimal medical care and minimal clothing allowances are in addition, and paid for by the placing agency directly to the vendors). With this cost differential, despite potential benefits of a different type of placement, there is little question that the growing shrinkage of service dollars will result in as much (if not more) use of foster care than in the past, unless efficient, effective, proven means of keeping families together at less expense can be developed.

Examination of particulars relating to the issues of placement in foster care, duration of stay in foster care, results of placements in foster care and efforts to reach the goals of providing the best possible placement for the child's development, the family's welfare, and the community's approval will be considered in the rest of this chapter. First, descriptive information on the participants in the foster care service system will be presented.

BRIEF HISTORY AND SOME DEFINITIONS OF TERMS

Estimates of children currently in foster family homes range around 350,000 (Sibbison, 1978). Some 50,000 more are in foster care group homes (U.S. News and World Report, 1979). Generally, a foster family "shall not have more than a total of six children, including foster children and foster parent(s)' own children, in the foster home" (American Public Welfare Association, 1975, p. 46). More typically a foster *group* home will have six to eight children who are *not* those of the foster parents. The "parents" may, in fact, be paid workers hired to serve as house parents. What remains unchanged in the foster group home is the atmosphere of a home and the functioning of members as a "family-type" group.

In this chapter, we will focus on the foster family home, the most widely used facility and the one for which most data is currently available. Generally, the foster home is in a setting typical of the area and differs little from other homes in the community. This is considered an important part of the normalizing aspect of the foster home upon which a great deal of the strength of foster care is considered to be based. Children in foster family care presumably have the opportunity to live a normal life in a normal family. This, in turn, is expected to enhance the development of the foster children who, by definition, have had some atypical, if not downright destructive, family experiences.

The notion of placing children, not known as orphaned, but deprived of life in their own families for other reasons, into the homes of other families has a long history. The most recent and relevant history in the United States dates to the early 1800s when there was great public concern about abandoned children roaming unsupervised in the streets of large Eastern cities. A minister, Charles Brace, of the New York Children's Aid Society, developed a "Placing Out Program" which involved finding homes on farms for these children. Farmers, looking for labor, took in these children with the expectation that they would work in exchange for support (Langsam, 1964).

The Free Home Movement, the name given to Brace's program, was described by Hutchinson (1972):

> Social workers carried out the program with little conflict
> or guilt in the face of mass auctioneering of children to
> unknown foster parents. The rescuing of unknown chil-
> dren from their unknown parents for placement with
> unknown foster parents was unquestioned (p. 18).

After much criticism of the Free Home Movement, Charles Birt-well, Director of the Boston Children's Aid Society, developed systematic plans for studying foster home applicants and for the supervision of children once placed. Birtwell attempted to develop a system which permitted the return of the child to the natural parents, as opposed to the quasi-adoption of the Free Home Movement (Kadushin, 1967). Birtwell's approach became the historic model for the current Child Welfare System, through which it has been institutionalized.

Foster Care Versus Adoption

At this point, it might be wise (although perhaps redundant for some readers) to draw a distinction between foster care and adoption. A child who is adopted goes to live with a new family permanently. There is no plan or even hidden hope that this child can return to the natural or birth family. The child takes the name of the new family and is legally a member of that family forever. A child can be adopted only after s/he has been "freed" from his/her parent(s) by the court. The court also gives the new parents full responsibility and rights in relation to the child. The biological parent(s) agree to surrender or relinquish the child, which removes all their rights in regard to the child. The short-term or temporary quality inherent in the model of foster care derived from Birtwell, is in stark contrast to the notion of leaving one's birth family permanently and joining a different family. Foster children are not the children of their foster parents in that parental rights are not transferred to the foster parents. The nature of parental rights and children's rights will be discussed in other sections in this chapter describing the various participants in the foster care system.

Subsidized Adoption. In recent years, some states have passed legislation permitting adoptive parents to receive subsidies from tax monies to support children they adopt. The subsidies can be in cash, medical, educational, or other services needed for the child and continue until no longer needed or the child is 18-years-old. The legislation has been passed in the hope that adoptions will be facilitated in instances where limited financial resources prevent an otherwise suitable adoptive family from accepting a child.

Long Term or Permanent Foster Care and Foster-Parent Guardianship

Long term or permanent foster care is a *planned* arrangement to maintain a child in a given foster family for the foreseeable future. Such an arrangement is made when a long, hard look ahead by the responsible agency indicates that the child will not be returned to the natural family or freed for adoption. It is preferred that an agreement be written to underline the commitment on the part of foster parents and agency and, if possible, the natural parents and/or the child who is old enough to do so. The purpose of this agreement is to establish stability for the child and to strengthen the foster parent-child relationship. Agency support and rights over the child continue.

Guardianship operates in the same way except that the rights regarding the child are placed in the foster family. Except for financial and resource assistance to the family by the agency, the foster family operates as the child's own family. Guardianship is always a formal, legal, court-approved action, although a guardian may be terminated and replaced by another if a situation arises to make the original guardianship inappropriate.

Specialized Foster Care

Because many children coming into the foster care system today are older and have more medical, emotional, and educational problems than those of years ago when the system was used primarily to deal with children whose parents were the major clients, a new concept has been introduced into the system. This is the notion that specialized care, i.e., more than routine nurturance and training, is required to meet the needs of the children. The concept includes the implicit, if not explicit, understanding that the foster parents will need to be skilled and effective in dealing with difficult or impaired children. Training is given more often to specialized foster parents than to those dealing with traditional foster children. Presumably, caseworkers working with specialized foster care caseloads have fewer families, are able to be more involved in the management of these cases, and provide more support to the foster parents. If the children are delinquent or mentally ill or retarded, special treatment programs, often very behaviorally oriented, must be devised and supervised. The concept of therapeutic foster homes has been introduced where the foster parents are intended to create a therapeutic environment (Tavormina and Hampson, 1978; Engel, 1980; Horner, in press). Foster families generally are reimbursed at higher rates for providing these more demanding services.

THE PARTICIPANTS IN THE FOSTER CARE SYSTEM

The Foster Children

Two classifications of children are generally served in the foster care system. The first represents the smaller number. These are children whose own handicaps or behavior have placed greater demands on their birth families than the families can meet. Experts in the field (e.g., Gruber, 1978; Fanshel, 1979) seem to agree that child-related problems account for fewer than one quarter of child placements. In New York State, 14.1 percent of the children from New York City and 10.6 percent of children from up-state samples were in this group (Sibbison and McGowan, 1978). Conversely, 78.6 percent of the placements were a result of parent-related problems in the New York City group and in 74 percent of the up-state group.

Of the parent-related problems across all of New York State including New York City, mental illness of the caregiver accounted for the largest number (35.3%). Abandonment or desertion of the child account for the next largest (34.2%). Either adjudicated or alleged neglect was third (28.3%). Other causes cited were parent-child conflict and no natural home because of death of parents or other reasons.

When child-problems are the placement basis, children are more likely to be voluntarily surrendered by their parents. When parents seek outside help in caring for a mentally or physically handicapped child, agencies may help arrange foster care. In such instances, the agencies may not be child welfare agencies, those usually engaged in placement services, rather they are mental health, mental retardation, or other services to handicapped or dysfunctional children.

Children in the second category may also be surrendered voluntarily because the parents feel unwilling or unable to care for them, particularly those under one year of age (Fanshel, 1979). However, when parents are the problem, most children are placed at the instigation of an agency. Families may seek professional help, with or without placement in mind, or the agency is contacted through "abuse hot lines," schools, neighbors, or other agencies who have dealt with the family.

Description of the Children

More males than females were found to be in placement in the New York state study, particularly in New York City. In a survey of demographics of children in placement in Western Pennsylvania (Guerney, 1976), boys again outnumbered girls. Girls were significantly older, with a mean age of 11.1 compared to the mean age of 9.9 for the boys. Differences in age/sex pattern in placement may occur because boys prove more difficult to control at younger ages, whereas the concern about girls appears to increase as they reach sexual maturity (Guerney, 1976).

For New York state, approximately twenty percent of the children were under school age, while about eight percent were under two years of age. In New York City (Fanshel, 1979), 24.6 percent of all children who came into care were under one year of age while the total state sample was 18.1 percent under one year of age. Clearly, these children were placed because of parental inability to care for the children, as demonstrated by the abandonment or neglect of the children (20.5%) and drug-addiction of the parent(s) (10.14%). By contrast, in the Western Pennsylvania region, which has only one large metropolitan area, only 3.3 percent of the children in care in 1976 were under one year of age. These are very different regions, with only one large metropolitan area in Western Pennsylvania. In Western Pennsylvania it would appear that infants either are adopted or remain with their mothers who are not, as a group, exhibiting inadequacy as frequently as those in inner-city samples. In the upstate New York sample (which also includes several large cities, e.g., Buffalo and Syracuse, 36.9 percent of the parents of these infants requested that the children be placed. Foster care was used as the entry into what was considered to be the adoption system.

Older children and specialized care. Characteristics of teenagers in foster care may be somewhat different. Fanshel (1979) observed that "in recent years the foster care system in New York City has increasingly had to absorb teenagers from *intact* families who cannot remain in the community because of *their* acting out behavior" (p. 790). This trend reflects the recent increased use of foster care by both departments of welfare and juvenile justice. Actually, keeping a child in foster care "has always been a relatively inexpensive way of providing for children separated from their own parents and not placed for adoption" (Fanshel and Shinn, 1978), which is the case with these youths. The new element is the notion of foster care as a treatment alternative rather than a custodial alternative as with the younger children.

About 23 percent of the children in the total New York State foster care system were 15 years and older. Approximately 20 percent of them were categorized as adolescent behavior disorders, runaways, and school problems, e.g., truancy. While such behaviors in the children result in a classification of child rather than parent-problems as the basis of placement, there is little doubt that with this group, the placement also reflects problems in family and community life (Sibbison and McGowan, 1978).

Native American children. Statistics gathered by the Association on American Indian Affairs (Horejsi, 1979) revealed that 25 percent of all

Native American children are in adoptive or foster homes, or boarding schools. Further, the number of these children taken from their parents is grossly disproportionate to their percentage in the population. For example, in the state of Washington, the rate at which Native American children are placed in non-familial care is 19 times that of other children of the state. In 1969, 85 percent of the children were in homes of non-Native Americans. Needless to say, this situation is having serious effects on the abilities of Native American communities to maintain the integrity of family and tribal life. Without agency intrusion, Native American families generally are able to care for neglected children within the circle of the family, with grandparents or other relatives taking over (Horejsi, 1979). Thus, there are serious questions about the use of foster and adoptive care, and even boarding schools which are usually far away from the family. Does it not needlessly interfere with the natural helping networks of the already tenuous culture of the Native American tribes?

The *Standards for Foster Family Service Systems,* published by the American Public Welfare Association (APWA) (1975), asserts that it does, by including special standards for Native American children and their families. They state,

> The Responsible State Agency shall serve Indian children and their families who need foster family services living within the boundaries of the state, including those under the jurisdiction of the tribal courts (p. 21).

They continue with the guideline that these services "will be made available with recognition that Indian Tribal Courts and Courts of Indian Offenses are courts of competent jurisdiction with respect to removing children from their own home" (Basic Guideline 3, p. 21). Basic Guideline 4 states "...services shall include provision for meeting the child's needs relative to Indian heritage, Indian status, and tribal culture" (p. 21).

Problems of Children at Entry

> There is a trend toward a changing composition of children coming into foster family care. The development of services to children in their own homes implies that many situations that once led to foster care may not today. This suggests that the families of children needing foster care are those that demonstrate the greatest disorganization, the greatest pathology. Children who have lived under such conditions for sometime have suffered more deprivation and have more emotional difficulties than was true of children who came into foster care earlier in our history (Kadushin, 1967, p. 423).

Children placed in foster care as a result of mental and physical handicaps, only, are hard to sort out because these problems, particularly mental retardation and emotional illness, may be at the root of acting out and other socially undesirable behaviors. However, as an estimate, mental retardation, physical conditions, and emotional problems residing in the child were given as the primary reasons for placement for about 10 percent of New York City children and five percent of Upstate children.

Regardless of the primary reason for entry, a survey of New York State's foster children indicated that diagnoses of mental and medical problems were made for many foster children. Approximately 20 percent of the children across the state were diagnosed as mildly to profoundly retarded. Neurological disorders were diagnosed in two percent, and visual, severe, and disabling medical conditions were reported for 13 percent of the Upstate sample and 10 percent of the New York City children. The most frequently reported specific medical problems affecting the child physically were speech disability and visual disability. It is interesting to note that these two conditions were also most frequently reported as affecting the child socially. Similarly, the presence of psychiatric or psychological conditions was high, occurring more commonly in the New York City youngsters (18.2%), possibly because psychiatric evaluations were more frequently reported for them. For the Upstate sample, 13.2 percent were reported as psychologically disturbed (Sibbison and McGowan, 1978).

Types of Families Most Commonly Involved in the
Foster Care System

According to Hanton (1980) four types of families are most likely to reach the level of requiring formal agency assistance. These are families who:

1) Abuse or neglect their children

2) Move frequently to keep up with employment and are never fully integrated into a community

3) Reside permanently in the community but because of poverty and/or lack of social status never gain full acceptance

4) Experience a major crisis beyond the assistance of the informal helping networks in the community (p. 422).

It is interesting to note that Hanton's classification of families really is along two dimensions--1) the severity of the problem (abuse and neglect and major crises--loss of both parents, for example) and 2) the status of the family in the community. Families with low status, which is an indicator that few resources are available to them--of both a material and social nature, are likely to have family problems resolved by social agencies and utilize foster care more often than families of higher status who command greater financial and social "wealth." In disorganized families, joblessness, inadequate housing, parental alcoholism, and mental illness are all prominent factors in entry into the foster care system. In more organized families of higher status, only the more severe problems, inescapable from official response once apparent, will tend to bring children into foster care.

Even in the minority of cases where child rather than parental-problems are the precipitants of foster care, families with greater resources are more likely to be able to meet the demands of a hard-to-manage child--whatever the cause. Private institutions and group homes are generally available, if one can afford the price through help from loans and relatives, if not one's personal resources. Caretakers can be brought in to assist or replace the primary caregivers and thus prevent placement outside the home. Some advocacy groups such as the National Association for Retarded Citizens will support community living arrange-ments which reduce the enormous expense to parents of providing adequate care for their children without formal foster placement.

What we have then is a disproportionate number of children entering foster care with lower socio-economic status, from minority groups, and from families with only one parent. In New York state samples (Sibbison, McGowan, 1978), 64 percent of families were in these categories; 15 percent of the children had unwed mothers. In summary, it might be said that the families tend to be economically deprived, socially deviant, and inadequate in controlling their children. Represented also dispro-portionately are children whose parent(s) receive Aid to Families of Dependent Children (AFDC). The amount of money alloted to such families places them in the poverty group, making any problem more likely to crack the family. Further, since families in the welfare group are usually in contact with social workers and other representatives of public agencies, they are more likely to be firmly entrenched in the formal agency system which, like the more informal networks, tends to resolve problems within its own system. Since the formal system involves foster care--and since the reason for being known in the formal system to begin with was a result of family dysfunction--a relatively closed system emerges (Horejsi, 1979).

The Placement Agencies

Type and staffing of agencies. About 95 percent of foster place-ment is made by public child welfare agencies (Horejsi, 1979). The remaining placements are made by private social work agencies or juvenile justice and mental health agencies. The amount of placement done by the latter may be deceptively small because in some states, Pennsylvania for instance, placements recommended by other types of services, such as mental health, are frequently channeled through child welfare. When special grant programs exist in the other systems for placing children into their own foster care programs, greater use of foster care service can be expected. However, competition among agencies for the limited number of foster parents in a community can develop.

Placement services, with the exception of special grant programs for mental health or juvenile justice agencies, are supported by county funds and supervised and supported financially to some degree by parallel state agencies. Supplemental funds are generally available to the local children's service agencies through various federal title programs.

Some large, overburdened public agencies subcontract foster care services to private agencies, e.g., the Children's Aid Society. In this instance, the private agency charges some overhead to the child welfare agency for providing the services. This financial practice has been cited as a factor in extending foster care unnecessarily. Very difficult research would need to be done in order to demonstrate this unequivocally. In the state of Pennsylvania, reimbursements from the State to the agencies for providing either foster care or subsidized adoption are the same in order to make the placements equal financially and, thus, remove the influence of financial considerations in making judgments about what is best for a child.

Placement agencies are expected to meet licensing and accreditation standards for their respective states, generally based on guidelines published by the American Public Welfare Association (1975) and the Child Welfare League of America (1975). However, placement agencies are notoriously understaffed with young, inexperienced workers generally fresh out of college, the only kind who can be hired for the low salaries that are paid. "Burnout" in children's service workers is a common outcome of the stress and frustration in dealing with such enormous decisions and the execution of them. Two years is the average length of employment as a child caseworker in public agencies (Foster Care and Adoption in North Carolina, 1979; Pennsylvania Task Force, 1978). In its executive summary, the North Carolina report states, "The average child stays in foster care longer than the average foster care worker stays on the job" (p. xii).

As a consequence, placement decisions about children are often made by persons poorly equipped to make them. There is some quality control exercised in agencies fortunate enough to have experienced supervisors. In studies made in Oregon (Emlen et al., 1976) about decisions regarding placement, experience was identified as the crucial element in the use of placement outside the home. More experienced workers were less likely to make a decision to place children outside their own home than the inexperienced.

According to Horejsi (1979), the average caseworker in a foster care public agency carries about sixty families. With such a large caseload, it is nearly impossible for most agencies to track progress and supervise cases with the care that would be most conducive to rapid movement out of the system. The work of Cautley and her co-workers (Aldridge and Cautley, 1974) indicates that intensive effort on the part of the agency in the early weeks of placement is critical to the success of the foster placement. Since few agencies have time for this, workers are frequently engaged in removing and replacing children after the initial placement which prevents their doing casework and is detrimental to the development of the children (Palmer, 1976).

Agency Responsibilities to Children

The agency usually serves as the community's representative to the foster family and the natural family, as an advocate for the child, and manager of the child's case. In addition, the agency takes on the legal guardianship of the child. Except for emergency placements, a child must become a ward of the state, that is, have his/her custody in the hands of the child placement agency representing the state, generally the local public children's service. As guardian, the agency is empowered to make most decisions in relation to the child, such as the school s/he should attend, the home s/he lives in, and even whether s/he will be returned to the natural parents. When natural parents are available, some major decisions may be made in consultation with them; for example, permission for surgery, joining the armed forces, and getting married. Unless the child is discharged to family or elsewhere, the agency remains the guardian until s/he is emancipated, which is usually at age 18.

The Foster Family

An administrator of a major foster care placement agency testifying at a hearing on foster care (National Action for Foster Children, 1979) stated:

> Foster parents are probably the most valuable, flexible, single human resource in the Commonwealth, but there are times when you would never know it from the way we act (Boston transcript, p. 171).

Foster parents are selected by the agency to provide the services required of guardians--care, protection, and training. It should be emphasized that the foster families are not paid for their services. In many states they must pay themselves for liability insurance to cover foster child damage (Gruber, 1978). They are given only reimbursements for expenses, but most foster parents pay more money out in support of the foster children than is received from the agency (Settles, Culley, and VanName, 1977; North Carolina Report, 1978). Families frequently pay for orthodontia work, class trips, and so on in order to permit the foster children to share the family life style and that of the community in which they reside. Sometimes community groups and foster parent associations raise money to give gifts and other extras to foster children to supplement what agencies and foster parents cannot afford.

A daily room and board rate is paid to families for each child placed with them, and clothing and medical care is provided in addition by the agency. Medical cards (Medicaid) are generally issued for each child. However, a common complaint of foster parents is that the medical care provided by medical cards is often deficient or even unavailable in communities where cards are not readily accepted by the local professionals. Foster parents again are either forced to pay for medical care out of their own pockets or settle for inferior care for the foster children, which they are loathe to do. Since most foster parents have working class incomes, there is a limit to how much subsidizing they can actually do. Agency failure to provide adequate support and needed resources for foster children is one of the major reasons cited for attrition of foster families (Stone, 1969).

Selection. Such problems as those cited above result in foster parent "burnout." The median length of service for a foster family is approximately five years (Stone, 1969). As a consequence, most agencies are interested in recruiting foster parents on an ongoing basis. Aggressive efforts to increase their ranks are constantly urged upon agencies since active recruitment strategies do seem to work, particularly if done regularly as opposed to staging an "annual drive" (Horejsi, 1979). To recruit, agencies typically present programs to churches and other socially-minded groups, explaining the need for and responsibilities of foster parenting. For persons expressing interest, home studies are conducted by agency personnel, or sometimes personnel of private agencies, contracted to do home studies through "special home-finding units."

Foster families tend to be working class people with high school educations. Most frequently, they have children of their own who are teenagers or older and are approaching the empty nest stage in the family life cycle. On other characteristics, (i.e., race and religion) they tend to be representative of the area in which they reside (Guerney, 1976).

Research findings are available and many guidelines exist for agencies attempting to select foster parents who will function as loving, caring substitute parents (Cautley, 1980). While occasionally a scandel erupts about abusive parents, for the most part they provide adequate care and emotional support. In New York City, experienced social workers rated nearly all foster homes as good or excellent for physical care and 85 percent of them as also "warm and affectionate" (Fanshel and Shinn, 1978).

Workers look for experience in rearing or relating to children, knowledge of children, tolerance of children and prosocial reasons for wishing to become involved as foster parents. Numerous studies (Cautley, 1980; Fanshel, 1972; Weinstein, 1960) have indicated that altruistic motives of helping and sharing resources with those might need them, tend to be associated with more successful foster parents, whereas reasons such as companionship for their own children, or companionship for themselves, tend to be associated with less successful parents. Other factors related to success as foster parents are: coming from a family with young siblings, knowledge and understanding of children based on previous experience, and ability to see children as individuals and permit them to function as such (Cautley, 1980).

While recent casework practice will permit individuals, as opposed to couples, to serve as foster parents, this is still uncommon. When both husband and wife are in the foster home, an attitude of interest and support from the husband is viewed as an important factor. The most outstanding single feature descriptive of successful foster families is a shared view by the couple that child-care is a critical life task to be continued throughout marriage (Babcock, 1965).

Role responsibilities. Foster parents take the responsibility for all of the day-to-day needs and activities of the foster children. They are expected also to work with the agency and to cooperate in promoting relationships with the foster children's own families to the extent advised by the agency. Foster parents have few rights in relation to foster children beyond making decisions within their purview which implement the goals of the agency. Recently, foster parents have pressed via their organizations for rights commensurate with their responsibilities.

The foster parent role is a paradox in that parents are expected to be warm and caring to the foster children, involved and concerned, and yet at the discretion of the agency, able to release the child for replacement or discharge to family or adoption. It is a tribute to foster parents that they meet these opposing demands as dependably as they do.

Training foster parents. The most common method of training foster parents has been via "on the job supervision by caseworkers" (Stone, 1969). Because of the low level of training and experience of the average caseworker, experienced foster parents are likely to be better qualified regarding decisions about the child's daily and future needs than the workers. Consequently, agency help is sometimes of little value.

While some formal training of foster parents has been done for many years (Goldstein, 1967), more recently greater emphasis has been placed on the need for and value of education and support for foster parents. Several factors have contributed to this movement. First was the recognition of the deplorable state of affairs in the foster care field by governmental officials, primarily HEW Children's Bureau, and secondly the rise of foster parents' organizations. The National Foster Parents Association (NFPA) as well as state foster parent associations were formed to provide foster parents with an identity and to assist parents in becoming more effective in their roles. NFPA adopted an 11-point Code of Ethics for Foster Parents (1975). These organizations function also as advocates of foster children and generally seek to upgrade the entire system. They hold conferences at least annually at which training workshops are provided. Frequently, parents must shoulder expenses themselves, or raise money through local foster parent associations to support or subsidize the attendance of a few members.

Funding for developing and delivering more systematic pre-service and in-service training programs has been provided by both national and state governments to many universities and agencies through demonstration grants and title programs. Most widely known are those of the Child Welfare League of America (CWLA), which received several million dollars from the U.S. Children's Bureau to develop training packages for foster parents, in general, and for those working with adolescents and the mentally retarded. Training programs have been very well received by the foster care community. Parents attend them in large numbers, even when they are asked to pay for some of the costs. They regard them as an important adjunct to "on-the-job" supervision and rate them as instructive and supportive. Evidence that training is having desirable effects has been demonstrated in at least four extensive evaluations (Guerney, 1976; Guerney and Wolfgang, in press; Brown, 1980; Tavormina and Hampson, 1978). Foster parent associations are pressing for a standard of both pre- and in-service training for all foster parents. Currently, many foster parents cannot count on agencies providing more than a cursory orientation to their responsibilities prior to receiving a child. Title XX of the Social Security Act does cover many training expenses for parents and agency personnel, and most state foster care offices are trying to facilitate their use to increase training opportunities.

Licensing. As of 1980, nine states have passed legislation requiring that foster families be licensed by an appropriate state agency before being permitted to take children into their homes. In its *Standards for Foster Family Service Systems* (1975), the American Public Welfare Association sets forth a "Goals Standard" (as opposed to a "Basic Standard") which calls not only for initial licensing but for renewal for each foster family home. Exactly what standards should be set to obtain a license is left to the states; however, conformance is advised to national standards (such as theirs and those published by CWLA, 1975) and state standards for safety. Six states have passed legislation requiring foster parents to receive training before they can be licensed.

While foster parents are clearly functioning as important service providers, they are not necessarily regarded as such. Their role has remained ambiguous, so that they have been regarded by agencies variably from client to paraprofessional. Recommendations have been made that they become a "career" (Fanshel, 1972) or "quasi-professional" (Goldstein, 1967) group. The Pennsylvania Task Force (1978) recommended that foster parents be accorded the same authority that service-providers receive in other spheres. Desirable clarification of foster parent status should include full team membership and acknowledge authority on issues where autonomy for foster parents would facilitate service delivery (Cautley, 1980; Fanshel, 1972; Stone, 1969).

PLACEMENT ISSUES

Factors Involved in Successful Placement

   Work with the foster family.   The most extensive work on the
success of foster placements has been done by Patricia Cautley and her
colleagues at the University of Wisconsin (Aldridge, Cautley, and Lichstein, 1974; Cautley and Aldridge, 1975; Cautley, 1980).   They made an
empirical study of 115 placements which they followed over a period of 18
months from their beginning.   Duration and quality of the placements
were investigated.   All were in two-parent families who were serving as
foster parents for the first time.   A number of casework factors were
identified which correlated with successful placements: (1) The extent of
preparation for the placement by the social worker in terms of number,
length of contacts, and inclusion of the foster father (Cautley, 1980, p.
251).   Aldridge et al. (1974) developed a list of items which should be
shared by the agency with foster parents to facilitate the parents'
abilities to function effectively.   These include information about the
child's health, educational situation, habits and unusual behaviors, reason
for placement, guidance on parental visiting, length of expected stay with
the family, and financial arrangements.   (A common complaint of foster
parents is that insufficient information is provided at the time of placement, particularly if it is a hurried one Gruber, 1978; Horejsi, 1979); (2)
The age of the foster child in relation to the children of the foster parent.
In 56 percent of the 23 placements ending in nine months or less, foster
parents described problems between the foster child and their own
children.   Some of these related to the foster child's becoming the oldest
in the family group; placement of the child in a home where s/he would be
the youngest in the family group was a positive item.   The more
preschoolers in the family, the more negative the effect; no preschoolers
at all was best; (3) Early and continued support and reassurance from the
agency.   "If provided without fail during the early part of the placement
and when the foster parents later indicated some doubts, this might make
the difference between success and failure" (Cautley, 1980, p. 238); (4)
Casework with foster parents to help them accept their critical feelings
toward the child's family was facilitative.   Their role as foster parents
does not permit them to express any negative feelings about the natural
family in the earshot of the foster children.   Therefore, such assistance in
turn helps foster parents to support children in maintaining their ties to
their natural families while including them as members of the foster
family.   An interview guide developed by Aldridge et al.   (1974) is
recommended for use in eliciting problematic concerns in this and other
areas before they grow into crises; (5) Treatment of foster parents as
members of the child team, seeking out their opinions, and including them
in planning for the child; (6) Placement of foster child siblings in the same
home can be facilitative to the children, but may be difficult for the
foster parents unless they value family ties.

The findings and recommendations of Cautley and her co-workers (1980) focus on the process of inter-relationships in successful placements. Other writers have cited other kinds of factors as contributing to the success of placements. For example, there is general agreement that children under six should be placed in foster family care, but there are serious questions about the use of foster family care for adolescents, in spite of its growing use. Because it is important for the adolescent to try to develop independence, adapting to a foster family creates an unnecessary hardship for all. Foster group homes are considered preferable (Horejsi, 1979; Radinsky, 1972). Age of the foster mother has also been related to successful placement, with women beyond 40 given the advantage (Trasler, 1960; Weinstein, 1960). Parent attitudes related to success have been referred to earlier in this chapter in the section on selection of foster families.

While it is a recommended casework practice to try to place children with foster parents who match with them on race, ethnicity, and religion, the relationship of such matching or, more importantly, the lack thereof, has not been cited as a reason for either failure or success. Fanshel (1978) found no differences on variables related to success for black children in white homes versus black children with black parents. With no counter-evidence, continued efforts to match on these factors would seem wise in light of the normalization goals of foster family care. APWA (1975) guidelines do specify that special efforts should be made to find suitable American Indian foster families for all American Indian children in need of services.

Horejsi (1979) makes the point that the expectations of the foster family for certain kinds of children are important in achieving success. For example, if they wish young children, adolescents should not be placed with them. He suggests that they may have "intuitive awareness of their own abilities and limitations" and often function selectively with regard to different age groups of children (p. 178).

A method which has been demonstrated to facilitate successful placements is the use of contracts or formal agreements among the various parties involved in the placement including foster children when old enough and the agency. These eliminate ambiguity regarding rights and responsibilities and clarify goals. Revisions in the contracts should be provided with both foster parents and agency having equal rights to suggest or refuse changes (Pennsylvania Task Force, 1978; Stein, Gambrill, and Wiltse, 1974).

The Appropriateness of Placement Decisions

In determining whether a child should be placed into a foster family in preference to his own family, which must be a court decision for any stay beyond an emergency placement of very short duration, the standard generally applied by judges is the "best interests of the child." This

standard has long been used to decide matters of child custody, particularly in disputes between parents. According to Mnookin (1973), who
wrote a widely read treatise on the legal issues involved in foster care,
the best interests test is applied more appropriately in divorce cases because the strengths and weaknesses of both parents can be evaluated and
comparative outcomes for the child with each parent predicted. However, in making a decision to place a child into foster care, the court must
decide between one known factor and an unknown one--i.e., the foster
home is rarely known at the time of these decisions and its relative merits
for the child's future development cannot be assessed. Also, more
frequently than in divorce cases, the decision requires predicting the
effect of removing the child from home, school, friends, and familiar
surroundings, and predicting the child's experience while in the foster care
system, including the number of foster homes in which the child ultimately will have to be placed. Even if the judge had substantial information about all of these factors, "our knowledge of human behavior
provides no basis for predictions called for by the best interest standard"
(Mnookin, 1973, pp. 174-175).

In a seminal work in the field of child placement, *Beyond the Best
Interests of the Child*, Goldstein, Freud, and Solnit (1973), proposed that a
different standard, "the least detrimental alternative for safeguarding the
child's growth and development," be used. The least detrimental alternative, is "that specific placement and procedure for placement which
maximizes, in accord with the child's sense of time and on the basis of
short-term predictions given the limitations of knowledge, his or her
opportunity for being wanted and for maintaining on a continuous basis a
relationship with at least one adult who is or will become his psychological parent" (p. 53). Goldstein et al. (1973), reject the best interest of
the child standard because they believe that it works "primarily to meet
the needs and wishes of competing adult claimants or to protect the
general policies of a child care or other administrative agency" (p. 54).

The psychological parent, a concept publicized through Goldstein et
al. (1973), is defined as

> ...one who, on a continuing day-to-day basis, through
> interaction, companionship, interplay, and mutuality, ful-
> fills the child's psychological needs for a parent as well as
> the child's physical needs. The psychological parent may
> be a biological parent, adoptive, foster, common-law
> parent or any other person (p. 98).

Thus, the principle was advanced that biological parents have no greater
claim to a child if they do not fill the psychological and physical needs of
the child than any other available person who can function as the
psychological parent. Both biological parents are still recognized as the
primary parents in courts of law, necessitating freeing children from both
before any others can become the legal parents of a child. However, in

recent years, there has been a growing use of the concept of the psychological parent in custody decisions, along with the usual legal considerations.

Preplacement Family Services

An agency seeking to have custody of a child transferred to it must prepare evidence that this action is the only viable alternative. This presumes that conditions in the child's family are so unmodifiable, at least for the immediate future, that only removal could result in the best interests of the child being served. The best interests of the child standard, while fraught with confusion about the basis on which the judgment is made, e.g., the child's financial future, health future, social and emotional maturity, properly places the focus on the future welfare of the child. However, it does tend to ignore other genuine considerations. First, there is the question of the possible *detrimental* effects of removing the child from parental custody (Mnookin, 1973).

The evidence is equivocal that a child's life is improved when s/he is removed from home unless the dangers of remaining are immediate and substantial and there are no effective means of protecting the child against them. Thus, placing a child away from home is supposed to be done only as a "last resort." Is this in fact the case?

In 1967, a survey conducted by the American Humane Association concluded that "no state and no community had developed a child protective system program adequate in size to meet the service needs of all reported cases of child neglect, abuse, and exploitation." More recently, a survey in Massachusetts (Gruber, 1978) indicated that "virtually no effort is made to keep the biological family together and to prevent children from being placed into foster care...82 percent of the parents saw a social worker six times or less before the placement, and 60 percent were in contact with the foster care agency two weeks or less before the child was removed from home" (p. 176).

In North Carolina, about one-half of the biological parents approached agencies voluntarily seeking help with a pre-placement problem. Only about 21 percent of all cases were provided services. Where provided, the most common services were AFDC income support payments (21%) and medical care (15%). Services were rarely offered to help parents deal with child-rearing problems (13%) or marital problems (1%). Many counties had no such services available. When parents were asked what services might have made it possible to keep their children at home, they most often listed financial assistance (North Carolina Report, Dec. 1978). In Massachusetts, parents stated that services such as day care, counseling, and homemaking would have prevented placement had they been offered (Gruber, 1977).

The validity of the parents' notion that help with home conditions might serve to reduce the need for placement, gains some support from the research of Horowitz and Wintermute (1978) at Rutgers University. This preliminary study had shown that 43 percent of the families involved with abuse and neglect were on public assistance and an additional 13 percent were receiving supplementary public assistance. In response to this evidence of gross poverty, many of the state's child welfare offices attempted to maintain emergency supplies of clothing and small emergency funds collected through the worker's own contributions. While effective, such token efforts were too limited. As a consequence, an emergency fund of $11,000 per year was created for one large agency in a heavily populated, metropolitan area. The fund was used to provide emergency financial aid without delay to alleviate a crisis situation, prevent out-of-home placement, or provide a step toward eliminating abuse or neglect. These funds were dispersed as a cash grant to individual clients, to meet some significant child care expense, e.g., emergency food, housing, electricity restoration, or health care, when other assistance was impossible. Funds could not be given on a recurrent or continuing basis. In the six month period studied, having disbursed *only $5,800*, the following conclusions were reached:

> 1) ...in many cases the funds eliminated a clear and present danger to the child's health or well-being... 2) often the availability of emergency funds prevented placement of a child outside the home; 3) the ability to provide funds in an emergency demonstrated to the family the worker's intention to work with the family on a wide range of problems (including financial) that affect child care. Later stages of the project evaluation will examine the relationship of the emergency fund to overall improvement in parental functioning (p. 436).

If such a small amount of money can make such a big difference, it would not seem radical to assume that there is a largely untapped potential for bypassing foster care in perhaps nearly as many cases as the extreme critics of foster care claim would be possible.

A study conducted in Canada, where the foster care system operates in the same way as in the United States, has revealed that many situations leading to admission to foster care represent "the need of the family for support rather than the need of children for protection" (Palmer, 1976, p. 75). Results of the study led to the conclusion that the problem has been largely defined incorrectly because "agencies are not used to knowing how to hold the family together as much as they are able to provide placement help" (p. 75). The Oregon Project (Emlen et al., 1976) and Kadushin (1967) have shown that placement in foster care tends to be an easy solution for agencies, relatively speaking, satisfying short range goals.

TABLE 1

Services Required for Children/Families in their Homes
Instead of Inappropriate Foster Placement
(Adapted from material in Sibbison and McGowan, 1978, p. 12.)

Type of Service Required	Percentage of Families Requiring the Service	
	Upstate New York Sample	New York City Sample
Comprehensive Family Services	75%	41%
Casework Services	55%	43%
Child Guidance Services	40%	14%
After School Recreation	44%	30%
Assistance with Housing	44%	32%
Alternate Special Education Program	31%	21%
Family Day Care	22%	12%

Palmer (1976) describes two "pre-care" variables which correlate with family dynamics and casework outcomes: parental inadequacy, and emotional rejection of children. Emotional rejection seems to be associated with situations where parents are feeling psychologically threatened. Parental inadequacy relates primarily to economic deprivation and inadequate physical care, complicated by drinking and socially unacceptable behavior. Rejection is more likely to be associated with physical abuse of the child and/or when the child is not the natural child of both parents. In Palmer's view, because these latter problems cannot be improved in a reasonable length of time, together with the relatively good outlook in placement for children who were emotionally rejected, these children should be taken into care without a prolonged period of work with the family. In contrast, Palmer suggests that parental inadequacy is an indicator that all the financial and casework support possible should be given to improve the care of the children, and only if this fails should the children be taken over by the agency (pp. 79-81).

In an extensive study, *New York State Children in Foster Care* (Sibbison and McGowan, 1978), the data indicated that approximately 14 percent of the children "should not have been in foster care at all, but rather could have remained at home with supportive services made available to the youngsters and/or parents" (p. 15). Table 1 indicates the type and frequency of services which would have prevented placement in the opinion of the experts who evaluated the cases. Data on children from New York City and those from Upstate New York were analyzed separately for this study. Multiple services would have been necessary in most instances, hence percentages sum to more than 100 percent.

Demonstration that appropriate supportive/protective services have failed after a reasonable number of them have been tried for a reasonable time is legislated in many states before the argument that "foster care is the only alternative" can be recognized by a court. The Pennsylvania Task Force (1978) states this position as follows:

> Such decisions are intended to follow after a reasonable time to work with natural parents toward resolution of the problems... Parental conduct should justify state intervention only when it has clearly negative impact on the child's development. Standards for intervention... should focus on the emotional and physical needs of the child rather than on parental fault alone (p. 12).

However, the report continues,

> the status of parent exists only so long as it is real in terms of the health and well-being of the child (p. 12).

While controlled studies of the comparative effectiveness of foster care versus at-home services offered on a routine basis (as opposed to demonstration studies) have not yet been reported, there is little question that the costs to taxpayers for an average stay in foster care of approximately five years at approximately $5,000 per year per child, are greater than what would be required to help a family in crisis in their own home. However, multi-problem families living in what might be called continuous crises, may present problems beyond the management of ordinary casework, necessitating placement in order to meet the goal of protecting the rights of the child to a stable family life, with an opportunity for adequate growth and development.

Adjustment During Placement

Child adjustment. Ratings by caseworkers reflected a surprisingly low degree of maladaptive behavior and even homesickness in children in the study of New York City children conducted by Fanshel and Shinn (1978). Children who showed a greater degree of awareness of the reason for placement tended to be those who showed more troubled responses. Also, children who "felt that placement was to be temporary, found continued tenure in care beyond 30 days to be a hardship" (p. 377).

In analyzing ability to relate to others, Fanshel's group found that children related surprisingly well to foster parents and others in their new environment. Scores on relationship measures tended to decline with age, but older children are more likely to be placed as a result of their own problems or to have developed problems before entering care. Relationship problems with people in the foster care setting were associated with more frequent parental visiting. Implied in this "....is that children from intact families remaining in foster care have increased difficulty in establishing satisfactory human relations, especially when they maintain closer ties with their own family. The possibility emerges that they are caught in a web of relationships that may be difficult to fathom" (Fanshel and Shinn, 1978, p. 401; Reistroffer, 1971).

Parental visiting. Parental visiting can be a stressful experience for the foster children, natural parents, and foster parents. Fanshel and Shinn (1978) write,

> It is not easy for the child to juggle two sets of relationships, and the caseworkers report that some children show signs of strain in the process. We maintain, however, that this is a healthier state of affairs than that faced by the child who must reconcile questions about his own worth as a human being with the fact of parental abandonment (p. 488).

However, these researchers report that there are positive factors related to parental visiting: (1) Highly-visited children showed significantly greater gains in emotional adjustment, behavioral adjustment, and nonverbal I.Q. scores from Testing Time I to Time II; (2) Significantly

greater gains in verbal I.Q. scores over the full five years of the study; (3)
Higher level of parental visiting was a significant predictor of an overall
positive assessment by the child's classroom teacher (pp. 486-487).
Earlier, Weinstein (1960) found that visited children showed a better sense
of well-being and higher self-esteem.

The most critical and powerful case for parent visitation is that is
relates more strongly than any other single variable with discharge rate.
According to Fanshel and Shinn (1978), this pattern holds across ethnic
groups and persists over time. About 43 percent of foster children studied
were the recipients of a high degree of parental visitation. They were
never exposed to foster care without the active presence of their parents.
Of these children, 86 percent were discharged by the end of the five-year
study. Of those receiving uniformly low visitation, close to 41 percent
were discharged. Of children whose parents showed mixed visiting
patterns, i.e., low changing later to high, 52 percent were discharged to
their families, and of those with a mixed visiting pattern of high
decreasing to low, only 35.8 percent were discharged. Of children not
visited in the first year, 66 percent were still in care five years later (p.
110).

Correlates of parental visiting indicated that older children and
those admitted for their own behavior (which correlates with age) tended
to be visited more frequently. Black children were "under visited"
(Fanshel and Shinn, 1978, p. 118).

Fanshel and Shinn (1978) conclude "that the finding that discharge
rates are quite closely linked to the frequency of parental visits underscores the need to assign high priority to monitoring this phenomenon.
Further work needs to be accomplished in illuminating factors that deter
parents from maintaining contact with their children. System variables
that discourage visiting should be removed, ...and agencies should be held
accountable for efforts made to involve the parent in more responsible
visitation" (p. 111). Finally, Sibbison and McGowan (1978) note, "Youngsters in institutional settings were more likely to have been visited than
those in foster homes". However, they also point out that children were
in institutional settings most commonly for 0-3 months, corresponding to
the most frequent visiting period for children in foster care. These
researchers suggest that "infrequency of biological parent visiting is
undoubtedly related to the extended period of time in which children in
foster homes stay in care" (pp. 3-4). After five years, 43 percent of the
New York City children were still being visited (Fanshel and Shinn, 1978).

In attempting to evaluate the contribution of parental visiting to
discharge, the reader should take special care not to convert correlation
to causality. It is possible that parents show their inability to function as
responsible and involved parents to their children in foster care by not
visiting. Similarly, a high degree of visiting may indicate the opposite.
Perpetuating the notion that visiting in some way *in and of itself* will

bring about return might be a grave mistake. Rather, all of the above findings are consistent with the view that it is *desired* involvement with the child and continued *concern* about him/her that heralds a return to the family. To assume that visiting per se is the major factor can promote unnecessary stay in foster care by delaying attempts to make a permanent alternate plan for the child which does not include a family incapable of responsible parenting. On the other hand, even subtly discouraging parent visitation or failing to support parents in every way to carry out what is often a very threatening effort for them should be viewed as unprofessional and unethical--even illegal.

In the conclusion of their book, Fanshel and Shinn (1978) state,

> The termination of parental rights reflects one of the most extreme forms of state power.... People should not be penalized because they are poor, because they are mentally ill, or because they are afflicted with drug addiction or alcoholism. They should not be penalized because it is less expensive for society to terminate their rights and allow others, endowed with better economic means, to replace them as the parents of their children (p. 490).

By implication, we can conclude that they can be "penalized" only when, in spite of all reasonable efforts to encourage it, they refuse to show interest in their offspring. It is this author's view that it is questionable if termination in such instances is in fact a penalty since, for some conscious or unconscious reason, the parents do not seem to value their parental relationship to the children. Conversely, children *are* penalized by such parents, and consideration of their welfare must also be entered into the decisions.

Number of Placements While in Foster Care

Most children in foster care experience what is considered a "normal transfer" from a temporary emergency or receiving home, in which they generally spend a few days at the beginning, to a regular foster home where they are expected to remain while in care. It is difficult to compare the number of placements among the various studies that have tracked them because of differences in reporting. However, it appears that, even in the first year, it is not uncommon for children to experience one transfer once placed in regular care. Cautley (1980) reported that within 18 months, 43 percent of the children placed with new parents experienced transfers to second foster homes. Over the five year span of Fanshel's study, 10 percent of the children experienced four or more transfers, whereas 72 percent experienced only the "normal" transfer or none (i.e., did not first go into an emergency home) (Fanshel and Shinn, 1978). In less than four years, North Carolina children averaged two placements. About 10 percent had been in five or more homes, and three of the 326 studied had been in ten or more (North Carolina Report, 1978). Palmer's study (1976), which covered a ten year span, indicated that 40 percent of the children had had five or more placements. Most commonly, the longest placement in a foster home was three years, but half the children spent six years or more in one placement. Regardless of the comparability of studies, it is clear that a fair amount of moving around goes on for close to half of the children.

Factors Related to Replacement

Palmer (1976) noted that children with initial problems seemed to be particularly vulnerable to placement changes. She concluded that it is impossible, however, to determine whether more placements (when length of time in placement is controlled) result from the child's behavioral difficulties or vice versa. However, she does suggest that some replacement problems can be controlled by assigning experienced workers to problem children. Casework skills were identified as a positive correlate of a low number of replacements, particularly worker ability to help the child handle separation feelings and worker ability to relate to foster parents. Frequent parental visits were also associated with fewer replacements.

Correlates with replacements identified by Fanshel and Shinn (1978) were entry into the system because of family problems, minority group membership, and frequent visitation by natural parents, the reverse of Palmer's finding. Apparently, "the involvement with their parents contributed to less stability or poorer relationships in the foster family" (Fanshel and Shinn, 1978, p. 139).

In the North Carolina Report (1978), records revealed that reasons forcing the child to change foster homes were usually circumstances that had nothing to do with the child. In more than 60 percent of the cases, the reason was that the foster family had an illness, moved, had a death in the family, divorced, had a parent begin full-time work, abused the child, or didn't want to be foster parents anymore. However, when foster parents were surveyed, they indicated that transfers were most common for *child* related reasons, e.g., unable to discipline the child (most frequently given). Requests for change from the child accounted for only 8 percent of the moves (pp. 52-54). Cautley (1980) found that there were three times more replacements initiated by foster parents than by the agency.

Effects on Children of Replacement

Palmer (1976) sees effects on the child's ability to relate to parent figures and to feel worthy as the most troublesome consequences of replacement. Noting that 50 percent of the children experienced four or more moves, with one long placement following three short-term ones, or failures, she asks,

> Would it be possible to locate this long-term foster home earlier, so that some of this damage could be avoided? It seems that any child who is able to last for six years in one foster home should not have to experience several unsuccessful placements first. Some of these early breakdowns could probably be avoided by a more careful diagnostic job at the outset and greater conviction about the need to move more slowly on replacement (pp. 128-129).

In the New York City Study (Fanshel and Shinn, 1978), no significant relationships were found between the number of placements experienced by children and the measures of symptoms (p. 452). However, Palmer (1976) found that poor academic progress, poor adjustment in school and community, emotional problems at discharge, and behavioral problems were related to both a high number of changes and a short time in the longest placement.

Specialized Foster Placements

Children with special problems place added stress on the placement, resulting in frequent failures (Horejsi, 1979). Matching child needs and problems with foster parent strengths appears to increase success. Tavormina and Hampson (1978) have developed quantified rating scales and behavioral observation techniques for evaluating foster parents for the developmentally disabled. Horejsi and Gallacher (1977) have published a set of guidelines for selection of parents for the same children. For the emotionally disturbed, Horner (in press) has a non-quantitative "formula" for matching foster parents and children. Foster parents serving these children are sometimes labeled "therapists", and their homes "therapeutic foster homes" (Engel, 1980). Engel among others, e.g., CWLA (1978), have developed parent training programs commensurate with the specialized status.

EFFECTS OF FOSTER CARE ON CHILDREN

It is generally believed that separation from a child's own family (or foster family) creates serious psychological damage. The view is expressed by Glickman (1972) as follows: "All foster care children (except adopted infants) experience trauma on separation from natural parents and on severing subsequent ties to foster families, etc. This trauma exists even for the older child, who may feel relief at leaving undesirable parents, yet still wishes painfully that the need for separation did not exist. If such trauma is not dealt with directly for healthier integration, the effects of it will appear in self-damaging symptoms and behavior" (p. 97). Writers have likened the reaction of children to the mourning stages spelled out by Kübler-Ross (1969).

Even if the child makes a satisfactory adjustment to foster care, the haunting question remains of whether damage "goes underground." Among others, Glickman (1972) expressed the judgment that

> Adolescence can rupture the weak defenses developed for the earlier pain. Even if the child weathers this stormy period, ...his close, meaningful relationships in later life, in marriage, and with his children, are hampered by the residuals of fear and anger, and such feelings may cause him to repeat the separation trauma for his children (p. 97).

There is little recent empirical data on the later life adjustment of children who leave foster care. However, it, too, is equivocal (McCord, McCord, and Thurber, 1960; Meier, 1965). In a study published in 1924, Theis reported that 77.2 percent of the 910 former foster children surveyed could be classified as 'capable' persons at age 18 or older.

Interviews of young adults who had been in foster care as children spell out the deep sadness and suffering of poor foster care experiences (U.S. News and World Report, 1979). One must be aware that these stories are selected to make a realistic point, that the foster care system is deficient. However, one must remember that many children have found enriching and fulfilling experiences in foster care, ones which would have been most unlikely except for the placement. These persons are chosen to make testimonials at foster parent annual dinners...again a selected group. Obviously, the picture is very cloudy at this point. Unless we as a society can protect children from critical deficits while with their own families (if, indeed, that is possible) external placement will be needed regardless of the nature of the long-range effects.

It must be understood how very difficult and expensive adequately controlled studies of long-term effects would be. First, there is the question of the psychological adjustment of the subjects when they enter foster care. Undoubtedly, some of them have problems prior to the separation. Secondly, there is the question of uniformity of experience in the foster care system--how many moves were made while in it and why? What was the quality of the foster home and the casework? Were supplementary services provided in the school or the community? Did the natural parents maintain contact? All are factors considered relevant to adjustment of children in foster care, which one could assume would have effects on later outcomes as well. Finally, if such a study were conducted at adulthood when the full and permanent effects, or lack thereof, would be most telling, how would one control for unlike experiences following foster care?

Studies of Child Adjustment

Possibly the biggest problem in addressing the effects of foster placement, either long or short term, is the selection of criteria for making the evaluations. Later trouble with the law or in keeping jobs may reflect socioeducational problems as opposed to placement effects. Other criteria, e.g., presence of psychosocial problems, fall short also. Some studies have been conducted of children while in placement. These studies suffer from their "one-shot" approach, sampling problems, and lack of non-placed peer controls. It has been reported that foster children look more poorly adjusted than children who were returned home or adopted (Eisenberg, 1962; Littner 1956; Maas and Engler, 1959).

New York Longitudinal Study. The advent of computer capability for monitoring, along with a recognition by leaders in the foster care field in government and in the academic, professional, and citizen sectors, has led to a massive undertaking to get more accurate information about the impact of foster care on children. David Fanshel (Fanshel and Shinn, 1978), a professor of social work at Columbia University and one of the outstanding authorities in the field, along with other colleagues, conducted the first reported longitudinal investigation of long-range placement.

Studying 664 children in New York City who were placed into foster care between the years of 1966-1971, Fanshel's group directed their attention to the impact of several variables on cognitive development, school achievement, and psychosocial adjustment. They reasoned that if foster care had negative impact on children, the longer they were in care, the greater would be the evidence of problems. Data were gathered for the same subjects at three points in time. Time I, from 90 days in placement through one year in placement; Time II, after two and a half years in placement; and Time III, five years from the time of the child's entry into care. In addition to time in placement, the variables examined were the age of the children at entry, the number of changes in foster homes, the developmental condition of the children at entry, the quality of natural parents and their visiting frequencies, and the amount and quality of casework.

Intellectual functioning. Reporting on the final results of this study in *Children in Foster Care,* Fanshel and Shinn (1978) observe the following: "We do not find that the longer a child spends in foster care, the more likely he is to show signs of deterioration...tenure in care was related to enhancement in I.Q." (pp. 490-491). This was not true of white children (one-third of the sample), who declined in I.Q. over the five years. Further, "Length of stay in foster care was not a significant predictor of change in school performance for any of the three spans considered" (p. 491).

A Canadian study (Palmer, 1976), included some different measures and reported somewhat different findings than those of Fanshel (1978). Assessing progress of 200 children in the areas of behavior, emotional adjustment, task performance (adjustment to school, work, and community), and academic progress, Palmer found that children improved in behavior, remained as a group unchanged in emotional adjustment, and actually increased in the number of task performance problems. Academic progress was poor; children with average I.Q.'s lagged at least a grade behind. Palmer suggests that some aspect of foster care status may depress intellectual functioning. However, she did not compare academic progress to that of non-foster children from similar socioeconomic backgrounds. There appears to be more basis for her suggestion that task performance may be more uniquely a foster care phenomenon, since task performance problems were unrelated to problem status at entry, or contact with own parents while in care. Palmer studied case records of the same children over a period of five to ten years.

A non-longitudinal study of the intelligence of 163 foster children in care for an average of 5.2 years with the Children's Aid Society of Philadelphia, conducted by Fox and Arcuri (1980), indicated that the children had low average I.Q.'s with a mean of 90.18. When 140 of the children were administered the Wide Range Achievement Test, a mean score of 95.51 (normative mean is 100) was earned. The authors concluded that "foster care in and of itself does not adversely affect learning and other cognitive functions" (p. 491).

Psychosocial Adjustment. Finally, length of stay in foster care "failed to emerge as a significant predictor of change with respect to figure-drawing scores (a test of psychosocial and intellectual adjustment) and the global assessment of the emotional condition of the children by our examining psychologists" (p. 491).

Fanshel refers to a study by Langner and colleagues (Langner, Green, Herson, Jamison, Goff, Rostkowski, and Zykorie, 1969) of low-income children for a comparison of adjustment status. Langner's group identified 12 percent as in need of immediate intervention; 36 percent had moderate developmental impairment, and 20 percent had symptom impairment. Langner found there was greater prevalence of impairment among black children and welfare families. Fanshel and Shinn (1978) state:

> Our report of emotional impairment of 25 to 33 percent of our sample, depending on the source of information, seems to be quite in line with his data. Our sample was three-fourths black and Puerto Rican. Given the social circumstances of these families, our estimates of impairment are not surprising.

In sum, Fanshel states:

> While we suggest that foster children tend to reflect the populations from which they derive and also point out that children who remain in foster care appear to fare no worse than those who return home--we do not wish this to

become a source of complacency....We are particularly mindful of the fact that our study was limited to five years. It is possible that the problems faced by these children will unfold and their impairment show greater severity as they move into young adulthood (pp. 494-495).

Behavioral status. In a study of change in foster children resulting from the training of foster parents in parenting skills, it was found that foster parents viewed their foster children as having fewer problem behaviors than children in an unselected sample of school children. Using the Problem Check List developed by the Wichita Guidance Center (Brewer, 1958), Guerney, Wolfgang, and Vogelsong (1978) found a mean number of 7.19 problems as compared to the norm of 8.52 for the typical children, and 22.91 for children coming for help with emotional problems. In relation to the scores on another checklist for parents, the Filial Problem List as modified by Horner (1974), foster parents' mean rating of foster children was 9.85, whereas the average for clinic samples was 29.40 (Sywulak, 1977).

Concerned that perhaps the problems of foster children were of a special kind, Guerney et al., (1978) devised a measure comprised of foster parents' own experiences of child problem behaviors obtained from them in earlier program evaluation interviews. This instrument, the Foster Child Problem Questionnaire (FCPQ), had a pretraining mean score of 17.9, out of 87 possible problem behaviors. The single pretraining score would indicate problem status prior to any changes in foster parent attitudes resulting from training. However, these encouraging results are limited because of the single administration. Longitudinal ratings by social workers of child behavior during five years in placement indicated that behavioral difficulties tended to increase with age and time spent in care. Behavioral status of discharged children was not obtained as a comparison (Fanshel and Shinn, 1978).

Health status. A cross section of children (N = 668) were given physical and psychological examinations in the New York City area on a one-time basis to determine their health status (Swire and Kaveler, 1978). In addition, some research was carried out to see what sort of follow-up had been provided for previous medical recommendations. The majority of these children had been in foster care for four or more years. Most had entered care as preschoolers because of family dysfunction, primarily maternal mental or physical illness. Immunizations against most childhood diseases had not been provided for the majority of the children. Incomplete physical examinations had been conducted for the group as a whole, with screenings for visual, hearing, dental, and mental problems absolutely missing for at least half the children. Further, 40 percent of those found in need of dental care had not been seen by a dentist for treatment. Of the 334 children who presented symptoms of emotional or developmental problems, only one-quarter had been seen for treatment. When glasses had been prescribed, 61 percent of the children were found to have the wrong prescriptions. Swire and Kaveler (1978) concluded that:

>These findings clearly suggest deficiencies in the level of
>care provided to the study's urban foster care group.
>Moreover, they indicate that the availability of medical
>funds does not assure that these children obtain what they
>need to stay well...or that services are adequate (p. 567).

They point out that these children were found to be less healthy than a
random sample of comparably aged youngsters drawn from more widely
based study groups. "It is likely that they are in need of more health care
than most children" (p. 568). Since most of the children had been in foster
care for four or more years, it is not appropriate to assume that all of
these conditions had been present prior to placement. Sibbison and
McGowan (1978) also found a similarly high incidence of mental, physical,
and sensory problems in their Upstate New York samples.

DISCHARGE FROM FOSTER CARE

Whether a child should be reunited with his/her parents, placed with
other relatives, or adopted and when, is a decision of grave consequence.
Agency personnel are actually responsible for determining the life future
of foster children. Aside from the problems involved in evaluating and
pronosticating by the largely inexperienced workers, this awesome responsibility is complicated further by the personal stress for workers
carrying out plans. For example, in The Oregon Project (Emlen et al.,
1976) it was found that the workers most experienced in handling
termination of biological parents' rights were the least likely to initiate
them when appropriate because of the distasteful aspects of the task. In
this section, we will review studies of the exit of children from the foster
care system and the major factors involved.

The fate of children in foster care can be measured by alterations in
personal and social adjustment (already discussed in previous sections) and
by status changes. Status changes are usually classified as follows:
discharge to own family, which can include relatives as well as parents;
adoption; discharge to an institution; planned long-term or permanent
foster care; unplanned long-term foster care. The two latter categories
are not, in fact, a discharge from the system, but represent, rather, an
outcome in terms of change in status from the anticipated temporary
foster care.

The classical study on discharge from foster care was conducted by
Maas and Engler in 1959 in nine communities of different sizes. They
stunned the world of children's services when they reported that, once in
foster care, only one of four children would, in fact, rejoin their families.
They predicted that "better than half" of the more than 4,000 children
they studied would be "living a major part of their childhood in foster
families and institutions" (Maas and Engler, 1959, p. 356). Average length
of stay in foster care was five years. Maas and Engler (1959) came to the
disturbing conclusion that "...unless children move out of care within the

first year and a half of their stay in care, the likelihood of their ever moving out sharply decreases" (p. 390).

Wiltse and Gambrill (1974) found in their San Francisco study of 772 foster children that the discharge rate ran about the same as was found by Maas and Engler. In Massachusetts, Gruber (1977) indicated that 83 percent of the children were not returned to their parents even for trial periods. Most children stayed in foster care from two to six years. In North Carolina (North Carolina Report, 1978), it was reported that children were out of their homes for an average of 3.9 years.

A summary of status changes of the 624 children in the New York City study (Fanshel, 1976) as of December 31, 1971, five years after the study was initiated, is presented below (see Table 2).

Over the five-year period, approximately 10 percent of the children in Fanshel's (1978) study experienced one or more discharges and were subsequently returned to foster care. Two had experienced four such discharges with three re-entries but were out of the system at the five year mark.

Status at One Year

There seems to be general agreement that about one quarter of the children in foster care, regardless of entry circumstances, are out of the system by the end of one year. They may be returned either to own family or adopted (Emlen et al., 1976; Fanshel and Shinn, 1978; Sibbison and McGowan, 1978; Wiltse and Gambrill, 1974).

TABLE 2

Summary of Status Changes of Foster Children in New York City Study
(Adapted from material in Fanshel, 1976, p. 145)

Status	*Percentage of Cases*
Discharged to Own Families	56.1
Adopted	4.6
	60.7 Actually Discharged From the System
Discharged to Institutions	2.9
Remaining in Foster Care (planned and unplanned)	36.4
	100%

The New York State Study (Sibbison and McGowan, 1978) evaluated the appropriateness of the placement status of children still in care beyond the one year mark. Of the 75 percent remaining in care, 80 percent were expected to be in long-term care, according to their agencies. Evaluators, who were placement experts, agreed that 47 percent of the children were appropriately placed. Two groups dominated the inappropriate placements: children who should have been in the adoptive process (62.9%), and those who should have been in general institutions (20%). Case evaluators indicated that placement alternatives, i.e., return to own home, group homes, residential treatment centers, adoptive care, were greatly underutilized to meet child needs. In general, appropriate one-year placements were somewhat more likely to be associated with younger children and with black or white children rather than Puerto Rican or "other" children (pp. 8-11).

Factors Related to Discharge

Problem at placement. The reason for the placement is strongly related to eventual discharge. Fanshel (1976) found that children who were admitted for their own problems were the most frequently discharged. Over 75 percent of them were discharged by the end of five years, and 8 percent were discharged by the end of the first year (the highest first-year rate of discharge in relation to entry problem). Children whose parents were mentally and physically ill were discharged next most frequently. Children whose parents abandoned, deserted, neglected, or abused them were the least likely to have been discharged in Fanshel's (1976) sample. Children slated for adoption because of parental disinterest (abandonment, relinquishing for adoption, etc.) were adopted more frequently than the rest of the children in the sample, 15 percent versus 4 percent. It is interesting that the differential discharge rates support Palmer's (1976) view that the prognosis for family reunion is greatest for admissions related to parental health or financial problems. (See section in this chapter on reasons for entry into foster care.)

Demographics of children. Children under the age of two fared less well in terms of discharge: 50.3 percent were still in care at the five-year mark. Of children 9- to 12-years-old, 75 percent were discharged. Somewhat fewer boys than girls were discharged. Out-of-wedlock children were discharged less frequently than children from married parents. White children were discharged more frequently than black: 71 percent to 54 percent, respectively (Fanshel and Shinn, 1978).

Changes in family circumstances. Children are most often returned to their own families when there has been a change in the family's or child's personal circumstances or behavior, in addition to the most predictive factor of parental visiting, already discussed (Fanshel, 1976; Gambrill and Wiltse, 1974).

The following list (Table 3) indicates the most frequent types of family changes for the 350 children (56.1%) returned to their families in the New York City Study (Fanshel and Shinn, 1978, p. 150).

Progress of younger children. In a more recent report, Fanshel (1979) shared his results of the progress of 12,736 youngsters, tracked through a computerized management system, in New York City. These children were admitted to foster care up to 7½ years earlier at ages of less than one year up to five years. Youngest children were slated for adoption more frequently than older ones, primarily because of parental intent in placing the children. However, as children remained in the system for additional years, placement plans called for adoption more frequently for older children as well (10 to 13 years, 73.5%). Conversely, the number of children said to be headed for discharge to their families fell to 12.4 percent for the 10- to 13-year-olds.

Returning to see how these plans materialized one year later, Fanshel found that there was "modest movement" out of the system. Of children who entered care under one year of age, 25.1 percent had moved out; 8.6 percent of this entire age group had been adopted. Of those who had entered at four to five years of age, 29.2 percent had left. Most of these were discharged to parents or were home on trial discharge.

TABLE 3

Changes in Families Leading to Return of Children
(Adapted from material in the New York City Study,
Fanshel and Shinn, 1978, p. 150.)

Type of Change	Percentage of Cases Discharged
Recovery of mother from mental illness	17.3
Parent(s) worked out job training treatment or other plans	12.2
Relatives offered acceptable plan for child	9.3
Improvement in parental health	8.8
Child improvement	5.7
Other child-related reasons (refused to return to foster home, court ordered return, etc.)	12.0

Fanshel (1979) concludes that:

> A special programmatic emphasis appears called for to safeguard the rights of infants and babies entering foster care...that 6,000 children who were infants at entry have spent almost 7½ years in care, in the aggregate, contradicts reason. The goal of permanency more clearly applies to them than to any other group of children (pp. 79-81).

FACILITATING CHANGES IN STATUS

A successful placement can facilitate an ultimately favorable outcome. A problematic placement may be interpreted as a deficiency on the part of the child and/or natural family and be detrimental to their reunion. However, successful placement can also lead to complacency, slowing down progress toward making permanent arrangements. Promotion of a good adjustment to foster care should be seen by the child, natural and foster families, and case worker as only the first step in facilitating exit from the system, and not as an end in itself.

If a child has been removed from a functional family (although it may be behaving dysfunctionally), good casework practice, as well as legislated regulations in some states, require that a plan should be in place for the child within 90 days, frequently less. This plan typically would be aimed toward the return of the child to the family members with whom s/he resided prior to placement. This being impossible, other relatives are next considered. Where no kin appear to be reasonable possibilities, or the child's condition will not allow it, an alternate plan is required for permanent substitute care (i.e., guardianship, institutionalization, or freeing the child for adoption), preferably with a time limit. Some states require review of plans and their implementation every six months to prevent inaction and drift.

In this section, we will describe the activities aimed toward an exit from temporary foster care.

Agency Activities

Work with the natural parents. Work with the natural families toward the return of their children should not go on indefinitely. Goals should be worked out specifying the objectives to be reached for family reunion (Pennsylvania Task Force, 1978). The more operational these objectives and the more they are placed in formal contract form with deadlines, the better (Gambrill and Wiltse, 1974b).

Most agencies attempt to provide support to the natural family both to meet behavioral objectives and to encourage visiting of the child. Objectives in a contract might include such activities as attending parenting classes, visiting the child twice a month, and moving to quarters where the child's safety would not be endangered, e.g., moving out of a dirt-floor shack with unsafe water. Unfortunately, because of their limited psychological and material resources, many parents realistically find it quite difficult to meet these objectives, regardless of their intent to do so, and agency problems limit the amount of assistance to parents. The common agency practice of using parental success in meeting these objectives as an assessment of motivation and fitness for the return of children appears to have questionable validity. It would seem that the means to meet the objectives, and clear consequences of not doing so, need to be provided before failure to do so can be viewed as a valid indicator of parental incompetence and/or indifference.

Sometimes the interim help provided can be very meaningful. Homemakers or parent aides may be sent to the home to relieve and instruct the parent; day care arranged for children; financial aid given; health care and counseling arranged. This type of assistance, together with the mere absence of a child whose presence increased family stress, can improve family coping.

Unfortunately, the norm for agency involvement includes few of the activities mentioned above. Contacts with natural parents in North Carolina were nonexistent in half the cases once children were in foster homes (North Carolina Report, 1978); in Massachusetts, six-month intervals were not infrequent (Gruber, 1978). Gambrill and Wiltse (1974a) discovered that even in cases where the agency's stated goal was restoration to the family, visits were scheduled months apart, and then were likely to be devoted only to arranging parental visits to the children. All this occurs in spite of the fact that there is an empirically established correlation between frequency of contact and case progress. However, contact per se without meaningful skills is not sufficient with families that require more than agency attention and concern (Sherman et al., 1973).

Services to children. Services to children are offered primarily in an indirect way through foster parent consultation. Some agencies do attempt to provide behavioral management or other programs designed to deal with child problems. Accurate assessment of children's problems and procurement of appropriate services are more commonly the goals. However, these go largely unfulfilled all too frequently (Gambrill and Wiltse, 1974a; Gruber, 1978). At the meta-level, the worker assumes the role of advocate for the child, seeking to facilitate the child's adjustment and development in relation to all other involved parties. Preoccupation with the success of the placement can overshadow, unwittingly perhaps, the advocacy for an exit from the system.

Contact with families following child's discharge from foster care. Whether the child is returned to the birth family, adopted, or remains in permanent foster care, casework practices require follow-up on a systematic basis to help maintain the placement. Commonly, any work of this type is either not done or provided on a demand basis only. Gambrill and Wiltse (1974a) cite agency pressure to close cases and overreliance on mental health professionals as reasons for failure for adequate follow-up.

Permanency Planning

A movement called Permanency Planning has developed in the past five years and generated great excitement and hope for reduction of problems of the foster care system. Fanshel and Shinn (1978) describe it as a revolution akin to the closing down of large institutions. The term refers to systematic case planning for permanency (Emlen et al., 1977; Maluccio, Fein, Hamilton, Klier, and Ward, 1980). The concept has been translated into practical application, demonstrated, evaluated, and followed-up primarily through "The Oregon Project." Financed through HEW, the project was conducted by the Regional Research Institute for Human Services of the Portland State University under Victor Pike's leadership. Permanency Planning is most succinctly described by Maluccio et al. (1980) as:

> A set of guidelines useful in arranging stable placements
> for children which usually include: (1) early intervention
> and early consideration of long-term plans for each child;
> (2) examination of different alternatives to move the
> child out of temporary foster care; (3) delineation of a
> time-limited casework plan to achieve an appropriate
> placement...; (4) organization of legal evidence for a plan,
> if necessary (e.g., termination of parental rights); and (5)
> periodic case review (internal, external, or a combina-
> tion).

Emlen et al. (1977) spell out the value of the Permanency Planning concept as follows:

> (1) The home is intended to last indefinitely with resulting
> commitment and continuity in the child's family life; (2)
> the family is one in which the child has a real sense of
> belonging with 'a respected social status' (pp. 10 and 11).

This is in contrast to the second-class status typical of temporary foster care.

Since any approach is only as good as the skills and understanding of the workers intended to implement it, guidebooks have been published by The Oregon Project staff (Emlen et al., 1977) both for caseworkers and agency administrators. Inservice training and workshops are proliferating around the country through the aegis of many training groups to teach the methods. Essentially, what is taught are decision making skills, be-havioral objective writing, monitoring practices, and legal procedures.

Effectiveness of Permanency Planning

In commenting on effectiveness, Maluccio et al. (1980) state that, "There is no question that the concept of Permanency Planning has been influencing service delivery, beginning by 'raising consciousness' about the needs of children in substitute care and leading to changes in the programs of particular agencies" (p. 523). Empirical studies have been conducted primarily by The Oregon Project. A summary report and follow-up issued in 1978 (Emlen, Casciato, Clarkson, Downs, Lahti, Liedtke, and Zadny), 18 months after the project ended, included the following results.

Originally involved in the project were 239 children selected essentially on the basis of their adoptability, e.g., under 12 years of age and unlikely to return home. They were compared to 233 randomly selected cases carried by non-project agencies. Of these, 52 were culled who most resembled the project children in adoptability. Project staff provided technical assistance. By the end of the three years, 66 percent of the project children were established in a permanent placement as compared to 46 percent of the non-project children and 43 percent of the most comparable non-project children. Comparing types of permanent placement, differences were sharpest on adoption by "new" parents; 20 percent for project children and 11 percent and 12 percent, respectively for the most similar groups. The fate of the 52 non-project children casts a revealing light on the effectiveness of the usual casework practices. Also revealed was the fact that only 10 percent of this group returned to their own parents as opposed to 26 percent of the project children. Children were adopted by foster parents in equivalent proportions in both groups. Children in foster care in project counties were reduced by 31 percent as opposed to a 4 percent reduction in the rest of the state.

Follow-up studies. Comparisons for follow-up contrasted only project versus non-project children as a whole. Both groups had about 90 percent stability in their placement. Child adjustment and health were assessed by interviews of parents and children. The single most important finding was that a sense of permanence was one of the best predictors of a child's well-being. However, sense of permanence was not necessarily related to the legal permanence of the placement. Whether the child was in legally permanent foster care, returned home, or adopted, made very little difference in level of adjustment or health. "Perception of permanence was the key. Permanence accounted for large proportions of the differences between high, medium, and low adjustment" (Lahti, Green, Emlen, Zadny, Clarkson, Kuehnel, and Casciato, 1978, p. 7). The child's adjustment and health when s/he left foster care were the best predictors of adjustment and health at follow-up. Unrelated to adjustment were the number of foster care placements, the length of time in foster care, and placeability (assessment of extra-familial placement likelihood) of the child. Providing information about the child's past to new and foster parent adoptive parents was positively related to superior adjustment.

Studies of related approaches. A smaller scale version of "The Oregon Project," actually initiated before it (Jones, 1978), is the "Aggressive Adoption" program in Cumberland County, PA, which after five years, resulted in a reduction of the number of children in foster care by 50 percent. The entire staff was trained in goal-oriented case management and review. It has been estimated that the program has saved $668,000 in foster care costs in the five years. In summing up the advantages of the program, Jones (1978) adds,

> The estimate of savings is low in that it considers only the direct costs...and does not consider medical and dental costs or administrative costs related to keeping a child in foster care. The agency continues to serve about the same number of children each year but because of the redistribution of caseloads, it has been able to develop day care and other service to children in their own homes. Other benefits have included a reduction in turnover rates of foster care caseworkers and fewer foster placements per child (p. 577).

This program had no special grants or legislative support.

A study of intensive services to families was conducted with the goal of reducing foster care (Jones, Neuman, and Shyne, 1976). Families who had one child under age 14 in foster care or likely to enter foster care within six months were the target group. Randomly assigned to the intensive service group were 663 children and their families; 329 were assigned randomly to regular child welfare programs. Caseloads of workers in the intensive program were reduced to 10 families. Each of the experimental units was required to make available to families, counseling, homemaker, day care, vocational or educational services for parents or children, and information and referral services. After one year, fewer children in the experimental group required placement. A significantly greater proportion of children from the experimental group were already back at home after having spent a significantly shorter time in foster care.

A six month follow-up indicated that a significantly higher number of children were then at home. Researchers indicated a proportional reduction in costs and recommended that such services be made widely available on a decentralized basis without restrictive eligibility requirements (p. 293).

Subsidized Adoption. Evidence supports the belief that subsidies will increase the number of adoptions. In Washington state, 534 children were randomly assigned to a subsidized adoption group or a nonsubsidized adoption group. Forty-one percent of the subsidized group were adopted, as opposed to 19 percent of the nonsubsidized group (Horejsi, 1979).

Concerns expressed about the "Permanency Movement".   In a thoughtful response to the new directions, Maluccio et al. (1980) raise several issues. They cite the dangers involved in giving up too quickly on natural parents in the rush to effect a permanent plan.

> There is already some indication that permanency plan-
> ning is becoming synonymous with adoption planning and
> that insufficient efforts are made to involve and help
> biological parents. For example, manuals and resource
> books are being developed for child welfare workers
> through demonstration projects on rights and planning for
> adoption, while paying limited or no attention to methods
> of helping biological parents (p. 526).

Finally, note is made of the failure to appreciate that in some instances, because of family circumstances, a sense of permanence may best be provided by long-term foster homes. They cite a need to develop guidelines useful to workers to achieve different types of "permanent plans" for different children at different points in their life cycles. They point out that a study conducted by some of the writers of the article found that only 66 percent of emotionally disturbed children discharged from time-limited foster care to "permanent" placements remained in them, regardless of whether they returned to adoptive or biological parents (p. 521).

Non-Programmatic Approaches to Reducing Foster Care

Experimental evidence does not exist for non-programmatic ap-proaches, but records of movement through the system have documented their effects. Non-programmatic approaches generally are actions taken at state administrative levels. Such efforts to reduce foster care drift are concerned with whether case plans are made and implemented.

Several states have mandated "Foster Care Review" procedures by the agency itself or by outside reviewers--courts or government ap-pointed citizen review boards, or a combination of both. The responsible reviewers are charged with periodic reviews of all cases in foster care. The process is generally initiated by state legislation specifying the frequency of the review. The first such legislation, passed in New York State in 1971, called for court review, which placed an overload on the courts, sometimes keeping children in care longer than necessary. When judicial review resulted in court orders for agencies to take action, agen-cies failed to comply in 17 percent of the cases. Monitoring of agency compliance was then ordered. In spite of the problems, more children were placed in permanent homes who had already been in care for two to five years than had ever been placed before (Jones, 1978; Pennsylvania Foster Care Task Force, 1978).

In South Carolina, laws have been enacted to help children move through the system. One law expanded the grounds for termination of parental rights; the second permitted continuation of state medical benefits to adopted children; and the third established a system of citizens' review boards. Significant reductions have occurred in the number of children in placement and a rise in the number of adoptions (up 44%), including children who previously were considered unadoptable (Jones, 1978; Pennsylvania Task Force, 1978).

The states of Virginia, Ohio, and New Jersey have enacted judicial review laws. Improvements have been incorporated in their procedures as a result of New York State's early problems. The number of children in foster care in Virginia was reduced by 1,000 in six months after the reviews were begun. The states of Pennsylvania and North Carolina are attempting to adopt review procedures (Jones, 1978; Pennsylvania Task Force, 1978).

In an analysis of review approaches, Jones (1978) reported on The Concern for Children in Placement Project (C.I.P.), developed by the National Council of Juvenile Court Judges. Trainers were sent to 12 courts throughout the country to assist judges in selecting and training volunteers to review the cases of children in court-ordered foster care. In some of the trained courts, petitions for adoption increased 100 percent and for involuntary termination by 50 percent in one year. C.I.P. also included review by a representative of the Court, who could quickly identify cases that required a judicial hearing, reducing court intervention to a minimum.

Other Promising Developments

As of 1976, 25 states have been engaged in special projects to overcome barriers to permanency, with the technical assistance of the staff of The Oregon Project. Funding for this effort is from the Children's Bureau's National Center for Child Advocacy.

> Even though it has always been considered desirable to maintain the child in his own home, only recently have increased efforts been made to do so through protective and other services to families (CWLA, 1968, p. 2).

For example, in New Jersey in-home services have increased from 18 percent in 1961 to 78 percent in 1976 (Horowitz and Wintermute, 1978). In-home services can be used either with voluntary participation by family members or with their non-voluntary participation in the case of protective services. Since placement services account for the majority of local agency expenses (Watson, 1980), the costs of in-home services are considerably less.

The innovative and promising concept of the Emergency Protective Services Fund (Horowitz and Wintermute, 1978), mentioned in an earlier section as a successful means of maintaining some children in their own homes, is now being extended to all of New Jersey's counties.

The development of computer-based tracking systems is having an impact on the foster care system as demonstrated by Fanshel's 1979 report on preschoolers in foster care.

There is growing interest in providing legal protection of children's rights when removal from the home may be a possibility. Several states recommend the appointment of a *"guardian ad litem."* This is a court appointed person who takes responsibility for acting on behalf of the child in all legal matters, making his/her rights more viable in custody decisions.

Cautions in Relation to New Approaches and Developments

1. All of the promising program developments, with the exception of "Aggressive Adoption" (Jones, 1978) and the Temporary Foster Care Project in five county agencies in Michigan which successfully replicated the permanency planning model (Boyd, 1979), have been externally funded demonstration projects. Much attention, technical assistance, increased financial and community resources have accompanied the projects. How new methods will operate on an everyday basis, without the secondary benefits accompanying involvement in a closely monitored study atmosphere, is yet to be known (Maluccio et al., 1980).

2. There is no certainty that funds to train workers to respond to case review recommendations will be available on the large scale necessary. Two factors seem to be crucial to the successful operation of efforts to stop foster care drift. *Both* the review process and the implementation procedures must be functional. Training in goal-directed casework has been demonstrated as necessary for appropriate implementations, as well as the training of administrators, judges, and others involved in making the review recommendations (Jones, 1978). This author would add training of legislators and elected officials to the list.

3. Computer tracking systems and case review systems must have a goal of permanence to have impact on the system. Otherwise, there is danger that their only product will be a tally of where cases are (Jones, 1978).

4. Funding sources often impose restrictive guidelines making it impossible for agencies to provide discriminating care based on case need. Care must be exercised to see that the principle of "least restrictive environment" is not abused and become merely a money saving device which sacrifices service.

5. Quality controls should be built into the system to be certain that the emphasis on adoption does not result in the same type of misplacement problems currently experienced in foster care.

6. There is a danger that children will be forced to fit into foster homes who really belong in a *more* restrictive environment as some

research has indicated does happen (Sibbison and McGowan, 1978). The national mood is bent on reducing public expenditures for human services. Legitimate as this might be in the case of the foster care system which costs about a billion dollars a year (U.S. News and World Report, 1979), a trend might develop to limit the amount of money spent per child or to create non-functional criteria for reimbursements, which would cut into the substance of service, rather than cut out "fat" as would be the intent.

EVALUATIVE SUMMARY

How does the foster care system stack up as an effective supplement to parenting? In respect to its performance in serving the larger society, it has fulfilled its purpose in providing homes to children when there are genuinely no others for them. Abandoned, deserted, orphaned children will be cared for at least minimally, in spite of serious deficiencies in the services, namely, too few homes, too few knowledgeable workers, too little monitoring of the system.

In relation to the biological parents of foster children, the foster care system has not functioned so much to provide supplemental parental care as it has served to supplant the parents--forever for about half of the families. Foster care has consistently failed to demonstrate respect for natural families of foster children. "Placement programs reflect a pervasive antifamily bias...." (Maluccio et al., 1980, p. 527). The reasons for the majority of children being admitted into foster care seem to reflect lack of resources in the families. Such resources frequently could be readily provided if the public's legislative representatives had the will to do so. It is shocking that in New Jersey the sum of $108,000 for approximately 20,000 child clients (roughly only *$5.00* per child) is seen as making the difference for many of them in eliminatng "a clear and present danger to the child" and/or "....preventing placement outside the home" (Horowitz and Wintermute, 1978). If this is all that may be needed, what is stopping us?

Many parents do not wish to admit their children into care but have no choice when health breaks down. Even while suffering mental illness, some nevertheless retain a strong commitment to their children. Five years after admittance to foster care, 43 percent of the parents are still visiting the children (Fanshel and Shinn, 1978). This statistic indicates that the intended temporary nature of foster care has too frequently been put aside; that children are being torn between two sets of parents and, thus, denied a sense of permanence. In contrast, planned long-term foster care, particularly with foster parents as legal guardians, a "seldom occurrence" in the system, has the advantage of truly supplementing parents, in that it acknowledges the existence and ties to the natural parents. At the same time, it permits the foster parents to function legitimately as psychological parents. Thus, the child does not suffer the fate of divided parenthood and can gain the sense of permanence needed (Wiltse and Gambrill, 1974). Of course, when adoption is clearly the first option, achievable without pushing functional natural parents out of the picture, this would be preferable. It has the greater advantage of genuine permanence and costs less.

It is again shocking to learn that "the state of North Carolina is willing to pay 150 percent more to keep a child outside its own home than it is to permit the child to stay there." Further, "once the state has removed the child from his home, it has little contact with the natural parents and provides few services to help stabilize and reunite the family" (North Carolina Report, 1978). Granted, as Fanshel and Shinn (1978) point out, there are adults who are "undeveloped as parental figures" as denoted by their abandonment of their children either prior to or while they are in foster care. However, the data would seem to support the thesis that these are a minority. It would appear that the greater part of the problem stems from deficiencies in the foster care system and in society's commitment to expend resources to facilitate the functioning of the children's families.

Until recently, foster care has been offered as an alternate to at-home services and therefore classified as a more restrictive environment. It has begun to be used heavily in the past 10 years as a less restrictive and less expensive alternative for youngsters who in the past would have been placed in residential treatment settings. This new function of the foster home as a treatment site seems very promising if adequate training for foster parents and staff are provided and ancillary services are readily available. Research assessing the effectiveness of such placements in meetings child needs in controlled comparison to other treatment approaches has yet to be published.

Promising new developments have burst forth in the past five years. Some important longitudinal and quasi-experimental studies, including follow-ups, have been conducted with large numbers of children (Fanshel, 1979; Emlen et al, 1978) yielding a more accurate profile of the strengths and failings of the system and demonstrating what appears to be a potent remedy to reduce the average length of stay in "temporary care" from five years to a time-limited, planned period of much shorter duration. The proposed remedy involves primarily the use of goal-oriented case management, with a quick exit from temporary care into a permanent family situation as the goal. This kind of planning implicitly stresses the child's rights, since it emphasizes termination of parental rights when the risk is high that the natural family will not be able to provide a stable home for the child within a reasonable time.

Related developments have increased the available routes to stability--subsidized adoption, guardianship, adoption by foster parents, and foster care under long-term contract. Systematic review procedures being developed to monitor the exit from temporary care arrangements should also be useful, if cautions are observed.

Results are not yet in on all of the changes. At present, the foster care system appears to be experiencing a spurt of growth in very positive directions. In the meantime, the system--like the children it was designed to provide care for--is being pulled in two ways: to reduce its numbers of conventional children and to accept greater numbers of special children. Since more children from the latter group come from intact, functioning families, and the reasons for placement are more likely to stem from special deficiencies in the children, the possibility exists that the system will, in time, provide primarily paraprofessional treatment services and shift away from simply providing substitute parenting. Whatever way it goes, it is most unlikely that it will slip back into its former state. Shortages of funds on the one hand, documentation of abuses and promising new approaches to remove them on the other, are working against that. Whether a whole new set or problems will emerge as it evolves remains to be seen.

Research Directions

Empirical evaluation of an entire delivery system and comparative program evaluation within the system are extremely difficult to conduct. While limitations exist in the research conducted on the general func-tioning of foster care as a system, the amount accomplished in the past 15 years has been impressive. Large samples spread over large geographical areas have been studied. Continued evaluation of the system's functioning via accurate reporting and computer monitoring should provide necessary data on whether stated goals are being met. Fanshel and Shinn (1978) recommend that this type of evaluation should become part of the operations of every agency, not something relegated only to academic researchers.

When it comes to the evaluation of the effectiveness of comparative programmatic approaches, it would seem that extra-agency assistance will continue to be required. Service delivery places demands on agencies which work against their generating experimental or quasi-experimental research. Nonetheless, the comparative effectiveness of some different, currently controversial approaches must be subjected to empirical evalu-ation, namely, (1) the use of at-home services versus foster care; (2) foster family care versus foster group settings for adolescents, the emotionally disturbed, and the developmentally disabled; and (3) actual stability of placement of adoption versus permanent foster home ar-rangements, and their differential effects on child adjustment. Many crucial placement decisions are being made everyday in relation to these approaches, based on some data but, essentially on unproven assumptions about short-range effects.

Research related to decision making which has critical, immediate and long-range effects on the lives of children cannot take 15-20 years to be accomplished. It must be done immediately and done well so that the generalizations made will be valid.

The U.S. Children's Bureau funding of large research and demonstration projects has contributed invaluable data which has had profound impact on the system in a relatively short time. Continuation of such projects, preferably with vigorous expansion, should result in more knowledge about priority issues.

REFERENCES

Aldridge, M., and Cautley, P. The importance of worker availability in the functioning of new foster homes. *Child Welfare*, 1975, 54(6), 444-453.

Aldridge, M., and Cautley, P. Placed siblings in the same foster home. *Child Welfare*, 1976, 55(2), 85-93.

Aldridge, M. J., Cautley, P. W., and Lichstein, D. P. *Guidelines for placement workers.* Madison, WI: Center for Social Service, University of Wisconsin-Extension, 1974.

American Public Welfare Association. *Standards for foster family services systems.* Washington, D.C.: American Public Welfare Association, 1975.

Babcock, C. G. Some psychodynamic factors in foster parenthood--Part I. *Child Welfare*, 1975, 55(7), 478-490.

Boyd, P. They can go home again. *Child Welfare*, 1979, 58(9), 609-615.

Brewer, J. A checklist of child behavioral problems for use by parents. Unpublished manuscript. Wichita Child Guidance Center, Kansas, 1958.

Brown, D. *A comparative study of the effects of two foster parent training methods on attitudes of parental acceptance, sensitivity to children and general foster parenting attitudes.* Doctoral dissertation, Michigan State University, 1980.

Cautley, P. *New foster parents.* New York: Human Sciences Press, 1980.

Child Welfare League of America. *Standard for foster family services* (revised ed.), 1975.

Child Welfare League of America. *Preliminary statement on social work service for children in their own homes.* New York: Child Welfare League of America, 1968.

Commonwealth Child Development Committee. *Summary report: State task force on foster care services.* Harrisburg, PA: Commonwealth of Pennsylvania, Governor's Office, Office for Human Resources, 1978.

Eisenberg, L. The sins of the fathers: Urban decay and social pathology. *American Journal of Ortho Psychiatry*, 1962, 32(1), 5-17.

Emlen, A., Casciato, J., Clarkson, D., Downs, S., Lahti, J., Liedtke, K., and Zadny, J. *Outcomes of permanency planning for children in foster care.* Portland, OR: Regional Research Institute for Human Services, Portland State University, 1978.

Emlen, A., Lahti, J., Downs, G., McKay, A., and Downs, S. *Overcoming barriers to planning for children in foster care.* Portland, OR: Regional Research Institute for Human Services, Portland State University, 1977.

Emlen, A., Lahti, J., Liedtke, K., Sullivan, M., Clarkson, D., Casciato, J., and Downs, G. *Barriers to planning for children in foster care.* Portland, OR: Regional Research Institute for Human Services, Portland State University, 1976.

Engel, J. *Foster parent therapist training: A manual for trainers.* New York: Episcopal Mission Society, 1980.

Fanshel, D. The role of foster parents in the future of foster care. In H. Stone (Ed.), *Foster care in question.* New York: Child Welfare League of America, 1972.

Fanshel, D. Status changes of children in foster care: Final results of the Columbia University longitudinal study. *Child Welfare,* 1976, 55, 143-171.

Fanshel, D. Preschoolers entering foster care in New York City: The need to stress plans for permanency. *Child Welfare,* 1979, 58(2), 67-87.

Fanshel, D., and Shinn, E. *Children in foster care: A longitudinal investigation.* New York: Columbia University Press, 1978.

Fox, M., and Arcuri, K. Cognitive and academic functioning in foster children. *Child Welfare,* 1980, 59(8), 491-496.

Gambrill, E., and Wiltse, K. Foster care: Plans and actualities. *Public Welfare,* 1974, 32(2), 12-21. (a)

Gambrill, E., and Wiltse, K. Foster care: Prescriptions for change. *Public Welfare,* 1974, 32(3), 39-47. (b)

Glickman, E. Treatment of the child in foster care. In H. Stone (Ed.), *Foster care in question.* New York: Child Welfare League of America, 1972.

Goldstein, H. Group learning for foster parents. *Children,* 1967, 180-184.

Goldstein, J., Freud, A., and Solnit, A. *Beyond the best interests of the child.* New York: The Free Press, 1973.

Gruber, A. *Children in foster care.* New York: Human Sciences Press, 1978.

Guerney, B., Jr., Wolfgang, G., and Vogelsong, E. *Second year evaluation of foster care systems training project.* State College, PA: IDEALS, 1978.

Guerney, L. F. *Foster parent training project, final report part I, Descriptive information about foster parents associated with public child welfare agencies in the Western region of Pennsylvania.* CHSD Report #94. University Park, PA: The Pennsylvania State University, September 1976.

Guerney, L., and Wolfgang, G. Long-range evaluation of effects of foster parents of a foster parent skills training program. *Journal of Clinical Child Psychology,* in press.

Hanton, S. Rural helping systems and family typology. *Child Welfare,* 1980, 59(7), 419-426.

Horejsi, C. R. *Foster family care.* Springfield, IL: Charles Thomas, 1979.

Horejsi, C. R., and Gallacher, K. *Guidelines for screening homes for developmentally disabled children.* Missoula, MT: University of Montana, 1977.

Horner, P. L. *Dimensions of child behavior as described by parents: A monotonicity analysis.* Master's Thesis, The Pennsylvania State University, 1974.

Horner, P. L. Family vulnerability to child-individual stress: Additional considerations for foster placement of "difficult" children. *Journal of Clinical Child Psychology,* in press.

Horowitz, B., and Wintermute, W. Use of an emergency fund in protective services casework. *Child Welfare,* 1978, 57(7), 432-437.

Hutchinson, D. *Cherish the child: Dilemma of placement.* Metuchen, NJ: Scarecrow Press, 1972.

Iowa Department of Social Services, Foster Care Research Project. *Increasing the effectiveness of foster care through the use of the service contract with children, natural parents, foster parents and workers.* Des Moines, IA: Iowa Department of Social Services.

Jones, M. Stopping foster care drift: A review of legislation and special programs. *Child Welfare,* 1978, 57(9), 571-580.

Jones, M. A., Neuman, R., and Shyne, A. *A second change for families.* New York: Child Welfare League of America, 1976.

Kadushin, A. *Child welfare services.* New York: MacMillan, 1967.

Kübler-Ross, E. *On death and dying.* New York: MacMillan, 1969.

Lahti, J., Green, K., Emlen, A., Zadny, J., Clarkson, D., Kuehnel, M., and Casciato, J. *A follow-up study of The Oregon Project: A summary.* Portland, OR: Regional Research Institute on Human Services, Portland State University, 1978.

Langner, T., Green, L., Herson, J., Jamison, J., Goff, J., Rostkowski, J., and Zykorie, D. Psychiatric impairment in welfare and non-welfare children. *Welfare in Review,* March-April, 1969, 10-21.

Langsam, M. Z. *Children West.* Madison, WI: Cushing-Malloy, Inc., 1964.

Littner, N. *Some traumatic effects of separation and placement.* New York: Child Welfare League of America, 1956.

Maas, H., and Engler, R. *Children in need of parents.* New York: Columbia University Press, 1959.

Maluccio, A., Fein, E., Hamilton, J., Klier, J., and Ward, D. Beyond permanency planning. *Child Welfare,* 1980, 59(9), 515-530.

McCord, J., McCord, W., and Thurber, E. The effects of foster home placement in the prevention of adult anti-social behavior. *Social Service Review,* 1960, 419-430.

Meier, E. Current circumstances of former foster children. *Child Welfare,* April 1965, 205-215.

Mnookin, R. H. Foster care: In whose best interest. *Harvard Educational Review,* 1973, 43(4), 599-638.

National Action for Foster Children. *Foster care in Massachusetts.* Boston, MA: National Action for Foster Children, 1979.

National Foster Parents Association. *"Code of ethics for foster parents."* St. Louis, MO: National Foster Parents Association, 1975.

North Carolina Report. Governor's Advocacy Council on Children and Youth. *Why can't I have a home?: Foster care and adoption in North Carolina.* Raleigh, NC: Department of Administration, 1979.

Palmer, S. *Children in long-term care--their experiences and progress.* London, Ontario: Family and Children's Services of London and Middlesex, August, 1976.

Pennsylvania, State Task Force on Foster Care Services: Summary Report. Commonwealth Child Development Committee, 1978.

Radinsky, E. In *Foster care in question.* New York: Child Welfare League of America, 1972.

Reistroffer, M. *What you always wanted to discuss about foster care but didn't have the time or the chance to bring up.* New York: Child Welfare League of America, 1971.

Settles, B., Culley, J., and VanName, J. *How to measure the cost of foster family care.* DHEW Publication No. OHDS77-30126. Washington, D.C.: U.S. Government Printing Office, 1977.

Sherman, E., Neuman, R., and Shyne, A. *Children adrift in foster care: A study of alternative approaches.* New York: Child Welfare League of America, 1973.

Sibbison, V., and McGowan, J. *New York State children in foster care: Executive summary.* Albany, NY: Welfare Research, Inc., April, 1978.

Stein, T., Gambrill, E., and Wiltse, K. Foster care: The use of contracts. *Public Welfare,* 1974, 32(4), 20-25.

Stone, H. *Reflections on foster care: A report of a national survey of attitudes and practices.* New York: Child Welfare League of America, 1969.

Swire, M., and Kaveler, F. Health of foster children. *Child Welfare,* 1978, 57(9), 563-569.

Sywulak, A. *The effect of filial therapy on parental acceptance and child adjustment.* Doctoral dissertation, The Pennsylvania State University, 1977.

Tavormina, J., and Hampson, R. *Issues in foster placements for the developmental disabled.* Paper presented at the annual convention of American Psychology Association, Toronto, Canada, September 19, 1978.

Theis, S. *How foster children turn out.* New York: State Charities Aid Association, 1924.

Trasler, G. *In place of parents: A study of foster care.* London: Rautledge and Kegan Paul, 1960.

U.S. News and World Report. A hard look at America's foster homes. February 19, 1979.

Watson, T., Director, Centre County Children and Youth Services. Personal communication, 1980.

Weinstein, E. *The self-image of the foster child.* New York: Russell Sage Foundation, 1960.

Wiltse, K., and Gambrill, E. Foster care, 1973: A reappraisal. *Public Welfare,* 1974, 32(1), 7-15.

RESIDENTIAL HOMES AND INSTITUTIONS

Hyman Grossbard

School of Social Work
Columbia University
New York, NY 10025

INTRODUCTION

Some Theoretical Considerations of Child Rearing and Its Biases

It is generally recognized that our perception of any given phenomenon is influenced to a significant degree by its subjective meaning to us. Styles and patterns of child rearing being emotionally charged as they are, are inevitably colored by our particular bias. Our appraisal of their relative effectiveness and value is frequently askew. Constant vigilance and soul-searching are necessary prerequisites to deal with the subject on a detached and objective level.

Ideology appears to play an important role in describing and evaluating various modalities of child rearing and the potential impact of certain socializing processes on personality development. Our concept of the ideal person, of the optimal society that we would like to create, our aspirations and value systems, constitute our frame of reference from which we judge the processes and the institutions of parenting. There is a recurring tendency to polarize, to view the individual and society as adversaries, with antagonistic interests and loyalties, when concerned with the study of the upbringing of man.

One may not subscribe to the point of view of the extremist who advocates the unbridled freedom of the individual, even at the expense of the many, nor bow to the other view--the repression of the individual, and the surrender of his uniqueness for the welfare of society.

However, one inevitably struggles with the wide gray area where the interest of the individual and those of society, though not on a collision

181

course, are not harmonious. Objectivity about child rearing becomes particularly precarious during certain periods of history when people are faced with, or perceive, threats to national security, and the repression of individual needs appears to be a condition for survival. The tilting of the goals and the destiny of man begins in the social-political domain, but gradually filters into the crib and child rearing concepts.

Our perspective of continuity and change, of ideologies and institutions are thus continuously in flux. It sways from one extreme to another, from the ecclesiastic observation that there is nothing new under the sun to the idea of future shock that men and institutions are undergoing continuous metamorphosis. Our concepts about child rearing and the role of residential homes and institutions are typical.

There are some who view the phenomena of children being brought up in group facilities outside of their biological home as a relatively recent development. They tend to see it as a product of the industrial age, the invasion of technology, and the foreboding of the breakdown of the traditional fiber of our society. Their prediction is, the dehumanization of man or, at best, the evolution of new man whose behavior will be mechanistic and undifferentiated. Others, however, view it as a positive progression in the normal evolutionary process. They see in it the evolution of a new life-style, an emerging social being with a promising potential in human growth and empathic social relationships which will culminate into a more tolerant and harmonious world.

These divergent perceptions as to the future of children brought up in group facilities seem to stem from different points of departure as to the optimal society to be molded and consequently to the dynamics and processes that go into shaping the ideal man. This may partially answer the intriguing rather puzzling question, why child rearing, the oldest preoccupation of man, is still the subject of so much controversy and diametrically opposing views.

Those engaged in the care of children outside their home have been observing a gradual but distinct change of the population in children's institutions. As usual this awareness of variations and difference is partly related to our growing diagnostic knowledge and skill. We have become more sensitive to the more subtle nuances of human behavior and their implications. Certain manifestations that in the past would have been dismissed as childish mischief, or growing pains, are now viewed suspiciously as deviance in disguise. The predominance of youngsters in institutions who are basically normal but in need of a benign home has been continuously on the decline. The overwhelming majority of children in institutions in the United States today, with minor exceptions, as a result of racial, religious or regional factors, present emotional problems of a degree that affect their functioning. While in the past they have been described as children coming from problem homes, their appropriate designation now is problem children. They no longer respond to the

traditional ingredients of an institution, a benign environment with opportunities for socialization and education.   Consequently, a new type of
institution, the residential treatment center has emerged, offering complex and wide range programs consisting of an integrated mesh of people
and services designed to provide growth, educational and therapeutic
experiences. Though the residential treatment center still constitutes a
minority, it is serving a significant role in the expansion of theory, in
standard-setting, and in formulating programs for other institutions to
follow.

The change of the nature of institutions has been brought about by
the diversification of factors that dictates placement. In the past, the
predominant causes for placement were external to the child: poverty,
physical or mental illness or death of parents. The locus of the problems
was primarily the home. However, with the advent of social legislation,
particularly the social security system, the problem home with its main
features of poverty and illness is no longer the determining factor. Financial assistance and various services directed to the home help maintain
the family and prevent the uprooting of children. Consequently, negative
selective processes have been set into motion forming new criteria and
impetus to the need for separating children from their home.   It is
basically when the external disturbances at the home have registered
their impact upon the child, affecting his functioning in a number of
areas, home, school, and community, usually in various combinations.
Thus one can see, even with the naked eye, the preponderance of problem
children in the institutions of today.

HISTORICAL VIEW OF PLACEMENT

Placement is an umbrella term. It encompasses a variety of types
of rearing of children outside of their homes. It represents a broad
spectrum, and is predicated on a variety of needs necessitating a wide
range of technics, disciplines facilities and manpower. The only common
denominator is that of parenting and treatment away from the biological
or legal parental figures. Placement includes foster homes, group homes,
mini and large institutions, residential treatment centers and mental
hospitals.

The foster home is probably the oldest form of placement, being
home grown and unplanned but gradually gaining legitimacy and sanction.
It is a natural improvisation and bears close kinship to the traditional
home and nuclear family. It usually consists of parental figures, siblings
living under one roof, with the continuity of the sacrosanct traditional
family life style. Foster homes have built-in advantages. They come
ready made and often within the community. They do not require special
design nor an investment in cement and bricks. However, the foster home
which has been considered the panacea to meet the needs of children
deprived of natural homes, has been subjected to the vicissitude of reality
and changing theoretical concepts and ideologies. The reduction of the

rural population where children could be left to live on green pastures, the urbanization of the U.S.A. with the resulting shrinkage of space in the home, and the restructuring of family roles, (mother being employed outside of the home) have contributed to a serious decline in the number of foster homes.   Coincidentally, the gradual percolation of mental hygiene concepts into childrearing practices and the growing recognition of the emotional disturbances of the children in need of placement made it obvious that the traditional foster home cannot meet their needs and resources had to be explored or designed.

Subsequent to, and parallel with, the existence of the foster homes, the child care institution came into being.   Historically, the institution had a rather infamous origin.   It began as an undifferentiated facility caring for the indigent, old, feeble, and insane, together with the foundling and urchin, euphemistically known as the Almshouse.   Institutions persisted to grow indiscriminately.   They were propelled by community needs tempered by the resources that were available and the prevailing social and cultural mores, and with more than a mix of political considerations.   Not infrequently, it was a matter of convenience masked by philanthropic and humanistic labels.   Consequently, there emerged institutions housing a conglomeration of diversified and undifferentiated groups of children whose living in close proximity was inimical to their growth.

However, the influx of humanistic and reform movements and the introduction of psychological concepts into the main stream of American life had a profound effect on our methods of child care and began to filter into the consciousness of philanthropy.   The concept of the importance of a one-to-one relationship, the need for attachment and bonding during the developmental years have been having a positive effect on children's institutions.   They served as an inhibiting factor on the expansion of institutions caring for children during their early developmental stages. Community boards and administrative staff have been placed on the defensive in justifying the need for, and the right of, existence of group care for children of toddler age.   Consequently, in spite of the population explosion, there are less children within normal range in institutions today than there were at the turn of the century.   The presence of the wholesome, blond, blue-eyed, smiling youngster is becoming a rarity. However, institutions for normal children cannot be totally dismissed as a vanishing species.   They still show enduring power, and at times, even vitality.

Children's institutions thus began to develop an identity of their own confining themselves to children only, with little awareness of their individual problems and needs.   Children were viewed as little adults rather than different beings with specific and intrinsic needs.   Traditionally but to a lesser extent today, the stated objective of institutions is to create a benign environment and to design a program, a carbon copy of the normal home, for the education and socialization of the child.

However, these programs are based on the assumption that when a significant prerequisite to growth has been lacking in the child's environment; life has been standing still, marking time until the necessary element comes along. When it does, it is readily accepted, assimilated and the normal course of progress is resumed.

Actually, during the intervening period, certain processes are put into motion. They invoke defensive measures to anesthetize the child against pain, and thus make future normal positive experiences alien and unassimilable. The severe deprivation of meaningful relationships, of nurturing experiences during certain developmental phases, give rise to pathological defense mechanisms. They are manifested in diverse forms: in suspiciousness, emotional numbness, in distancing, or attack. The presence of the most caring, giving adults may bring about minimal results and often a hostile negative response. A two-fold approach is necessary; one, directed to the psychological mechanisms that distort and contaminate, and the second feeding of meaningful nurturing relationships and experiences in appropriate dosages.

In view of the implied finality of the proceding formulation, a qualifying note is indicated. Unequivocal dogmatic predictability of human behavior is risky. Those who had the opportunity to observe the stream of children in placement have often been confronted with a puzzling phenomenon. A number of youngsters who have experienced continuous and abrupt shifts in relationships, settings, early placement, movement from foster homes to a sequence of institutions, appear to function within normal range. Though they may manifest some emotional problems, they are not commensurate with the traumas they have experienced. These children appear to raise questions about our theoretical assumptions that the human species need a continuous one-to-one relationship for its optimal development and the inevitability of doom if these conditions are lacking. They lead to speculation of the existence of yet unidentified genetic factors that might be in operation. One may also wonder what is the intangible price incurred in terms of future growth and personality development? What are the possibilities of problems surfacing during latter life passages. However at the risk of being simplistic, one may suggest a partial uncomplicated explanation of the apparent normalcy of certain emotionally deprived youngsters. It is our lack of authentic data, detailed history of their early developmental years. They might have had meaningful experiences with peripheral people which are not recorded nor recalled but have played an important prophylactic role. Cursory examination of the past of some youngsters reveal information that tends to substantiate this hypothesis but more careful research is necessary.

HOSPITALS FOR CHILDREN

With the increase of, or rather due to the sharpening of our awareness of, the presence of many emotionally disturbed children in our midst, the use of mental hospitals for extensive periods of their treatment has become rather common. The presence of a children's wing as an integral part of a large mental hospital appears to be a natural phenomenon. Without delving into the broader issue of the pros and cons of prolonged stay of adults in mental institutions, it seems imperative to question this use for children.

Unlike adults their growth has to run parallel with their treatment needs. Growth usually flows from exposure to new stimuli necessitating new coping patterns. However, it is in the very nature of the hospital that the horizon is limited, reality is clearly defined, coping stereotyped. The hospital rhythm is monotonous, encouraging passivity and apathy--both growth retarding agents. While an emotional moratorium is essential and therapeutic for adults, it causes a serious gap in the child's developmental and maturational processes when the hospital stay is prolonged. Residential treatment centers by virtue of the wider range of their population are able to create a less artificial atmosphere with more diversified stimuli and demands. The pulse of life is quicker with built in opportunities for experimentation, competition and growth. Special procedures should therefore be devised to monitor and control the length of the child's stay in a mental hospital.

DIAGNOSTIC CLASSIFICATION OF CHILDREN

In attempting to classify behavior, one tends to resort to diagnostic schemes. However, one is soon faced with the realization that it is the few and select that fall neatly into the well defined categories. The majority overlap a number of diagnostic classifications, though often the concentration of symptoms falls into one. The process of diagnosing is particularly complex in dealing with children during a period of rapid growth. Their coping patterns are still fluid and their defense mechanism transitory. Confronted with pressures outside of the normal and familiar range of experiences, children improvise with a variety of coping mechanisms and defenses. These may take on characteristics foreboding severe pathology, which not infrequently prove to be of a transitory nature.

At times there are numerous variations and changes in the symptom picture they present. The same stress experience may produce diametrically opposite responses. Fight or flight is in continuous flux. Tension that at one time is dealt with as sulkiness, passivity, and withdrawal, may at other times provoke aggression and unbridled acting out. These modes of operation often work simultaneously and interchangeably. Apparently it is through the process of experimentation, of testing which is more palpable to the ego, acceptable to the super-ego, available by reality and tolerated by society, that defensive patterns take on shape and symptoms become crystalized. This capricious symptom picture of children is a continuous source of confusion and embarrassment in the field. It is evidenced by the multiplicity and contradictory diagnostic statements that characterized the record of youngsters though they are made by experts from a common frame of reference. It is only through the observation of current functioning with a historical perspective that diagnosis may be ventured.

PROFILES AND CHARACTERISTICS OF INSTITUTIONAL CHILDREN

Faced with the phenomena of diversity of children residing in today's institutions, presenting a wide range of behavior difficulties, and in spite of the expressed reservation about diagnosing children, attempts toward identifying common characteristics, and causation are relevant. Viewing deviant behavior along a continuum one would place a significant minority of these youngsters at the very beginning of the line. Their deviance is basically a reaction to social and environmental factors. Their problematic conduct does not stem from inner characterological pathology, from a distorted perception of themselves or of the world around them, but is rather a direct reaction to external pressures. The aggression and violence they manifest has adaptive functional and, at times, survival value. Their defiance of the generally accepted code of ethics is reality based and of a more recent adaptive nature. This behavior essentially evolved in a malignant social environment and is often a normal adjustment to an abnormal surrounding. It is the street, the peer pressure rather than the early familial experiences, that created the need for the deviant behavior. It is therefore often circumscribed and localized and not consistent--violent outburst and treachery to some, affection and loyalty to others. There are indications of the existence of a functioning superego in some areas and suspended in others.

One may assume that their earliest developmental stages occurred within the context of relative security and have thus achieved a basic ego and superego structure, though there is some characterological vulnerability that makes them more readily responsive to external pressure. Their acting out is primarily a result of a later learning process, in pursuit of attaining maximum pleasure and avoidance of pain. True, not infrequently their behavior boomerangs on them and instead of attaining pleasure it ricochets with pain. Usually this type of behavior is not hermetically sealed and not yet integrated with their basic personality structure. It is still in a state of flux and transitory under optimal conditions. When placed in a benign environment, exposed to caring mature adults with age appropriate stimuli, they gradually shed their deviant behavior and develop socially acceptable coping patterns. They, on the whole, do not require specific psychotherapeutic intervention. Ideally in these cases, all our efforts should be mobilized and directed toward the economic and social factors that are impinging on the home and school and thus present the need for placement.

However, a larger percentage of institutional children seem to fall into the center of the continuum. Their deviant behavior is of a two-fold nature. Some is outwardly directed, impinging on the welfare of others. It is asocial or antisocial, but more often than not is is also turned against their self. It is manifested in floating or localized anxiety, hyperactivity, feelings of depression, suicidal thoughts and attempts. The symptom picture is not crystalized, it is rather fluid, fluctuating from aimless, aggressive activity to passivity and depression. One has difficulty in placing them in fine diagnostic categories since their deviance appears in many shades and colors and classifications are overlapping. However, unlike the previously described children, these youngsters do not react primarily to environmental factors. Their behavior basically stems from inner pathological processes at work, though it may be triggered off by current external factors.

The face value of their antisocial behavior is usually minimal and at times nonexisting. It has symbolic meaning, a hidden agenda and scenario. It nurtures on experiences removed in time and space. The connecting links between past and present are repressed, unconscious, and at best, rather hazy. The deviancy at times appears in clear-cut neurotic symptoms. They are tangible, identifiable and ego-alien. Their fears, their anxieties, their depressive moods appear puzzling to them and so are their extreme unprovoked violent outbursts and their delinquent activities. More often, the disturbance is diffused and diluted into their entire personality. It is ego syntonic and all pervasive. They view their behavior as idiosyncratic and their acting out is fragmented, projected and rationalized. Unable to tolerate the anxiety generated by awareness of conflicts within themselves, they resort to various defenses and alibis. These are often directed more to themselves, to their own nagging conscience than to others. They hate school because the subjects are boring, the teacher unfair, and at times with a sweeping generalization, "Who cares for school anyway?"

Background studies reveal that these youngsters have experienced basic relationships and have advanced to a fairly high level of ego and superego development (Bowlby, 1966). Through their identification and internalization of parental values they have incorporated a superego, but a severe and rigid one. They are still in bondage of their earlier conflictual experiences. Their history is characterized by meaningful relationship with parental figures, however, with some dangling strings in the form of unquestioning obedience and big expectations. When these are exacerbated, they generate fear and hostility and give rise to a love and hate relationship which results in the need for achievement and sabotage--a fine web for obedience and rebellion from which they cannot extract themselves without resorting to symptomatic behavior. They are thus overwhelmed with conflict and guilt. Their defensive mechanisms are overtaxed. Repression is ineffective and anxiety rampant. To ease their anxiety, they resort either to the traditional varieties of symptoms, such as phobias, compulsions, etc., or acting out in the form of aggressive and antisocial behavior. Though the manifestations seem to be poles apart, the dynamics are basically identical, an inner conflict between what they are (id) and what ideally they would like to be (superego).

They present the typical neurotic conflictual behavior; proclamation of high goals, drive for perfection, parallel with limited functioning and extremely poor study and work habits. Being inhibited in dealing with aggression and hostility spontaneously and directly, anger does not follow the socially accepted forms. It accumulates and takes on abnormal dimensions of an antisocial and self-destructive nature. The shy pensive youngster unpredictably responds with violence to little provocation from his peer or to the mild criticisms from his teacher. These generate problems in his class to the point that he cannot be maintained in a regular school setting culminating eventually in some form of placement, often through the intervention of the juvenile court system. In spite of an apparent tough exterior, scratching the surface may reveal a sensitive youngster, buffeted by diametrically opposed feeling which he is unable to reconcile, repress or express. Parenthetically, it is this very struggle for closeness and distance, love and hate that generates the spark and thrust that not infrequently evolves into emotional sensitivity and depth of personality.

The two types described, the first who basically reacts to external social factors and the second who struggles with inner conflicts, as well represented in the nondifferentiated institutions and constitute a considerable segment of the populations of residential treatment centers. However, the most prevalent single type of the population of the residential treatment centers is the character disorder often subsumed under the umbrella of the borderline syndrome (Kernberg, 1975). His conflicts are not internal, but external; his adversary is not his inner self, but the outside world. He is impulsive rather than compulsive. His behavior is not compelled by unconscious circuitous dynamics but rather by direct instinctual needs impulsively expressed. Unlike the hidden agenda of neurotic behavior, his has unambiguous face value. It is pervasive and is manifested in all of his activities (Redl and Wineman, 1957).

One of his most salient characteristics is a low threshold for frustration tolerance. He cannot delay gratification, nor is he able to tolerate anxiety, whether it stems from an external threat or from an awareness of his own limitations. When confronted he reacts with rage, panic or aimless fortuitous activity. He uses a wide range of infantile primitive mechanisms. When experiencing tension stemming from physiological or psychological needs, he does not sufficiently pause to identify its nature, consequently he cannot localize it. It appears infinite and takes on undue intensity. With the need, the hurt, the source of the tension blurred, he is unable to direct rational restorative efforts planfully. He acts out, follows dead ends, attacks innocent targets and, not infrequently, himself.

His sense of time is limited. He is present-oriented. The future, even the immediate one, seems to be hazy and meaningless. At best it is intellectually perceived, devoid of emotional charge. Past experiences become distant, drained of meaning and of little nutritive value. He is thus pathologically dependent on the present and its immediate gratification. His reality testing is selective and precarious. Fantasy and reality often merge. He indulges in magical thinking drawing on infantile omnipotence. As a result he engages in dangerous activities. He is unable to evaluate the odds against him, particularly when the consequences are not immediate and when some escape hatch looms in the distance though inoperative. He can bypass his limited archaic superego with the greatest of ease and is not ruffled by guilt. Responsibility is denied by projection and rationalization. He uses Orwellian language legitimatizing antisocial behavior with philanthropic motives. Though it may appear that he is lying he is actually the believer, immediate consumer and victim of his aberrations. It is basically self-deception, an ego rather than a superego deficiency. Reality is malleable, shaped and molded at his wish (Grossbard, 1962).

His object relationships are shallow. He views people as sources of supply, means to gratify his narcissism. He does not attribute to them human qualities and needs and is, therefore, able to commit violence against them without anger and with complete equanimity. The background reveals severe developmental deficiency, shifting parental figures, a lack of lasting meaningful relationships and thus limited opportunities to humanize people. He had been deprived of the stable figures that give the child a sense of continuity of past and future and the security to give up infantile omnipotence and to face life realistically. Not infrequently the background is of a diametrically opposed nature, extremely indulging parental figures overstimulating, narcissism feeding, thus depriving the child of opportunities to cope and master with resulting poor frustration tolerance and unbridled narcissism (Bowlby, 1966; Reimer and Kaufman, 1959).

MILIEU THERAPY AND DYNAMICS OF GROUP LIVING

The impact of group living on a youngster during his formative years is generally recognized, however, its dynamics and implications for growth lend themselves to diverse interpretations. Group life offers socializing opportunities for the normal youngsters and therapeutic possibilities for the disturbed. It involves experiencing common needs and problems which, in turn, creates a sense of communality, kinship and mutuality. Common problems predicate common solutions which demand the cooperation of the group. Thus concern for others is based, not just on altruism, but also on the realization that cooperation is not a moral dictum but a reality imperative; the route to self-fulfillment runs through the neighbor's domain. As summed up in one of the institutions' credos: "it takes more than one to get a game going."

However, due to the very nature of the dynamics of the group, many processes are set into motion which generate opposite results, promote and retard growth, having a healing and hurting effect. The wide range of alternatives, stimulating to some may be overwhelming to others. The group offers the child a number of coping patterns to be accepted or rejected. He observes diverse patterns of responses, and under optimal conditions, a fine balance is achieved assimilating group mores while shaping his individual identity. He becomes aware of self, of his impact on others and the image he projects by the repetitive reactions of the group to him and reinforced when similar behavior is displayed by his peers.

Peer support and criticism which are intensified in group living are significant socializing dynamics contributing to the education and maturation of the normal child (Bettelheim, 1969; Bronfenbrenner, 1970; Rabin, 1965). Appreciation of a member's achievement has stimulating and mobilizing effects, and disapproval may transform the omnipotent self-centered youngster into a realistic social being. Negative criticism expressed by peers, directly and unequivocally painful as it may be, has a sobering effect. The lingering attempts to hold on to one's omnipotence are shaken and a more realistic self-assessment gradually emerges. This course of events propels the child to risk himself into activities which do not guarantee unconditional success. It helps him to accept compromises and to tolerate the inherent frustration in the process.

Constructive as these group processes are to the youngster within the normal range, they prove overwhelming to the sensitive fragile youngster and mobilize primitive regressive mechanism in the delinquent character disorder type. It is through the adult understanding and monitoring of these processes, in accordance with the various developmental vicissitudes of the individual child, that group living can be used educationally and therapeutically (Mayer, 1971).

In identifying the potentialities of residental group care, the cross-fertilization inherent in its wide range of relationships, one often loses sight of one indigent problem. The continuous reverberation of stimuli emanating from the many active pulsating youngsters living in close quarters may generate serious impediments to growth. A child is in need of "emotional elbow room." It is essential that he has moments of privacy and solitude, to reflect, to daydream, to weave fantasies within his own life space. Constant exposure to external stimuli interferes with the process of one's integration of his own tempo. Working through the past, its linkage with the present, is tempered by the gushing intruding present which blurs and obscures the past. Through horizontal expansion, increased information is facilitated, vertical growth in depth is jeopardized. Creativity, the product of a fine interplay of earlier and current experiences is thus stunted.

The avalanche of group stimuli is particularly overwhelming to the fragile sensitive child who needs more outer space for his inner world. His fortuitous attempts to defend himself by distancing self from others and withdrawing often culminates into pathological mechanisms. It is manifested in the not infrequent institutional scene of a forelorn looking

child in the midst of the noisy restless activities surrounding him.   In
planning group care facilities, it is therefore imperative to build into
settings private nooks and corners, safe oases to assure a modicum of
privacy and solitude for each youngster.

However, even the advanced residential treatment centers, in
structuring group living, tend to focus on its socializing potentials often
at the expense of the preservation of the privacy and rights of the
individual. It is not often that one comes across a well-balanced facility
providing the apparent contradictory, but equally important needs of the
growing child. In defense, it may be suggested that the reluctance on the
part of administration to provide for more privacy is not a result of lack
of awareness of its significance, but rather due to concern of the
therapeutic misuse and realistic abuse of solitude of the disturbed child
when not carefully monitored.

LEARNING, PSYCHOTHERAPY AND THE MILIEU

Psychotherapy may be defined as an educational/re-educational
process, verbal and experiential. With the adult, one may suggest it is
predominately unlearning with learning being secondary.   It is the
relinquishing of disfunctional modes of behavior and the sequential
learning of new more effective coping patterns. Children who are still in
the process of growth, require more learning than relearning and more of
an experiential than of a verbal nature. Proceeding from this assumption,
the therapeutic learning possibilities inherent in group living must meet
certain prerequisites.

It is generally conceded that learning is not just a cognitive process
or a result of accretion, the accumulation of observations and transmitted
information. It is predicated on affective elements in one's life space
which serve as catalytic agents that transform perception into concepts,
and synthesizes fragments into a whole. The significance of the emotional factors in learning, whether of academic nature or of life experiences, varies in accordance with one's levels of maturity. The earlier
in the development stages, the more indispensable and decisive are their
role. Observations of children in group care, devoid of adult relationships,
where the primary nuturitive relationships are provided by peers seems to
validate this thesis. Learning appears to be fragmented. There is little
transfer learning from one situation to another, similar as they may be.
Behavior is repetitive even if counter productive. It appears that it is
within the context of a caring adult that experiences get connected and
registered.

The term milieu therapy is frequently mentioned in identifying the
educational therapeutic factors operating in child care facilities. Milieu
is the gestalt, the sum total of the institutional forces that converge upon
the individual child.   The process of the interaction of these given,
generate as original entity with its own attributes and dynamics as

expressed in the familiar epigram: the whole is more than the sum of its parts. The crucial characteristic of the therapeutic milieu is the integration into a fine balance of the diverse and contradictory elements--flexibility and structure, authority and permissiveness. It is achieved through a process of individualization and custom-tailoring of programs to meet the specific needs of each child, in accordance with the zigzag course of treatment, of progress and retrogression. In the treatment of the disturbed child, whose reaction to the normal stimuli and demands may be "fight or flight," the milieu is responsive and flexible. Reality pressures are cyclically lowered and raised. Demands to which the youngster is particularly allergic, be it social contact, intellectual effort, are modified within a diagnostic frame of reference and with realistic outer limits (Burmeister, 1967).

Lacking inner structure, the absence of external limits is anxiety provoking to the child and destructive to the group. Unlike the treatment of the adult who by virtue of life experiences has inevitably reached a certain level of ego and superego development, therapeutic intervention may focus on intrapsychic processes often bypassing reality and its demands, the treatment of children requires a real awareness of and allegiance to reality demands. The child may be allowed to deviate from reality structures but he is not to be confused by what they represent and their rationale. The therapeutic milieu focuses on the minutiae that represents the authenticity of life in its various ramifications. The agonizing question with which staff is confronted is where and when does one draw the line; when are expectations and demands stimulating and when overwhelming, what type of deviancy is to be tolerated and which to be discouraged.

One of the basic tenets of the residential treatment center is that its therapeutic program is not an isolated, localized process but is integrated in every aspect of its being: the cottage, the school, the dining room, etc. Feedback takes place in the cottage setting, confrontation occurs in the athletic field, interpretation is often given gratuitously but effectively by the teacher, and multiple transferences of varying quality are rampant in the total setting. A twofold question is therefore raised in some quarters; if such is the case, is there a need for the distinct role of a psychotherapist, for a verbal formal procedure identified as psychotherapy and which discipline has the prerogative to carry this mantle? Experience points to the need for a central figure who sees the child as a whole with his needs and conflicts, conscious and unconscious, as they are manifested in his overt and covert functioning, the responses he provokes, and how he is perceived, by the group around him. From this strategic point of vantage, the therapist is particularly qualified to intervene psychotherapeutically and coordinate and integrate the various resources available in the program. With his understanding of the dynamics, the coping mechanisms and the level of the child's ego strength, he is able with the participation of the other members of the team, to design the necessary approach to be taken by each one in his respective field, when one is to get close or distance oneself at any given juncture in the course of the child's treatment.

An indigent problem is how to prevent the treatment strategies based on collective planning from deteriorating into formalized edicts imposed upon the lower echelons in the institutional hierarchy. Periodic reviews and discussion, direct verbal communication and confrontation emanating from and circulating through all levels of staff, built into the program and sanctioned administratively, are prophylactic measures. But most importantly, while the direction is formulated centrally and collectively, each member is to be encouraged to be himself, to think independently and to devise his own methods of translating with the tools available to him, the general goals in his sphere of operation. This is predicated on a significant degree of elbow room granted the each discipline to operate within its own domain. When this freedom is tampered with, the inevitable consequences are apathy, lack of creativity and not infrequently sabotage in subtle and not so subtle forms.

ISSUES CONCERNING PERSONNEL--PARENTAL SUPPLEMENTS

Who is to be the central figure to be vested with this role of omniscience is more polemic, but as we succeed in emancipating ourselves from the burden of tradition, it seems self-evident that he may represent any profession that concerns itself with human behavior, be it psychiatry, psychology, social work, or education. He has to possess the ability to visualize ways of translating concepts pragmatically, to be able to delegate responsibility--a quality predicted on one's connectedness with others, and the capacity to experience the pleasure of creativity vicariously. Obviously, he must be ready to submerge himself completely to the obliquity of institutional life and to be able to shift gears constantly in relating on different levels to patients and colleagues. He has to play a dual role as his areas of concern are not only the inner psychic processes but also the realities that trigger the deviant behavior. He deals with the internalized conflicts and with the current realities that feed the early distortions. Without the psychotherapist's intervention, experiences, positive as they may be intrinsically, become contaminated, lose their therapeutic potential and, at times, are counter productive. The child whose early experiences with parental figures have been negative, tends to view the adults with suspicion and will repeatedly respond to the warm overtures of the staff with unprovoked anger. It is through the psychotherapeutic efforts, by identifying the child's patterns of responses, and by tracing their origins to the child they will enable him to view the world more objectively and use the institutional resources constructively. It is self-evident that with this role being complex and demanding, the number of youngsters that each coordinating therapist can encompass must be limited; according to some, not to exceed ten; with five optimal.

It is generally conceded that the child care person is the backbone of the institution, one of the most important single factors that determines its quality. Nevertheless, his therapeutic role is not clearly conceptualized and his status is often on the lowest rung of the institutional hierarchy. While his physical responsibilities are concrete and clearly defined, his real image and symbolic meaning to the children under his care are rather ambiguous. In some agencies he is identified as counselor, big brother, friend or referee, with the assumptions that the basic ties, the socializing and growing experiences are generated by the peer group and the many other single task professionals that constitute the staff. The term cottage parent is in some quarters in disrepute. It is considered well meaning naivete to attribute to the child care worker a parental role. However, when we examine the needs of children in placement, the term cottage parent with its attributes emerges as the appropriate name. The very fact that it was necessary to remove the child from the home is *prima facie* that he has missed, during his developmental stages, a meaningful relationship. He is pathetically in need of basic emotional anchorage of a nature inherent in a one-to-one relationship.

It is widely accepted that this relationship is to consist of two dimensions, continuity and intensity; when continuity is interrupted and intensity diluted, normal growth is stunted. The periodic shifting of parental figures, the imposed sharing of the mothering person with many siblings of similar age competing for identical needs, generates intense jealousy and hostility and, in their wake, apathy and withdrawal. Undeniably, peer relationship is a potentially stimulating and socializing factor. But it is effective only sequentially. It can compliment but not substitute an intense one-to-one experience. Normally, the need for exclusive, possessive relationship progressively diminishes. With maturation and widening prospectives, the child becomes interested in more diversified contacts. The need for friends appears to loosen the early bonds. Actually, they are elaborations of the original patterns of relationships, and in the absence of originals, there is little to copy, or rebel against. With the disturbed, the process of emancipation from parental figures and dependency on peer relationship is retarded. Because of their inner chaos and insecurity, the infantile need for parental omnipotence is still very alive and active. Peers, with their own vulnerability and demands, are in no position to meet this need and there remains a certain void, when the primary relationship is with contemporaries.

It seems, therefore, imperative that children's facilities providing group care offer opportunities for individualized, one-to-one intense and continuous experience with an adult. It would be presumptuous to designate a specific staff member for this task. Occasionally the child selects appropriately and then, if possible, his choice should be respected and reinforced. Usually, it is the child care worker by the very nature of his responsibility who emerges as the logical person and the child's choice. His round-the-clock presence, sharing the same physical living space, his catering to the basic primitive needs, of food, clothing, etc., his ever readiness to protect him from outer and inner threats, from the world around him and from his uncontrollable impulses, contribute to the fostering of an intense gut level relationship. It forms an emotional base that facilitates the development of secondary relationships.

One of the agonizing questions that residential treatment centers face is how to reconcile the child's needs for one-to-one relationship (Fraiberg, 1977; Goldstein, et al., 1973) with group care living where it is inevitable that the adult is shared and spread thin. Though no panacea is yet on the horizon, some ameliorative procedures have been experimented with. One is the subgrouping of groups. It is the breaking down of a cottage unit into small groups with the adults being assigned primary and secondary responsibilities in each group. Thus a group of ten children supervised by two adults is divided into two groups with each adult having primary relationships with only five children and a substitute secondary relationship with the rest.

This mode of organization has particular implications in the structuring of the currently expanding day care centers. These facilities serve children who are in their early developmental stages in need of one-to-one relationships. Their grouping into small units may temper the harm inherent in the repetitive daily separation and adaptation to many new faces and rhythms. This is all the more imperative where the home base is wanting in caring and warmth. However, logical as this structuring may be, it has been having slow, at best ambivalent, acceptance. Its resistance has been coming from many quarters, administrative, because of logistic problems but primarily from front line staff. It takes considerable self-awareness and discipline to relate differentially to children and to accept an auxiliary role as being secondary in importance serving only as an extension and substitute for the primary person.

RECENT PERSONNEL CHANGES IN INSTITUTIONS

One of the recent significant changes in the complexion of the institutional child care staff is that the traditional couple, husband and wife, "mom" and "pop" is becoming a vanishing species. They are being gradually replaced by the single unattached worker. He is usually young, with an academic background, in a state of moratorium, and in the process of defining his professional goals. His stay at the institution is thus a period of transition. Some view this change as a positive development replacing old burned out staff with enthusiastic and vital young people. This perception is based on the thesis that "burning out" is inevitable, outweighing the value of experience and stability. Others view this negatively. The undefined self-image of the young worker, his groping for self-identity, even with his best intentions, is unable to meet the disturbed child's needs for stability and emotional anchorage. Furthermore, a couple may offer a modality of relationship in its realistic manifestation with its strains and pulls, a segment of life that many of these youngsters have never experienced. The single parental figure deprives the growing child of the very complex, developmentally significant experience of relating to the opposite sex with its concomitant intricacies, and to learn to tolerate the sharing of loved ones.

INSTITUTIONAL SIZE AND POPULATION PATTERNS

A primary concern in designing residential group care, is what constitutes an optimal size and range of diversity of its population. Obviously size, be it beast or institution, defines its impact. In our contemporary civilization, we are inclined to view bigness with a positive bias. The concept of the advantages of bigness that emerged in the wake of technology and gave rise to gigantic industrial plants and organizations spilled over to other areas where bigness is counterproductive and alien to their very nature. The existence of children's institutions rambling over wide expanses with populations running into hundreds is illustrative. Here the size may negate the basic needs of children. Wide and open spaces may be stimulating and therapeutic to adults but often are frightening to children. Compactness generates an intimate and binding atmosphere. A familiar, well-defined space, a limited number of structures that can be encompassed in a single glance, convey a sense of stability and permanence and offer a kind of a home base that these uprooted youngsters are woefully in need. The picture of a forelorn looking child, making his way over the long distance separating his cottage from the dining room, is recalled with a sense of poignancy by a former resident of an institution. Even more bewildering is the number of people, staff and children, typical of a large institution that the youngster has to cope with and relate to. His world is viewed kaleidoscopically, with a constant stream of people passing by. Impressions are not given a chance to register and linger and object constancy is seriously impaired.

The range of children, in terms of their educational and therapeutic needs, sex and age, who can be physically maintained and emotionally nurtured within the confines of one institution or under one roof, has been a perennial topic of discussion and experimentation. When is heterogeneity growth producing and when is it stunting, and at what point does it become therapeutically negative and realistically not feasible? The pros and cons are legion and sound equally convincing. In an age-mixed population, some maintain the younger child is often intimidated and exploited by the older ones. He may tend to emulate the senior experienced ones and their delinquent behavior. Aggression takes on a desirable quality to the child who feels insecure and unprotected. On the other hand, age gaps offer opportunities for differential patterns of relationships. For the younger one, a soothing experience of being dependent and protected, for the older one, an emerging sense of identity as a grown up and protector. The exposure to various age levels and functioning offers the group a sense of movement, a process of growth and change.

The stepladder structuring on the cottage level, evokes contradictory reactions on the part of the child care staff. Some express concern that they are running a three-ring circus simultaneously and unable to plan any program of common interest. Others appear to be challenged by having to be continuously on the alert, to be sensitive to varying demands and to operate on many levels. These diametrically opposite responses are often the best indices of the potential and creativity of the child care worker.

Assuming that a modicum of heterogeneity is desirable, the right mix of various degrees of deviant and normal behavior is mystifying. Observation points to the phenomena of psychological osmosis, particularly among children with fragile and not yet coalesced egos. The chaos that follows in the wake of the admission of a disturbed child into a group of relatively well-behaved children is common. However, a neutralizing and determining factor is the group's psychological threshold. Those whose ego boundary lines are still fluid, are readily sparked by psychic stimuli, are easily swayed and prone toward identification and fusion with others from the outside. When homeostasis is precarious, the introduction of a disruptive element upsets the applecart. On the other hand, the gradual exposure to deviant behavior and the opportunity to observe different ways of coping with inner and outer pressure has educational and therapeutic possibilities. The child sees a wide range of modalities of expression and methods of control and sublimation.

It is vis-a-vis the variety of manifested deviancy that the ego consciously and unconsciously senses their meaning to the actor and perceives their impact on others. Self-observation and criticism is then enhanced. With a clearer definition of self, functioning is improved. The presence of the passive, inhibited youngsters in close quarters with the aggressive, explosive one, often results in the lessening of extreme behavior of both. One learns to risk oneself to experiment with bolder ways of coping and the other sees the possibilities and the rewards of restraint. Obviously, this generalization has some limitations. In situations where there is extreme polarity of behavior, a no man's land is created with little contact for interactions with the opposite. Mutuality is limited or sterile. An additional qualifying note is in order. Mixed groups do not tolerate minorities of one or two. A prerequisite for mixing is that each group is represented if not with equal but with substantial numbers.

However, in spite of the assumption of the potentials of blending, there is a tendency both on the institutional and cottage level to form homogeneous groups. Our technological credo of specialization may be directly playing a role. The more obvious reason is that optimal constructive mixing is predicated, again, on the creativity and skill of the staff who have to respond continuously, selectively and discriminately to the unique interest of the individuals that constitute the group.

COEDUCATION IN THE INSTITUTIONAL SETTING

In the effort to reconstruct a normal setting for children away from their parental home, the tendency is to create a facsimile of the traditional home.   However, in the process there comes the sobering realization that a home away from home inevitably develops unique characteristics of its own demanding modifications and adjustment.   The attempts to meet the child's needs for exposure and interaction with the opposite sex during their formative years are illustrative.   Child care facilities have undergone fluctuations in their philosophy and practice about coeducation or even cohousing of preadolescents and adolescents. Periods of rigid segregation of sexes in separate institutions have been followed by mixing sexes in a single institution on separate campuses and gradually on one campus in adjoining cottages and, occasionally, even in the same cottage.

Theoretically, the positive values of coeducation can hardly be challenged.   Early contact between children of the opposite sex offers the opportunity to become sensitive to the differences and sameness of their needs and reactions, and to learn to relate to one another in a nonsexual but sexually determined manner.   It is through this exposure that they acquire a gradual awareness of their drives toward, and fears of, the opposite sex and, most significantly, learn to channelize their impulses in socially acceptable ways.   The growing awareness of control of their drives generates a sense of comfort and capacity to deal and experience sexuality, in its various manifestations in distance and proximity.

However, this concept cannot be literally transposed from the normal home setting with its constancy of siblings, neighbors and peers to the ever-changing institutional population.   Unlike the home where sexual taboos and controls are gradually and painlessly developed vis-a-vis a fixed community, the institutional child is continuously confronted with new objects, fresh stimuli against whom he had little opportunity to build up defenses.   He is thus faced with alternatives for coping with stimuli none of which is conducive to mental health.   He may engage in a struggle of conscious self-control consuming considerable psychic energy, indulge in excessive sexual fantasy if not actually acting out, or resort to pathological defenses of denial or distortion of his sexual drives.

If the nongradual sexual exposure presents a problem to the normal adolescent, it may prove overwhelming and destructive to the disturbed one whose ego is fragile and the defense mechanisms deficient.   He feels powerless to deal with strong stimuli generated by his close proximity to sexual objects.   He is more likely to resort to pathological ways to defend himself.   This additional struggle puts further drain on his psychic energy which is being depleted by his having to fight on so many fronts.   Contrary to the therapeutic approach aiming to narrow the battle lines, unplanned exposure extends them.

STAFF COMMUNICATION AND TEAMWORK

It is one of the ironies of our complex society that solutions create problems, affluence generates wants. In their early primitive stages, children's institutions were manned by a small staff attracted to the calling by their inclinations or the exigencies of the day. Many played a triple role, combining administration, education and child care. With increase of our material resources, the expansion of knowledge of human behavior with the consequent burgeoning and differentiation of disciplines, children's institutions became the domain of a variety of newly evolving professions, child care, social work, recreation, psychology, psychiatry, etc. While, theoretically, these disciplines are complementary to one another, with the optimum welfare of the child as their goal, in reality, they tend to become warring partners. An extraordinary amount of time and energy is drained off in the process of "cooperation". Not infrequently, personal ambition deflects the needs of the child, each discipline defending its turf with the child lost in the shuffle.

Good team work is therefore acknowledged as one of the basic prerequisites of a well-functioning institution. The dilemma is how to achieve this elusive state of bliss, though many are in its pursuit, often with good intentions. Though this problem is germane in all bureaucratic organizations with hierarchical structure, it takes on particular intensity and poignancy in child care institutions. As usual it feeds on insecurity, threat of status, and exacerbated when roles are not clearly defined. Specific factors inherent in work with children accentuate rivalry within staff. Those who gravitate to this work consciously or unconsciously have some penchant for children. They have a strong need to be liked by them, to monopolize their affection, to the exclusion of others who are perceived as intruders if not spoilers. As usual, this possessiveness has ready-made rationalizations, "for the good of the child."

The child care person takes the primary role for himself. The therapist, be it social worker, psychologist or psychiatrist, tends to devaluate the basic rearing processes of feeding, disciplining, protecting which are in the domain of the child care worker and assigns for himself the primary role as the therapeutic agent. In various degrees this infiltrates into the very fabric of the agency. The child inevitably senses the friction and exploits it by playing one against the other. His infantile sense of omnipotence is thus pathologically reinforced. More significantly, he perceives the world around him at war. With his loyalities in constant conflict and turmoil; his need for a firm emotional anchorage is thus severely threatened.

There is a growing awareness of this insidious problem among institutional personnel. One may find solace in that this genuine concern is in itself a partial resolution. More significantly, efforts are being made to define each discipline's role vis-a-vis the other, with the formalized recognition of the indispensibility of each task. Staff training is built in to facilitate directly and indirectly team cooperation. Obviously, this is predicated on the administrative conviction and sanction of everyone's contribution concretized in status and material terms.

INSERVICE TRAINING

Though every discipline operating in residential treatment centers has to follow a specific inservice training program, there is a common unifying point of departure from which all have to proceed. It is the realization of the depth of the needs of children and the inability of any single individual to meet them. The interdependence of staff, the sharing of responsibilities within the context of a clear definition of one's own role, the understanding of the role of others, and the mutuality of their goals is a *sine qua non.* The ability and the willingness to depend on others is thus constantly and severely tested. Obviously this state of mind is predicated more on emotional maturity than on intellectual conviction. An inservice program, then, requires more than a didactic approach. All professionals proceed through a period of orientation, and follow the traditional course based on their specific frame of reference.

Inservice becomes open-ended with the child care worker whose tasks are all-encompassing. He is responsible for the daily twenty-four hours that makes up the world of the child and has to react continuously to his fluctuating moods and needs. The very nature of his responsibility makes him more vulnerable. His constant contact with children, with their provocative behavior and primitive instinctual drives stirs up in the adult his own aggressive and sexual impulses. The homeostasis built up in the course of years is shaken. He reacts with anger at the loss of his balance and complacency. To regain his equilibrium, he often resorts to various defenses becoming overly virtuous or vindictive. These reactions are often observed, in miniature, in the interplay accentuated in dealing with the disturbed, whose primitiveness are more pronounced. To deal with this professional jeopardy, special emphasis has to be placed on the recruitment and selection of the child care worker. Special personality attributes, equanimity, and perspective are basic. Training and supervision is then to be focused on, helping him to accept and make peace with his own aggressive and sexual impulses. Theoretical indoctrination about normalcy and pathology is of limited value though it universalizes needs, and perspectives are widened. The optimal goal is to generate tolerance of one's self, and then of others, and thus to free him to use self with greater ease and imaginativeness.

The child care worker's directness and candor in dealing with children will be in direct proportion to his self-awareness and acceptance of himself. A more realistic perception of self and how he is viewed by others, how he comes across to the children will thus follow. It will hopefully reduce the use of double-bind messages to which children are very sensitive (and skillful in deciphering) and to which they react with hostility and with confusion. The wide disparity between an adult's image of himself and his perception by others has a corrosive effect on the observing growing child.

PLACEMENT

The placement of a child, his removal from his habitual setting, is an agonizing and complex process. It connotes separation from the known and facing the unknown. Nevertheless the criteria for this procedure are rather vague. Decisions are often arrived at precipitously and are haphazardly practiced. Only in a relatively small percentage of cases is the need for placement unconditional and inevitable. More commonly, whether the underlying cause is a problem home or a problem child, the recourse to placement presents a professional and ethical dilemma. The typical characteristics of the problem home, physical neglect, chaotic conditions, lack of structure and even bodily abuse, visible and concrete as they may be are not necessarily decisive. They have to be viewed from a cultural and social milieu prospective. The parental threatening voice, even the physical attack, does not necessarily convey the intensity of rejection and the corrosive message encapsuled in the suave sarcastic remarks sometimes encountered in the so called "good homes." The first may connote contact, the latter distancing. Styles and modes of communication dealing with anger and aggression are to a considerable extent culturally determined and vary from direct body language to verbal symbolic modes. Children are amazingly perceptive of their nuances, sensitive to the gradations of feelings projected, and react accordingly.

It is therefore the total functioning of the child, his perception and interpretation of his home, the range and quality of his relationships that are the reliable indices for the need of placement. Parallel with these factors, the parents' capacity for caring, for relationships and particularly, their potential for change has to be explored. Not infrequently, one comes across child neglect, and even abuse, where the parental deep and meaningful involvement with their children is contaminated by ambivalence stemming from unconscious conflicts which inhibit caring and is manifested in outright cruelty. Therapeutic intervention may prove effective and prevent the need for placement. Diagnostic skill is necessary to differentiate this type of parent from the one who is basically infantile, preoccupied with his own need with little capacity to give, who is burdened and angered by the normal demands his children make. In the latter efforts to stimulate parental capacity to care may be an unrealistic goal, though some modifications on a conscious behavioral level may be achieved.

While the lines of demarkation between normalcy and pathology of the growing child is rather fluid one is often at a loss to differentiate deviant behavior which is a developmental phase, a reaction to external provocation and that which stems from inner conflict. Theoretically, when behavior is primarily reactive, intervention is to be directed to the environmental factors. When it is an expression of internalized conflict, the child is the focus of attention and, in extreme pathological cases, removal from home is indicated. However, reactive behavior may take on such intensity that the child's immediate removal from his environment is imperative for his safety and for the protection of the community. On the other hand, deeply rooted problems may not necessitate the procedure of placement and treatment in his usual habitat may be most effective and obviously more desirable financially and psychologically. At the risk of over-simplification, it may be suggested that it is not the severity of the pathology, either in terms of the symptom picture of how deep rooted and widespread the underlying dynamics are, that should be considered the sole determining criteria for placement. It is the interaction between the child, the immediate family, and the environment that is decisive. It is the extent to which the ongoing familial interplay and the environmental pressures feed the pathology. When the daily friction at home constantly reactivates deeper conflicts, defensive pathological mechanisms are placed in operation. They cause wear and tear of the child's coping capacity and drain off much psychic energy so that there is little available for growth and less for insight and emotional reorganization. Occasionally, one may observe a seriously disturbed child whose pathology has been sufficiently crystalized to feed on itself. He has marks of a no-man's land between himself and his immediate environment and is consequently relatively immune to the external pressures in his ambiance. In such situations placement is to be seriously questioned and possibly avoided. The main emphasis then is to be placed on therapeutic intervention and the provision of diverse services in the home and the environment.

Optimal placement is a two-fold process, it is a means to an end and end in itself. It is preliminary to treatment and a therapeutic experience within itself. It is predicated on the active participation of the parent and child with the worker at times confining himself to the role of a catalytic agent, maintaining a distance to allow his input to percolate, to gain greater perspective, and to evaluate the pros and cons objectively. The workers' understanding of the conflict gives them direct access to their feelings and facilitates more realistic planning. In the process, the parents are to learn that under the given circumstances, placement is not an act of rejection and abdication of responsibility, but rather an expression of their parental role and the positiveness of their attitude toward placement will determine its meaning and use.

A child's attitude toward placement even under realistic tangible duress such as illness or death of parents is heavily charged with fantasies. Not having yet relinquished his archaic egocentric omnipotence, he views himself as the manipulator of the course of events around him. He tends to interpret any phenomenon affecting him as if it were of his own making. Illness and death are his fault, hence--guilt and unworthiness. Variations of these distortions or similar themes are coupled with the normal realistic feeling around separation, relinquishing the familiar and the fear of the unknown, feeling of rejection, etc.

However, placement by its very nature, a period of crisis, makes submerged conflicts more accessible for resolution and can therefore prove to be an effective preliminary and distinct phase of treatment. It can serve as a psychological shock to the parent and child, confronting them with the seriousness of the deviant behavior and make inoperative the mechanism of denial that lulled them into wishful thinking and inactivity.

However, some qualification is in order. Though stressing the roles of the parent and child in placement and the distancing of the therapist, occasionally the latter's direct role is indispensible. Often, in spite of prolonged preparation, a sufficient residue of unresolved conflict lingers on which blocks a voluntary decision. The extension of time and renewed procedures are counterproductive. The clients are submerged in a mire of doubts, and thought processes are immobilized. The imposition of an external decision is helpful and even merciful. It relieves guilt and doubt by sharing of responsibility. Diagnostic skill is a must, to discern the point when direct intervention is wise.

Discharge and Reentry

In examining the literature on placement, one is impressed with the professional concern about the traumatic effects of separation and the relative paucity of data of the phenomena of reentry and its implication. The child's return to his family and community, after having spent a significant period of time during an important maturational phase away from home, is a painful and disturbing experience. He is faced with a new physical setting, new social demands, and more complex emotional relationships. From the institutional, structured, and regimented life, he enters a world where the boundary lines are far apart and the options and alternatives-legion. He no longer has the external structure to protect him from the daily temptations. Inner discipline and a degree of immunity to the inevitable frustrations and disappointments inherent in a period of transition are required.

A problem is the necessary reorientation within the immediate family and the need to define new ways of relating and new styles of communication. Frequently, during his absence, parents and siblings have reorganized their relationships and his emotional space has been sub-divided and reallocated. There is hardly elbow room left and a period of shove and squeeze follows. He has to adapt himself to a new type and quality of relationship. From the more impersonal, diluted style of relating characteristic of group life, he is now confronted with intense giving and demanding characterized by strong ambivalence and conflict. Unfortunately, insufficient professional attention has been given to this crucial period. It is reflected in the paucity and quality of services designed for this period of transition. Public funding providing for sophisticated and costly inpatient programs, offer little and at best token services for aftercare services. This serious gap is manifested in the excessive rate of recidivism and the revolving doors of institutions for the delinquent and emotionally disturbed. Research studies pointing to the ineffectiveness of the therapeutic programs of the institutions would do well to turn their attention to the void in services of aftercare. This lack reduces, if not cancels, the effect of the inpatient treatment, positive as it may have been.

SUMMARY

In conclusion, the child rearing and education implications of group care for children outside of their natural homes vary in accordance with a society's concept and image of the ideal man. The traditional institution for children of problem homes is gradually being replaced with residential treatment centers for problem children. The populations of today's institutions may be classified into broad overlapping categories, reactive, neurotic and character disorder youngsters. In the wake of changing social conditions, mental hygiene concepts and population, a gradual reconstruction of objectives and programs is taking place, with the increase and diversity of staff and disciplines operating in the institution.

The danger of fragmentation and dilution of basic adult-child relationships is to be faced. Special emphasis on recruitment and training, particularly of the child care staff, and the development of cohesive team work is imperative. The pros and cons of heterogeneity in group living in terms of age, sex, and pathology is to be further explored. The educational and therapeutic potentials of the transitional periods to and from placement have not been fully identified and even less utilized. The relative neglect of parents in the programs for children and the serious gaps of services during the children's reentry to the community, threaten to diminish if not negate the effectiveness of our residential child care programs.

REFERENCES

Bettelheim, B. *The children of the dream.* New York: McMillan, 1969.

Bowlby, J. *Maternal care and mental health.* New York: Schocken, 1966.

Bronfenbrenner, U. *Two worlds of childhood: U.S. vs. USSR.* New York: Russel Sage Foundation, 1970.

Burmeister, E. *Tough times tender moments.* New York: Columbia University Press, 1967.

Fraiberg, S. *Every child's birthright.* New York: Basic Books, 1977.

Goldstein, J., Freud, A., and Solnit, D. *Beyond the best interest of the child.* New York: The Free Press, 1973.

Grossbard, H. Ego deficiency in Delinquents. *Social Case Work,* 1962.

Kernberg, O. F. *Borderline conditions and pathological narcissism.* New York: Jason Aronson, Inc., 1975.

Mayer, M. E., and Blum, A. *Healing through living.* Springfield, IL: Charles C. Thomas, 1971.

Rabin, A. *Growing up in The Kibbutz.* New York: Spring, 1965.

Redl, F., and Wineman, D. *The aggressive child.* New York: The Free Press, 1957.

Reimer, B., and Kaufman, I. *Character disorders of parents of delinquents.* New York: Family Service Association, 1959.

CHILD NURTURANCE IN OTHER CULTURES: A PERSPECTIVE

Emmy E. Werner

Department of Applied Behavioral Sciences
University of California at Davis
Davis, CA 95616

INTRODUCTION

Among the earliest fossil finds of genus "homo" are the remains of two young children and of a group of related adults who were discovered by the French-American archeological team of Don Johanson and Maurice Taieb.

They lived some three million years ago in the Omo Valley in Ethiopia, in close proximity to each other, in one or two domestic groups (Leakey and Lewis, 1977). Lionel Tiger in his book *Optimism: The Biology of Hope* (1979) has called them the "first family."

Since prehistoric times, child care has taken many forms among kin and neighbors, and, more recently, among strangers as well. Cross-cultural studies provide us with a perspective across space and time: They enable us to see that the children and their caretakers who live in the context of modern industrialized societies, such as the U.S.A., are a select group and probably unrepresentative of the human species in most other cultures and during most of human history (Lozoff, 1977).

Once we step outside of our own familiar world of childhood into other cultures where four out of every five children on this planet live, we note that exclusive nurturance of the young by their parents, especially their mothers, is an *exception* rather than the *rule*.

In this chapter, I will briefly introduce some conceptual models and research methods that have guided the cross-cultural study of child-rearing, and then review several patterns of shared child care found in other cultures, with different economies and household structures than our own.   This includes care by related adults and child nurses and by adoptive parents, foster parents and godparents as well.   Some attention will also be paid to a phenomenon that arises in societies which are stratified by social class, race, or both: child care, for pay, by unrelated persons, i.e., nannies, "au pair" girls, and their kindred.

I will examine the fragmentary evidence of what we know about the effects of supplementary parenting on children's behavior and development in traditional societies, and conclude with a review of some cross-cultural findings on the effects of rapid social change on caretakers and children.

SOME CONCEPTUAL MODELS

Within the last decades, cross-cultural studies of child-rearing have been successively influenced by the perspectives of cultural anthropology and social learning theory, and, more recently, by ethology and socio-biology.

Cultural Anthropology and Social Learning Theory

Whiting's (1977) model for psychocultural research divides the environmental determinants of personality into two parts: The maintenance system which is the institutionalized ecologic, economic, socio-political, family and household structure for the survival of the *group*, and child training and socialization which operates within the constraints set by the maintenance system, shaping children's dispositions in accordance with the adaptive needs of the *group*, but often against the needs of the *individual*.

Among the key variables in the child's learning environment on which Whiting and his associates have focused their attention are the frequency and strength of reward and punishment during the socialization process; the relative salience of the mother and father as socializing agents, and the role of alternate caretakers.

Ethology

Our species, as other primates, has been able to survive within a wide range of environmental settings as a result of its adaptability.   This capacity is correlated with a very complex central nervous system and a long and relatively helpless period of infancy.   The biological determinants of social behavior, both infantile and parental, that favor the maintenance of physical proximity, protection and nurturance are of particular interest to ethologists (Blurton-Jones, 1975).

Highly recommended to students of cross-cultural child development is a thoughtful discussion of the evolution of human behavior development by Konner (1977) which touches on aspects of human social behavior that have undergone relatively recent changes in the transition from a nomadic hunter-gatherer existence to sedentary agriculture to a modern industrial way of life, and whose evolutionary consequences are still not well understood.

Sociobiology

A number of books, such as E. O. Wilson's *Sociobiology: The new synthesis* (1975) and *On Human Nature* (1978), R. Dawkins' *The Selfish Gene* (1976) and D. P. Barash's *Sociobiology and Behavior* (1977) have combined the perspectives of ethology and population biology in their discussion of general laws of the evolution and biology of social behavior. They contain provocative extrapolations from comparative studies of animal behavior about strategies of being a parent, the relationship between the generations and the sexes, and the development of altruism and aggression. These speculations should yield some testable hypotheses in future cross-cultural studies.

Among the key concepts of sociobiology that are relevant to child care are the terms "inclusive fitness," "kin selection" and "reciprocal altruism" (Fox and Fleising, 1976).

"Inclusive fitness" theory, also known as "kin selection" theory, predicts that altruistic behavior is a function of two factors: The degree of relatedness between altruist and beneficiary and the benefit-cost ratio of the altruistic act to recipient and altruist (Van den Berghe and Barash, 1977). Altruistic acts (e.g., nurturant, protective behavior) that ensure the survival of the young of close kin (kin selection), will also ensure the preservation of the genes of the altruist among the beneficiaries (inclusive fitness). If individuals are only slightly related, however, or totally unrelated, altruism will most likely occur when the individual can expect at some time in the future an altruistic act in return (reciprocal altruism). If the cost to the altruist is relatively low, if the individual in need is well known, if interactions are frequent, and if the population at large is exposed to a common risk, the probability of an altruistic act is increased (Trivers, 1974).

The interested reader is referred to *The Sociobiology Debate* (Caplan, 1978) for an excellent summary of scientific and ethical issues that have been raised by both advocates and opponents of sociobiology, and to a book by Freedman, *Human Sociobiology: A Holistic Approach* (1979) for an application of kin selection theory to cross-cultural studies in a number of human societies.

Kin selection theory does not necessarily preclude conscious motivation and cognition. Thus altruistic behavior can be a combination of early experience, social learning and direct, genetically mediated predispositions. It does not deny the importance of culture in humans, but puts culture in the broader context and constraints of biological evolution (Van den Berghe and Barash, 1977).

CROSS-CULTURAL METHODS

Ideally a cross-cultural researcher would like to draw conclusions about universalities in childrearing that are applicable to children everywhere in the world.   Only a pancultural design, drawing a large representative sample from the universe of human societies, will permit such broad generalizations.   The cross-cultural surveys by John and Beatrice Whiting and their associates (Whiting and Child, 1953), relating childrearing practices to ecological, economic and socio-structural factors have come closest to this pancultural approach by summarizing and integrating data from ethnographies in the Human Relations Area Files (HRAF).   The main difficulty with this kind of research is the lack of dependable data on a large and representative sample of world cultures.   Reliance on data already collected for other purposes severely limits the kinds of hypotheses that can be tested.

More realistic than the pancultural approach is one in which a limited sample of cultures is drawn that maximizes desired variations wit⁵ regard to a dimension of special interest.   For example, as a follow-up to their cross-cultural surveys, the Whitings (Whiting, 1963; Whiting and Whiting, 1975) and their associates (Minturn and Lambert, 1964), chose six cultures in Africa, Asia, Latin America, Oceania and a New England village, and conducted field studies on childrearing practices and the development of prosocial behavior in children, using comparable methods in each culture (Whiting et al., 1966).

The most common type of cross-cultural study involves only two societies, usually the United States and one other complex society, such as the longitudinal studies of Caudill and associates on caretaker styles and infant behavior in the United States and Japan (Caudill and Plath, 1966) and by Holtzman and his associates in the United States and Mexico (Holtzman, Diaz-Guerrero and Swartz, 1975).   Here the possibilities of misinterpretation are greater: as Campbell and Narroll (1972) have pointed out, comparisons between only two cultures are generally uninterpretable, because many cultural differences operate that might provide alternative explanations of the findings.   In order to control for this possibility, the systematic use of subcultural variations, by social class or rural/urban residence, replicated across two or more cultures, appears to be the most promising approach for the study of cultural factors in child development.

PARENTAL GOALS

LeVine (1977) proposes the following universal goals of parents vis a vis their children: 1) The physical survival and health of the child, including the normal development of his reproductive capacity; 2) the development of the child's behavioral capacity for economic self-maintenance in maturity; and 3) the development of the child's behavioral capacities for maximizing other cultural values, such as morality, intellectual achievement, etc., as formulated and symbolically elaborated in culturally distinct beliefs, norms and ideologies.

The economy, woman's workload and composition of household put certain constraints on child-caretaker relationships that provide fewer options, but more continuity in traditional than in modern societies.

MODE OF SUBSISTENCE

The availability of alternate caretakers, besides the parents, is related to both settlement patterns and population unit size, which, in turn, are tied to the basic economy of a society (Berry and Annis, 1974). Thus, hunting and gathering societies, the prevailing mode of human subsistence during more than ninety-nine percent of our existence, are predominantly nomadic, with small population units and small-sized families; agricultural and pastoral societies are predominantly sedentary, with much larger population units and domestic groups.

A rather striking example of how a culture's basic economy effects childrearing goals may be found in the work of Barry, Child and Bacon (1959). These investigators rated over one-hundred societies in HRAF on the relative stress placed by parents on various aspects of socialization. They also classified the subsistence activities of these societies by placing them in four categories, differing in extent of food accumulation. Societies with agricultural and pastoral pursuits represented the highest extreme, and hunting, fishing and food-gathering societies represented the lowest extreme. Caretakers in societies with high accumulation of food were found to put strong pressures upon their children to be responsible, obedient, and compliant, and were correspondingly low in stressing individual achievement in both boys and girls. Caretakers in societies with low accumulation of food emphasized achievement, self-reliance, independence and assertiveness for *both* boys and girls. Rohner (1975) also found that the latter societies accepted their children more readily than societies with a secure food base.

WOMEN'S WORKLOAD

Textor (1967) reports from a sample of HRAF ethnographies that societies in which women dominate subsistence activities, are low in indulgence of the child, and that children in these societies have high anxiety over the performance of responsible behavior. In an analysis of maternal interviews from the *Six Cultures Study*, Minturn and Lambert (1964) found vigorous responsibility training and severe punishment for mother-directed aggression among societies in which women made a financial contribution to the family.

Whiting and Whiting (1975) noted that non-egoistic, *altruistic* behavior ("offering help, support, suggesting responsibility to others") was typical of children in societies in which women had heavy work responsibilities. Here children were assigned tasks upon which the welfare of the household depended, including infant and child care. *Egoistic* child behavior ("seeking attention, dominance, help") was seen most frequently among children in the United States who were not assigned work on which the welfare of others depended.

It appears that if responsible and helpful behavior toward others is considered of positive value, then societies in which mothers have less specialization for child care produce children with "healthier" personality patterns (Greenfield, 1974).

HOUSEHOLD STRUCTURE AND COMPOSITION

An examination of the households of 565 societies representing a sample of world cultures (Whiting and Whiting, 1960) indicates that the *nuclear* family consisting of a mother, father and unmarried children, is the sole form of the family kin group in only about a quarter of all human societies. In the majority of the world's cultures, children grow up in large domestic groups that consist of either *extended* or *polygamous* families. Children are raised in such households with grandparents, aunts, uncles, cousins and siblings who assist in child care (Minturn, 1969).

In a *patrilocal* type of extended family, boys continue to live after their marriage in or near the dwelling of their father, adding their wives and children to the father's kin group. The sisters of these brothers go to live with or near their husband's family.

A *matrilocal* type family is created when girls remain in or near the family of their mother after marriage, adding their husbands and children to that kin group, while their brothers, after marriage, go to live with or near the families of their wives.

Polygamous families are created through an extension of the marriage relationship. Quite common around the world are *polygynous* families where a man marries two or more wives and becomes husband and father to several nuclear family kin groups. If a man marries sisters, all co-wives tend to live in the same household and share in the rearing of all children. If a man marries women who are unrelated, each wife with offspring has her own *(mother-child)* household, and the husband may have a domicile of his own or sleep in a men's house.

Societies that practice *polyandrous* marriages, the marriage of one woman to several husbands, usually brothers, are extremely rare, and we know little about their impact on children (Peter, Prince of Denmark and Greece, 1963).

PARENTING BY RELATED ADULTS

In most traditional societies there is no extreme role specialization of child care, such that it constitutes the major or exclusive task for a whole group of people--mothers.   In their analysis of the mothers' interviews from the *Six Cultures Study,* Minturn and Lambert (1964) found that "Proportion of time mother cared for infant" shows large cross-cultural variations; most of this was due to the fact that *only* the New England mothers spent most of their time in infant care.   In the other five cultures, mothers had other adults or children take over the care of their infants while they attended to other chores.

Three features of enculturation, (1) a large number of adult sur-rogate parents; (2) balancing of competing kin group demands through stress on common descent; and (3) grandparents as principal portrayers of cultural history and "ethos", are found in the majority of the world's societies which are non-industrial and non-urban (Williams, 1972).

For example, among the Arunta hunter-gatherers of the central Australian desert, who live in *patrilocal* extended families, a young child learns that the woman his mother calls "sister" will also care for him, even nurse him.   He also learns that his father's mother will serve him as mother as well.   A boy learns that there are many men besides his biological father whom he will call "father," who will address him as "son" and who will act toward him as his father does, when he cares for him, protects him or disciplines him (Williams, 1972).

The majority of the Ashanti, a West African agriculturist tribe, live with their *matrilineal* kin.   Ashanti children learn that their mother's sisters are to be treated and responded to as their own mother, and expect that their unruly behavior will be dealt with by their mother's brother as the mother's disciplinary representative (Williams, 1972).

Grandparents

Because of her position as the link between the children and their matrilineage, the maternal grandmother has a great influence on Ashanti children.   She cares for them regularly during infancy and provides her grandchildren with plenty of affection. This finding is not unique for the Ashanti.   A worldwide study of the effects of parental acceptance and rejection by Rohner (1975), based on an intensive analysis of the ethno-graphies of some 101 societies notes that children the world over tend to be given a fair amount of warmth when grandparents are significant child-rearing agents within the domestic group.

An examination of the social structure of grandparenthood, based on some 75 societies, the majority of which were contained in the HRAF files, found that an indulgent, close and warm relationship with the grandchildren is fostered by the dissociation of grandparents from family authority.   A grandmother who is titular head of a household is likely to function more as a discplinarian, whereas one with less status is more likely to function in a nurturant caretaking role (Apple, 1956).

Grandparents play an important role as supplementary caretakers in the largest of the developing nations, the People's Republic of China. Even today, the majority of Chinese children under the age of seven are cared for by grandmothers and other relatives rather than in collective institutions. According to Kessen (1975) a number of factors continue to place Chinese grandparents in a prominent position as caretakers:

1. Mothers and fathers are expected to work full-time, but places in nurseries and kindergartens are in short supply, especially in rural areas;

2. Though both men and women work, there are different retirement ages for the sexes. Grandmothers retire in their early fifties, just at the point when their sons and daughters have young children in need of care;

3. Grandparents have acquired status and prestige as victims of prerevolutionary "bitterness" and as teachers of the history of Maoist revolution.

With industrialization and urbanization, the number of parent-surrogates tends to be progressively reduced; kin groups' demands are increasingly replaced by the demands made on the individual by technological institutions from which s/he derives his livelihood, and schools and the mass media take over the special role of grandparents in transmitting cultural history.

However, even in the contemporary United States, among urban Black families (Robins, et al., 1975) and among Oriental and Polynesian families in rural Hawaii (Werner and Smith, 1977; Werner and Smith, in press), grandparents continue to be a major source of nurturance and support, in the midst of poverty, family instability and the dissolution of marital ties. For lower-class working mothers, they are major providers of child care and for single teenage mothers, they often serve as adoptive or foster parents.

Adoptive Parents

Adoptions are especially common in Polynesian island societies, for example, among the Tahitians (Levy, 1973), the Melanesians (Scheffler, 1965), and throughout Eastern Oceania (Carroll, 1970). Adoption was also an important aspect of traditional Hawaiian culture, and research among modern Hawaiians demonstrates that it is still prevalent (Werner and Smith, 1977). Many Polynesians adopt other children after their own have grown up, or to complete a family with young children of a single sex, or to substitute for deceased children.

Whereas adoption is often a transaction involving total strangers in the United States, adoption in Oceania is generally a transaction between close relatives. In the typical case, the adopter is related to one of the natural parents of his or her adopted child as a full or classificatory "sibling" or "parent."

Prospective adopters in Oceania are rarely denied the privilege of adoption because of economic circumstances, old age, ill health or personality characteristics. On the other hand, natural parents, as well as unwed mothers, who give up their children in adoption are not stigmatized. Despite the great value attached to child nurturance, parents can be prevailed upon by relatives to relinquish their offspring as part of a more general set of obligations between kin.

However, there appears to be little effort to sever legal and social relations between a child and his natural parents. Thus, Oceanic adoptions might be thought of more as creating an *additional* parental relationship for the adopted child rather than replacing the bond between parents and their natural children (Carroll, 1970).

Foster Parents

In most Oceanic societies, there is a clear distinction between "fosterage" (temporarily taking care of others' children as an obligation of kinship) and "adoption." An American adoption in which a couple takes an orphaned young relative would in Eastern Oceania be considered "fosterage."

Both "crisis" and "voluntary type" kinship fostering is prevalent in a number of West African societies. Children of both sexes are sent to relatives (men take care of kinfolk's sons, women of kinfolk's daughters), either in the case of the dissolution of the conjugal family by death or divorce, or to be taught the technical skills and moral values necessary for survival in the adult society.

Goody (1970) has examined the institution and the consequences of kinship fostering among the Gonja in Northern Ghana. The majority of the adults in her sample had been exposed to "voluntary" kin fostering. After the age of six, both boys and girls were sent to stay with relatives for a few years to be taught domestic and farming skills. Fostering always meant a change of residence, either to the home of the mother's brother (for the sons) or to the father's sister (for the daughters), or to the homes of maternal or paternal grandparents.

The foster-parent/foster-child tie is a direct one, based on a reciprocal relationship of service and training with respect to tasks which are central to adult roles in the Gonja society. The role model (and discipline and instruction) is provided by the child's kinsman and kinswoman. Thus the institution of fosterparent helps reinforce ties between kin.

Godparents

The initial ties of kinship can be reproduced by acts of individual will as well. A well known form of ritual kinship is the "compadrazgo" (coparenthood) prevalent in the Mediterranean countries and in Latin America (Pitt-Rivers, 1973). Godparenthood or "compadrazgo de Bautismo" is numerically and socially the most important form of ritual kinship in Latin countries. Every child at Catholic baptism must have godparents who are chosen by his parents. In case of death or disability, the godfather has the moral obligation to take over the economic maintenance of the godchild and to look out for his spiritual welfare as well.

In the world of urban marginality in Latin America, godparenthood can become a legitimation of a network of mutual assistance that is essential for the survival of the individuals. For example, in all cases studied by Lomnitz (1977) in a Mexican shantytown, compadres were involved in a regular daily exchange of goods and services. A majority of the instances of godparenthood were contracted between neighbors, and a large number of godparents were relatives, i.e., brothers and sisters, or parents or parent-in-laws of the child's parents. Among relatives, those who lived in the same household or in a mutual network of assistance were preferred.

PARENTING BY SIBLINGS AND CHILD NURSES

In the most basic human subsistence type, among nomadic hunter-gatherers, there is a great deal of non-maternal *contact,* but less non-maternal care of infants and young children than in agricultural and pastoral societies (Konner, 1975). Most of this non-maternal contact takes place in multi-age play groups made up of siblings and cousins of both sexes, as can be found among the Kung San (Bushmen) of the Kalahari Desert (Konner, 1977). These play groups provide invariably, though *incidentally,* protection, care and teaching of infants and young children by older children, though children are not *expected* to take care of infants, and mothers are always within shouting (or crying) distance.

The "farming out" of the actual care of infants and young children to "child nurses," often only four years older than their charges, is more common in horticultural agricultural societies in the world. Typically, an older child is designated as a regular caretaker for the infant born second or third after him (Rosenblatt and Skoogberg, 1974).

Caretaking of children by older children appears to be most common in societies where women make a substantial contribution to the subsistence economy, where the work takes the mother away from home and/or is difficult to interrupt, and where circumstances of residence, birthorder and family size make such alternative caretakers available (Minturn and Lambert, 1964).

Most common in the world is informal child and sibling care which is part of the daily routine of children within the family, and which is carried out without formalized organizational rules. Under these circumstances child caretakers are frequently operating under two simultaneous sets of pressures: one from their small charges, the other from their parents.

In all non-Western societies in the *Six Cultures Study,* children were expected to do some child-tending. There were striking differences, however, in what type of caretaking mothers were willing to delegate, and the amount of supervision considered necessary. No question on the mothers' interview indicates the value placed on the help given by the child nurse (Whiting and Whiting, 1975): The mothers were asked who had helped them care for the sample child when s/he was an infant. Sixty-nine percent of the mothers from the East African community, 41 percent of the mothers from the Mexican barrio, 25 percent of the Filipino, 21 percent of the North Indian, but only 12 percent of the Okinawan and New England mothers reported having been helped with infant care by a child. The three highest ranking societies, the East African, the Mexican and the Filipino communities, were also the societies who ranked highest in the nurturant behavior of their children.

Most, but not all caretaking of children by other children is done within the child's own domestic group, but there are also instances of extra-familial child caretaking. Some societies use hired child nurses, or exchange young children between households in order to provide for caretaking. Specific kin of the mother (such as a younger sister or female cousin) are often preferred (Weisner and Gallimore, 1977).

Rogoff, Sellers, Pirotta, Fox and White (1975) made a cross-cultural survey of the age of assignment of roles and responsibilities to children, based on ethnographies of 50 cultures from the HRAF files. They find pan-cultural trends in the age of assignment of child-care roles, centering on the 5-7 year period. This is the same age when Western bureaucracies introduce formal schooling, a phenomenon that is spreading in the developing countries. The process of modernization may bring about some unexpected side effects in infant care that are created by the greater educational opportunities for older children, especially for girls.

Leiderman and Leiderman (1977), in their study of an East African agricultural community, noted that families who send their children to school lose the services of an important infant caretaker of the requisite age for at least part of the day. Some families with sufficient economic resources can pay *both* the school fees and hire a non-familial caretaker. Less affluent families who send their daughters to school quite likely have the disadvantage of a less mature infant caretaker, a still younger sister or girl cousin. Since the stimulation of more mature caretaker seems to contribute to higher infant performance on psychomotor tests, even when the family economic level is controlled, the decrease of age of infant caretaking under the impact of schooling has important implications for a modernizing society.

It remains to be seen what positive roles siblings can play in helping the younger child adapt to changes brought about by modernization, since older children appear more open and exposed to modern influences than younger ones. In recognition of the fact that the mother-surrogates for young children in the developing countries are in many cases older children, a UNICEF sponsored child-to-child program was initiated during the International Year of the Child to teach children the rudiments of nutrition education, health care, safety and child development. Such "child-to-child" projects are now in operation in more than forty countries of the Third World--from Afghanistan to Zambia (Morley, 1979).

PARENTING BY STRANGERS: NANNIES AND THEIR KINDRED

Within the past decade some new perspectives on "surrogate" mothers have been provided by anthropologists interested in the study of sex roles and social inequality (Yanagisako, 1979) and by historians who have traced changes in parent-child relationships through Euro-American history (De Mause, 1974).

"Motherhood," it turns out, is not everywhere construed in the same manner and unequal access to the resources of complex societies (education, money, social status) allows some women to acquire full-time mother-surrogates.

During a period of unprecedented economic and population growth that began with the onset of the industrial age in Europe, there arose in British society a peculiar surrogate mother, the "nanny." Nannydom flowered between the years 1850 and 1939, then virtually disappeared from England after World War II. However, nannies survive today among the wealthy families of Latin America, Switzerland, Austria, France, Italy, Spain, and among upper-upper class families in the United States.

In a fascinating account of the rise and fall of the British nanny, Gathorne-Hardy examines the influence that some one-and-a-half million lower-class nannies exerted on the values and actions of the offspring of the entire British upper-class and of a large part of the middle-class as well:

> Nanny wiped bottoms and washed penises.
> Nannies fed. Nannies wiped up sick.
> Nannies gave baths and tucked up in bed.
> It was Nanny's arms that went round
> little boys, Nanny's breasts and lips
> they felt, Nanny they smelt. And
> Nannies were lower-class (Gathorne-Hardy,
> 1972:98).

Mother-surrogates who are not kin seem to arise in other complex societies that are stratified by class, caste or ethnicity (Boon, 1974). Examples of the transatlantic journey of the nanny is the Black nurse or "mommy" in the West Indians plantation society (Drummond, 1978) or the foreign "au pair" girl who provides child nurturance for the offspring of upper middle-class European families, in exchange for language lessons (Moore, 1975).

In contemporary American life we have contractual arrangements for mother-surrogates as well, be they babysitters, or providers of day or family care for young children. What distinguishes the "nanny" type surrogate from a surrogate parent who is kin is a theme of *separation* from, rather than *incorporation* into, the family.

CORRELATES AND CONSEQUENCES OF SUPPLEMENTARY PARENTING

While we know relatively little about the *specific* effects of auxilliary caretakers, varying in age and status, on the social development of the child, we *do* know that in traditional societies the responsibility for child care is shared among members of a *homogenous* family group. Although the child may have a number of caretakers, they will all have a common set of socialization goals and a common set of practices in relation to childrearing. Childrearing is thus a *collective* rather than an *individual* responsibility. This aspect of socialization has been recreated in the Israeli kibbutz, in the Soviet Union, in Cuba and in the People's Republic of China. These modern experiments show also a similarity with socialization in traditional societies for explicitness of desired behavioral outcomes.

What are the gains and losses from a system of child care involving multiple caretakers? Let us look at some of the available cross-cultural evidence.

Pattern of Infant-Caretaker Interaction

The pattern of caretaker-infant interaction among multiple care-takers was studied in a group of ten Wolof infants in Senegal. Using observational techniques as well as standard testing procedures, Lusk and Lewis (1972) found that it was more strongly related to *age* of *infant* than any other variable investigated. In the first year of life, there was no relationship of interaction patterns to *age* of *caretaker* or to the *relationship* of *caretaker* to *child*. It appeared to make little difference in either treatment of the infant or infant response to its treatment, whether the caretaker was 7- or 70-years-old, or whether she was his natural mother, his mother's mother, his sister or a distant cousin. Whiting and Whiting (1975) have reported complementary results from their *Six Culture Study*: nurturance was the most common response to infants by *both* adults and children in all cultures.

Sex differences in the care of infant boys and girls in the first year of life have, however, been noted by Super in a comparison of observational data from 13 societies in Africa, Latin America, Europe and the United States (1977). Generally, in households where mothers shared the daytime care of their infants with others, they were more likely to turn over the daytime care of their infant daughters to someone else, such as an older (girl) sibling, or the grandmother. Mothers were more likely to retain the primary caretaking role themselves, if the baby was male, and male babies appeared to receive more attention and physical stimulation from their mothers than female infants.

Infant-Indulgence

Whiting (1961), using judgments on the family and household structure for a large number of the world's societies found the degree of infant indulgence roughly proportional to the number of adults living in the household. Extended and polygynous families where there were more than two adults living in the household tended to be predominantly indulgent with their infants. Nuclear households with two adults were unpredictable. Finally, in the mother-child household where one woman alone had to care for her children, the probability of high indulgence was slight. Munroe and Munroe (1971) investigated whether this effect is present within a single culture as well as across cultures. Working with twelve Logoli infants in Kenya, they visited their households and noted (a) whether or not the infant was being held and (b) how long it took for someone to comfort an infant after he started to cry. They found that infants were significantly more often held and more promptly attended to in large households than in small households.

Attachment

Attachment behavior may be significantly influenced by the number of persons in a household. Ainsworth's data (1967) from a careful longitudinal study of a sample of 28 Baganda babies in Uganda, East Africa, observed in their natural habitat over a time period from 2 to 15 months, indicated that these babies, who spent most of their time on their mothers' backs, but also interacted with a number of other caretakers appeared to be accelerated in attachment behavior.

Ainsworth (1967) observed that nearly all the babies who became attached to their mothers, also became attached to some other familiar figure--father, grandmother, some other adult in the household, or an older sibling. In some instances, these other attachments were formed to persons who shared in the routine care of the child, although it was the mother who undertook all the feeding. Differential responses to the mother were followed fairly rapidly by differential responses to other caretakers. Actual attachment to other caretakers emerged in the third quarter of the first year, in the same quarter in which the first clear-cut attachment to the mother was observed.

Short-term longitudinal studies of Kikiyu and Gusii infants reared in a modified polymatric system (in which the mother remained the central figure and was helped substantially by other caretakers) also showed that infants form multiple attachments, to the mother as well as other caretakers, such as older siblings and grandparents. Infants reacted more positively to the approach of the mother and more negatively to her absence than they did to the approach and absence of other caretakers (Leiderman and Leiderman, 1974; Reed and Leiderman, 1981).

There may also be sex differences in the security of attachment to the mother and in subsequent exploratory play in cultures, where sons are greatly preferred to daughters. Graves (1978), in a study of maternal interaction patterns with 7- to 18-month-old infants in West Bengal, noted a more distinct pattern of reciprocity between mothers and infant sons than between mothers and infant daughters. These differential maternal attitudes toward boys and girls became more marked during the second year of the child's lives. Mothers initiated interaction more and were more responsive to the social and exploratory behavior of their sons than their daughters. The girls, in turn, showed less secure attachment behavior, a heightened need for physical closeness and reduced exploratory behavior in free play.

Stranger Anxiety

Reactions to the approach of strangers tends to be more negative among infants reared in a polymatric system than among infants reared in a monomatric setting. Reports from a number of African societies in which child care is shared, i.e., among rural Ganda (Ainsworth, 1967) and Kikuyu (Leiderman and Leiderman, 1974), among nomadic Kung San (Konner, 1972) and in urban Zambia (Goldberg, 1972) as well as from Guatemalan Ladino families (Lester et al., 1974) all indicate that familiarity with many persons in the domestic group does not preclude strong stranger anxiety.

Psychomotor Development

A distinct acceleration of psychomotor development has been reported among more than fifty samples of infants reared in traditional, preindustrial communities in Africa, Asia, Australia, and Central America, with the African samples showing the greatest acceleration, followed closely by Central American infants and samples from different parts of the Indian subcontinent.

In spite of a great deal of cultural and geographical diversity, all of the infants shared certain common experiences during the first year: membership in an extended family system with many supplementary caretakers; breast-feeding on demand, day and night; constant tactile stimulation by the body of the adult or child nurse who carried the infant in a sling on her back or side, and slept with him; and participation in all social activities (Werner, 1972). Thus, a polymatric infant care system appears to enhance the infants' psychomotor performance during his first year (Leiderman and Leiderman, 1974). Social stimulation from a number of alternate caretakers, appears to compensate for a relatively impoverished environment, at least for a limited period during infancy.

Transition from Infancy to Early Childhood

The age of transition from infancy to early childhood appears to be also affected by the number of caretakers in the household. Cross-cultural surveys indicate that *nuclear* households are *earliest* for *both* weaning (median: 2 years) and independence training (median: 2 years, 9 months) and *mother-child households* are the *latest*. *Extended* and *polygynous* households fall between these two extremes for *both* weaning and independence training (Harrington and Whiting, 1972).

"Transition anxiety," an estimate of the degree of pressure exerted upon the child during his change of status from infancy to early childhood, appears significantly *more severe* with *nuclear* households than in societies with *extended* families.

Early to Middle Childhood

Dependence-Independence. Let us now move to a consideration of the effect of multiple caretakers on children in the age range from three to eleven years: Whiting and Whiting (1975) systematically sampled the social behavior of children in that age range in the *Six Cultures Study*. Only in the American sample did first-born children seek attention (by showing off, boasting, requests to look at me) more than later brothers and sisters. The Whitings hypothesize that this attention-seeking of the first-born in our society represents a conflict over dependency needs and consider it a negative effect of upbringing in the isolated nuclear family, with an inexperienced mother as the sole caretaker. In the non-Western cultures of the Whiting study, children engaged in less attention-seeking when grandparents were living in the household. A similar trend was found by Goldberg in Zambia (1972). In the Polynesian, African, Asian and Latin American societies where shared child care has been investigated, it appears that early parental demand for non-dependence serve, in part, to shift independence training to older siblings. Thus, refusal of help by parents redirects the child's overtures to older siblings, who provide nurturance and training and, in turn, pressure for independence.

Sex Role Training and Identification

In a cross-cultural survey of ethnographies of 50 cultures from the HRAF files, Rogoff et al. (1975) noted that a number of cultures around the world change the social place of the children at the age when Western societies place them in school: Girls typically assume responsibility for the care of younger children and carrying out of household chores; boys tend to assume responsibilities that take them out of the house, such as the tending of animals (Minturn, 1969; Rogoff et al., 1975).

Minturn (1969) notes that household composition makes a significant impact on sex role training and identification. Large differences in sex typing of work roles and sex role training of boys and girls are generally found in *polygynous* and *extended* families, while smaller differences tend to occur in *nuclear* families, where adults must be prepared to take over at least the essential work roles of a member of the opposite sex, in case of illness, death, or separation. *Polygynous* family societies tend to be more *feminine* in orientation, *nuclear* family societies, like ours, tend to be more *masculine* in orientation, and *extended* families fall somewhere in between. *Extended* families are in some ways the *easiest* for *both* sexes to learn the expectations for typical masculine and feminine behavior and to internalize these norms.

Prosocial Behavior

The Whitings, in their *Six Cultures Study* (1975), noted that children who interact with infants were more nurturant and less egoistic than children who did not care for infants. Caretaking of infants appears to affect overall interaction toward peers. This becomes quite apparent when we take a look at the consequences of sex differences in child caretaking. Whiting and Edwards (1973) compared boys and girls in seven societies, the *Six Cultures* plus the Kikuyu of Kenya and observed incidences of nurturant and responsible behavior. Older girls, ages seven to eleven, offered help and support to others more often than did boys. There was no such sex difference for children ages three to six. The authors interpret the increased nurturance of older girls as due to the assignment to girls of increased childrearing duties, particularly infant caretaking.

Ember (1973) also observed Luo boys in Kenya who were expected to perform child caretaking chores, usually assigned to girls. Such boys displayed more feminine social behaviors than boys not needed for such tasks. Thus, it appears that sex differences in nurturance and responsible behaviors may only occur at particular ages and are not uniform across all cultures. The critical factor for the development of nurturant behavior seems to be the demand of the child care tasks within the home.

Caudill and Plath (1966), in a study of sleeping arrangements of urban Japanese families, were impressed with the role of siblings in the instruction and care of the younger babies, and how this responsibility for parenting appeared to diminish any sibling rivalry and to create close bonding between brothers and sisters. They ascribe the strong affectionate bond and interdependence between different members of the family to the sleeping arrangements. When the baby is new, he sleeps with the mother; when another baby comes, the child sleeps with an older brother or sister. This phenomenon of sleeping with another member of the family, apparently strengthens family bonds and contributes to a strong nurturant family life. The same appears to be true for Hawaiian-American families (Gallimore, Boggs, and Jordan, 1974). Both the giving and receiving of sib-care characterized the resilient children of Kauai who surmounted poverty and/or parental mental illness to grow into young adults who "loved well, worked well and expected well" (Werner and Smith, press).

Aggression

A strong association between severity of aggression training and household structure has been reported, *both* from cross-cultural surveys as well as from individual difference studies across cultures. Ninety-two percent of the extended families and 61 percent of the polygynous and mother-child households in a worldwide sample of HRAF ethnographies were found to be above the median in punishment for aggression in contrast to only 25 percent of the nuclear families (Harrington and Whiting, 1972).

Minturn and Lambert (1964), in their analysis of the mothers' interviews in the *Six Cultures Study* found two aggression factors: one concerning the mother's reaction to aggression directed *toward her*, and one concerning her restrictive and punitive handling of aggression *against other children*. The second factor showed large differences between societies. Generally, children were severely punished for fighting with each other in those communities and cultures where many people share cramped living quarters. Thus, overcrowding in household and courtyard appears to be *the* crucial ecological variable. Data collected by LeVine, Klein and Owen (1967) in Nigeria, point in the same direction: 87 percent of traditional Yoruba mothers with large extended families, but only 43 percent of elite Yoruba mothers with smaller families, living in the suburbs, were found to strongly discourage aggression against other children.

Psychological Differentiation and Cognitive Style

Several authors, including Levy (1968) and Ritchie (1956) have made an attempt to generalize about the effects of shared child-care, especially of child caretakers, on the development of individual differences in children. These authors have dealt with ethnographic accounts of child caretaking in Polynesian societies and have argued that sibling caretaking restricts the development of individual differences in both children and adults. In an excellent review article entitled "My Brother's Keeper" (1977), Weisner and Gallimore suggest that these consequences need to be interpreted in terms of the social context in which the child will live as an adult. The socialization goal of the societies in which these observations were made is the integration of the child into the *social context* as opposed to the fostering of *individual achievement* and independent skills. Thus it may be that children raised by multiple caretakers develop psychological and behavioral characteristics which are adaptive in some settings and not in others.

There is some indirect evidence from cross-cultural studies, reviewed by Witkin and Berry (1975) and by Werner (1979), based on reports of school-aged children from Hong Kong, Korea, Mexico and the West Indies, that the extended family and the polygynous family are linked to a less differentiated cognitive style. However, a direct relationship between shared family functions, child caretaking style and field dependence remains to be demonstrated. It should be noted that among adults, field-dependent persons are more alert to social stimuli, are able to achieve unanimous consensus in significantly less time than is required by field-independent individuals, and are more skilled at the art of interpersonal accommodation.

PARENTAL ACCEPTANCE AND REJECTION

A worldwide study of the effects of parental acceptance and rejection has been undertaken by Rohner (1975), based on an intensive analysis of the ethnographies of some 101 societies. Both acceptance and rejection were rated on a five-point scale, ranging from the presence of a warm and accepting parent-child relationship, characterized by much fondling, cuddling, and demonstration of love and affection to the child by parental words and actions, to rejection that either took the form of indifference and lack of interest in the child's development or frequent and severe physical punishment and withdrawal of warmth and affection.

One of Rohner's principle hypotheses, explaining the worldwide variability of parental acceptance-rejection, relates to the intensity of interaction between parents and their children. Mothers or major caretakers are likely to reject their children whenever they are unable to break the intensity of continuous interactions with them.

Rohner (1975) found a significant worldwide relationship between parental behavior and household composition. Mothers who are home alone all day with their children are more likely to reject them than mothers who have someone else in the household, especially another adult, to share the burden of child care.

A significant worldwide relationship appears to exist between parental acceptance-rejection and households where fathers are present to varying degrees during a child's first few years of life. Children tend to be accepted more often in homes where fathers are present on a day-to-day basis, as in nuclear family households, than in households where fathers are present less often, as in mother-child households where women live alone with their children. The more time fathers spend tending their children in relation to other caretakers, the more likely the children are accepted. Thus, fathers the world over are important and effective nurturing agents.

EFFECTS OF FATHER ABSENCE

In the Western world, most infants are reared in a nuclear family setting, and a boy, therefore, receives adequate contact with adult males in the person of his father. Recently, concern has been expressed about the increasing number of families in which the father is absent because of separation, desertion, divorce or death.

It may come as somewhat of a surprise to us to learn that, among as many as 40 percent of traditional societies, a significant segment of the infant male population has very little contact with adult males (Munroe and Munroe, 1975). This is especially pronounced among the polygynous societies which predominate in Africa (LeVine, 1973) and is probably on the increase in the developing world as men leave their homes and families in the rural areas in search for work in the big cities.

In an excellent summary of research on the father done in the West, Lynn (1974) has reviewed the predominantly negative consequences of father absence on the sex typing of the young boy. What cross-cultural evidence do we have that may support these findings in societies other than our own?

Beatrice Whiting found "machismo" or "compensatory masculinity" more often in societies where the father has low salience in infancy, but high status in later life (Harrington and Whiting, 1972). The glorification of warfare may also be considered an exaggerated need for men to defend themselves against femininity. This particular phenomenon can be found more commonly in societies with an exclusive boy-mother relationship in infancy, but without initiation ceremonies in adolescence to resolve a possible conflict between primary and secondary sex identity.

Whiting, Kluckhohn and Anthony (1958) consider juvenile delinquency to be another form of exaggerated masculinity. We have some cross-cultural evidence that suggests that this particular phenomenon is common in non-literate societies, in which there is little contact between the father and the young son. Bacon, Child and Barry (1963), surveying a sample of 48 non-literate societies in HRAF, found that lack or limitation of opportunity for the young boy to form an identification with his father was associated *both* with frequency of theft and personal crime.

Father absence during the first two years of their son's life is especially critical. This, at least, is suggested by the findings of a study on cross-sex identity in Barbados (Burton, 1972). In this Caribbean culture both conflicts about cross-sex identity and feminine identification occurred more frequently in males of school age when their father had been absent during the first two years of life.

One would expect a continued striving to identify with femininity in males in societies in which there is *both* an exclusive mother-infant sleeping arrangement and matrilocal residence, since in such societies the initial status of the mother inherent in the mother-infant sleeping arrangement is later supported by the matrilocal living arrangement. Such societies tend to provide males with some means to act out at least symbolically, the feminine role, such as the "couvade" (Burton and Whiting, 1961; Munroe, Munroe, and Whiting, 1973). Sometimes called "male child bed," the couvade consists of taboos and restrictions observed by the father around the time of his child's birth, taboos that are not unlike those observed by the mother.

Most of the cross-cultural studies of sex role learning have been limited to males. Females rarely lack for a same sex adult in the critical early years, and it is therefore predictable that they would display fewer problems of sex typing than males. There are few studies on the effect of father absence on sex role development in females, and their results do not demonstrate any detrimental influence.

SOCIAL CHANGE AND PARENTING

Inkeles (1969) has called attention to the role that parents play through both purposeful and unconscious adjustments in their childrearing practices, in mediating the influences of social change in their children. Ideally, to test these assumptions we would need detailed information about the childrearing practices utilized by two consecutive generations of parents in the same culture, the first of which lived and raised children in a period of relative stability, whereas the second lived and brought up children under conditions of rapid social change. We do not have any second generation longitudinal studies of childrearing behavior in developing countries, but we can learn from comparisons of sub-cultures within the *same* country that have been exposed to different rates of social change.

One of the most extensive studies of changing life styles and parent-child relationships has been reported from Nigeria by LeVine and associates (1967) and by Barbara Lloyd (1970). Two contrasting Yoruba groups in Ibadan were studied: One group, called the "Oje," lived in a compound, in a cluster of extended families and practiced traditional professions; the vast majority of the adult women were illiterate. The modern "elite" families in the comparison group contained women with secondary school education who were married to men with postsecondary education in highly prestigeful occupations, residing in the modern suburban sections of Ibadan in a one-family home. Its size was dependent on family income, but afforded a good deal of privacy for the nuclear family. Most of the "elite" men in the father study were only a generation away from the "Oje" men in level of acculturation. Many of their own fathers had been illiterate and lived in polygynous families.

A total of 40 interviews were conducted with *both* mothers and fathers from the traditional and elite groups. Asked what they valued most in a well behaved child, the *traditional* mothers mentioned *obedience* most frequently, whereas *elite* mothers mentioned *self-reliance* and *sociability* as well as *responsibility*. The proportion of traditional and elite mothers who gave first mention to tasks involving achievement socialization were significantly different, with the *elite* mothers stressing *achievement* more.

In comparison with the *traditional fathers*, the *elite fathers* not only appeared to be *less restrictive* of their children's aggressive behavior, but also warmer, less demanding of household chores, more permissive in occupational choice, and *more egalitarian* in their relations with their wives.

Thus, in this exploratory study of two groups of urban Yoruba parents, representing traditional versus modern poles on a modernization continuum, there is evidence of a change toward a *more intimate* and *affectionate* parent-child relationship, oriented towards the raising of *fewer*, more *self-directed* children. This shift has taken place in the context of a general *decline* in *social* distance between the husband and his wife.

Traditionally this social distance was related to age and sex segregation in the compound of an extended or polygynous family. Its sharp diminuation under the changed conditions of the nuclear family has made husband-wife relations *more egalitarian,* given *more paternal atten-tion to the child,* and made the amount of this attention dependent *not* on the *external* structure of the family, but on the amount of *time* the father's extrafamilial roles allow him to spend with his family. Most impressive is the fact that movement from the traditional end of the continuum to the modern end can be accomplished in a culture in only one generation. Similar findings have been reported from other studies in Africa (Grindal, 1972), Mexico (Holtzman et al., 1975), Puerto Rico (Mussen et al., 1969) and Indonesia (Danzinger, 1960 a, b).

Studies of the *rural poor* in transition to *urban poverty* indicate that it may be the lack of skills required in making a living in urban, industrialized settings that has the most *disorganizing* effect on child care in the slums and shanty towns of the developing world. An excellent cross-cultural study of *urbanization* by Graves (1969) indicates that when poor mothers, be they Mexican-American or Ugandan, move to the city they develop a realistically based sense of powerlessness that has, in turn, adverse effects on the development of their children. At the time of the Graves study, the general cultural norms for childrearing were not different from country to city, either among the Baganda or the Mexicans. Yet in the urban groups, mothers had a lower belief in their efficacy and less confidence in their ability to produce the kind of child they desired. Interviews also revealed that urban mothers were far less likely than rural mothers to believe that their preschool children were capable of understanding or being taught various skills. These unedu-

cated, poor *urban migrant* mothers rated their children lower in potentialities for independence, self-reliance and ability to help within the
family than their *rural* counterparts.

Acculturation in this group was associated with an increase in the
use of power assertive techniques, commands, demands and threats on the
part of the mother.   Thus, ironically, mothers reacted to their *own*
powerlessness by asserting power over their children.

CHANGES IN CHILDREN'S SOCIAL BEHAVIOR

The Whitings (1973) predict that urban living will affect the
behavior of children in consistent ways because it confines them to a
setting where it is impossible for them to participate in family subsistence activities, but brings them in contact with strangers, specialists
who furnish the goods and services ordinarily acquired self-reliantly by
rural families. City life should decrease a child's contact with altruistic
and self-reliant models and reduce his opportunity to learn and to practice
responsible and helpful behavior.

What evidence do we have from the actual behavior of children that
might support or contradict these predictions?   Most of the evidence of
the effects of urbanization and cultural complexities on children's social
behavior comes from the Whiting's (1975) *Six Cultures Study.* On the basis
of naturalistic observations of the behavior of children in these communities the Whitings classified their social behavior along an *"altruistic-
egoistic"* dimension.   On the *altruistic* end of the dimension the primary
beneficiary is the *other,* the two types of behaviors with the highest
positive loadings being "offers help," and "offers support." By contrast,
the *ego* or the actor himself primarily benefits from the following types
of behaviors: "seeks dominance," "seeks attention," and "seeks help,"
representing the *egoistic* pole of the dimension.

The "altruistic-egoistic" dimension of children's social behavior
appears to be strongly related to the degree of cultural complexity of the
communities in which they were reared.   The American community
produced children who were rated very high on the "egoistic" end of the
pole, displaying a lot of dominance and attention seeking in their social
behavior.   The other two cultures (Okinawa, India) in which children
displayed egoistic behavior were likewise characterized by a rather
complex social system that included occupational specialization, a class
system, and an indigenous centralized government.   None of these
features were present in the simpler societies in Kenya, Mexico and the
Philippines.

So far, there is only one longitudinal investigation that has examined
the effects of shared child care from infancy to adolescence in an
advanced urban society. Moore's (1975) investigation focused on the later
development of London children who had either exclusive care by their

mothers up to age five or daily substitute care, i.e., "diffused mothering" in a day nursery, or with a private individual, either in the child's home or elsewhere.

The groups did not differ significantly in their behavior as infants, so far as the psychologists' observations and the mothers' reports showed, but from about age three on (when "diffused mothering" began for many), the differences began to emerge progressively, especially for the boys.

For (middle class) boys, exclusive mothering up to school age was correlated with a significant tendency toward adult orientation, academic interests, introversion and a strong superego, whereas diffused mothering was correlated with greater peer group orientation, social and sexual interests, extraversion and aggressive, "acting out" behavior. These tendencies were relatively consistent through childhood and adolescence.

Intergroup differences in social behavior between exclusively and diffusedly mothered girls, were fewer, less significant and less consistent. In both sexes, the exclusively mothered children tended to read better, especially when mental age was held constant, but the differences reached significance only in the boys.

Other studies of the effects of non-maternal care on children in industrialized Western societies, predominantly the United States, but also Canada and Israel--reviewed by Etaugh (1980) have indicated that males may be more affected than females by variations in caretaking environment.

SUMMARY AND CONCLUSIONS

Viewed from a cross-cultural perspective, exclusive care of children by their mothers is an *exception* rather than the rule. Worldwide, children tend to be accepted more when mothers can share the burden of child care with at least one other adult, such as a grandparent or close kin, and when fathers are present on a day-to-day basis in the child's first years of life.

Mode of subsistence, household structure and the workload of women put constraints on parental childrearing goals and practices, providing fewer options, but also more continuity in the socialization of children in non-urban, non-industrial societies than in modern societies.

Shared childcare in traditional societies and among the poor in contemporary societies tends to be practiced by related adults, older siblings or neighbors who are kin; only in complex societies which are stratified by class, race or both, do we find supplementary parenting, for pay, by strangers, such as nurses, nannies or "au pair" girls.

Cross-cultural surveys find a pan-cultural trend in the age of assignment of child-care roles, especially for girls, which coincides with the introduction of formal schooling in the Western world. Sibling and child caretaking is most common in societies where women make significant contributions to the economy, where the work takes the mother away from the domestic group and where circumstances of residence, birth-order and family size make such alternative caretakers available.

Cross-cultural studies report a number of significant differences between extended, nuclear and mother-child households in indulgence, attachment, stranger anxiety and the psychomotor development of their infants, and in independence, sex role training, prosocial behavior, aggression control and psychological differentiation of older children. Boys appear to be more affected by variations in caretaking environments than girls.

The introduction of schools, mass media and urban life opens up more options for parents and children, but can also lead to greater discontinuity in the caretaking environment.

Social change has led to consistent changes in child care in the developing world. Within a generation, a shift toward a more intimate, affectionate and egalitarian parent-child relationship has been noted, which is oriented toward the raising of fewer, more self-reliant and achievement oriented children. This occurs in the context of greater equality between husband and wife and appears to lead to increased participation in child care among educated fathers.

Negative consequences, including a greater sense of powerlessness and less confidence in parenting skills, have also been reported--mostly among rural migrants in the slums of large cities, who lack the skills to make a living in an urban, industrialized setting and among their sons, especially when fathers were absent during the boys' early years.

Across cultures, the complexity of the socioeconomic system appears to be related to the prosocial behavior of children: In simple stratified societies in which children have important household and child-care tasks to fulfill, and where they interact mostly with kin and neighbors, they tend to be more altruistic, nurturant and responsible. In more complex societies, where children interact with strangers and school attendance fills part of the day, they tend to display more aggressive, dominant and self-centered behavior.

Diffuse mothering in contemporary societies by strangers tends to lead children to orient more toward their peers than toward adults. Surrogate parents in such societies are often excluded from family life rather than included--as they were in traditional societies.

Shared child-care needs to be viewed within the context of rapidly changing sex roles in the contemporary Western world. Greater social equality between the sexes may lead to increased male investment in parenting, but it may also have negative consequences, the introduction of greater social inequality among women, pitting those who can afford to hire surrogate mothers, the "nanny takers," against the "nanny givers" who provide care for their children.

The future, I hope, will see the results of some well-designed longitudinal studies, both here and abroad, which (1) assess the long-term consequences of shared child care, (2) explore the specific effects of alternate caretakers, such as fathers, grandmothers, older siblings, and "hired help" on children's behavior, and (3) monitor the differential effects of such care on the development of boys versus girls.

REFERENCES

Ainsworth, M. D. S. *Infancy in Uganda: Infant care and the growth of love.* Baltimore: The Johns Hopkins Press, 1967.

Apple, D. The social structure of grandparenthood. *American Anthropologist,* 1956, *58,* 656-663.

Bacon, M., Child, I. L., and Barry, H. A cross-cultural study of correlates of crime. *Journal of Abnormal Psychology,* 1963, *66,* 291-300.

Barash, D. P. *Sociobiology and behavior.* New York/Amsterdam: Elsevier, 1977.

Barry, H., Child, and Bacon, M. Relation of child training to subsistence economy. *American Anthropologist,* 1959, *61,* 51-63.

Berry, J. W., and Annis, R. C. Ecology, culture and psychological differentiation. *International Journal of Psychology,* 1974, *9,* 173-193.

Blurton-Jones, N. Ethology, anthropology, and childhood. In R. Fox (Ed.), *Biosocial anthropology.* New York: Halsted Press, 1975.

Boon, J. A. Anthropology and nannies. *Man,* 1974, *9,* 137-140.

Burton, R. V. Cross-sex identity in Barbados. *Developmental Psychology,* 1972, *6,* 365-374.

Burton, R. V., and Whiting, J. W. M. The absent father and cross-sex identity. *Merrill-Palmer Quarterly of Behavior and Development,* 1961, *7,* 85-95.

Campbell, D. T., and Naroll, R. T. The mutual methodological relevance of anthropology and psychology. In F. L. K. Hsu (Ed.), *Psychological anthropology.* Cambridge, MA: Schenkman, 1972, pp. 435-468.

Caplan, A. (Ed.) *The sociobiology debate: Readings on the ethical and scientific issues concerning sociobiology.* New York: Harper and Row, 1978.

Carroll, V. *Adoption in Eastern Oceania.* Honolulu: University of Hawaii Press, 1971.

Caudill, W., and Plath, D. W. Who sleeps by whom? Parent-child involvement in urban Japanese families. *Psychiatry,* 1966, *29,* 344-366.

Clignet, R. Environmental change, types of descent, and childrearing practices. In H. Miner (Ed.), *The city of modern Africa*. London: Pall Mall Press, 1967, pp. 257-296.

Danzinger, K. Independence training and social class in Java, Indonesia. *Journal of Social Psychology*, 1960, *51*, 65-74. (a)

Danzinger, K. Parental demands and social class in Java, Indonesia. *Journal of Social Psychology*, 1960, *51*, 75-86. (b)

Dawkins, R. *The selfish gene*. New York: Oxford University Press, 1976.

de Mause, L. The evolution of childhood. In L. de Mause (Ed.), *The history of childhood*. New York: The Psychohistory Press, 1974, pp. 1-74.

Drummond, L. The transatlantic nanny: Notes on a comparative semiotics of the family in English-speaking societies. *American Ethnologist*, 1978, *5*, 30-43.

Ember, C. R. Female task assignment and social behavior of boys. *Ethos*, 1973, *1*, 424-439.

Etaugh, C. Effects of nonmaternal care on children: Research evidence and popular veiws. *American Psychologist*, 1980, *35*, 309-319.

Fox, R., and Fleising, U. Human ethology. In B. J. Siegel, A. B. Beals, and S. A. Tyler (Eds.), *Annual review of anthropology*, Vol. 5. Palo Alto, CA: Annual Reviews Inc., 1976, pp. 265-288.

Freedman, D. G. *Human sociobiology: A holistic approach*. New York: The Free Press, 1979.

Gallimore, R., Boggs, J. W., and Jordan, C. E. *Culture, behavior and education: A study of Hawaiian-Americans*. Beverly Hills, CA: Sage, 1974.

Gathorne-Hardy, J. *The rise and fall of the British nanny*. London: Hodder and Stoughton, 1972. Published in the U.S.A. under the title *The unnatural history of the nanny*. New York: Dial Press, 1973.

Goldberg, S. Infant care and growth in urban Zambia. *Human Development*, 1972, *15*, 77-89.

Goody, E. Kinship fostering in Gonja: Deprivation or advantage. In P. Mayer (Ed.), *Socialization: The approach from social anthropology*. London: Tavistock Publ. Ltd., 1970, pp. 51-74.

Graves, N. D. *City, country and childrearing in three cultures*. Unpublished manuscript, University of Colorado, 1969.

Graves, P. L. Infant behavior and maternal attitudes: Early sex differences in West Bengal, India. *Journal of Cross-Cultural Psychology*, 1978, *9*, 45-80.

Greenfield, P. M. *What we can learn from cultural variation in child care*. Paper presented at the American Association for the Advancement of Science, San Francisco, 1974.

Grindal, B. *Growing up in two worlds: Education and transition among the Sisala of Northern Ghana*. New York: Holt, Rinehart and Winston, 1972.

Harrington, C., and Whiting, J. W. M. Socialization process and personality. In F. L. K. Hsu (Ed.), *Psychological anthropology* (2nd ed.). Cambridge, MA: Schenkman, 1972, pp. 469-508.

Holtzman, W. H., Diaz-Guerrero, R., and Swartz, J. D. *Personality development in two cultures: A cross-cultural longitudinal study of school children in Mexico and the United States.* Austin: University of Texas Press, 1975.

Inkeles, A. Making men modern: On the causes and consequences of individual change in six developing countries. *American Journal of Sociology,* 1969, 75, 208-225.

Kessen, W. *Childhood in China.* New Haven: Yale University Press, 1975.

Konner, M. J. Aspects of the developmental ethology of a foraging people. In N. Blurton-Jones (Ed.), *Ethological studies of child behavior.* London: Cambridge University Press, 1972.

Konner, M. J. Relations among infants and juveniles in comparative perspective. In M. Lewis and L. A. Rosenblum (Eds.), *Friendship and peer relations.* New York: Wiley, 1975, pp. 99-130.

Konner, M. J. Evolution of human behavior development. In P. H. Leiderman, S. R. Tulkin, and A. Rosenfeld (Eds.), *Culture and infancy: Variations in the human experience.* New York: Academic Press, 1977, pp. 69-118.

Konner, M. J. Infancy among the Kalahari Desert San. In P. H. Leiderman, S. R. Tulkin, and A. Rosenfeld (Eds.), *Culture and infancy: Variations in the human experience.* New York: Academic Press, 1977, 287-328.

Leakey, R. E., and Lewis, R. *Origins.* New York: E. P. Dutton, 1977.

Leiderman, P. H., and Leiderman, G. F. Affective and cognitive consequences of polymatric infant care in the East African highlands. In A. D. Pick (Ed.), *Minnesota symposia on child psychology,* Vol. 8. Minneapolis: University of Minnesota Press, 1974, pp. 81-110.

Leiderman, P. H., and Leiderman, G. F. Economic change and infant care in an East African agricultural community. In P. H. Leiderman, S. R. Tulkin, and A. Rosenfeld (Eds.), *Culture and infancy: Variations in the human experience.* New York: Academic Press, 1977, pp. 405-438.

Lester, B. M., Kotelchuck, M., Spelke, E., Sellers, M. J., and Klein, R. Separation protest in Guatemalan infants: Cross-cultural and cognitive findings. *Developmental Psychology,* 1974, 10, 79-85.

LeVine, R. A. Patterns of personality in Africa. *Ethos,* 1973, 1, 123-152.

LeVine, R. A. Child-rearing as cultural adaptation. In P. H. Leiderman, S. R. Tulkin, and A. Rosenfeld (Eds.), *Culture and infancy: Variations in the human experience.* New York: Academic Press, 1977, pp. 15-28.

LeVine, R., Klein, N. H., and Owen, C. R. Father-child relationships and changing life-styles in Ibadan, Nigeria. In H. Miner (Ed.), *The city in modern Africa.* New York: Praeger, 1967.

Levy, R. I. Child management structure and its implications in a Tahitian family. In E. Vogel and N. Bell (Eds.), *A modern introduction to the family.* New York: Free Press, 1968.

Levy, R. *Tahitians: Mind and experience in the Society Islands.* Chicago: University of Chicago Press, 1973.

Lloyd, B.   Yoruba mothers' reports of childrearing: Some theoretical and methodological considerations.   In P. Mayer (Ed.), *Socialization: The approach from social anthropology.* London: Tavistock, 1970.

Lomnitz, L. A.   *Networks and marginality: Life in a Mexican shanty town.*   New York: Academic Press, 1977, pp. 159-174.

Lozoff, B.   *The sensitive period: An anthropological view.*   Paper presented at the Biennial Meeting of the Society for Research in Child Development.   New Orleans, March 19, 1977.

Lusk, D., and Lewis, M.   Mother-infant interaction and infant development among the Wolof of Senegal.   *Human Development,* 1972, *15,* 58-69.

Lynn, D. B.   *The father: His role in child development.*   Monterey, CA: Brooks/Cole, 1974.

Minturn, L.   A survey of cultural differences in sex-role training and identification.   In N. Kretschmer and D. Walcher (Eds.), *Environmental influences on genetic expression.*   Washington, D. C.:   U.S. Government Printing Office, 1969.

Minturn, L., and Lambert, W.   *Mothers of six cultures.*   New York: Wiley, 1964.

Moore, T. W.   Effects on the children.   In S. Yudkin and A. Holme (Eds.), *Working mothers and their children.*   London: Michael Joseph, 1963.

Moore, T. W.   Children of full-time and part-time mothers.   *International Journal of Social Psychiatry,* 1964, Special Congress Issue No. 2.

Moore, T. W.   Stress in normal childhood.   *Human Relations,* 1969, *22,* 235-250.

Moore, T. W.   Exclusive early mothering and its alternatives: The outcomes to adolescence.   *Scandinavian Journal of Psychology,* 1975, *16,* 255-272.

Morley, D.   The child-to-child programme.   *Assignment Children,* 1979, *47-48,* 171-185.

Munroe, R. H., and Munroe, R. L.   Household density and infant care in an East African society.   *Journal of Social Psychology,* 1971, *83,* 3-13.

Munroe, R. L., and Munroe, R. H.   *Cross-cultural human development.*   Monterey, CA: Brooks/Cole, 1975.

Munroe, R. L., Munroe, R. H., and Whiting, J. W. M.   The couvade: A psychological analysis.   *Ethos,* 1973, *1,* 30-74.

Mussen, P. H., and Beytagh, L. A. M.   Industrialization, childrearing practices and children's personality.   *Journal of Genetic Psychology,* 1969, *115,* 195-216.

Peter, H. R. H.   Prince of Greece and Denmark.   *A study of polyandry.*   The Hague: Mouton, 1963.

Pitt-Rivers, J.   The kith and the kin.   In J. Goody (Ed.), *The character of kinship.*   London: Cambridge University Press, 1973, 89-105.

Reed, G., and Leiderman, P. H.   Age-related changes in attachment behavior in polymatrically reared infants: The Kenyan Gusii.   In T. Field, P. H. Leiderman et al. (Eds.), *Culture and infant interaction.*   New York: Lawrence Erlbaum, 1981.

Ritchie, J. E.   *Basic personality in Rakau.*   New Zealand: Victoria University, 1956.

Robins, L. N., West, P. A., and Herjanic, B. L. Arrests and delinquents in two generations: A study of black urban families and their children. *Journal of Child Psychology and Psychiatry*, 1975, *16*, 125-140.

Rogoff, B., Sellers, M. J., Piorrata, S., Fox, N., and White, S. Age of assignment of roles and responsibilities to children: A cross-cultural survey. *Human Development*, 1975, *18*, 353-369.

Rohner, R. P. *They love me, they love me not: A world-wide study of the effect of parental acceptance and rejection.* New Haven, CT: HRAF Press, 1975.

Rosenblatt, P. C., and Skoogberg, E. Birth order in cross-cultural perspective. *Developmental Psychology*, 1974, *10*, 49-54.

Scheffler, H. W. *Choiseul Island social structure.* Berkeley: University of California Press, 1965.

Super, C. M. *Differences in the care of male and female infants: Data from non-American samples.* Worcester, MA: Clark University, October, 1977 (mimeo).

Super, C. M. Cross-cultural research on infancy. In H. C. Triandis and A. Heron (Eds.), *Handbook of cross-cultural psychology*, Vol. 4. Rockleigh, NJ: Allyn and Bacon, 1980.

Textor, R. B. *A cross-cultural summary.* New Haven, CT: HRAF Press, 1967.

Tiger, L. *Optimism: The biology of hope.* New York: Simon and Schuster, 1979.

Trivers, R. L. The evolution of reciprocal altruism. *Quarterly Review of Biology*, 1971, *46*, 33-57.

van den Berghe, P. L., and Barash, D. P. Inclusive fitness and human family structure. *American Anthropologist*, 1977, *79*, 809-823.

Weisner, T. S., and Gallimore, R. My brother's keeper: Child and sibling caretaking. *Current Anthropology*, 1977, *18(2)*, 169-190.

Werner, E. E. Infants around the world: Cross-cultural studies of psychomotor development from birth to two years. *Journal of Cross-Cultural Psychology*, 1972, *3*, 111-134.

Werner, E. E., and Smith, R. S. *Kauai's children come of age.* Honolulu: University Press of Hawaii, 1977.

Werner, E. E. *Cross-cultural child development: A view from the planet earth.* Monterey, CA: Brooks/Cole Publ. Co., 1979.

Werner, E. E. *Vulnerable, but invincible: A longitudinal study of resilient children and youth*, (in press).

Whiting, B. B. (Ed.) *Six cultures: Studies of childrearing.* New York: Wiley, 1963.

Whiting, B. B., and Edwards, C. A. A cross-cultural analysis of sex differences in the behavior of children aged three through eleven. *Journal of Social Psychology*, 1973, *91*, 188-191.

Whiting, B. B., and Whiting, J. W. M. *Children of six cultures: A psycho-cultural analysis.* Cambridge, MA: Harvard University Press, 1975.

Whiting, J. W. M. Socialization process and personality. In F. L. K. Hsu (Ed.), *Psychological anthropology: Approaches to culture and personality.* Homewood, IL: Dorsey Press, 1961, pp. 358-359.

Whiting, J. W. M.   A model for psycho-cultural research.   In P. Leiderman, S. R. Tulkin, and A. Rosenfeld (Eds.), *Culture and infancy: Variations in the human experience.* New York: Academic Press, 1977, pp. 29-48.

Whiting, J. W. M., and Child, I. L.   *Child training and personality: A cross-cultural study.* New Haven: Yale University Press, 1953.

Whiting, J. W. M., Child, I. L., and Lambert, W. W.   *Field guide for a study of socialization.* New York: Wiley, 1966.

Whiting, J. W. M., Kluckhohn, F., and Anthony, A. S.   The function of male initiation ceremonies at puberty.   In E. E. Maccoby, T. Newcomb, and E. Hartley (Eds.), *Readings in social psychology.* New York: Holt, 1958, pp. 359-370.

Whiting, J. W. M., and Whiting, B. B.   Contributions of anthropology to the methods of studying childrearing.   In P. Mussen (Ed.), *Handbook of research methods in child development.* New York: Wiley, 1960, p. 935.

Whiting, J. W. M., and Whiting, B. B.   Altruistic and egoistic behavior in six cultures.   In L. Nader and T. Maretzki (Eds.), *Cultural illness and health* (Anthropological Studies No. 9).   Washington, D. C.: American Anthropological Association, 1973.

Williams, T. R.   *Introduction to socialization.*   St. Louis, MO: C. V. Mosby, 1972.

Wilson, E. O.   *Sociobiology: The new synthesis.*   Cambridge, MA: Harvard University Press, 1975.

Wilson, E. O.   *On human nature.*   Cambridge, MA: Harvard University Press, 1978.

Witkin, H. A., and Berry, J. W.   Psychological differentiation in cross-cultural perspective.   *Journal of Cross-Cultural Psychology,* 1975, *6,* 4-87.

Yanagisako, S. J.   Family and household: The analysis of domestic groups.   In B. J. Siegel, A. R. Beals, and S. A. Tyler (Eds.), *Annual review of anthropology,* Vol. 8.   Palo Alto, CA: Annual Reviews, Inc., 1979, pp. 161-206.

FAMILIES AND CHILD CARE: A GLOBAL ECOSYSTEM PERSPECTIVE

Verna Hildebrand

Family and Child Ecology
Michigan State University
East Lansing, MI 48824

INTRODUCTION

We are all citizens of the world. In this day of modern technology, one's neighbors are not only next door but, also, on the opposite side of the globe. We now keep in touch with our world neighbors through instantaneous communications via satellites stationed around the planet. Jet travel takes us to the opposite side of the planet in a matter of hours. The world's families, their successes and problems, are more closely linked to each of us each day.

Nurturing children is a primary function of families throughout the world. Whether nurturing is done by the natural parent, in an extended family, or in some form of group care depends on historical, cultural, and political-economic factors within each society. *The objective of this essay is to provide a global perspective on caring for children in groups.* To provide essential background, we'll first explore families in a global perspective, then turn to group care and education of young children.

Educated citizens of the decade of the 1980's must be concerned about all families around the globe. The world is now like an apartment house. What we do affects the world's families and what they do affects us. Human development professionals around the world are dedicated to helping nurture children and improve life for individuals and families. There is much knowledge to share through written materials and public service, i.e., knowledge of child development, and early childhood education, nutrition, housing, clothing, family decision making, and interpersonal relationships. This knowledge can be utilized to enhance life for our world neighbors as well as for ourselves. In addition to sharing knowledge and our personal energy we can assist our world neighbors

239

through taxes to support national and international agencies that work for and with families. Also, some professionals may accept challenges such as service in the Peace Corps, or with the American Friends Service committee, or in other internationally minded volunteer groups organized to serve families. Colleges and universities open their doors to students from around the world. Various scholar-exchange programs are available that encourage exchange of knowledge throughout the world. World peace and the well-being of each of us hinge on the very insights and services to families that can be provided.

To focus on the issue of caring for children in groups requires looking at the context within which families in today's world are living and rearing their children. Using an ecological system framework is helpful in analyzing many of the factors affecting the world's families today. If we want to help families--our own or those on the other side of the globe--this ecological system or ecosystem framework will help us consider where, when, and how we might try particular inputs. Before proceeding let's answer the question. What is an ecological system framework?

THE ECOLOGICAL SYSTEM FRAMEWORK

The ecological system framework has long been used in the biological sciences to define, explain, and predict the interdependence among biological organisms and their environment. This framework is also useful in the social sciences for helping study resources, social institutions, individuals, families, and the interdependence between families and the various environments within which they function and use resources.

Bubolz, Eicher, and Sontag (1979) have proposed a model of the human ecological system. The environments discussed are 1) the natural environment; 2) the human constructed environment; and 3) the human behavioral environment. The family is an *open system* that functions in these environments. An open system means that interaction proceeds from the family toward the environment and also from the environment toward the family. As in biological systems, a human ecosystem such as a family seeks to come to some equilibrium or balance within its system. The authors define *natural environment* as that environment formed by nature with space, time, physical, and biological components. The *human constructed environment* refers to environment that is altered or created by human beings; for example, educational environments including group child care, medical, political, and economic institutions which humans organize to meet their physical, biological, social, and psychological needs and desires. The *human behavioral environment* includes 1) people's interaction with each other; 2) people's thoughts, emotions, values, attitudes, and sentiments; and 3) people interacting in groups in short- and long-term relationships.

Keeping this human ecosystem framework in mind will be helpful as discussion proceeds concerning the world's families and their need for group care for their children. For our purposes a family is defined as two or more people who share common resources and have some common commitment over time. Family forms vary widely throughout the world. Each society probably would be able to make a strong case to support its family form or forms. The future depends on the ways families of the planet care for their children and the supports the human constructed environment provides for families and for children. Limitations may be placed on the human constructed environment due to inadequate resources in the natural environment with the result that families do not receive supportive inputs from the human constructed environment. For example, poor countries lack resources to construct and operate schools; therefore, families cannot receive free public education as do the families in resource abundant countries. Further, individuals who lack educational opportunity can not most effectively utilize information in their behavioral environments to improve their lives or solve problems.

POLITICAL SYSTEMS

Political systems are designed by people and are part of the human constructed environment. Political systems have significant influence on the human behavioral environment and on the allocation of resources from the natural environment. Governments affect families throughout the world. History is replete with examples of how decisions of a government in a remote corner of the world have turned tranquility to turmoil in the homes of families many thousands of miles away.

Throughout the following discussion, there are references and implications regarding political decisions of governments that affect families and their decisions. Public policy and its effect on families is a growing area of study in the United States and Europe. Many believe that a family impact statement should be required for every legislative action, just as an environmental impact statement is required for technical proposals.

Of course, there are many governmental forms throughout the world. Some countries have many political parties; others have few. Some have a parliament, others a congress, and others a politburo. Some are democratic while others are authoritarian. The rights of free speech, freedom of the press, and voting do make differences to individuals and families. The interested reader can pursue more information on the issue of governmental public policies affecting families around the world. In addition to unilateral governmental decisions, the effect of the United Nations and other multilateral international agencies on behalf of families should be kept in mind. Suffice it to say that the reader needs to be aware of political overtones as the ecological system of the world's families is discussed further.

NATURAL RESOURCES

Let's consider the natural environment which is the home of the world's families. We've all seen the breathtaking beauty of the photographs of the planet Earth taken from outer-space and from the moon. A familiar song goes, "This land is your land, this land is my land." In a global perspective, the planet Earth belongs to all the world's families regardless of national boundaries. The resources for sustaining all our lives must come from the planet with the help of the sun, the atmosphere, and the oceans. That's our bank account for today and for the future. Our world's resources are finite. Many are depletable. For too long we have acted as if our natural resources are unlimited or readily renewable or replaceable.

The natural environment includes land and various natural resources such as oil and minerals. This is the ecological system that provides living organisms the basis for their livelihood. The amount of land per person is decreasing as rapid population growth proceeds. Many of the world's poor families would feel fortunate indeed if they could own and cultivate the land that many Americans keep in ornamental grass around their homes.

In many parts of the world, peasants notch out small terraces on steep hillsides to grow precious grains. The unknowing American says, "Why don't they mechanize their agriculture?" However, once you travel there and see how low wages are and the type of land being farmed you begin to understand some mechanization difficulties.

The United States is in an extremely favorable position with respect to good land suitable for producing food for its families. Flying over the midwest and looking down on fields of corn, wheat, and soybeans, one sees a sample of the wonderful bounty in the United States. Try to imagine how many African, Latin American, or Chinese persons would feel when they first see those wide vistas of productive cropland. The type of terrain and mechanization linked with know-how make American farmers particularly efficient. About 1.5 percent of the U.S. population are employed in agriculture (U.S. Department of Commerce, 1980). These workers are able to feed the 220 million Americans with much to spare for export.

In the People's Republic of China where about one billion or one fourth of the world's people live, the country is about the same size as the U.S. However, more of their land is dry, mountainous, and not well suited for crop production. There are over four times more Chinese than Americans and most Chinese are densely settled on the eastern one-third of their country where the land is more productive. They cultivate every inch of land like one might take care of a flower box. No weeds are allowed to grow. In the warmer regions the farmers grow three crops a year through diligent effort. Eighty percent of the Chinese people are rural peasants, though some work in commune industries that have been established in the countryside to provide essential products and to keep the workers from migrating to the crowded cities. For example, farm workers in one commune make cement and adobe bricks during slack seasons. These bricks are needed on the commune and on neighboring communes (Hildebrand and Hildebrand, 1981).

Energy, another component of the natural environment, is commonly derived from fossil fuels. Petroleum may indeed be the hottest topic of the late 20th century. Hopefully, it can be kept cool enough that conflicts can be resolved peacefully and fairly. Energy--its cost, availability, and distribution--affects each of the world's families.

POPULATION

Population is a topic that must be discussed in relation to the resources of the natural environment. The number of families is one important aspect of the human behavioral environment of the human ecosystem model. The number in each family determines the relationship with each family's ecosystem. World population is reported to have reached 4.5 billion people in early 1980. One billion people have been added to the planet in the last 15 years. It took 32 years--over twice as long--from 1933 to 1965 to add the previous billion. By projecting these population growth figures, you can readily see that our spaceship earth may be in danger of filling up soon beyond its carrying capacity.

The population explosion is most severe in the less developed countries of the world that have achieved modern death rates with the aid of modern medicines, but which still maintain the traditional high birth rate. The largest proportion of the population in many countries is younger than 21 (McHale and McHale, 1979).

FAMILY PLANNING

Looking at the world as a whole, the population explosion is obvious. In the United States, the families of today's adult generation are generally smaller than those of their parents' generation. Today in the United States, fertility stands at 1.8 births per woman. However, in the less developed countries, families are much larger than formerly because more children are living to maturity. A Guatemalan doctor once told us, "The typical Guatemalan woman used to be pregnant about twelve times--the outcome being three miscarriages, three stillbirths, three infant deaths, and three reaching maturity. Now, with modern health care, all twelve reach maturity. Our economy is unable to provide decent opportunities for so many." The U.S. Agency for International Development at that time was helping the Guatemalan government expand education; yet with the additional money and expertise the number of illiterate Guatemalans was growing. School expansion (part of the human constructed environment) was not keeping up with the population explosion.

Family planning includes aspects of the most intimate human behavioral environment. It also requires and utilizes information and technology from the human constructed environment; for example, from the medical and educational systems. Family size has an impact on the natural environment in terms of the resources each new human needs such as food, clothing, housing, education, and eventually a job. There are also related pollution effects on the natural environment from each new person.

A popular myth is that the women of the underdeveloped world won't limit their families. It is said that men need many children to show their masculinity and parents need children to care for them in their old age. In a powerful little book, *Message from the Village,* Perdita Huston (1978), who is today a Peace Corps director, published the results of a study she undertook through interviews with third world rural women of Southeast Asia, Africa, and Latin America which put to rest many of the myths surrounding conventional information about the acceptance of family planning. Huston's interviews show how trapped the village women feel. She reports that not once did they mention that they wanted more children for their "old-age security." The women do want to stop having so many children. Most would never opt for more than three or four children, yet have eight to thirteen. Many tell how worn out their bodies are from giving birth every year. Some tell how they know about family planning, yet are not allowed to practice it because of their husband's ego image in the village. A few courageous women have decided that what happens to their bodies is their business, and they use contraceptives without their husband knowing. Huston found little evidence of inter-personal communication between husbands and wives on the subject of family planning. Women in these villages expected and received very little help from their husbands in child rearing. Most were forceful in a desire for their children to have an education and a better life than they've had. Most of the women see the world changing and recognize that they are being left behind. Huston concludes that the women are ready but some men need to be persuaded to limit family size.

Family planning policy in the People's Republic of China is one that many countries might study and consider adapting to their own situations (Hildebrand and Hildebrand, 1981). To eliminate the starvation that was common during the "bitter past"--before liberation--and to have adequate resources to share among a large population that has now reached about a billion people, China's leaders soon realized that population growth had to be reduced. China has carried out one of the world's most effective family planning programs. The adequate provision of food, clothing, housing, health care, education, and capital for productive jobs was believed to be dependent on stopping the population explosion. Excessive child-bearing would cause the country's development plans to fail.

The following slogan is widely posted in Chinese health clinics and in neighborhoods, "One child is not too few; two are okay; but three are too many." The family planning program has been strikingly effective in limiting family size. People seem to appreciate the urgency of the population problem. Today, there is additional encouragement through special benefits for couples who have no more than one child.

The Chinese have trained paraprofessionals called "barefoot doctors" who take major responsibility for family planning education and for the utilization of family planning methods among the people in the neighborhoods. In addition to birth control measures, the Chinese also advocate late marriage for both men and women. Couples desiring to marry consult with several peer groups before they are allowed to marry. Tubal ligations and vasectomies are available for couples with the desired family size. Abortion is available but is not a desired form of family planning.

Since 1972, the American Home Economics Association has had a grant from the U.S. Agency for International Development to combine family planning education with education in home economics. The project has served 36 countries in Asia, the Mid-East, Africa, Latin America, and the Caribbean. According to a report on Nepal, the work is carried on in isolated villages. For example, "in the mountainous kingdom, young village girls and chief women workers receive a year's training by home economists at Women's Affairs and Training Centers. They then travel, often by foot, to live for three months in isolated villages where they work with mothers on nutrition, kitchen gardening, and poultry raising, clothing construction, family planning, and literacy--then move on to the next village." In other countries, the work is part of the formal school setting and the cooperative extension service.

The Population Reference Bureau (1979) estimates that many countries in Asia, Africa, and Latin America will double their populations in 20 to 25 years. Western and northern European countries generally are approaching zero population growth with doubling projected in 693 years. For the Soviet Union and Canada, the doubling projection is 87 years, for the United States 116 years, and for southern European countries 99 years.

Etinenne van de Walle and John Knodel (1980) in an interesting report titled, *Europe's Fertility Transition: New Evidence and Lessons for Today's Developing World,* trace the turndown in fertility rates in Europe starting in the 1840's. They also report corresponding decline in infant mortality and morbidity. These data may give new insights to those searching for causes of child abuse and those with traditional views on birth control acceptance. When children are expected to live, families tend to have fewer children and to treat them better. Apparently, with decreasing family size, the situation improves for those children who are produced. The writers conclude that, "In many cases a greater payoff might well result from concentrating efforts on improving and extending existing family planning programs" (p. 39).

Stressing family planning by reliable medical contraceptive methods is beginning to be viewed in many countries as a preferable alternative to the dangerous, self-inflicted, and frequently illegal back-alley abortions that are the last resort when women do not have access to contraceptives. Some of Huston's (1978) village women reported inflicting themselves with knives and sharp glass to make their fetus abort. In some Latin American countries, the governments are accepting family planning, in part, because self-induced abortions are filling too many hospital beds and destroying women's lives.

It is clear that firm population policy requires a serious commitment from both the behavioral and human constructed environments. Some countries in the developed world have made this commitment, but few in the developing world have, as yet, made the commitment. The population-family planning factor is very important when assessing the place of children in a society and for understanding the provision of care and education for children in the community or at home.

DIFFERENTIAL TREATMENT BASED ON SEX

In many parts of the world, inferior treatment is given daughters and women compared to that given to sons and men. Male children have been valued more highly than females even to the extent that infanticide was practiced on girls much more than boys. In some cultures, boys and men in a family are given food first with women and girls eating last--frequently to the nutritional disadvantage of the females. In some societies, the girls and women are confined to the family compound with very little opportunity to move out into the outside world or to become educated. This treatment is similar to that of American girls and women in the early years of our history. Females were "protected" by keeping them home where they served the needs of men. Only when the men began to realize that these uneducated women might have a negative influence on their sons did they begin to provide education--elementary education for girls. Our country was more than 100 years old before girls in large numbers had access to upper levels of education. As recently as the 1970's, women still fought for a toe-hold in some professions.

The rights of women have received worldwide attention during the 1970's. Consciousness raising has been almost as dramatic for women as it has for men. Because of our expressed ideals for human rights and equality in this country, the discrimination pointed out with respect to girls and women has been surprising to many. Could there really be so great a disparity between theory and practice? There could and there was, as case after case helped break the barriers of sexism. There is still much to do here at home.

Do women and girls around the world face the same discrimination? The new Chinese constitution has the equivalent of the Equal Rights Amendment (Hildebrand and Hildebrand, 1981). In practice the Chinese women are finding success in educational and labor systems, but have yet to crack the top political layers--a familiar theme for women except in England, India, and Israel where women have headed governments. Similar reports are received from the Soviet Union and Cuba, two socialist countries where equal treatment was high on the agenda following their revolutions.

HEALTH CARE

Health care as provided by the human constructed environment has improved steadily during the last century. The latest in immunizations reaches remote areas of the planet--so successfully that smallpox is now believed to be erradicated. Yet, some knowledge and service still eludes families. In Kenya in 1976, young children whose limbs had been crippled by polio could be seen in a special school. This was a startling reminder of the fight nearly won in the United States in only a few short years, thanks to the Salk vaccine. If parents who today are neglecting this simple and painless protective measure could have viewed the Kenyan children, they'd surely have hurried their children to their nearest clinic.

The family's access to many health care measures curtailing mass killers of the young has been largely responsible for the population explosion. Health care measures providing for a modern birth rate to accompany the modern death rate would seem to merit serious attention.

Education in sanitation and personal hygiene was an early objective of public health agencies in the industrialized nations. Some old timers remember well the U.S. campaigns to stop spitting on the sidewalks or to remove the common drinking cup in public schools. Today, similar effort is needed in the developing world.

There are some who believe that health care has been so largely turned over to the medical profession that people are unable or insecure about taking care of themselves. Professional medical care is so expensive that many people actually lack care. In some countries, such as England, Canada, and the socialist countries, governments finance most health care for all citizens. China's barefoot doctors program mentioned earlier in the discussion on family planning is an example of grass-roots health care that is affordable, effective, and probably could be adapted to work in many countries.

NUTRITIONAL STATUS

What is the nutritional status of families around the world? Here, the three environments are linked, the natural environment with its land and climate, the human constructed environment with its institutions fostering food production, marketing, and utilization, and the behavioral environment, including cultural preferences and the technical know-how of family members for utilizing available foods efficiently.

In 1980, a report from the Presidential Commission on World Hunger was released. One statistic, particularly appropriate to cite here, is that there are 230 million badly nourished children in the developing world. Now, 230 million is a statistic that you can conceptualize because it is close to the number of people in the United States. Think of enough children to populate the United States--children whose parents have hopes for them just as you have hopes for your children. Within each child there is a marvelous unique human potential--sort of a diamond in the rough--that must be nourished, polished, and developed to make contributions to society. These 230 million children are malnourished in ways that often cripple their mental development and make them weak physically and frequently subject to illness. Think of the work undone, the treasures that are undiscovered, the books unwritten, and the songs unsung because these individuals lack normal physical and mental capabilities.

Children aren't the only ones who suffer from malnourishment. There is a very high incidence of malnutrition in women of childbearing age. Many are anemic, lack calcium, protein, and calories to sustain their constant pregnancies and lactation and to provide energy needed for the heavy physical work their society requires. In their condition many can never properly nurture their children.

On a study tour to the People's Republic of China, I was particularly impressed with the healthy appearance of the people. The children's eyes are bright, their teeth strong and straight, and their hair shiny. They have energy for many activities including hikes to school, bicycle riding, and daily physical fitness routines. Since the 1949 victory of the revolution, the Chinese leaders have been particularly committed to providing the people an adequate diet, and it shows on the faces of the populace.

As Americans, we have an enlightened self-interest in a well-fed world. President Carter said when giving the charge to the Presidential Commission on World Hunger, "We cannot have a peaceful and prosperous world if a large part of the world's people are at or near the edge of hunger" (1980). Many of our foreign aid dollars help poor countries improve their food production. An example is a Michigan State University project known as the "Bean and Cowpea Project" where plant breeders will cooperate with scientists in Africa and Latin America to improve the subsistence foods of the poorest people. As part of these aid projects, the Congress has mandated, through the Percy amendment to the foreign aid bill, that the concerns of women and children be an explicit part of the project plan. In some African countries women are actually the farmers growing these subsistence crops. Women also store, cook, and feed these crops to their families. Rather than aiming agricultural programs toward men, women should be the focus in many countries.   Knowing the sociological aspects of the environment is essential for helping people, because sex role division of labor and responsibility may be rigidly set. For example, it is considered inappropriate for men, particularly strange men, to teach women in some African countries. Such considerations may call for training more women agriculturalists.

Using the human ecological system framework, one notes that if bean breeders make inputs into the natural environment and ignore the human behavioral or human constructed environments, we can predict that they will achieve less of their objectives from the project, e.g., linkages to storage, marketing, local tastes, and customs.

An appreciation of the function of world trade in our own agri-cultural and commercial ecosystem is essential. The U.S. grain exported helps pay for needed imports of oil and raw materials.   Political restrictions on food exports, such as the grain embargos, are unfortunate. When food imports are undependable, the importing countries will grow more of their own food at higher costs in order to keep from starving in times of emergency. Thus, all nations become poorer as limited resources are used less wisely.

HOUSING

Housing also interrelates the three environments of the human ecosystem--the natural environment, the human constructed environ-ment, and the human behavioral environment.   Housing the world's families is a major problem as population increases and as families crowd into the cities to find work and to seek a better life than the one they have known. You've all seen slums in this country. Clearly, America has much more to do in order to house its families adequately. Yet, until you've seen the shanty towns that have sprung up in cities such as Buenos Aires, Rio de Janiero, or Mexico City, you can't really understand the magnitude or severity of the problem. In some cities, the slums are in the same neighborhoods as elegant homes, the squatters simple taking over vacant lots and building their lean-to shacks out of scraps of junk materials. Without any of the normal human constructed environmental services, for example, water, light, or sewerage, these settlements become cancers on the society.

Of course, housing, population, and income are all related. If you have traveled in Mexico throughout the last 30 years you may have observed a great deal of economic development in that country. How-ever, progress has not touched many families, and one still sees much housing without water, lights, or sewerage. Economic progress has passed these families by.

The Chinese have been building many apartments for their people since 1949. I found housing crowded but neat, clean, and modest. Often, several generations of one family live together.   Bath and kitchen facilities are often shared by families in adjoining apartments.   In a Shanghai housing project, a small park was visited containing an exhibit of pre-revolution housing, which prevailed in what they call the "bitter past." One house was typical of the housing our 72-year-old guide had lived in before liberation. He said he, his wife, and five children lived in such a "straw ramshackled house." The park helps teach the Chinese youth an appreciation of the progress the families have made since 1949.

In many parts of the world, families have done a good job of using natural available materials in their home construction. In Guatemala, for instance, the monaca palm tree is protected by laws because it is the source of roofing materials for native homes. These roofs are cool in the hot tropical sun. When housing experts of the U.S. Agency for International Development decided to help those native families, they built small wood or block houses with tin roofs. The tin roofs collected too much heat and air circulation proved to be inadequate; consequently, people couldn't stay inside comfortably during the heat of the day. Careful studies of housing in use by families and more discussions with residents might have resulted in house designs more appropriate and even less expensive.

In the larger cities in many parts of the world, the homes of the wealthy families are large and constructed with the assumption that cheap maid service and gardeners will always be available. However, as industrialization brings jobs and household workers choose other employment, the owners are less successful in securing the labor required to keep up their homes. They adapt by turning to machines and to a type of housekeeping that the owners can do themselves.

For much of the less developed world, the drinking water and the firewood for cooking must be carried long distances--often by women and children. They carry heavy loads on their heads and backs that we can hardly imagine. It may take one adult two days of labor to provide the family firewood for seven days. The source of wood for cooking is receding farther and farther from many of these villages. Besides the labor of obtaining the wood, the centuries of cutting the vegetation for firewood is leaving lands barren and increasing loss from wind and water erosion.

In Kenya, while visiting a village in 1976, the women proudly showed us the "women's well." After hearing this reference numerous times, we asked why they called it the "women's well." They replied, "Because when the man or the children want a drink it is the woman who must get it for them." The women had organized a cooperative and had gotten water pumped about a half mile up the hill to the village. One spigot served the families of the village.

PRODUCTIVE JOBS FOR ALL

The economic sector of the human constructed environment has a direct and sometimes drastic influence on the family and the opportunities available for family members. Income is closely related to all the factors already discussed and to schooling and child care which will be discussed later. The ability of a country to generate sufficient capital essential for productive jobs for everyone is where a poor country faces an almost insurmountable problem if rapid population growth can not be curtailed.

A characteristic of an interdependent system is the migration of job seekers from one region to another in search of better opportunities with respect to human rights and income possibilities. International migration is occurring at both the higher education levels as well as at the lower education levels. When an African student studies in the U.S. or Europe and decides to emigrate rather than return to his or her own country to work, that is referred to as the "brain drain." That person's human resources--knowledge, skills, and talents, will not be available to improve directly life in the home country. Also, a drain in skilled laborers may occur. "Jordan, for example, had 28 percent of its labor force working abroad in 1975....," according to Kathleen Newland (1979, p. 11) of the Worldwatch Institute. In the same report Newland writes, "The example of South Africa illustrates starkly the dark side of the benefits of immigration to the receiving country..." (p. 20). Blacks work in white South African homes, factories, mines, and farms. They are not allowed to have their families accompany them. The wives and children of workers are relegated to various restricted areas called "homelands" hundreds of miles from the husband-worker and his job. The men are housed in crowded dormitory-type housing in segregated areas. The women eke out an existence in the arid homeland and wait for some funds to be sent back occasionally by their husbands. South African policy shows little concern for the family life of blacks. Whites have a very high standard of living.

Many Americans are having guilt feelings in relation to the plight of the South African blacks and believe our ideals concerning human rights should be translated into action by U.S. policy and by pressuring U.S. multi-national corporations in South Africa to give more leadership for change. Without more rapid change, many observers believe South Africa is locked on a collision course which will result in tragedy for both black and white families.

The industrial economic development, which today differentiates the developed and the less developed world, began in England in 1760 with the dawn of the industrial revolution. With the invention of machines to speed hand processes, for example in spinning and weaving, and the development of such energy sources as steam and coal, machines began production of goods that had never been possible when human power was all that was available. Products were produced that were sold around the world. Leading the way was Britain with its rich coal deposits at home and an extensive colonial system providing needed raw materials and markets for industrial goods.

People moved from a subsistence economy, similar to the economies in the underdeveloped countries today, to a market economy. The European industrial system was adapted in the United States. As states were added, the U.S. became the world's largest common market free of trade barriers and with freedom for laborers to move where jobs were available. In both Europe and America, workers were needed for factories, and large numbers of people moved from their pastoral rural life styles to the industrial centers. After World War II, Japan joined the group of highly industrialized exporting countries.

Women workers were common in early factories, especially in textile manufacturing. Children were also utilized as labor until the countries passed legislation outlawing child labor. World War II brought women into the labor force in greater numbers in the industrialized countries where they worked in defense plants. Many of these women went back home following the war. However, since 1970, the most startling labor statistics are the increase in women workers, especially women with young children. The legislation for equal educational and employment opportunities has helped women hope for a career ladder rather than dead-end jobs. The fulfillment of this hope is still on the horizon because even today women receive 59 cents for every $1.00 that a man earns (U.S. Department of Labor, 1979).

SCHOOLING

Schools are provided by the human constructed environment. Most governmental leaders would say schools are essential and believe that investment in the human agent is crucial for socio-economic development of a country. Once schooling was considered the domain of the family; however, since the beginning of the industrial revolution there has been an increase in the provision of schooling by the public sector in the industrial countries. Today industrial nations such as the United States, Canada, Europe, Israel, Japan, and Australia require parents to send their children to school.

Historically, boys were educated before girls because the prevailing attitude was that girls were stupid and needed the protection of men--an attitude we are still coping with today. Racial discrimination, too, was practiced extensively in educational institutions. Few job opportunities were available to minorities. Racism is also a continuing problem, with many changes still needed throughout the world.

Simple literacy is a luxury in much of the developing world. The wealthy in many of the developing countries send their children to private schools. As leaders, the wealthy often ignore the educational needs of the less affluent children. The United States has long accepted compulsory school attendance as basic for improving society. Public funds are used to provide schools, although private education has usually remained available.

In the developing world, many children will be very lucky if they are able to receive three years of primary schooling taught by a sixth grade graduate. The village women in the Perdita Huston (1978) survey often mentioned how unreliable the schooling had been when they were young. Teachers sometimes were not provided or did not show up when they were supposed to. Children got discouraged easily and quit school. Most of the women interviewed felt strongly that education was a way out of poverty.

In some developing countries today, child labor interferes with education. Some societies depend on children to be helpers of women in the market or on farms. Consequently, a compulsory school attendance law may be unpopular. Though many of these women work hard to get money to send their own children to school, they import a child from a rural area and use his or her labor in peddling or in household tasks. Fifty-two million children, ages seven to fifteen, are paid and unpaid workers throughout the world, according to the International Labor Organization (Newland, 1979).

The People's Republic of China, however, requires attendance at primary school, and many children are able to attend secondary schools (Hildebrand and Hildebrand, 1981).   China is still a developing nation trying to catch up from years of neglecting its educational system. Education is believed to play a big role in the current modernization plans for China. To help teach children how to work with their hands as well as their heads, Chinese children do some hand labor in schools--sometimes in a factory run by the school.   The Chinese are expanding educational institutions as rapidly as possible. In 1979, following diplomatic recognition by the United States, the People's Republic of China began sending scholars to the United States in an effort to secure the latest scientific information available there.

CHILD CARE OUTSIDE THE FAMILY

Caring for young children, like educating children, was once considered the responsibility of the family and the extended family. In Europe during the Industrial Revolution, mothers and their older children began to work in factories. Young children were frequently left uncared for and unprotected. According to Forest (1927, pp. 154-183), the first caregiving institution for children of working mothers was founded in Germany in 1802. Thus, to provide for certain human needs the human constructed environment evolved a new form of child care--group child care.   An infant school was established in Scotland in 1816 by Robert Owen. In France in 1833, Jean Frederic Oberline founded a nursery school. Creches were organized in Vienna, Austria in 1847, in Spain in 1855, and in Russia in 1864. The United States had its first center for children of working mothers in New York City in 1854.

Historically in Europe and the United States as well as in many countries, parallel development occurred in both the provision of nursery school and kindergarten education, and in the provision of group child care. A German philosopher, Fredrich Froebel, influenced the early childhood education movement. In 1837, Froebel coined the term *kindergarten* meaning "garden of children." Froebel believed that children should be allowed to play, but that teachers and mothers could arrange play for them that developed their minds, bodies, and senses. Froebel's writings provided the philosophy for the early kindergarten movement in America and in most European countries (Forest, 1927).

Dr. Maria Montessori founded schools bearing her name in Italy in the early 1900's (Montessori, 1966). Montessori was trained as a physician and psychologist. Her major work centered around training feebleminded children in an Italian slum housing project. She stressed cleanliness and self-help and taught children to use especially designed self correcting educational materials using repetitive methods. Many of the methods Dr. Montessori developed are still used in schools bearing her name today; however, the chidren today are generally those of the wealthy who can afford high tuition costs, rather than poor children as were the original Montessori students.

In England, the McMillan sisters, Rachel and Margaret, organized the first nursery school in London between 1908 and 1910 (Macmillan, 1921). The McMillans' school and writings were also inspirations for American schools.

Today, in Europe, as in the United States, group child care is increasing as more and more women with children are employed outside the home. Kahn and Kamerman (1979) are researchers who have studied the social systems of various countries with child services being one portion of that research. Their report covers the Federal Republic of Germany, France, Israel, Poland, the United Kingdom, Yugoslavia, Canada, and the United States. Because Israel and the United States are discussed in other chapters, details of these two countries will be omitted here.

Kahn and Kamerman (1979) discovered 1) that most children between three and six-years-old were already in a preprimary program with an educational base, 2) that educational agencies operated and administered the programs rather than personal service agencies, and 3) that the policy and program distinctions for children under age three generally indicate a day care concept in the usual custodial sense (pp. 147-148).

The Federal Republic of Germany

Kahn and Kamerman (p. 175) reported concerning the Federal Republic of Germany that, by 1977, kindergarten was expected to be available for 75 percent of three- and four-year-olds and 90 percent of the five-year-olds. The kindergarten program covers the child's day from 8 a.m. to 1 p.m. A small percent of the children are in full-day kindergarten or a combination of kindergarten and organized day care. The authors report growing pressure for the expansion of the later programs to cover all children of working mothers. The Federal Republic of Germany has few child care centers for children under three. Experiments are being carried out encouraging family day care and giving mothers a cash allowance to stay home with their children.

France

"In France there is a clear recognition that preschool is a *social utility*," according to Kahn and Kamerman (p. 176). Social utility programs are "programs available at the initiative of the potential user, who should be thought of as a 'consumer,' not as 'patient' or 'client'. These researchers found that,

> In France there is a clear recognition that preschool is a social utility for all children aged two and over and that it serves a basic child care function as well as an educational function, even though satisfactory fulfillment of this dual function may require supplementary programs beyond the standard school day (p. 176).

Parents are charged for supplementary care for the periods 7:30 a.m.-8:30 a.m., the lunch, 4:30 p.m.-7:00 p.m., Wednesdays (when school is closed), and school holidays. France has one of the most comprehensive full-day preschool programs, called *ecole maternelle*, which enrolls 100 percent of the five-year-olds, 93 percent of four-year-olds, 72 percent of three-year-olds, and 22 percent of two-year-olds. The child care programs became part of the public school program in the late 19th century (p. 176).

Poland

Poland, according to Kahn and Kamerman (p. 170), has two systems --nurseries or creches under the health department for children under the age of 3; and kindergartens under the education department for children 3 to 6 years old. However, these systems are jointly located though not integrated into one program. Children of all preprimary ages can receive services in one location prior to entering primary school. Preschool is provided for about 50 percent of the children in a full school day program with some supplementation available to cover the mother's working day. Ninety percent of these children have working mothers.

Belgium

"Guarderies" for young children were started in Belgium under governmental auspices in 1832 (Austin, 1976, pp. 242-244). By 1850 the pedagogical ideas of Fredrich Froebel of Germany were influential in Belgium giving emphasis to instruction in addition to child care. Later, the philosophy of Maria Montessori was influential.

Organization and control of education in Belgium is on a national basis. There are two ministries of education, one representing the Dutch part of Belgium and the other representing the French. In preprimary education 61 percent of the children are Dutch and 38 percent are French. Preschools admit children from two and a half years up to the time of primary education. There is in Belgium a downward trend in births, an upward trend in the number of children enrolled in preschool, and an upward trend in the number of women in the labor force.

Netherlands

According to Austin (1976, p. 301), there have been day nurseries in the Netherlands since about 1870, mainly in the larger cities. Froebel and later Montessori both influenced early education in the Netherlands. Children from age one to four from poor families have, since World War II, been eligible for special nursery schools financed by the community. These day care centers have psychohygienic aims. The typical Dutch family now has one child. Early statistics showed a large portion of children attending private preschools. Though there has been an increase in children attending preschools the private schools still enroll the larger portion of young children.

Sweden

Austin (1976) reports that Sweden's "child-minding" facilities came into existence in the late nineteenth century during periods of increased industrialization. The kindergarten developed out of these "child-minding" institutions (p. 141). Today, the employment of mothers of young children is also on the increase in Sweden, as in other developed countries. The family size in Sweden averages just slightly over one child per family. According to the Kahn-Kamerman report (1976, p. 175), the Swedish government operates an integrated child care program, the care of the very young being an integral part of the program.

In Sweden today the socio-emotional objectives of "child centres" and kindergartens are as important as the educational objectives, according to Austin (1976, p. 141). He also reports further, that the day nursery receives children as young as six months to age seven. Seven is the compulsory school age. The facilities are open 11½ hours daily, Monday through Friday and for 7½ hours on Saturday. Apartment complexes with 200 units or more are expected to provide preschool facilities (pp. 154-155).

Italy

Preschool education in Italy began with a Catholic priest who established an infant school in 1825, according to Austin (1976, p. 207). The priest wrote a manual in 1833 stressing moral habits, intellectual stimulation, and physical activities as necessary ingredients in infant education. Another Italian, Montessori, whose philosophy was mentioned earlier, gave leadership to Italian preschool education from the early 1900's. Also, according to Austin, "In 1894, the Agazzi sisters opened a home for preschool children. They developed methods for working with poor children, especially the "museum of humble things" composed of the objects the children treasure (and that come out of their pockets), things that a child can look at, touch, recognize, distinguish, and enumerate. These humble things can be used for all exercises in sensory development, distinguishing qualities, color, contents; recognizing forms, material, size, and graduation. Thus, in a poor school and with scant-resources, a clever teacher can find ways to provide a very adequate educational experience for the young child" (Austin, 1976, p. 232).

Up to 1968, Italian preprimary education was organized under private auspices (primarily Roman Catholic churches). Since 1968 the government has taken increased responsibility and is especially concerned for children who are disadvantaged due to social, economic, or geographical circumstances (Austin, p. 216).

Soviet Union

Creches were first organized in Russia in 1864 (Forest, p. 154). Preschools were parts of the educational reform following the 1917 revolution. They offered children protection and socialization in the new idealogy. The systems of kindergarten and creche were integrated with new emphasis added on the potential for young children to learn.

The Soviet government holds the political and administrative authority over the preschools. Preschools are provided throughout the country on state farms and collective farms, as well as in the cities. They are often in or near a factory, enabling mothers to nurse the infant during time-off periods. Many women are employed outside the home in the Soviet Union. Ending discrimination against women by providing equal opportunity was part of the improvements sought by the new regime. However, with many male casualties during World War II, women had to work in factories both during and following the war. This created a major need for child care services. According to Bronfenbrenner (1970), an American child development authority who was a visiting scholar in the Soviet Union in the 1960 to 1967 period, the Soviet Union's child care program served over 10 percent of all children under two years of age and about 20 percent of three- to six-year-olds.

The curriculum for the early childhood center has been given serious attention by Soviet researchers. Henry Chauncey (1969) has translated into English the Soviet Union's program of early childhood instruction providing us a detailed look at the volumes that are read throughout Russia by early childhood "upbringers" and teachers. Bronfenbrenner (1970), indicated that he saw the books in use in several localities and that they provide the base for numerous other publications related to providing child care and education for young children. The books show many similar activities to those of European and American preschools. There is an emphasis on nature, fresh air, physical activity, and working for the common good.

Yugoslavia

Yugoslavia has two types of child care, according to the Kahn-Kamerman report (1976, p. 177). Preschool is under the education agency; however, day care for children age three and younger, is under the social welfare agency. For the limited spaces available families with problems are given preference. Yugoslavia provides both types of programs in one location for children up to the age of seven, the age for entering primary school.

United Kingdom

In the United Kingdom, the Department of Health and Social Security regulates day care programs which are established and operated by local governments, according to the Kahn and Kamerman report (1976). Nursery schools for three- to five-year-olds are established by local governments with policies set by the Department of Education and Science (p. 167). In the United Kingdom compulsory education begins at age five. "The official government position is that preschool education is an essential program that should be available to most, if not all, children aged three and over" (p. 173).

Canada

There are 2.2 million Canadian children under age six, according to Kahn and Kamerman (1976, p. 172). About one-fourth of the total number of children under age three have working mothers. There is an immediate need for 200,000 all-day places for children in the birth to age five group. Present facilities and programs are largely privately operated in the day care and kindergarten-nursery school categories. According to the report, there is little coordination among centers or between day care centers and kindergartens; nor, are there formal linkages with other categories of service.

The Canadian kindergarten or preschools are for four to six-year-olds and are under provincial departments of education and local school boards as part of the public school system. These programs were designed to enhance the child's education rather than to serve as custodial care. More than half of the day care centers and nursery schools are privately operated, the rest coming under provincial public school systems. Most are part-day only (p. 164).

Japan

Lebra (1974), writing in *Women in Changing Japan*, indicates that child care centers have been set up throughout the country since World War II. Preference is given to working mothers and when applicants outnumber spaces available, income also becomes a criterion for entrance. According to Lebra, private centers are often expensive, inadequate, and unlicensed, whereas, women teachers are the main users of public child care facilities (p. 171).

DEVELOPING COUNTRIES

In the countries of the developing world, the rural nature of the economies, the low rates of industrialization, the low rates of literacy, high unemployment, and poverty are factors which relate closely to the almost non-existence of child care centers, except in a few of the larger cities. Most of the developing countries today are still in the stage of trying to provide elementary and secondary education for their children. However, the children of the most affluent families attend private schools. Leaders in these countries probably have given little consideration to extending services to preprimary children needing child care. These developing countries where the population explosion is most threatening already face a severe strain on very limited resources.

Africa

In Africa, some authorities see a need for group child care developing. For example, based on a 1975 survey of 824 working mothers, Professor Eleanor R. Fapohunda (1979) of the University of Lagos in Nigeria reported, as a result of difficulty finding relatives or domestic help to care for children, that working women of Lagos were turning to commercial businesses, largely unregulated by government agencies to take care of their children.

Also in western Africa, a Liberian educator indicated a proposal for child care facilities for market women's children was being discussed. She knew of one child care center in the capital city of Monrovia (Hildebrand, 1976).

In Kenya in East Africa, child care is considered the province of the social agency while preprimary education is considered an educational function and the domain of the education agency. Only a small percent of the children of the very poor in the large cities can be served by the few existing child care centers. These centers are expected to provide only the simplist necessities--a protected environment, food, and rest (Hilde-brand, 1976).

Latin America

In Central and South America, the distinction between male and female roles is well drawn. Until recently, few middle and upper-class women worked outside the home. Whenever these women leave home to work or to socialize, their children are cared for by domestic servants. Middle and upper-class children tend to be enrolled in private kinder-gartens. On the other hand, many poor women have always worked as domestic servants and peddlers. Children often accompany the mother; for example, sometimes an infant sleeps in a a box under a table in the peddler's stall at the market, and the preschoolers run up and down the aisle. Relatives are at times called upon to rear the child of a domestic servant. Today, a few child care centers called "guardarieas" are available for younger children of low income families in the larger cities such as Mexico City, Guatemala City, San Salvador, and Panama City. The few centers, organized by governmental social service departments, are crowded, short-staffed, under-equipped, and unable to serve many children who need care (Hildebrand, 1978).

China

The government of the People's Republic of China has taken considerable responsibility for providing nurseries and child care centers for infants and young children (Hildebrand and Hildebrand, 1981). Many of these facilities are attached to the factories where members of a child's family work. It is easy for the mother to drop by the nursery to nurse the infant, for instance. Most mothers do work outside the home; however, some infants remain in the care of grandparents rather than attend a child care center. This work gives a useful occupation to the elders, which is important in Chinese culture. There are no elite private schools in China as there are in most other developing countries.

Chinese children frequently sing in the schools. In one center, when this observer walked through the various rooms occupied by two or three adults with a group of children, the children would stand by their seats and sing while the teacher played on an electric organ. On a number of occasions, a well organized program was presented to visitors by the school. Each program was complete with costumes and well-choreo-graphed dance routines. The words to songs and the dances depicted political themes and current concerns. People from the children's environment were depicted in programs, such as the barefoot doctors, a farmer carrying fodder to the pigsty, and People's Liberation Army soldiers. The children presented a very healthy appearance. Several ob-servers, including this one, have commented on the docile and conforming attitude of the children. This behavior is undoubtedly rewarded from birth. One should remember that the press of population is ever present in China, on the streets, in child care centers, and in homes where many people occupy a small space. A controlled child is, undoubtedly, an asset.

Cuba

Marvin Leiner (1974) revisited Cuban day care in 1971 after having made a study of the day care system in 1968 and 1969 when he lived in Cuba. Leiner reports that The Children's Institute was established in 1971 with the duty of performing research, supervising the early childhood institutions, and raising the quality of day care personnel (pp. 167-168). A strong central control was placed over all early childhood programs which had previously been decentralized. The school was expected to stress academic subjects--even reading, rather than free play type activities. Leiner reports that, between 1969 and 1973, the number of day care centers rose from 364 to 610 (pp. 56-57). Current demand far outstrips available space (p. 13). The population explosion continues in Cuba, though at a slower pace than in other countries of Latin America (*Demographic Yearbook*, 1979).

FAMILY SECURITY AND PEACE

The human constructed environment is responsible for promoting well-being, peace, and security for families residing on the planet. If political systems are inadequate and fail, with resulting international nuclear war and its aftermath, all families in our global habitat will suffer. Hundreds of millions of families will not survive. For families sharing our planet, there is a powerful lesson to learn from visiting the Hiroshima Peace Park in Japan and seeing the effects of the first atomic bomb which destroyed Hiroshima and killed several hundred thousand people. Today's super hydrogen bomb with over 10,000 times more explosive force relegates the Hiroshima bomb to a pop-gun category.

One stands in empathetic mourning upon observing a busload of Japanese people stop at a common tomb for tens of thousands. They light candles for their loved ones killed in the atomic holocaust of August 7, 1945.

So that a Hiroshima or Nagasaki holocaust will never happen again, we must all work to create a human constructed global political environment with appropriate international institutions to maintain peace with justice, thus making a nuclear holocaust impossible. Peace and justice can be promoted with the help of human developmentalists and others working for the common interests of families and children around the globe.

CONCLUSION

Nurturing children is an obligation and privilege of families around the globe. Their need for, desire for, or willingness to accept assistance with their nurturing function, such as child care, depends on many factors in their environment.

As human development professionals, and, in our efforts to prepare the next generation of human development professionals for the 80's, 90's and beyond, we must become fully cognizant of the planetary context within which families live. There are many problems with world-wide ramifications close to home as well as in Asia, Africa, or Latin America that need attention. First, we must grow out of our "me-ism" and nationalistic approaches and help develop "we-ism" and global approaches that acknowledge every family's close links with the planetary ecosystem and with all families around the world. Human developmentalists must forge linkages with other professions that will help foster justice, economic well-being, and peaceful change benefiting families wherever they reside on our planetary home. Knowledge and experience can make a difference as we push ourselves and our students to look at horizons beyond ourselves throughout our interdependent world. Whenever we confront a problem, we must learn to look at the many environments that impinge on the problem and to analyze the interrelationships from possible courses of action. A total ecosystem approach is essential.

Study and travel lead to the discovery that people learn, laugh, love, and cry much the same the world around. A sense develops that we are all citizens of the same spaceship Earth, sharing the same ecosystem so vital to the well-being of families and children everywhere.

REFERENCES

Austin, G. R. *Early childhood education: An international perspective.* New York: Academic Press, 1976.

Bronfenbrenner, U. *Two worlds of childhood: U.S. and U.S.S.R.* New York: Russel Sage Foundation, 1970.

Bubolz, M., Eicher, J., and Sontag, S. The human ecosystem: A model. *Journal of Home Economics*, 1979, 71(1), 28-31.

Chauncey, H. (Ed.). *Soviet preschool education volume I: Program of instruction.* New York: Holt, Rinehart and Winston, 1969.

Chauncey, H. (Ed.). *Soviet preschool education volume II: Teacher's commentary.* New York: Holt, Rinehart and Winston, 1969.

Demographic Yearbook. New York: United Nations, 1978.

Fapohunda, E. *The child-care dilemma of working mothers in African cities: The case of Lagos, Nigeria.* Unpublished paper presented at the conference on Women and Work in Africa, May 1, 1979, University of Illinois, Urbana, Illinois.

Forest, I. *Preschool education: A historical and critical study.* New York: Macmillan, 1927.

Hildebrand, V. Conversations with educators in Monrovia, Liberia and in Nairobi, Kenya, 1976.

Hildebrand, V. Conversations with authorities and observations in child care facilities in Central America, 1978.

Hildebrand, V., and Hildebrand, J. *China's families: Experiment in societal change.* Minneapolis, MN: Burgess Publishing Company, 1981.

Huston, P. *Message from the village.* New York: The Epoch B Foundation, 1978.

Integrated home economics programs: An international force for families. Washington, D. C.: American Home Economics Association International Family Planning Project, January 1980.

Kahn, A., and Kamerman, S. *Social services in international perspective.* Washington, D. C.: U.S. Department of Health, Education and Welfare, 1976.

Lebra, J. (Ed.). *Women in changing Japan.* Boulder, CO: Westview Press, 1976.

Leiner, M. *Children are the revolution: Day care in Cuba.* New York: The Viking Press, 1974.

Macmillan, M. *The nursery school.* New York: Dutton, 1921.

McHale, M., and McHale, J. *World's children data sheet of the Population Reference Bureau, Inc.* Washington, D. C.: Population Reference Bureau, Inc., 1979.

Montessori in perspective. Washington, D. C.: National Association for the Education of Young Children, 1966.

Newland, K. *International migration: The search for work.* Washington, D. C.: Worldwatch Institute, November 1979.

1979 World Population Data Sheet of the Population Reference Bureau. Washington, D. C.: Population Reference Bureau, Inc., 1979.

Presidential Commission on World Hunger. Washington, D. C.: 734 Jackson Place, N.W., 1980.

United States Department of Commerce. *Survey of current business.* Washington, D. C.: July, 1980, p. S-11.

United States Department of Labor, Women's Bureau. *The earnings gap between women and men.* Washington, D. C., 1979.

van de Walle, E., and Knodel, J. *Europe's fertility transition: New evidence and lessons for today's developing world.* Washington, D. C.: Population Reference Bureau, 1980.

SUPPLEMENTARY PARENTING IN THE KIBBUTZ

CHILDREARING SYSTEM

A. I. Rabin

Department of Psychology
Michigan State University
East Lansing, MI 48824

INTRODUCTION

Compared with many species in the animal kingdom, human beings arrive into the world rather ill-equipped to face its demands and requirements. It has been observed that evolution has endowed us with a large brain--with great potential. However, we have to "pay a price" for this gift. The price is the long period of dependence, following birth, during which we have to acquire the necessary skills for coping with the human, social, physical realities which we encounter. This period of dependence involves caretakers, parents and supplementary parents, who protect, guide, and teach the developing human being; they gradually aid in the development of independence and adult status in the community and society.

The term parenting, as it is understood generally and, especially in Western society, involves some major functions and activities on the part of adults, which aid and facilitate children's biological survival and development, their acquisition of the appropriate social skills and the achievement of a capacity for trust in others and psychological well being. However, the term parenting may be somewhat ethnocentric and representative of a limited view, reflecting Western society. For example, some anthropologists note that caretaking by nonparents is quite widespread throughout the world: "What cross-cultural evidence we can find indicates that nonparental caretaking is either the norm or a significant form of caretaking in most societies" (Weisner and Gallimore, 1977, p. 169).

In a similar vein, Werner (1979) points out that:

> ...we do know that in traditional families the responsibilities for child care are shared among members of a

homogeneous family group.   Although the child may have
a number of caretakers, they will all have a common set
of socialization goals and a common set of practices in
relation to childrearing (p. 171).

In the context of this chapter we shall, nevertheless, regard parenting as
we know it best in the setting of the Western family in which the
biological parents are the major caretakers, especially during infancy, and
consider care by others as supplementary.

Obviously, the most important aspect of early parental care is that
of physical care which assures physical survival of the young organism and
provides optimal conditions for its development.   Closely tied with this
process is the acquisition of trust and attachment to the caring figures
which are of utmost importance to the psychological development of the
infant.   These are at the basis of the most fundamental aspects of
personality development to which we shall return.

Of no lesser importance is the process of socialization in which
natural parents as well as supplementary parents are so intimately
involved.   "Socialization", according to Baumrind (1977), "is an adult-
initiated process by which developing children, through insight, training
and imitation, acquire the habits and values congruent with their adaptation to their culture" (p. 640).   Stated somewhat differently by Handel
(Anthony and Benedek, 1970):

> From a sociological point of view, the principal task of
> the parents is to prepare their children to become adult
> members of society.   This involves various kinds of care,
> the inculcation of values and norms, training in specific
> kinds of behavior, provision of models of adult roles upon
> which the child can draw informing his concept of himself
> and his place in society, and the fostering of appropriate
> self-regard--all of which are summed up in the concept of
> socialization (p. 95).

We can clearly see that this aspect of parenting is a rather complex
set of activities, behaviors, and relationships which are also at the root of
personality formation.   The term parenting is perhaps a bit too narrow to
describe the complexities involved.   What we must consider is not only a
series of operations and activities performed by parents which affect
children modify their behavior and attitudes, and mould them into
"civilized" people capable of living in the society of other people, but we
should also consider as parenting the innumerable interactions between
parent and child, which are not exclusively instrumental, from the very
beginning of the postpartum period through the years of childhood and
adolescence.

Parental interaction with children is not a one-way street which the
term parenting seems to imply.   We are increasingly aware of the child's

contribution in this relationship. The attention of theoreticians and investigators to the child's contributions to the parent-child relationship was directed some time ago (Bell, 1968). In discussing the parents' repertoires in the areas of "social response" Bell points out that:

> Reasonable bases exist for assuming that there are congenital contributors to child behaviors which (a) activate these repertoires (b) affect the level of response within hierarchies, and (c) differentially reinforce parent behavior which has been evoked (p. 93).

Much of the work on temperament and child development published in recent years is consonant with the viewpoint just referred to. Particularly the work by Thomas, Chess, and Birch (1968) on temperament and behavior disorders in children highlights the vicissitudes of the clashes and interactions between children's temperament and parental socialization demands and expectations. In their followup study in which "problem" children were identified, some interesting issues regarding parent-child relationships were raised. It is not solely the childrearing practices of the parent(s) that produce psychopathology in their offspring. Neither is a particular temperament characteristic, or set of such characteristics in the child the prime causative factor of psychopathology. However, the inadequacy of the "fit" between a child's temperamental pattern on the one hand, and the socialization demands and expectancies of the parents on the other, precipitate problem behavior. The friction, the clashes, the incompatibilities are the culprints in the formation of psychopathology.

At this juncture, it may be noted, parenthetically, that supplementary parenting holds considerable potential for the mitigating of the conflicts engendered between children and their natural parents. It is possible that the "supplementary" parent may have greater tolerance for, or provide a better "fit" with, some of the "odious" temperamental characteristics so unacceptable and rejected by the natural parent.

I do not wish to imply, by any means, that parental figures are the only significant ones in the formation of the independent adult personality. As children grow and develop, they come under the influence of an increasingly wider circle of figures and "actors" in the environment. However, I shall attempt to make the distinction between any kind of interpersonal interactions and that more strictly defined as *parenting*. As indicated above, the parenting function is that of protecting and socializing or teaching and transmitting cultural values. Some informal social contacts may have an impact in these areas, but are not intended, planned or consciously directed. Yet a good deal of informal parenting goes on in most societies outside the parent-child interaction. Older siblings and other relatives, especially in the extended family, fulfill some such functions. Caretakers, babysitters, albeit transitory in their function, participate in the process. However, in some settings, different patterns of supplementary parenting are planned and formalized. Some societies have considered supplementary parenting outside the family context-- broadly defined; while others are rather limited in this aspect.

The "sociological" aspect of parenting involves or impinges at "that point of the infant's development at which the explicit imposition of 'discipline' begins." However, the concerns of Mahler and her associates (1975) with the early infantile experience in the typical dyadic relationship with a mother or her surrogate which is viewed as "reverberating" throughout the life cycle of the individual is not of concern in the sociological orientation. Thus, in considering parenthood and parenting we end up with a bi-polar set of concerns--the social and cultural-adaptive issues on the one hand, and the intra-psychic, self-concept experiential one on the other. The former stems from the sociological orientation while the latter has its origins in psychodynamic theory and psychoanalysis.

From the foregoing, one gains the impression that what we may call "supplementary parenting" may depend upon the society and culture with which we are concerned. In the more traditional societies studied, "multiple mothering" seems to be the rule and thus the exclusiveness of the parental role is not as salient as is the case in most Western societies where the parental role and biological parenthood are one and the same. A rather antagonostic attitude to "multiple mothering," i.e., supplementary parenting emerged in our society where the exclusiveness of mother-child relationship, especially in the early years has been stressed. With the accumulation of additional knowledge and research data, this attitude has moderated considerably. Thus, in a review of "nonmaternal care of children" Etaugh (1980) concludes that "The available data indicates that high quality nonmaternal care does not appear to have adverse effects on the young child's maternal attachment, intellectual development, or social-emotional behavior....books and magazine articles appearing during the last 20 years have tended to present a more negative view of nonmaternal care. Between the 1960's and 1970's, however, a shift has occurred....more favorable" (p. 309).

Important social changes have taken place in the last decade or so in American society. The activities of the women's liberation movement, increased participation of women in the work force, single-parent families, etc., have increased the use of supplemental parenting. Also, of no small consequence have been the results of different cross-cultural studies in which the effects of different patterns of supplementary parenting have been investigated. One source of information regarding the possible long-term effects of a certain pattern or variant of family and social structure that involves supplementary parenting as well, is the setting of the Israeli kibbutz. A fairly detailed exposition of this setting appears in the following pages.

THE KIBBUTZ

The institution of the Israeli kibbutz is not a static phenomenon. During the more than six decades of its existence it has undergone numerous changes in structure, ideology and, of course, in its childrearing system (Beit-Hallahmi and Rabin, 1977). When one discusses phenomena related to this system, attention to the historical perspective is mandatory. Specifically, it is important to know which period during the last 60 years is being covered in the description of conditions and circumstances of childrearing in the kibbutz. This is closely related to the extent of parental participation in the nurturance and socialization processes of the growing child.

Although the term and meaning of the word kibbutz is generally widely known and understood, my personal experience has taught me that this knowledge is not universal. It is for this reason that I shall devote a few paragraphs to a brief description and definition of the term kibbutz. I shall then procede to greater detail with respect to the childrearing and educational system, and the aspects of supplementary parenting involved.

The kibbutz is essentially a voluntary organization--a village built on communnal economic and social principles. All of the wealth, real estate, means of production and capital are owned in common by all members of the kibbutz. Needs of each member, food, shelter, etc. are taken care of by the community to the best of its economic ability. All members are treated equally. There is no formal differential reward system; there are no salaries. Everybody receives according to his or her needs and, at the same time, is expected to give his or her best efforts in achieving the economic and social aims of the community. All major decisions are made by the exercise of "direct democracy"--by the entire adult membership of the kibbutz. Such decisions as to responsibilities for major parts of the economy, education, security, etc. are made at the weekly "town meeting," and tasks are delegated to specifically elected members of the community. Committees and individual job holders are appointed for specific time periods, providing for rotation of responsibilities. Patterns of economic production and consumption as well as social regulation, including childrearing and education are community decisions, arrived at democratically.

Not only does the economic structure of this society represent innovation and deviation from the commonly adopted system in Western society, but the social fabric, the structure of the family the cell of that fabric, is also modified and different. Generally, the kibbutz family does not meet most of the major criteria assigned to it by sociologists. In the usual Western societies, the family is viewed as an economic unit. This is not true in the kibbutz where the entire community is the economic unit; persons, married or unmarried, participate in, or are part of, the overall economic endeavor *as individuals.* In the kibbutz, the family's educational function, the socialization of the child, is largely relinquished by the biological parents and is in the hands of the community as a whole and its representatives. It is in this connection that the "supplementary parenting" issue is very salient and will be discussed in greater detail in the subsequent pages of this chapter.

Only the third major function (in addition to economic and socialization of the new generation) of the family stressed by sociologists remains characteristic even in the kibbutz. The sexual-reproductive function, the exclusiveness of the heterosexual affectional relationship is still characteristic of the kibbutz family. It may be remarked parenthetically that, despite the relinquishment of the economic and much of the childrearing functions, the kibbutz family is at least as stable as families in the larger Israeli society, or in Western society in general.

It can be stated that, until the middle 1960's, the couples of the vast majority of the 240 Israeli kibbutzim lived apart from their children. I have described the situation in another context (Rabin, 1965) as follows:

> Married couples live in individual living units consisting sometimes of a single room with no indoor toilet facilities; this may be the case in younger, less affluent kibbutzim. In the older, well established kibbutzim, the living quarters often consist of small apartments of one or two rooms, with private toilet, porch, etc. Kitchens are not included in the design of these living units, for the central dining room serves all the major meals of the day. However, most couples have a hot plate on which they prepare 'four o'clock tea' (or coffee) or late evening snacks (p. 8).

Although some of the conditions described above have changed for the better (all have indoor toilets, more cooking facilities, refrigerators, etc.), the basic space remains the same and does not include rooms for anyone (children) beyond the couple itself.

The question arises--where are the children of all these families? The answer is: the children reside in the various children's houses in the kibbutz. It is this fact that makes the kibbutz childrearing system unique and involves a division of labor as far as the parenting functions are concerned. However, as was implied above, the separate residence of parents and children is no longer a universal phenomenon in today's kibbutzim. In about one half of the kibbutzim of the nineteen-seventies, the children reside with their parents (Beit-Hallahmi and Rabin, 1977). Discussion in this chapter, however, will center primarily on the traditional or "classical" kibbutz conditions which involve early separation of children from their biological parents and residence in the children's houses, away from the parental home.

What I shall attempt in the following pages is a brief description of the classical" kibbutz childrearing system. I shall then comment on the relative importance of the biological parents and other parenting agents in the rearing process. Special attention to the major aspects of parenting--nurturance and socialization--will be given. Finally, I shall attempt an examination of the results or outcome of kibbutz childrearing: --its effects on child development and upon the adult personality; also, how and in what ways (if at all) does the childrearing experience with a higher degree of participation of non-biological parents in the parenting process make the person different from his peers who have been reared under conditions of family relations typical of the Western nuclear family. Some consideration of the implications of the findings in this area will also be presented.

CHILDREARING: INFANCY TO ADOLESCENCE

When the kibbutz baby is a few days old, it leaves the maternity ward in the regional hospital and comes "home" to the kibbutz, accompanied by the mother. Mother resumes her residence in her own quarters which she shares with her husband, while the infant is placed in a sort of creche--the "infant house." Thereafter, the child lives, with few interruptions, in the company of his peers almost continuously until he graduates from high school at the age of eighteen. The 1960's and 1970's brought some changes, however.

The situation described in the preceding paragraph is, in fact, no longer true even in the kibbutzim that maintain the "classical" childrearing system. Even in these settings, mother may keep the baby with her (in her apartment) for a short period of time (a week or two) before placing it in the infant house where the regimen of "collective sleeping arrangements" is instituted. In the kibbutzim that have abandoned this sort of arrangement, or where it never existed, there are the "family sleeping arrangements" where the child sleeps in the parents' apartment from infancy until adolescence. With exception of this caveat, the description of the arrangements for the children that follows still holds true at the time of this writing.

The infant house consists of several rooms and the necessary services. About four to five infants are placed in individual cribs in each of the rooms. The infants are usually within a few weeks of the same age. Each infant has toys in the crib and is exposed to considerable visual, tactile, kinesthetic and auditory stimulation provided by a variety of environmental inanimate objects and by the caretakers as well as by the age mates in the adjacent cribs. The infant resides in the house for about 15 months or so. At the end of that period, the infant is transferred to the toddler house.

Although the mother is free to come and go, to feed the infant periodically, to play, bathe, fondle and, generally, do much of the "mothering," especially during the first couple of months, the general physical care and supervision of the four or five infants is in the hands of a *metapelet*--the nurse--caretaker. The metapelet, usually a mature woman with some special training for the job including her own experience as a mother, is in many respects a "co-mother" of the children in her care. She feeds them, keeps them clean, comforts them when they cry and generally serves as a mother substitute during most hours of the day. At night, there is a watchperson who supervises the children's houses and is available to comfort the crying or restless infants. In the instances when the child continues to cry incessantly or in emergencies and sickness, the mother is contacted and provides individual care for the duration of the special conditions.

Thus, from the very beginning in the life of the child, parenting (i.e., mothering) is a function performed by, at least, two figures--the biological mother and the metapelet. Both provide care and nurturance of the young infant. In terms of sheer time, the infant is more in contact with the metapelet than with the biological mother. However, the relationship of the latter is more personal and specific (Rabin, 1965) when compared with that of the metapelet whose treatment of the several children in her care is somewhat more impersonal and "objective."

Compared with earlier years in the history of the kibbutz movement, the mother in recent years has been much more involved in the care of her offspring during the first nine months of life. Mothers are usually on "maternity leave" for about six weeks following the birth of the child and do not return to fulltime work until the infant is about four months of age. During those first four months the kibbutz mother spends a great deal of time in the infant house--feeding the baby, bathing it, and playing with it. Gradually the metapelet takes over these functions since mother is available for shorter periods of time during working hours and during the baby's daily visit to the parental apartment where considerable interaction with father and biological siblings takes place. These daily visits for about two hours in the afternoon, after working hours, and for longer periods on the sabbath, become the major opportunities for interaction with the biological family during the rest of the life of the child in the classical kibbutz childrearing system.

The other aspect of parenting--that of socialization of the child--is more heavily in the hands of the metapelet, especially during the early years of development. To quote kibbutz educators Katz and Lewin (Rabin and Hazan, 1973):

> Teaching the child to master infantile urges--the habit training so vital to his development--is a function carried out mainly by educators in the children's house. Because these educators are able to maintain objective and professional attitudes, fewer problems are encountered than is generally the case when childrearing takes

place in the conventional family setting and parents have
the fulltime responsibility (p. 11-12).

Whether we agree with the values expressed in the latter part of the
quotation or not, the fact is that the "educators," first the metapelet and
later other figures in the system, are charged with the bulk of "habit
training" and socialization. This process will become clearer when we
begin to describe the toddler of whom society begins to demand much
more than from the young infant during the first year of life.

We are now ready to continue with the next phase in the child's
development--after reaching age 12 to 15 months. By this time,
locomotion and some speech have been achieved. The entire group of
infants is usually transferred to a different building which is more
appropriately equipped to meet the new needs of the children. The
"toddler house" is equipped with large playrooms, that can accommodate
several children at a time, with ample floor space to "facilitate the child's
discovery of the wide world." The toddler house usually has an attached
enclosed playground with sandboxes and the usual "jungle gym" equipment
to allow considerable freedom for the expression of increasing needs for
motility. Children remain in the toddler house for about three years until
they are transferred to the kindergarten.

During this period (years 1½ to 4), the importance of the metapelet,
both in caring and especially in the socialization of the child is undeni-
able. Her supplementary parenting function reaches its peak in the
childrearing process. "The metapelet is available to the child when he
cries or is restless; she comforts him and plays with him in the absence of
the mother. She does this increasingly as the infant gets older and the
time of contact between mother and child decreases" (Rabin, 1965, p. 13).

It is in the area of socialization, however, that the metapelet's
involvement is paramount.

> Training in self-feeding and eating habits, toilet training
> and other habits of cleanliness are directly handled by the
> metapelet. She helps the child learn how to dress and
> undress and get ready for bed. She supervises the play of
> the children...the metapelet aids in transition from the
> individual, spontaneous play to more organized and co-
> operative types of activity... (Rabin, 1965, p. 15).

The metapelet takes the children for short walks, teaches them songs,
leads them in exercise and rhythmic games, and so on.

The fact that the metapelet is such a dominant figure in the life of
the toddlers does not mean that she is the exclusive socializing agent in
their lives. The parents also play a significant role. As the child gets
older the time spent with parents and siblings during their free hours, in

the afternoons and on the Sabbath (Saturday), also increases. The toddlers may spend about two or three hours daily in their parents' company. They are taken for walks, taught games and various skills, and manners as well, especially when they take light meals together. Parents also supplement the training self-feeding, toilet training, and reinforce control of aggression to which the children are exposed in the toddler house. There is, essentially, a coordination with, and reinforcement of, the guidance of the metapelet. Since they have similar aims, they do not ordinarily function at cross purposes. However, in terms of the amount of time involved (hours of the day), parental socialization of the child is secondary to that of the metapelet during those crucial years prior to entrance into the kindergarten.

Still another socializing influence upon the toddler must be mentioned in this context. I refer here to the peer group--the constant observers who represent a constant presence in the life of the kibbutz child. Fagin (1958) reported detailed observations of several groups of kibbutz toddlers aged 19 to 38 months. Following a description of an amicable settlement of a conflict between several children in the group, Fagin comments:

> The children from a very early age have thus taken over the values of the culture in which they are being reared and use these actively in setting standards for each other's behavior. Not only are these social controls used but they carry weight in controlling behavior of the children. So the group operates as a socializing agent upon its members from a very young age (p. 123).

She further concludes that the results of the study indicate:

> ...that group identification, sharing, and group control of individual behavior can be learned by very young children under conditions of group living (p. 123).

This study, as well as other systematic and unsystematic observation, certainly support the notion of the peer group as a socializing agent even at the tender age of two to four years. The group, and the children within it, transmit the values and expectations presented by the metapelet and the parents who, in turn, are bent on perpetuating the values of their community and culture. In addition, it should be pointed out that the group not only exercises control and "socializes" its members, but it also contributes to their nurturance and gives them security, support and affection. This is not to deny that intra-group aggression exists, but according to Fagin (1958) it correlates with the overall expression of affection within the group.

Another central figure, with supplementary parenting functions, is introduced into the life of the kibbutz youngster upon being transferred to the kindergarten at age three to four years.   The kindergarten group, consisting of 15 to 18 children, results from combining three to four groups which have "graduated" from the toddler house.   The children remain in the kindergarten for three years, with the same teacher and the same metapelet.   The metapelet continues with her housekeeping, care-taking and habit-training functions.   However, the new figure of cardinal importance is the kindergarten teacher.   Overall, according to Roth (Rabin and Hazan, 1973), the kindergarten teacher "is responsible for the general program, for enriching the content of the children's life, and for their many-faceted development."   The kindergarten staff, consisting of the teacher and metapelet, see their function beyond the maintenance of a secure and stable atmosphere for the child.   In Roth's words,

> ...the functions of the kindergarten staff assume addi-
> tional dimensions: the children see them as a source of
> information and knowledge, they turn to them for help
> with group difficulties and social rules, and they see in
> them an example of moral and well-manner behavior.   The
> staff is a bridge between the adult world and the kinder-
> garten group, and in the eyes of the children represent
> society and its values (p. 42).

Thus, particularly the kindergarten teacher seems to be concerned with the cognitive development of the children, with their enculturation as well as with their socialization, and serves as an identification model for them during the rather crucial period of their development.   It may be speculated that much of the "modeling" behavior that takes place in the conventional family in relation to the parental figures more often involves the teacher in the kibbutz kindergarten situation.   It can be said that her serving as an example and as a representative of the adult world is an aspect of parenting which ordinarily is the more exclusive domain of the biological parents in the nuclear family.   This situation, of course, contributes to the greater diffusion of identification noted in kibbutz children (Rabin, 1965).   Although kibbutz children continue with their daily contacts with their parents, the emotional ties are not so intensive and the identification with them is not as exclusive as in the nuclear family setting.   Also, the moral teaching on the part of the kindergarten staff is ordinarily an important part of conventional parenting.   It may be remarked parenthetically that some of the teachings are unique for children in the kibbutz setting.   The reference here is to the importance of cooperation and rules that must be observed to facilitate continuous group living in the kibbutz setting.

In conventional nonkibbutz society, the beginning of formal school-ing very often introduces a new experience in the life of the child as far as relationships with adults are concerned.   Teachers, viewed by the children as persons of knowledge and authority, become important figures in their lives for several hours a day.   Although teachers, in the ordinary school, may offer little nurturance to the pupils, they become extensions of the parents in the process of socialization. Not only do they introduce the children to the numerous rules and regulations that govern civilized society, but they also serve as models for imitation and identification. Increasingly, Western society has been relying on the school system and its influence as a socializer and a purveyor of the cultural values for the younger generation. Thus, to a considerable extent the teachers have taken over a good many of the moral and cultural transmission functions of the parents of yore.

In the kibbutz primary school, the teachers continue to exercise the influence similar to that of the kindergarten teacher. Each grade (from 1 through 6) is a little society by itself. Residences and classrooms are in the same building which is occupied exclusively by the children of the grade, presided over by a metapelet and a teacher. By the time the children have reached school age, the significance of the metapelet is reduced considerably and she recedes into the background. Her nurturance functions no longer are focal (except in some particular cases) and her work concentrates more on the supervision and housekeeping involved in the group's house.

On the other hand, the significance of the teacher in the grade school setting as a supplementary parent continues at a fairly high level. The teacher not only imparts knowledge or the relevant skills required by the educational system, but also serves as a guide and counselor to the children, individually and as a group. Lea Alterman, a veteran teacher in the kibbutz movement describes the teacher in relation to the group (grade class) as follows:

> The child treasures his group, as does the educator. The children are deeply concerned about the prestige of their group, and they preserve its unity at all cost. Herein lies a powerful educational force, which the teacher must respect and know how to channel. He respects their independence, stimulates them to initiative, and at the same time preserves his own leadership. Based on his knowledge, experience and personality, the children regard him as an authority. To them, he represents the society in which their parents live and with which they identify.... His authority is not assumed merely because of his status as teacher, it is something he must build up through his personality, behavior, and attitudes (Rabin and Hazan, 1973, p. 89).

At the beginning of the material just quoted, reference is made to the group--the same group that continues together from kindergarten through the 12th grade to maturity. An important function of the teacher-counselor is to minimize the friction between individuals and the group--to have the group a smoothly living and developing unit. A good deal of the guidance given by the teacher-counselor has to do with group cohesion and satisfaction of the individuals within it. Here, identification with group objectives, concern with "group prestige" highlight the group's importance as a socializer and a creator of what was dubbed as the "group superego" (Bettelheim, 1969). I have elsewhere (Rabin, 1965) summarized this issue succinctly by stating that "kibbutz education quite consciously builds upon the authority of the teacher and upon the social authority of the peer group" (p. 23).

As is the case in the kindergarten period, contacts with the biological parents continue, approximately to the same extent. Since the decision whether or not to go to the parents' apartment during the afternoon hours is increasingly that of the child, the amount of contact may vary from one family to another. The freedom exercised by primary school youngsters as they get older increases, and the amount of time they spend with the family varies accordingly. Their involvement with group activities increases and, as many parents complain--especially during the secondary school years--"we hardly see them." Thus, immediate direct contacts and parenting is reduced to a minimum at the beginning of the "teens."

During the primary school years and, especially when the child is in the secondary school, parents attempt to direct their academic activities, choice of subjects, etc. However, the dominant influences in this respect are the teacher-counselors and the peers.

As the child grows older, his contacts with other adults in the kibbutz increase. For example, he may have quite a few contacts with the adult supervisor of the children's farm. Or, as adolescents who are increasingly involved in the work force of the kibbutz (up to four hours a day), they interact with many adult members in the work settings. However, the influences of the adults at this stage are ordinarily not so significant in personality formation, but may be important in vocational choice and the acquisition of work habits.

SUMMARY OF PATTERN OF SUPPLEMENTARY PARENTING

In the table that follows (Table 1), I attempted to summarize schematically the relative importance of different figures in the life of the kibbutz child. The importance is based on the extent of supplementary parenting exercised through the developmental period--from infancy through adolescence. The table summarizes involvements of the biological parents and supplementary parenting persons at focal chronological stages of development. These correspond to the material discussed in the preceding pages.

TABLE 1

Relative Involvement of Different
Agents in the Care and Socialization of the Kibbutz Child

	Infancy (0 - 2)	Preschool (3 - 5)	School (6 - 11)	Adolescence (13 - 18)
Mother	High	Medium	Medium	Low
Father	Medium	Medium	Medium	Low
Metapelet	High	High	Medium	Low
Teacher	----	Medium	High	High
Peer Group	Medium	High	High	High
Work Group	----	----	----	Medium

The first period covers the first one or two and an half years of life--infancy and "toddlerhood." This, of course, is a very important period in the child's development; according to some, the most important period in basic personality formation. It includes the formation of an individual--separation from the mother and individuation--the "psychological birth" (Mahler et al., 1975) of the child. From our perspective, we noted the infant's great need for nurturance in the earliest stages of development. In earliest infancy (the first few weeks), it is almost exclusively supplied by the biological mother with some support from the metapelet. During the latter part of the first year, the metapelet and the mother share the nurturance function. However, during the second year of life the role of the matapelet in this respect is remarkably enhanced. Especially her socializing function is paramount during those first three years. Considering the total parenting activities, subsumed under the rubrics of nurturance and socialization, it can be said that both mother and metapelet evidence a high level of participation. The contribution of the father to the parenting process is relatively modest during those first three years, but is most likely greater than that noted in the ordinary Western family. Finally, another source of parenting activity, even this early in the child's life, is the peer group. As we noted earlier, the group supplies support (nurturance) even to the two-year-old as well as sanctions (socialization) of nonforming behavior and interpersonal aggression. Thus, in sum, during this earliest period of the child's development in the kibbutz, the main supplementary parenting agent is the metapelet and, secondarily, the peer group.

During the preschool years (3 to 5) which are spent in the kindergarten, the metapelet and the peer group appear as the most salient agents in providing care and nurturance, exercising control and the teaching of social behavior and morality. The kindergarten teacher gains an important position as one involved in supplementary parenting, but not as potent as that of the other two agents mentioned. The salience of mother is reduced, but both parents' influence remains undiminished. Thus, upon perusal of the table, we note that in the kibbutz system the extent of supplementary parenting in the preschool years remains at a high level with the metapelet retaining her pivotal position.

During the school years, with the reduction of the children's dependency needs and needs for nurturance, the centrality of the metapelet is reduced and the teacher as guide and counselor becomes a central figure. He or she becomes the central authority in the life of the kibbutz child, closely meshed with the all powerful peer group. The teacher may open up new horizons and the group provides the framework for their exploration. Both, control and guidance, sanctions and ideals are provided by these two agents. They represent the "collective superego" which vies strongly with the personal superego--the heir of the parents.

The last column of the table which covers the period of adolescence reports on some of the dominant socializing agents in the life of the kibbutz youngster on the threshold of adulthood. The term supplementary parenting may not be quite appropriate when considering this period, for even in the conventional family it is a period fraught with rebellion and ambivalence. Yet, even if this characterization holds, the socializing influences of the parents, albeit temporarily rejected, are quite recognizable and the parental effort in this direction is not inconsiderable. In the kibbutz setting, however, the youngsters' lives are centered in the organized "youth society" which is geographically, but more important, socially and psychologically, distanced from the family (parental) apartment and milieu. Little time is spent with the parents and their direct "parenting" is negligible. Here, the teacher-youth leader and the peers exert maximal influence and are responsible for the formation of the "Weltanschauung"--the ideology of the adolescent. Additionally, the workgroup which the kibbutz adolescent joins as his fulfillment of his work obligations in the secondary school becomes an important reference group. In this context, he meets adult members of the community who often serve as identification models; he learns the value of work and work habits and attains a good deal of insight about himself, his abilities and capacities. This knowledge becomes integrated in the self-identity and in his self-esteem. In a sense, this, too, is a parenting function, as especially in the old-fashioned farming families where the parents were the co-workers, the children-apprentices and the family economic unit--the stage upon which the adolescent proved himself on the way to adulthood.

Before closing the present section, it may be well to comment on a recent development in the kibbutzim that goes counter to the pattern discerned in Western society for the past several decades. Although the extended family has become a vanishing phenomenon in the various developed and developing countries, its revival and rejuvenation has become quite apparent in kibbutz society during the past decade or two. Many kibbutzim have provided homes for the old parents of the aging founders of the settlements. Thus, the founders, their parents, their own children and children's children frequently form multigenerational units within the kibbutzim. However, the parenting functions of the great grandparents or the grandparents in the childrearing process of the youngest generation is minimal, if at all, of any consequence.

STABILITY, CONTINUITY, AND CONSISTENCY

In the preceding pages, we have surveyed briefly the parenting activities and influences of various agents, in addition to the biological parents, in the kibbutz childrearing system. Most of these supplementary functions are not accidental, as they occur in other cultural settings, but are deliberately and consciously planned, albeit often modified, by the membership of the collective society in which they take place. In this connection, two important principles must be stressed for they characterize this system.

First, there is a great deal of consistency in the attitudes of the various parenting agents vis a vis the child. They all represent the ideology which is at the root of the foundation of their society and a prerequisite for its perpetuation.

Secondly, and this point is especially important in early infancy and childhood, although the situation may be described as that of "multiple mothering," there is a consistency and continuity during the earliest period of childrearing. The *same* biological mother continues her care over time; similarly, the *same* metapelet functions as the "co-mother" during the first year and a half or two. There is no shifting of personnel from day to day as is the situation in most residential homes. Thus, the stability and continuity are important factors in the outcome findings of kibbutz childrearing, to be discussed in the subsequent pages.

Not only is there a sense of continuity and stability in the early years of childrearing experience, but also a simultaneous consistency in the total social system itself. This aspect is especially important in the later development of the kibbutz child during the primary and secondary school years. Whereas these are rather difficult years for the child in the larger society in which he or she may contend with many conflicting attitudes and forces, the kibbutz child faces a much more consistent and stable milieu with minimal conflicting attitudes and values. The different socializing agents, the different supplementary parenting figures belong to the same voluntary collective society and social system at the basis of which is a fundamentally common ideology.

SOME RESEARCH FINDINGS--KIBBUTZ CHILDREN AND ADULTS

Over the years, the kibbutz form of life generally and its child-rearing system in particular, have been the focus of a good deal of clinical and research interest. Social scientists as well as psychiatrists, psychologists and other mental health workers, based in Western society, have been interested in the outcome or the product of a childrearing system that departs rather markedly from the one with which they were most familiar. The lack of exclusiveness in the earliest mother-child relationship has prompted some investigators to raise the issue of "maternal deprivation" (Bowlby, 1951) and has promoted speculation about similarities between the kibbutz and the residential institution. Other investigators were concerned with a wide variety of differences between the kibbutz and the conventional childrearing system, during childhood and adolescence, beyond the early infantile period.

Two types of investigations were published over the years. First were the detailed anthropological observational reports which were primarily concerned with descriptive accounts of kibbutz-reared children and adults. In this category fall some clinical descriptive and observational reports as well. Second is a series of systematic studies that have been comparing kibbutz-reared children and adults with comparable Israeli age-groups of persons reared in the conventional nuclear family setting, whether in cities or rural areas.

Spiro's *Children of the Kibbutz* (1958) is the most comprehensive description of the kibbutz childrearing system and a most detailed observational study of the "Sabras" (Israeli reared). Introversion, hostility, insecurity, and inferiority feelings were discerned as characterizing the kibbutz childrearing product. Bettelheim (1969), on the other hand, stresses the development of the "collective superego" (showing the decisive influences of group socialization) and the difficulties of the kibbutz reared child in achieving interpersonal intimacy or forming intimate relationships.

Looking at the more nomothetic comparative studies of kibbutz children and adults, a number of interesting results come to the fore. In one study, also completed in the 1950's, results indicate that kibbutz infants develop at a slower tempo than their nonkibbutz agemates; however, this delay in development is apparently temporary and is more than compensated for in childhood and adolescence (Rabin, 1965). The author reasoned that:

> Compared with the child born in the ordinary family setting, the kibbutz infant is immediately faced with a more difficult task, that of sorting out stimuli from, and coordinating responses to, more than one maternal figure. These frustrating demands...result in a slower tempo in intellectual growth and ego development (p. 208).

The results of a later study with similar populations do not agree with these findings (Kohen-Raz, 1968). Perhaps changes in the infant care system in the 10-year interim period are responsible for the discrepancy.

Some of the findings on older kibbutz children (Rabin, 1965), when compared with same age youngsters who were family reared, follow. The ego development and social maturity of the kibbutz child equals that or, to some extent, surpasses that of his peers in the ordinary family setting. Drive control, especially in the area of sexuality, is greater among kibbutz adolescents, although it becomes markedly reduced upon reaching young adulthood. From the viewpoint of psychodynamic theory, it is of interest to note that kibbutz children's attachment to the parent of the opposite sex is lower than that of nuclear family-reared children. Identification with the same sex parent is less clear-cut and it is more diffuse, encompassing peers and other adult figures. The identification of the kibbutz child is seen as less intense and less exclusive. A related finding is the development of a superego that is less punitive and less guilt ridden. This latter notion is consistent with the observations of other investigators (Bettelheim, 1969; Spiro, 1958).

Another interesting comparison is in the area of cooperation and competition. Compared with urban children (in an experimental study), kibbutz children behaved more cooperatively than competitively (Shapira and Madsen, 1969). This is also consonant with the higher level of drive control in kibbutz children, noted above. Speculations regarding the possible excessive conformity and greater similarity or uniformity in the personalities of kibbutz children reared under conditions of collective education, have not been supported by research data.

Finally, as far as the overall "adjustment" is concerned, there were no marked differences between the kibbutz and nonkibbutz groups of children studied. Neither is there a significant difference in the kinds of disturbance that occur when such diagnoses are made in some instances (Kaffman, 1965).

Recently, a systematic follow-up study of 146 individuals has been completed (Beit-Hallahmi et al., 1979). These represent nearly 90 percent of the children originally studied in 1955 (Rabin, 1965). They were re-tested and re-interviewed as adults 20 years later. Data on a number of demographic, personality, and sociopsychological variables are reported in the volume, *Twenty years later: Kibbutz children grown up* (in press). Some of the results are briefly summarized in the paragraphs that follow.

When the kibbutz adults are compared with a parallel group born into the conventional family setting and in the context of more conventional socioeconomic structures, very few differences in psychosocial adaptation are discernible. Most members of both groups, twenty years later, continue to reside in the type of community in which they were born and raised, show almost identical rates of marriage, parenthood, and levels of education attained. There are, however, differences in occupational aspirations. The kibbutz members are less specific about personal career ambitions, whereas the nonkibbutz subjects more often identify entrepreneurial and/or professional goals. These correspond to the expectations and demands of their subcultures.

Both groups are similar in their level of self-esteem, but kibbutz people tend to be more critical of themselves as well as of others. They also rate themselves as more anxious and tend to succumb to a greater number of psychosomatic disorders. The subset of 19 kibbutz-born adults who no longer reside in the communal setting does not differ to any extent from the majority that elected to stay in the kibbutz. This subgroup adapted well to the new and larger conventional community setting.

Our brief and, admittedly, incomplete review of the characteristics of kibbutz children and adults indicates that they are well prepared to cope with the demands of their own community as well as with the realities of the larger cultural environment. The particularly designed program of supplementary parenting, especially that of multiple mothering in the early years, does "reverberate" in later development. The effects are those of response styles rather than those of coping and general adaptation.

IMPLICATIONS

A natural question that is readily raised when cross-cultural material is reported involves the issue of the applicability of results to other societies, including our own. Is there a lesson to be learned from the outcome of kibbutz childrearing which is characterized by early multiple mothering and subsequent supplementary parenting?

First, we need to consider the flexibility of the human psyche which we infer from the positive changes that occurred in passing from infancy to later childhood. Stress on this matter has been placed by the Clarkes (1976) and their collaborators.

Second is the issue of multiple mothering. The term "lack of continuity in mothering," often applied when more than one mother figure is involved in childrearing, is not always appropriate, as in the kibbutz situation. There can be stability and continuity with more than one figure involved, as I indicated above.

This brings us directly to the raging controversy regarding the desirability of day care facilities for preschool children. With somewhat more qualifying language than Etaugh's (1980), Rutter (1981), in his recent review of "social-emotional consequences of day care," states that:

> Although day care for very young children is not likely to result in serious emotional disturbances, it would be misleading to conclude that it is without risk effects. Much depends on the quality of the day care...day care arrangements which lack both stability and continuity do appear to suffer an increased risk of emotional and social difficulties (pp. 4-5).

One might add that, as I pointed out at the outset of this chapter, what the child brings with him (Thomas et al, 1968) is an important part of the interaction (Bell, 1968) with parents, surrogates, or supplementary caretakers. Moreover, the constitutional factors should not be overlooked in judging consequences of variations in the childrearing process.

REFERENCES

Anthony, E. J., and Benedek, T. (Eds.) *Parenthood: Its psychology and psychopathology.* Boston: Little, Brown, 1976.

Baumrind, D.   New directions in socialization research.   *American Psychologist,* 1980, 35(7), 339-352.

Beit-Hallahmi, B., and Rabin, A. I.   The kibbutz as a social experiment and as a childrearing laboratory. *American Psychologist,* 1977, *32,* 532-541.

Beit-Hallahmi, B., Nero, B., and Rabin, A. I. Family and communally raised (kibbutz) children twenty years later: Biographical data. *International Journal of Psychology,* 1979, *14,* 215-223.

Bell, R. Q. A reinterpretation of the direction of effects in studies of socialization. *Psychological Review,* 1968, 75, 81-95.

Bettelheim, B. *The children of the dream.* New York: The Macmillan Company, 1969.

Bowlby, J. *Maternal care and mental health.* Geneva: World Health Organization, 1951.

Clarke, A. M., and Clarke, A. D. B. *Early experience-myth and evidence.* New York: The Free Press, 1976.

Etaugh, C. Effects of nonmaternal care on children: Research evidence and popular views. *American Psychologist,* 1980, *35*(4), 309-319.

Fagin, H. Social behavior of young children in the kibbutz. *Journal of Abnormal Social Psychology,* 1958, *56*(1), 117-129.

Kaffman, M. A. A comparison of psychopathology: Israeli children from the kibbutz and from urban surroundings.   *American Journal of Orthopsychiatry,* 1965, *35,* 509-520.

Kohen-Raz, R.   Mental and motor development of kibbutz, institutionalized, and home-reared infants in Israel. *Child Development,* 1968, *39,* 488-504.

Mahler, M. S., Pine, F., and Bergman, A. *The psychological birth of the human infant.* New York: Basic Books, 1975.

Rabin, A. I. *Growing up in the kibbutz.* New York: Springer Publishing Company, 1965.

Rabin, A. I., and Beit-Hallahmi, B. *Twenty years later: Kibbutz children grown up.* New York: Springer, (in press).

Rabin, A. I., and Hazan, B. (Eds.) *Collective education in the kibbutz.* New York: Springer Publishing Company, 1973.

Rutter, M. Social-emotional consequences of day care for preschool children. *American Journal of Orthopsychiatry,* 1981, *51*(1), 4-28.

Shapira, A., and Madsen, M. C. Cooperative and competitive behavior of kibbutz and urban chidlren in Israel. *Child Development,* 1969, *40,* 609-617.

Spiro, M. C. *Children of the kibbutz.* Cambridge, MA: Harvard University Press, 1958.

Thomas, A., Chess, S., and Birch, H. *Temperament and behavior disorders in children.* New York: New York University Press, 1968.

Weisner, T. S., and Gallimore, R. My brother's keeper: Child and sibling caretaking. *Current Anthropology,* 1977, *18*(2), 169-190.

Werner, E. E. *Cross-cultural child development.* Monterey, CA: Brooks/ Cole Publishing Company, 1979.

PARENTING: ALTERNATIVES AND CONTINUITIES

Louise J. Kaplan

New School for Social Research
Seminar College
New York, NY 10011

INTRODUCTION

As we examine the patterns of supplementary parenting described in this volume, we could lose sight of certain biological imperatives that shape the structures of family life and, thus, parent-child relationships. Similarily, our perspective on the significance of these explorations of supplementary parenting might be distorted if we were to ignore the social context that has given rise to them.

The previous chapters are not to be ranked among current broadsides on the nuclear family. Overall, each chapter supports the general theme that "something" basic has shifted in the traditional roles assumed by members of the nuclear family group of mother, father, child. In view of the observable changes in role definition, particularly the role of mother, the contributors have addressed themselves primarily to categorizing, defining and scrutinizing alternatives to the traditional forms of child nurturance and caregiving. These included day care, foster care and care of children through institutional means. A secondary theme of some chapters was the multiple socio-cultural phenomena that influence our present-day inventigations of the problems of child nurturance: population structure, family size, political systems, food production, occupational changes, values and ideologies, household composition, kin proximity, teen parents, divorce, and single parents. Finally, there were descriptions of existing variations in caregiving among varying multicultural groups.

Taking the license granted to a summary essay, I will indulge in one or two abstract issues. The family unit will be defined as a structure that mediates the tensions between biology and culture. As a result, this chapter will deal with some of the elemental meanings of the primary attachment systems: mother and child, mother-child-father, mother and father.   With such an approach, the presumed permanence of contemporary changes in family life and also the consequences of those changes for our conceptions of child nurturance are laid open for question and further examination.

Obviously, my own research on the significance of the primary attachment between infant and mother--the symbiotic and separation-individuation subphases during the first three years of life--weighs heavily in my examination of the sufficiency of any pattern of supplementary parenting. Although I cannot solve the numerous problems of how one might apply separation-individuation theory to evaluating caregiving alternatives, I thought it would be valuable to present a brief outline (Kaplan, 1978) of the emotional import of that process. Moreover, since I also strongly believe that our comprehension of infancy and childhood should play an important part in determining the appropriateness of various forms of child nurturance, I present a partial history of the Western-European discovery of childhood. Here, I raise the question of how we might resolve the tensions between our increased knowledge of the significance of parent-infant interaction and the antagonistic political and social demands currently placed on family life. Finally, I take stock of the contemporary cultural landscape for family life that is virtually barren of those essential generational transactions that enable the kind of trustworthy caregiving that promotes trust and hope in childhood.   In describing these final concerns, I have been influenced by Erikson's (1964) description of the cogwheeling of generations.

AN HISTORICAL PERSPECTIVE

During the last two decades, there has been a transformation in overt attitudes concerning the institution of the family and the individual's role in that institution. Rossi (1977) has described the transformation:

> What was defined as decade ago as "deviant" is today labeled "variant," in order to suggest that there is a healthy, experimental quality to current social explorations into the future "beyond monogamy," or "beyond the nuclear family." Not so long ago, many sociologists were claiming that the nuclear family was neither as fragile nor as isolated as had been claimed but was, in fact, embedded in a viable, if modified, extended kin network. Today, one is more apt to read that the nuclear family will oppress its members unless couples swap spouses and swing, and young adults are urged to rear their children communally or to reject marriage and parenthood altogether (p. 1).

Early twentieth-century sociologists were already agreed that the nuclear family was in a period of distressing decline. Some decreed that the patriarchal family was "...unsatisfactorily adjusted to twentieth-century conditions" (Goodsell, 1915, p. 497). Others were lamenting that the family had been "reduced to a temporary meeting place for board and lodging" (Dealy, 1912, p. 90).

Somewhat later, in the 1930's, the psychologist, John B. Watson, confidently predicted that the family, as it was then known, would be dead in fifty years (Montagu, 1956). Watson's premise for the demise of the family related to the dangers he saw stemming from the passions of family life:

> There is a sensible way of treating children. Treat them as though they were young adults. Dress them, bathe them with care and circumspection. Let your behavior always be objective and kindly firm. Never hug and kiss them, never let them sit in your lap. If you must, kiss them once on the forehead when they say good night. Shake hands with them in the morning. Give them a pat on the head if they have made an extraordinarily good job of a difficult task. Try it out....you will be utterly ashamed of the mawkish sentimental way you have been handling it... (p. 70).

Watson warned parents to expose children to corrective learning principles, thereby eradicating improper passions. Watson's thinking continued to be a major influence on how the family was perceived as the century progressed. The passions between parent and child and husband and wife were increasingly cited as the primary source of individual psychic strain and the principle enemy of social, economic, and personal progress. David Cooper's (1970) *The Death of the Family* stands as the most recent work supporting the view that it is the passions of the nuclear family that perpetuated individual pathology.

In response to these concerns, social experiments with the family-- that is, attempts to buttress particular political and religious systems through the manipulation of parent-child, husband-wife relationships--are legion. Indeed it has become a convention of social experimentation to associate the weakening of family ties with ideologies of social progress. For example: The Israeli experiment with communal child rearing was designed to dissolve family loyalties and promote the child's allegiance to the group. Inevitably, beneath the overt attitudes of compliance with such experimentation, there seems to exist a resistance to the dissolution of family attachment networks. An outgrowth of the kubbitz experience has been heightened peer attachment. However, there has been a failure to eradicate maternal possessiveness or the child's persistence in regarding the mother as the most salient attachment figure despite the number of hours and years spent in the care of a metapalet (Kagan, 1977).

This resistance was also apparent in the 1920's Soviet experiment which endorsed sexual permissiveness and serial monogamy. The experiment had been calculated to insure the child's allegiance to the state by eliminating possessive mother love and exclusive love between husband and wife. By 1936, the rampant vagrancy, delinquency, and crime rates among the youth ushered in an equally despotic counter-compaign to outlaw common-law marriages, bigamy, promiscuity and adultery (Fuchs, 1972, p. 190).

Similarly, in rural Chinese communities today, where the government has been unable to exert effective regulation over its 600,000,000 peasants, officially prohibited extended family arrangements, marriage by purchase, and kinship and village loyalties persist after nearly 30 years of communist control (New York Times, December 19, 1977).

A more dramatic and complex instance of the endurance of familial leitmotivs is provided by the ease with which the thunderous, fearsome, authoritarian Japanese father was transformed into the passive, shadowy, father figure of today's so-called "fatherless Japanese society." This was brought about by the advent of Westernization and Democratization. Investigations of this surprising conversion have led Japanese social scientists to conjecture that the maternal Taoism which lay beneath the surface orthodoxy of paternal Confucianism may have all along been the more influential family force, that, in fact, the Japanese mind had always been "maternally dominated." As the anthropologist Hiroshi Wagatsuma (1977) hypothesized,

> In short, what have changed are the cultural norms rather
> than the psychological characteristics of the Japanese
> fathers. In their personalities, I am inclined to see more
> continuity than change (p. 205).

Personal ideologies have been as ineffectual as the socially enforced in permanently eradicating monogamous bonding and close mother-child attachments.

> Of the many hundreds of experiments in communal living
> begun in the United States, only nine have lasted more
> than one generation...(Fuchs, 1972, p. 168).

Of these nine, eight have viewed sexual relationships as evil; in general, they were strictly celibate, permitting intercourse only insofar as it was absolutely necessary for the perpetuation of the species. In the single exception, the Oenida community, celibacy as well as monogamy were considered sinful. Group marriages and free sexual access of any consenting member to any other was the enforced rule. Under the charismatic leadership of John Humphrey Noyes, the Oenida experiment flourished. Fifty-eight children were born; nine fathered by Noyes. When Noyes died, the eldest children were 15 and 16. Though these young people did not appear to be emotionally scarred by the collective family system that absolutely and rigorously discouraged intense, close mother-child ties and long-term pair bonding between the sexes, the second generation did not choose to raise their own children in the collective method. Furthermore, many young people had to be publically ostracised for having formed "exclusive and idolatrous attachments" (Fuchs, 1972, p. 175).

A 1971 study of middle-class counter-culture alternatives in child rearing compared multiple mothering in communal families, single mothers who raise their children alone, unmarried couples who often live separately but raise their children together, and counter-culture two-parent nuclear families (Eiduson, Cohen and Alexander, 1973). None of these family styles were chosen out of consideration for parenting or child rearing. Initially, choices were made on the basis of desire for personal self-fulfillment and self-actualization. The major finding of the study was that there were virtually no differences in attitudes toward child rearing. Child-rearing behaviors prevalent across these family alternatives included: emphasis on breast feeding, intense mother-child contact during the first two years, encouragement of the direct expression of affectional needs, more sexual freedom and earlier sexual sophistication, a playing down of achievement striving and peer competitiveness, and enhancement of the intuitive over the rational.

The effects on the second generation of these most recent alternatives in family life cannot yet be evaluated. The results will depend largely on the social conventions in existence when these children reach maturity. It cannot be taken for granted that the second generation will choose the family style or child-rearing method of their parents. Nor can it be assumed that these children will be less competitive or less restricted in their affectional or sexual behaviors when they reach adulthood than children who have been reared by other means. All that can be said, with some degree of certainty, is that the conventionalization of these counter-culture approaches has temporarily normalized a wide range of personal possibilities in life style. These include some possibilities which previously would have been labeled "deviant;" and, in fact, currently represent a prevalent style of child rearing.

This scattered collage of experiments in family life should be taken as a simple demonstration that any short-range, historical view of changing parental-familial roles is bound to be deceptive. However, it can be said that the dynamic nature of the family has been, and will continue to be, influenced by both cultural and ideological factors.

THE WESTERN-EUROPEAN DISCOVERY

The family, as it is currently known, is a relatively new institution. It evolved in tandem with the discovery of childhood as a unique stage of life. That discovery had a profound impact on the nature of parenthood and society's expectations of the role of the adult.

Much of what we know about a society's conscious appreciation of infancy and childhood is through the representation of infants and children in painting, sculpture and poetry. From these sources, historians have dated the Western-European discovery of childhood at around three hundred years ago (Aries, 1965). The child-like figures of Cupid-Eros, the naked Pitti of Renaissance painting, and angels of illustrated manuscripts of the middle ages were representative of the few references to children prior to that time. A change in this approach can be noted during the Elizabethan age when children were depicted as miniature adults. Portraits of that time show children wearing the same clothes as adults and engaged in many of the same activities. Degrees of experience marked the primary difference between generations. As a result, men, women, and children shared a communal life--they worked at the same tasks, played the same games, and enjoyed the same sexual freedoms and moral excesses (Aries, 1965).

Children who looked like children began to appear in family portraits around the middle of the 17th century. In addition, for the first time, children's names and faces could be found on tombstones. These were certain signs that childhood was thought about as a period of life having a meaning of its own (Aries, 1965).

It was not until the 19th century that childhood emerged as a continuous theme in Western-European literature. The poets Blake and Wordsworth as well as the writers Dickens and Twain became preoccupied with the themes of childhood innocence and "natural piety." The creation of this romantic vision of childhood followed the dissolution of medieval society into nation states and the ensuing spiritual crisis brought on by industrialization and the impersonality of the state (Coveney, 1957).

The artist saw himself as alienated from society and, thus, the child became, for the artist, the symbol of free imagination--of nature set against the dehumanizing trends of social life. The artist was to use the idea of childhood to investigate the well-springs of the artistic vision and the origins of the feeling of selfhood. Through the child, the artist sought to encompass the nature of humanity itself. As might have been predicted, this metaphorical vision of childhood (which was devoid of any real understanding of actual childhood) was soon to deteriorate into the stultifying Victorian-Calvinist notion of the child who must be stripped of all passion. The child was to be purged of his inclinations away from the innocence and natural piety that were the prevailing mythologies of that epoch. The sentimental falsification of the child's true nature went along with a religious savagery toward the child (Coveney, 1957).

It is not surprising, therefore, for some contemporary historians to lament the discovery of childhood--a discovery that began as a revolution designed to protect the innocent child from his own natural sinfulness and the sinfulness of the adult world. This resulted first in harsh repression and then in the segregation of children into an artificial child's world unconnected with culture. Many historians long for the good old days of the medieval world and the possibility that life would be short, brutal, but also sweetly alive (Aries, 1965).

Within the past fifteen years of our continuing discovery of childhood, a new perspective on its meaning has begun to make itself felt. We have begun to appreciate some of the ways in which the child's innate maturational-developmental rhythms might shape the possibilities of parenthood. With this new perspective, we have become alert to the ways in which a child's innate energies and behavioral repertoires create his parent--particularly during the early months and years of life (Lewis and Rosenblum, 1974).

SEPARATION-INDIVIDUATION[1]

It is now widely believed that every normal human infant enters the world with a behavioral repertoire which profoundly influences the behavior of his caregiver--provided the caregiver consciously or otherwise is responsive to the underlying meaning of these behaviors. Every human infant is born with physical attributes and behavioral systems that evoke mothering responses, thereby insuring the survival of the infant and, by extension, the survival of the species. In separating from the mother, infants learn the conditions of actual love and, in doing so, simultaneously acquire the sense of own unique individuality. All later love and dialogue is an attempt to reconcile our longings to restore the unconditional love of symbiosis with our equally intense need for separateness and individual selfhood.

From the dialogue of symbiosis, infants become aware of their mother's presence out there in the world, and begin to *differentiate* from her. When an infant is approximately five months old, the mother's presence lights the child's way to the familiar world outside their commonly shared orbit. By the end of the first half-year of life, the harmonies of attachment and exploration will have been augmented by the affiliative and agonistic behaviors that also participate in the child's relationship to the cultural world outside the familial attachment system. During the *early practicing* period, the infant is wary with strangers and may often check back to the mother's face for reassurance. In this way, an eight-month-old lets us know that although he is intrigued with novelty, he is still fairly cautious about separating too far from mother.

Eighth-month stranger wariness is an expression of the interaction of all four biological systems (Bretherton and Ainsworth, 1974, p. 132). By this time, the child has learned to count on this specific attachment to the most salient caregiver(s) in order to regulate impulse life and an increasing urge to explore the world outside the Symbiotic orbit. By now, some basic distinctions between the animate and inanimate worlds have made themselves known to the infant. The human-animate stranger is a source of both intriguing fascination and a source of frightening uncertainty. An infant's wariness represents a newfound anxiety about being overcome by these impulses in the context of uncertain and unfamiliar dialogues (Spitz, 1955). The child moves toward the stranger and away, back to the home-base of familiar dialogue; and it is here that balances between affiliative and agonistic behavioral systems begin their meshing with attachment and exploratory systems.

By twelve months, moves away from mother are more courageous. The child stands up and walks away. The *practicing proper* period begins. And, as children are able to walk away on their own two feet, their minds have reached a moment of perfection. The world is theirs, and they are the mighty conquerors of all they behold.

However, at the height of this joyous period of life, infants are still not able to comprehend that they and their mothers are separate beings. Their exhilaration and grandeur are partly based on the illusion that the world is mother, that her presence pervades the world. Not until eighteen months, when the body-mind is joined by an imperfect thinking mind, will the toddler come to the full awareness that mother has an existence apart from the child's own. Then the child confronts the crisis of a second or psychological birth. We call this crisis "rapprochement" because the infant becomes involved once more in trying to be close to mother. The joyous mood of the previous months will be replaced by letdown, anger, sadness. The toddler would want to return to the unconditional bliss of symbiosis but now cannot give up an overwhelming desire to claim his body and mind as his own. The child begins his quest to comprehend the conditions of actual love. For the next year or two, he will be learning that it is possible to be a separate self without giving up inner wholeness, that he can retain the love of his parents and his self-love and still possess his own mind and his own body. An average three-year-old will have achieved an initial sense of separateness and identity. However the reconciliations of symbiosis and separateness have only begun.

Our dialogues of love derive from both aspects of separation-individuation. The first, or core, experience of love comes from the unconditional love of symbiosis, the dialogue of merging, body-molding unity when self and other have not yet differentiated. The second source of love is more complex. It derives from the achievement of separateness, from the formation of boundaries between self and other. It is the love that includes all the varied emotions, thoughts, fantasies, and values that are involved when we relate to down-to-earth, in-the-flesh, actual persons. In the perfection of symbiotic love, there is neither self nor other and, therefore, no true emotional relatedness.

Even as separate, whole persons, we never forget that core experience of symbiotic love. Whenever the challenges of separateness become too great, we all long to bring back the primary bliss of symbiosis. This basic longing to refind our core experience of selfhood is the essence of religion and poetry and the essence of the ecstacies of perfect love.

Though oneness is the essence of love, the vitality of love comes from the partnership of two, in-the-flesh human beings who respect one another's separateness.

Each phase of separation-individuation leaves its unique imprint on the reconciliations between narcissism and object-relating that characterize adult love. We call these reconciliations *constancy*. Without constancy, human love is impoverished. With constancy, we reconcile our longings for perfection with our strivings for separateness. Symbiotic-like love is probably just right for the beginning moments of a love relationship. However, when lovers do not go on from these ideal beginnings to appreciate one another's separateness, love stagnates. The vitality of love comes from a partnership between two such people, a partnership-- consisting of devotion, loyalty, respect, admiration, camaraderie-- qualities of love made possible through the various reconciliations of constancy. When constancy prevails, we go on loving the other even when he does not fill us up with the perfect harmony of unconditional love. Through constancy, the perfect is united with the actual.

The biological inheritance of the human infant, his innate attachment-seeking and exploratory urges, pretty much insure that an average baby from any of a multitude of diverse human societies will attain separate selfhood while simultaneously learning the first conditions of loving an actual other. However, this genetic insurance is not an absolute guarantee. It guarantees neither these first reconciliations of symbiosis and separateness nor any of the subsequent difficult reconciliations that will follow in the course of a life cycle. Subsequent life should be a series of fresh opportunities to enlarge on the initial potential for constancy that emerges from the separation-individuation process.

The issues of separation-individuation touch upon every aspect of our ordinary daily lives and also on our hopes for human perfectibility. An appreciation of the dilemmas of separation-individuation could serve as a bulwark against the anti-human forces that make us all a little deranged, detached, disenchanted, cynical. Every now and then we need reminding that a healthy respect for our biological roots is the best protection we may have against the invasion and domination of social forces.

Nevertheless, there is a danger in our sanctification of the biological roots, the first dialogue of human love--the infant-mother dialogue. In this contest, Erikson (1964) observed that a human being's survival

> ...is safeguarded only by vital virtues which develop in the interplay of successive and overlapping generations living together in organized settings (p. 154).

We cannot, therefore,

> ...derive the meaning of development primarily from a
> reconstruction of the infant's beginnings (p. 114). Trust-
> worthy motherliness needs a trustworthy universe (in
> which to be able to) ...give hope and establish trust in the
> newborn (p. 132).

SOCIETY AS A CONTEXT FOR GROWTH

Our most recent discoveries of infancy and childhood have tended to
focus almost exclusively on the early infant-mother bond.   These cele-
brations of primal love have obscured the direction given to a life history
by the transformations of later developmental phases.   While it is true
that the themes of symbiosis and separateness are reflected in subsequent
dialogues of love, adult love is diminished when we reduce it to infantile
origins.   Our increasing knowledge of the origins of love has burdened the
mother-child relationship with the entire responsibility for adult sanity
and morality.   We are tending to neglect the psychological transformations that come after separation-individuation and also the intricate
enmeshment of that early psycho-biological process in the social order.

Erikson (1964) described the interweavings of infantile life with
social order in the following ways:

> ...the vulnerability of being newly born and the meekness
> of innocent needfulness have a power all their own.
> Defenseless as babies are, they have mothers at their
> command, families to protect the mothers, societies to
> support the structure of families, and traditions to give a
> cultural continuity to systems of tending and training. All
> of this, however, is necessary for the human infant to
> evolve humanly, for his environment must provide that
> outer wholeness and continuity which, like a second womb
> permits the child to develop his separateness capacities in
> distinct steps...(p. 114).

These lines were written in 1960.   Erikson demonstrates an intuitive
appreciation of how our infantile reconciliations of perfection and ordinary life reverberate in all aspects of life.

> For along with a fund of hope, an inescapable alienation is
> also bequeathed to life by this first stage, namely, a sense
> of threatening separation from the matrix, a possible loss
> of hope, and the uncertainty whether the 'face darkly' will
> brighten again with recognition and charity (p. 154).

He also comprehended how our primary love relationships might be
reflected in social institutions.

> Even as the individual, in frantic search of his earliest
> hope-giving relationship, may end up lost in delusions and
> addictions, so are religions, when they lose their bonds
> with living ethics, apt to regress to the fostering of
> illusory and addictive promises or empty fantasy (p. 155).

We have only to take a look at two later phases of the life cycle, at old age and at adolescence, to confront the failure of our social institutions to support the cogwheeling of generations, the mutual dependence of generations which finally makes sense out of the hopes aroused by our primary dialogues of love. In order to establish and confirm hope, social institutions must nurture the individual throughout the life cycle.

The elderly in our post-industrial societies are castoffs, leftovers that, in the most charitable of circumstances, we neatly sweep away to their retirement communities. We certainly have ceased to look to the elderly for wisdom or hope. How could we? Their very presence is a nagging reminder of the despair and stagnation that await us at the end. Yet, such was not always the case for the elderly. In many traditional societies, it was intuitively recognized that the reconciliations of perfection with down-to-earth separateness come together at last in the wisdom of the elders.

In traditional Japanese societies, for example, adulthood was thought of as the road to an old age that would recapture the exhilaration of youth. They believed that, in old age, one finally attained that ideal combination of *kororo* and *ki* that defines a life well lived. *Kororo*, as they said, is the heart, core, essence, the universal spiritual understanding of life. *Ki*, on the other hand, is exhibited in the alertness and vitality directed to the forms of the outer world, the attitudes that express one's relationship to the practical, common sense, tangible, sensate daily life. An alert, self-disciplined posture announces an orderly and well-kept daily existence. The spiritual insights and universal truths of *kororo* are arrived at through the disciplines and rituals of daily life. It is *ki*, the daily life, that provides the connections between the down-to-earth self and the eternal truth that lies at the core (Rohlen, 1976).

Adolescence may be the phase of life that has become most endangered by a sense of hopefulness. To some extent, the 'darkened face' of adolescence is a reflection of society's treatment of the elderly. Erikson (1964) noted that, when any phase of life is doomed to be lived without vigor, the vitality of the younger generation would also be sapped (p. 133). The contemporary adolescent has been brought up to believe in self-fulfillment and the supreme value of individuality. Many find themselves alone and disenchanted as they scrutinize the actual workings of an adult world that is dominated by self-seeking individuality.

The word, "adult," is derived from the Latin, *adolescere*, "to grow up." To grow up in the United States must seem like a frantic uphill race that leads finally to an abrupt abyss. Adolescence should be a time of life when personal illusions temporarily bridge the disparities between the perfect and the actual. Yet, with the one hand we sponsor the second individuation (Blos, 1972) of adolescence, and with the other we under-mine the adolescent opportunity to truly grow up. *Many have lost the capacity to create* the illusions that might eventually change the world for the better. "Of what use," they say, "are illusions in an uncaring, impervious society?"

The paradox of adolescence in our post-industrial societies is another example of the derailment of dialogue between individual and culture. The invitation we offer the adolescent is a hypocritical one. Unlike many primitive and traditional societies, where the transition from childhood to adulthood is accomplished in rites and rituals that span a few weeks, we grant a stay of time where the real may be temporarily pre-empted by the possible. We allow the adolescent to rub against the grain of the adult world in order to refine his own edges. From this reforging of personal edges could come the possibility of changing the shape of the world. The adolescent would then be able to step into adulthood with a capacity of visionary reformations to the disappointing contradictions of the real world, the adolescent staves off madness and cynicism. From such adolescent visions, new worlds might emerge, as once more, possible perfection is reconciled with the actual.

However, in their hopelessness and disenchantment with the dis-orderly planet we have bequeathed to them, many adolescents have given up trying to engage the down-to-earth world. They devote themselves to ecstasies and longings for absolute perfection. What they mistrust most are the binding loyalties of personal intimacy. With infinite space and the possibilities of infinite new worlds, they will not put their faith in the finite world of personal dialogue. And who could blame them? Their own infantile experiences with intimacy may have inspired hope. But some-thing went awry. Our physical birth from the womb entails a definitive rupturing of bonds. However, our first psychological birth eventuates in a strengthening of the attachment between parent and child. In a similar way, the second individuation of adolescence *should* lead to renewed possibilities for the strengthening of attachments. Yet, we have come to view the adolescent opportunity to grow up and achieve a new level of personal Selfhood as a time for rupturing the bonds of family attachment.

Even the experts have fallen prey to this distortion. Psychologists have grown fond of analogizing the adolescent struggle to separate from the ties of family life to the 18-month-old's rapprochement crisis. However, this analogy is misleading. It confuses an inner process of separating self and other images--a process that occurs only once in life, during the first three years--with an adolescent's efforts to work out an optimal balance between distance and closeness to the parents. The adolescent search for optimal distance is *in the service of individuation* not separation. In fact, the intensity of an adolescent's despair and resistance to growing up may be gauged by how desparately and how far he must flee from the family in order to feel safely individuated.

An infant's separation-individuation is accomplished by gaining a relative independence from external love objects--from the actual parents--through taking in and internalizing the parental ideals, inhibitions, and authority. Adolescents, on the other hand, must gain independence from the very *internal* objects that they worked so hard to take in during infancy and childhood.

Internal love objects are not relinquished by fleeing from the intimacies of family life. The task of adolescence is not to get rid of the parents, but rather to transform the internal love objects into a new internal structure, the adult ego-ideal. An essential aspect of growing up is the creation of one's own adult ideals, inhibitions, and authority. In that way, we move on to new relationships with peers, children, and parents. The formation of this adult ego ideal is dependent on a social order that fosters the intimate cog-wheeling of generations, a society that recognizes the connections between personal dialogue and moral dialogue at every phase of the life cycle.

As we take stock of what has been happening to family life in the United States, we wonder about the ultimate value of our recent discoveries concerning the earliest dialogues of human attachment. We recognize that these dialogues are deeply rooted by a biological inheritance designed to insure the survival of the species. (However, it would seem that the more children become invested as an object of supreme value, the more they were simultaneously invested with the intense ambivalent attitudes of their parents.) Nineteenth century children became adults who carried within the over-idealization that derived from a burden of absolute goodness or absolute evil (Muller, 1969, p. 15).

In the 20th century, as individuality, personal achievement, and self-fulfillment ascended as reigning values, the inner eye of conscience relaxed its vigilance and was replaced by public opinion, general consensus, and pragmatic morality. The contemporary child and adolescent, upon whom this child-centered society has invested so much value, carry the combined burdens of an uncertain conscience and a sense of grandiose self-entitlement--a fanciful combination which virtually by definition leads to disappointment, cynicism, self-devaluation and narcissistic transformations of guilt and depression. It leads finally to a breakdown in the moral dialogue with culture.

The nuclear family has been a profound disappointment, both in its severely repressive Victorian-Calvinistic version and in its deceptive counter-version of self-gratifying permissiveness. This latter version has not eliminated the tyranny of the nuclear family cocoon; if anything, it has been intensified. This cocoon, which was originally thought to shelter the individual against the indignities of the Industrial Machine age, became a forbidding Alcatraz that sheltered its inmates by slamming the gates on the social and emotional realities outside the family. The more the family isolated its members from culture, the more the society surreptitiously but steadily invaded the cocoon. As Christopher Lasch (1977) aptly put it:

> At bottom, the glorification of private life and the family represented the other side of the bourgeois perception of society as something alien, impersonal, remote and ab-stract--a world from which pity and tenderness had fled in horror. Deprivations experienced in the public world had to be compensated in the realm of privacy. Yet, the very conditions that give rise to the need to view privacy and the family as a refuge from the larger world made it more and more difficult for the family to serve in that capacity (p. 8).

In the end, the family did not serve as a refuge. More and more it resembled the harsh world outside.

> Relations within the family took on the same character as relations elsewhere: individualism and the pursuit of self interest reigned even in the most intimate of institutions (Lasch, 1977, p. 34).

It is a pollyannish deception to believe that personal self-fulfillment and liberation can be achieved without commitment to the common good; that we can have the security of belonging without being bound to others by devotion and loyalty. Our urgent strivings for individuality have not helped us to become fulfilled or liberated. In trying so hard, "to do our own thing," many have ended up feeling empty, lonely, unloved, and unlovable.

What begins as a teleology of individual survival, achieving pleasure in a dialogue of love that protects individual narcissism should then later be transformed into a moral dialogue between individual and culture. Here the adequacy of dialogue also depends on a teleology of pleasure, narcissism, and respect for self-other dialogue. In cultural terms, such dialogue means the capacity to contribute to a culture (Winnincott, 1963, 1965). An individual's capacity to contribute to a culture is an indication of the depth of the moralization of character, an indication also of the viability and vitality of a culture.

In 1871, Darwin sought to evaluate the progress of the sympathetic regard of one human for another. Darwin predicted that, as feelings became more tender, they would extend to all humans, even to useless members of society and finally to the lower animals (pp. 15-17). Echoing Darwin's sentiments, J. C. Flugel (1921) stated:

> The increasing moralization of human character (in which the relationship between parent and child has probably played a leading part) has brought it about that at least some degree of attention is given in all civilized societies to the needs material and mental of those who are no longer able fully to support themselves or carry on their life without assistance.... The care of elderly, lonely or infirm parents by their children may perhaps legitimately be considered one of the most beautiful and touching expressions of specifically human morality--a point in which (Man) humankind has definitely risen superior to the conditions of a brutal struggle for existence (p. 240).

In the past two decades, it has been fashionable for the extremists, both feminists and anti-feminists, to perpetuate the myth that sexual equality would mean death to the family. The assumption was that what was good for children, men, or family life was necessarily inimical to the equality of women. The prevailing self-absorbed search for personal liberation dominated the women's movement. As more and more women fled from the binding intimacies of family life, the idea that the family was the principle enemy of personal and social progress was accepted by many. Most minor disagreements with this premise were quickly laid to rest. The family issue seemed to be momentarily settled.

However, the family is stirring again. In 1979, the National Organization of Women convened a National Assembly on the Future of the Family. It was announced that feminists at the end of the 70's were moving on to a new frontier--the family. One prominent feminist was quoted as saying:

> I think, in fact, that the women's movement has come just about as far as we can in terms of women alone...we are finding that its not so easy to live with--or without--men and children solely on the basis of that first feminist agenda (*New York Times*, November 20, 1979, p. B11).

Although there were some disputes about the specific form of the new family, the panelists were unanimous in the view that women needed children and men, men needed women, and in fact, that everybody needed everybody else. There was also general agreement that participation in family life was the best bulwark against the post-industrial work ethos that turned men *and* women into dehumanized corporate creatures.

One of the most prominent panels was called, "The New Third of Life." Here, the idea was promulgated that the dominant social revolution of the 1980's would be made by men and women in the last third of the life cycle.

> There will be demanding active participation in society instead of the diminished opportunities, low status, de-

humanization, discrimination, and passive roles as patients that our society now imposes on the aged" (p. B11).

As one listened to the voices of these conference participants, the majority of whom were, in fact, already entered into that last third of life, there was a pervasive sense of a longing for intimacy and for a restoration of the binding commitment of family life. Once again, visionary reformations and strivings for absolute perfection were being reunited with the actual, with the down-to-earth vitalities of partnership, devotion, and loyalty. One was reminded of that innocent and hopeful voice of Flugel (1921) who maintained that future war could be averted if we reaffirmed the values of family life. He had proclaimed that all schemes, from Plato onward, that set out to destroy familial attachments had failed and would continue to be doomed to

> ...practical failure, because these feelings are too strong, too intimate and essential a part of human nature to be successfully and permanently inhibited by alteration of environment; moral failure, because the development of certain of the most important aspects of human character are in their origin and first appearance, bound up with family feelings and would probably fail to ripen if these feelings were abolished (p. 220).

If we are to respect the lessons of the elders, those who assembled to reaffirm the future of the family, it would seem that Flugel might have been right, that familial attachments are too essential an aspect of human nature to be permanently eradicated. As Jane O'Reilly, (1980) one of the leaders of the new feminism suggests: "Maybe the greatest challenge now is to find a way to keep independence while also committing ourselves to the ties that bind people, families and ultimately societies together" (p. 20).

Undoubtedly, the present volume evolved out of a concern with providing infants and children with adequate emotional and cognitive nurturance in an increasingly demanding social environment where more and more parents require some additional support in the parenting role. Thus, the volume itself is at once a product of culture and an interpretor of a cultural dilemma. It is essential therefore to question how these various patterns of supplementary parenting might contribute to a strengthening or a weakening of familial attachments or commitment to culture. While there is nothing inherent in this examination of alternatives that would point to a weakening of human bonds, the current tendency to view the family in a negative manner could encourage some readers to interpret the volume as yet another acquiesence to the death of the family. However, as the title clearly states, the chapters are devoted to *supplementary* parenting. And, in fact, many of the papers directly consider the ways in which certain alternative modes might or might not promote personal attachment and cultural bonding.

In summary, I have attempted to place the preceding chapters in a context of the historical and psycho-social structures in which parenting *of any kind* necessarily takes place. In a volume of practical and factual papers I have allowed myself the liberty of a bit of polemics, knowing full well that the tone, my repeated emphasis on biology and history, my insistence on the centrality of the infant-mother relationship--might at first seem conservative and against the overall drift of the volume. So, I conclude by putting my concerns to rest with some further comments of Erikson (1964):

> The cogwheeling stages of childhood and adulthood are, we can see in conclusion, truly a system of *generation* and *regeneration*--for into this system flow and from this system emerge, those social attitudes to which the institutions and traditions of society attempt to give unity and permanence (p. 152).

> Human strength, then, depends on a total process which regulates at the same time the *sequence of generations* and the structure of society (p. 152).

REFERENCES

Aries, P. *Centuries of childhood*. New York: Vintage Books, 1965 (Paris: Librairie Plan, 1960).

Blos, P. The second individuation process of adolescence. *Psychoanalytic Study of the Child*, 1972, 22, 162-186.

Bretherton, I., and Ainsworth, M. D. S. Responses of one-year-olds to a stranger in a strange situation. In M. Lewis and L. A. Rosenblum (Eds.), *The origins of fear*. New York: John Wiley and Sons, 1974.

Cooper, D. *The death of the family*. New York: Pantheon, 1970.

Coveney, P. The image of the child in English literature. In A. Skolnick (Ed.), *Rethinking childhood*. Boston: Little, Brown and Company, 1976, pp. 62-67.

Darwin, C. *The descent of man, and selection in relation to sex*. New York: Appleton, 1962. (Originally published in 1871.)

Dealy, J. Q. *The family in its sociological aspects*. Boston: 1912. Cited in C. Lasch, *Haven in a heartless world*. New York: Basic Books, Inc., 1977.

Eiduson, B. T., Cohen, J., and Alexander, J. Alternatives in child rearing in the 1970's. *American Journal of Orthopsychiatry*, 1973, 43, 720-731.

Erikson, E. *Insight and responsibility*. New York: W. W. Norton and Company, 1964.

Flugel, J. C. *The psychoanalytic study of the family*. London: Hogarth Press, 1921.

Fuchs, L. H. *Family matters.* New York: Random House, 1972.

Goodsell, W. *A history of the family as a social and educational institution.* New York: 1915. Cited in C. Lasch, *Haven in a heartless world.* New York: Basic Books, Inc., 1977.

Kaplan, L. J. *Oneness and separateness.* New York: Simon and Schuster, 1978.

Lasch, C. *Haven in a heartless world.* New York: Basic Books, Inc., 1977.

Lewis, M., and Rosenblum, L. A. (Eds.) *The effect of the infant on its caregiver.* New York: John Wiley and Sons, 1974.

Mahler, M. A., Pine, F., and Bergman, A. *The psychological birth of the human infant.* New York: Basic Books, 1976.

Montagu, A. *Marriage: Past and present.* Boston: Porter Sargent, 1956.

Muller, P. *The tasks of childhood.* New York: McGraw-Hill, 1969.

(The) New York Times, Family ties in rural China seem more binding than party's rule, 1977, December 19, p. 1.

(The) New York Times, Women's movement sets its sights for the future of the family, 1979, November 20, p. B11.

O'Reilly, J. *The girl I left behind.* New York: Macmillan, 1980.

Rohlen, T. P. The promise of adulthood in Japanese spiritualism. *Daedalus,* 1976, *105*(2), 125-144.

Rossi, A. S. A biosocial perspective on parenting. *Daedalus,* 1977, *106*(2), 1-31.

Spitz, R. A. A note on the extrapolation of ethological findings. *International Journal of Psychoanalysis,* 1955, *36*, 162-165.

Wagatsuma, H. Some aspects of the contemporary Japanese family: Once Confucian, now fatherless? *Daedalus,* 1977, *106*(4), 127-140.

Watson, J. B. *Psychological care of infant and child.* New York: Norton, 1928.

Winnicott, D. W. Dependence towards independence. *The maturational processes and the facilitating environment.* New York: International Universities Press, 1965.

FOOTNOTE

[1]The stages of Separation-Individuation were discovered by Dr. Margaret S. Mahler. A full description of her methods of discovery and the complete rendition of each stage appears in *The Psychological Birth of the Human Infant,* Mahler, Pine, and Bergman.

Abbott, M. S., 109, 128
Abramovitch, R., 74, 91
Adams, B. N., 34, 41, 62
Adams, B. W., 4, 28
Adelson, J., 84, 93
Adler, A., 82, 86, 91
Adler, M., 86, 98
Ainsworth, M. D. S., 7, 16, 28, 220, 232, 293, 303
Albrecht, R., 38, 42, 62
Aldous, J., 34, 45, 62, 64
Aldridge, M., 142, 146, 177
Alexander, J., 291, 303
Allen, C. M., 4, 5, 29
Allen, V. L., 79, 91, 93
Ambron, S., 116, 124
American Public Welfare Association, 133, 138, 141, 147, 177
Andrews, M., 55, 56, 62
Andry, R. G., 205
Annis, R. C., 211, 232
Anspach, D. F., 56, 62
Anthony, A. S., 226, 237
Anthony, E. J., 266, 284
Apple, D., 38, 62, 213, 232
Arcuri, K., 160, 178
Aries, P., 292, 293, 303
Asher, S. R., 88, 97
Atchley, R. C., 33, 66
Auerbach, A., 112, 124
Austin, G. R., 256, 257, 262
Avis, C., 109, 125
Axin, N., 8, 11, 31
Babcock, C. G., 144, 177
Babijian, H., 87, 93
Bacon, M., 211, 226, 232
Bagarozzi, D. A., 21, 29
Baggiano, A. K., 86, 98
Bakawa-Evenson, L., 112, 129
Bane, M. J., 14, 22, 23, 29, 59, 65
Banks, S., 88, 91
Barash, D. P., 209, 236
Barker, R. G., 69, 91
Barry, H., III., 70, 91, 211, 226, 232
Bates, E., 80, 91
Beavin, J., 17, 31
Beit-Hallahmi, B., 269, 270, 282, 284
Bell, N. W., 21, 29
Bell, R. Q., 267, 284
Beller, E., 109, 124
Belmont, L., 80, 91
Belsky, J., 101, 114, 115, 116, 118, 124, 125
Beman, A., 52, 64
Bemis, J., 59, 62
Benedek, T., 266, 284
Benn, J., 113, 121, 127
Berbaum, M. L., 80, 91
Bergman, A., 268, 284, 304
Berry, J. W., 211, 225, 232, 237
Bettelheim, B., 191, 205, 277, 281, 282, 284
Beytagh, L. A. M., 228, 235
Bianchi, S., 50, 62
Biemiller, A., 109, 125
Bierman, K. L., 75, 79, 91, 94
Bigelow, B. J., 75, 91
Bigner, J., 86, 91
Billingsley, A., 51, 62
Binger, C. G., 87, 94
Birch, H., 7, 31, 267, 285
Birdwhistell, R. L., 4, 29
Blood, R. O., 4, 29
Blos, P., 84, 92, 297, 303
Blum, A., 205
Blurton-Jones, N., 208, 232
Boll, E., 70, 71, 72, 74, 83, 87, 92
Boger, R., 55, 56, 62
Bogg, J. W., 72, 94, 224, 233
Bonvillian, J. D., 75, 97
Boon, J. A., 219, 232
Bordon, B., 37, 62
Bossard, J., 70, 71, 72, 74, 83, 87, 92
Bowerman, C. E., 74, 75, 84, 92
Bowlby, J., 7, 16, 29, 72, 73, 92, 115, 125, 188, 190, 205, 281, 284

Boyd, P. 173, 177
Brainerd, C. J., 78 92
Brandt, E. M., 71, 92
Breland, H. M., 80, 92
Bretherton, I., 293, 303
Brewer, J., 161, 177
Bricker, W., 82, 97
Brim, O. G., Jr., 82, 92
Brittain, C. V., 84, 92
Broderick, C., 7, 29
Bronfenbrenner, U., 13, 27, 29,
    71, 84, 92, 104, 105, 112,
    117, 125, 191, 205, 257, 258,
    262
Bronson, W. C., 87, 92
Brooks, J., 75, 96
Brown, D., 145, 177
Brownell, C. A., 77, 96
Bruner, J. S., 78, 92
Bryan-Logan, B. B., 59, 62
Bubolz, M., 5, 30, 240, 262
Buckley, W., 11, 29
Burmeister, E., 193, 205
Burns, S. M., 78, 92
Burton, R. V., 226, 227, 232
Cairns, R. B., 73, 92
Caldwell, G., 104, 125
Campbell, D. T., 210, 232
Campos, J. J., 73, 93
Cantwell, D. P., 88, 96
Caplan, A., 209, 232
Carroll, V., 214, 215, 232
Casciato, J., 132, 169, 177, 178,
    179
Cattell, R. B., 86, 92
Caudill, W., 210, 223, 232
Cautley, P., 142, 143, 144, 145,
    146, 147, 155, 156, 177
Chandler, M. J., 88, 92
Charlesworth, R., 75, 97
Chauncey, H., 258, 262
Chennault, M., 88, 92
Chess, S., 7, 31, 267, 285
Child, I. L., 210, 211, 226, 232,
    237
Child Welfare League of Ameri-
    ca, 131, 141, 157, 172, 177
Chilman, C., 58, 63
Cicirelli, V. G., 79, 90, 93

Clarke, A. D. B., 283, 284
Clarke, A. M., 283, 284
Clarke-Stewart, A., 19, 29, 101,
    110, 125
Clarkson, D., 132, 169, 177, 178,
    179
Clavan, S., 44, 51, 63
Clignet, R., 233
Cloward, R. D., 79, 93
Cohen, J., 291, 303
Cohen, L. J., 73, 93
Commonwealth Child Develop-
    ment Committee, 177
Conger, J. J., 84, 93
Connell, D. B., 109, 125
Cooper, D., 289, 303
Cormack, T., 79, 93
Corter, C., 74, 91
Costanzo, D. R., 84, 93
Coveney, P., 292, 303
Cowen, E. L., 87, 93
Cox, M., 57, 64
Cox, R., 57, 64
Crane, W., 83
Crase, D. R., 40, 63
Crawford, A., 56, 63
Culley, J., 142, 180
Damrin, D., 88, 98
Dancy, B. L., 59, 63
Dann, S., 89, 94
Danzinger, K., 228, 233
Darwin, C., 300, 303
Davis, E., 51, 63
Dawkins, R., 209, 233
Dealy, J. Q., 289, 303
Decker, J., 54, 66
Deets, A. C., 87, 93
Dell, P. F., 59, 63
de Mause, L., 218, 233
Demographic Yearbook, 261, 262
Deutsch, F., 4, 11, 29, 79, 93
Devin-Sheehan, L., 79, 93
Diaz-Guerrero, R., 210, 234
Dickinson, K., 48, 63
Diers, E., 59, 62
Dixon, D., 78, 98
Dobash, R. M., 74, 92
Dodsworth, R. O., 73, 94
Doise, W., 78, 96

Douvan, E., 84, 93
Downs, G., 132, 169, 177, 178
Downs, S., 177
Drummond, L., 219, 233
Duncan, G., 48, 63
Dunn, J., 90, 95
Easterbrooks, M. A., 76, 93
Eber, H. W., 86, 92
Eckerman, C. O., 90, 97
Edwards, C. A., 223, 236
Egeland, B., 115, 129
Eicher, J. 240, 262
Eiduson, B. T., 291, 303
Eisenberg, L., 159, 177
Elardo, R., 123, 125
Elkins, D., 90, 93
Ember, C. R., 223, 233
Emerson, P. E., 17, 31
Emlen, A., 102, 103, 125, 132,
    141, 150, 162, 163, 168, 169,
    175, 177, 178, 179
Engel, J., 136, 157, 178
Engler, R., 159, 162, 179
Erickson, M. R., 79, 93
Erikson, E., 16, 17, 29, 228, 295,
    296, 297, 303
Essman, C. S., 72, 93
Etaugh, C., 230, 233, 268, 283,
    284
Fagin, H., 274, 284
Fagot, B. I., 81, 93
Fanshel, D., 132, 136, 137, 143,
    145, 147, 152, 154, 155, 156,
    157, 159, 160, 161, 163, 164,
    165, 166, 168, 174, 175, 176,
    178
Fapohunda, E., 259, 262
Farber, B., 49, 54, 63
Farley, R., 50, 62
Fein, E., 168, 179
Fein, G., 49, 65, 101, 110, 111,
    112, 113, 125
Feit, M., 54, 66
Feldman, N. S., 86, 98
Feldman, R. S., 79, 93
Feldman, S. S., 71, 93
Ferguson, L. R., 84, 99
Fine, G. A., 83, 93
Fink, R. S., 78, 93

Fitzpatrick, J. R., 53, 63
Fitzsimmons, S., 113, 125
Fleising, U., 209, 233
Fleming, V., 107, 125
Flugel, J. C., 300, 303
Foote, N., 34, 64
Forest, I., 253, 254, 257, 262
Fosberg, S., 110, 125
Fowler, W., 112, 113, 114, 123,
    125, 126
Fox, F., 37, 63
Fox, M., 160, 178
Fox, N., 217, 236
Fox, R., 209, 233
Fraiberg, S., 16, 29, 196, 205
Frankena, W., 17, 29
Freedman, D. G., 209, 233
Freud, A., 89, 94, 148, 178, 196,
    205
Fried, E. G., 37, 63
Friedman, D., 108, 126
Friedman, M. M., 6, 7, 11, 12,
    16, 29
Fuchs, L. H., 290, 291, 302, 304
Furman, W., 74, 75, 79, 85, 87,
    88, 91, 94
Furstenberg, F., 56, 57, 58, 63
Gallacher, K., 157, 178
Gallimore, R., 70, 72, 94, 99,
    217, 224, 233, 236, 265, 285
Gambino, R., 54, 63
Gambrill, E., 147, 163, 164, 166,
    167, 168, 174, 180
Gardner, A., 120, 128
Gathorne-Hardy, J., 218, 233
Gecas, V., 18, 29
Geiringer, E., 77, 98
Gibson, G., 34, 64
Gilutz, G., 86, 98
Glick, P., 56, 64
Glickman, E., 157, 158, 178
Goff, J., 160, 179
Goldberg, S., 221, 222, 233
Goldberg, S. R., 4, 11, 29
Golden, M. M., 87, 97
Goldfard, W., 115, 126
Goldstein, H., 148, 178
Goldstein, J., 144, 146, 178, 196,
    205

Gonso, J., 87, 94
Goodall, J., 71, 94
Goode, R., 45, 64
Goode, W. J., 4, 27, 29, 33, 64
Goodman, M. E., 52
Goodsell, W., 289, 304
Goodson, B., 109, 125
Goody, E., 215, 233
Gordon, I., 111, 126
Gordon, M., 33, 64
Gottman, J., 87, 94
Gove, F., 115, 129
Graves, N. D., 228, 233
Graves, P. L., 221, 233
Graziano, W. G., 70, 86, 96
Grebler, L., 52, 64
Greeley, A. M., 54, 64
Green, C., 111, 129
Green, K., 169, 179
Green, L., 160, 179
Greenfield, P. M., 212, 233
Grindal, B., 228, 233
Grossbard, H., 190, 205
Grotevant, H., 82, 94
Gruber, A., 132, 136, 142, 146,
     149, 163, 167, 178
Guerney, B., 145, 178
Guerney, L. F., 136, 137, 143,
     145, 161, 178
Guzman, R. C., 52, 64
Haines, A. C., 88, 98
Hall, O. A., 8, 11, 31
Hamilton, J., 168, 179
Hampe, G. D., 56, 66
Hampson, R., 136, 145, 157, 180
Hansell, S., 79, 98
Hanton, S., 139, 178
Harlow, H. F., 73, 82, 89, 94
Harlow, M. K., 73, 94
Harlow, R. G., 205
Harrell, J., 118, 126
Harrington, C., 222, 224, 226,
     233
Harris, L., 35, 64
Hartup, W. W., 7, 29, 69, 70, 74,
     75, 77, 81, 82, 83, 87, 88,
     92, 94
Harvey, D. L., 49, 63
Harvey, J., 84, 95

Harvey, O. J., 83, 98
Hathorn, S., 88, 95
Hazen, B., 272, 275, 276, 284
Heathers, G., 76, 94
Heber, M. E., 88, 94
Heber, R. F., 88, 94
Heinicke, C., 108, 126
Hendrickson, N., 40, 63
Herjanic, B. L., 236
Herson, J., 160, 179
Hetherington, E. M., 57, 64
Hildebrand, J., 243, 244, 247,
     253, 260, 263
Hildebrand, V., 243, 244, 247,
     253, 259, 260, 262, 263
Hill, C. R., 105, 126
Hill, R. B., 34, 40, 48, 49, 50, 51,
     64
Hitchcock, J., 25, 30
Hodges, W., 120, 128
Hofferth, S., 105, 118, 122, 126
Hoffman, D., 113, 118, 126
Holtzman, W. H., 210, 228, 234
Hood, W. R., 83, 98
Horejsi, C. R., 131, 132, 137,
     138, 140, 141, 143, 146, 147,
     157, 170, 178
Horner, P. L., 136, 161, 179
Horowitz, B., 150, 172, 174, 179
Horowitz, F. D., 86, 95
Howell, M. C., 48, 64
Howes, C., 75, 87, 95, 110, 126
Huang, L. J., 53, 64
Hughes, S. L., 48, 64
Huston, P., 244, 246, 247, 253,
     263
Hutchinson, D., 134, 179
Inkeles, A., 227, 234
Integrated Home Economics Pro-
     grams, 263
Iowa Department of Social Serv-
     ices, 179
Ipsa, J., 75, 95
Irish, D. P., 79, 87, 95
Iscoe, I., 84, 95
Izzo, L. D., 87, 93
Jackson, D., 17, 31
Jamison, J., 160, 179
Jessner, L., 65

Joffee, C., 109, 126
Johnson, A. S., 60, 64
Johnson, J., 78, 98
Johnson, R. C., 85, 97
Jolly, A., 78, 92
Jones, E., 108, 128
Jones, L., 118, 128
Jones, M., 171, 172, 173, 179
Jones, M. A., 170, 179
Jordan, C., 72, 94
Jordan, C. E., 223, 233
Kadushin, A., 123, 126, 132, 134,
    138, 150, 179
Kaffman, M. A., 282, 284
Kagan, J., 19, 30, 114, 126, 289
Kahana, B., 41, 64
Kahana, E., 41, 64
Kahn, A., 102, 103, 104, 120,
    123, 126, 254, 255, 256, 258,
    263
Kahn, M., 88, 91
Kamerman, S., 102, 103, 104,
    120, 123, 126, 254, 255, 256,
    258, 263
Kandel, D., 95
Kandel, D. B., 84, 96
Kantner, J. F., 58, 67
Kantor, D., 6, 7, 9, 11, 30
Kaplan, L. J., 288, 304
Karnes, M. C., 49, 64
Katz, A., 57, 64
Katz, P. A., 81, 95
Kaufman, I., 190, 206
Kaveler, F., 161, 180
Keasey, C. B., 85, 95
Keister, M., 111, 128
Keiter, L., 113, 126
Kelly, J. A., 88, 95
Kendrick, C., 90, 95
Keniston, K., 8, 11, 22, 23, 30,
    120, 126
Kennel, J. H., 16, 30
Kernberg, O. F., 189, 205
Kessen, W., 49, 65, 214, 234
Kikumura, A., 53, 65
Kinch, J. W., 75, 84, 92
Kinsey, A. C., 81, 95
Kirschner, Associates, Inc., 113,
    126

Kitano, H. H., 53, 65
Kivnick, H. Q., 46, 65
Klatzky, S. R., 34, 65
Klaus, M. H., 16, 30
Klein, E., 120, 127
Klein, N. H., 224, 234
Klein, R., 221, 234
Kleinman, C., 120, 127
Klier, J., 168, 179
Kluckhohn, F., 226, 237
Knodel, J., 245, 263
Kobasigawa, A., 81, 95
Kohen-Raz, R., 282, 284
Kohlberg, L., 85, 95
Kohn, M., 19, 30
Konner, M. J., 208, 216, 221, 234
Koppel, F., 115, 123, 127
Kostelnik, M., 18, 30, 124, 127
Kotelchuck, M., 17, 30, 221, 234
Kramer, M., 51, 65
Kreinin, M. M., 26, 30
Kritchevsky, S., 108, 128
Kubler-Ross, E., 157, 179
Kuehnel, M., 169, 179
LaBarre, M. B., 65
Ladd, G. W., 87, 95
LaGaipa, J. J., 75, 91
Lahti, J., 132, 169, 177, 178, 179
Lake, A., 105, 107, 122, 127
Lamb, M. E., 7, 16, 30, 70, 73,
    74, 76, 81, 93, 95
Lambert, W., 211, 216, 235
Lambert, W. W., 210, 213, 224,
    237
Lando, B., 74, 91
Landy, F., 87, 99
Langner, T., 160, 179
Langsam, M. Z., 134, 179
Langworthy, R. L., 84, 96
Lasch, C., 23, 30, 300, 304
Layzer, J. I., 109, 125
Lazerwitz, B., 54, 63
Leakey, R. E., 207, 234
Leaman, T., 20, 31
Leborici, S., 205
Lebra, J., 259, 263
Lee, G. R., 34, 65
Lefruge, W. G., 85, 96
Lehr, W., 6, 7, 9, 11, 30

Leichter, H., 54, 55, 65
Leichter, H. J., 18, 30
Leiderman, G. F., 217, 221, 234
Leiderman, P. H., 217, 221, 234, 235
Lein, L, 118, 127
Leiner, M., 261, 263
Lerner, R. I., 20, 30
Lesser, G. S., 84, 96
Lester, B. M., 221, 234
LeVine, R. A., 210, 224, 226, 227, 234
Levy, R. I., 72, 96, 214, 224, 234
Lewis, M., 49, 54, 63, 75, 96, 219, 235, 293, 304
Lewis, R., 54, 66, 207, 234
Lichstein, D. P., 146, 177
Lieberman, A. F., 76, 96
Liedtke, K., 132, 169, 177, 178
Lightfoot, S., 118, 127
Lindsay, A., 109, 125
Lippitt, R., 113, 118, 127
Littman, R. A., 82, 97
Littner, N., 159, 179
Litwok, E., 109, 124
Lloyd, B., 227, 235
Loban, W., 85, 96
Loda, F., 116, 127
Lornnitz, L. A., 216, 235
Lougee, M. E., 70, 86, 96
Low, S., 70, 96
Lowery, R., 112, 127
Lozoff, B., 207, 235
Lusk, D., 219, 235
Lynn, D. B., 226, 235
Maas, H., 159, 162, 179
Maccoby, E. E., 75, 97
MacDonald, R., 34, 64
MacMillan, M., 254, 263
Madsden, M. C., 282, 284
Mahler, M. A., 304
Mahler, M. S., 268, 278, 284
Maluccio, A., 168, 169, 170, 173, 174, 179
Mannarino, A. P., 86, 96
Markus, C. B., 80, 99
Marolla, F. A., 80, 91
Marshall, R. J., 86, 96
Martin, C. E., 81, 95

Martin, E. P., 50, 65
Martin, J. M., 50, 65
Martindale, C., 4, 30
Martinson, F. M., 14, 30
Masnick, G., 14, 29, 59, 65
Masters, J. C., 75, 85, 94
Mayer, M. E., 191, 205
McAdoo, H. P., 51, 65
McCall, A. M., 58, 65
McCord, J., 158, 179
McCord, W., 158, 179
McGowan, J., 136, 137, 139, 140, 151, 154, 162, 163, 164, 174, 180
McGuire, W. J., 86, 96
McHale, J., 243, 263
McHale, M., 243, 263
McKay, A., 177
McWhirter, N., 25, 26, 30
Mead, G. H., 86, 96
Mead, M., 36, 37, 65, 72, 96, 205
Meier, E., 158, 179
Merel, F., 83, 96
Michalson, L., 75, 96
Miller, D., 54, 65
Miller, M. V., 52, 65
Miller, N. B., 88, 96
Miller, S. A., 77, 96
Miller, S. J., 33, 66
Mindel, C., 54, 63
Minton, B. A., 86, 96
Mintum, L., 210, 211, 212, 213, 216, 222, 224, 235
Mirande, A., 52, 54, 66
Mitchell, G., 71, 92
Mitchell, W., 54, 55, 65
Mnookin, R. H., 148, 149, 179
Montagu, A., 289, 304
Montessori in Perspective 254, 263
Moore, J. 102, 111, 128
Moore, J. W., 52, 64
Moore, T. W., 219, 235
Moore, W. E., 21, 30
Moreland, R. C., 80, 91
Morley, D., 218, 235
Mott, P., 121, 127
Mueller, E., 75, 95, 99
Mugny, G., 78, 96

Muller, P., 299, 304
Munroe, R. H., 220, 226, 227, 235
Munroe, R. L., 220, 226, 227, 235
Murray, F. B., 77, 97
Mussen, P. H., 228, 235
Myers, J., 71, 97
Myers, L., 111, 112, 113, 118, 127
Naroll, R. T., 210, 232
Nash, S. C., 71, 93
National Action for Foster Children, 142, 179
National Foster Parents Association, 145, 179
National Research Council, 104, 127
Nelson, C., 88, 97
Nelson, O., 122, 128
Nero, B., 282, 284
Neugarten, B. L., 39, 41, 43, 65
Neuman, R., 132, 170, 179, 180
Newland, K., 251, 253, 263
Newman, D. M., 15, 30
Newman, P. R., 15, 30
New York Times, 290, 301, 304
North Carolina Report, 142, 150, 156, 163, 167, 175, 179
Nye, F. I., 18, 30, 58, 65
Oden, S., 88, 97
Oden, S. L., 87, 95
Offer, D., 84, 97
Offer, J., 84, 97
Office of Assistant for Planning and Evaluation, 105, 106, 127
Ogburn, W., 121, 127
O'Neill, O., 28, 30
O'Reilly, J., 302, 304
Orost, J. H., 78, 97
Owen, C. R., 224, 234
Padawer-Singer, A., 86, 96
Pagan, B., 123, 125
Palmer, S., 142, 150, 151, 156, 157, 159, 164
Paolucci, B., 5, 8, 11, 30, 31
Patterson, F. G., 75, 97
Patterson, G. R., 81, 82, 97
Paxson, L. M., 70, 91

Pederson, A., 87, 93
Pennsylvania State Task Force on Foster Care Services, 141, 146, 147, 151, 166, 171, 172, 180
Pepler, D. J., 77, 78, 97
Perry, L. 102, 103, 125
Peter, H. R. H., 212, 235
Peters, D. L., 101, 102, 103, 104, 111, 112, 113, 114, 115, 116, 120, 121, 123, 124, 127
Phenice, L. A., 44, 65
Phillips, J., 88, 95
Piaget, J., 77, 85, 97
Pine, F., 268, 284, 304
Piorrata, S., 217, 236
Pitt-Rivers, J., 216, 235
Plath, D. W., 210, 223, 232
Polsgrove, L., 88, 97
Pomeroy, W. B., 81, 95
Porteus, B. D., 85, 97
Powell, D. R., 113, 117, 118, 121, 127, 128
Prescott, E., 108, 109, 126, 128
Presidential Commission on World Hunger, 263
Prugh, D. G., 205
Puncel, C., 108, 126
Rabin, A. I., 191, 205, 269, 270, 272, 273, 275, 276, 277, 281, 282, 284
Radinsky, E., 147, 180
Rahe, D. F., 88, 94
Rasmussen, B., 87, 94
Rawson, J. A., 48, 65
Redhorse, J. G., 54, 66
Redick, R., 51, 65
Redl, F., 189, 206
Reed, G., 221, 235
Reese, H. W., 86, 97
Regan, R. A., 87, 99
Reimer, B., 190, 206
Reistroffer, M., 153, 180
Reynolds, P. G., 75, 97
Rheingold, H. L., 90, 97
Rhodes, S., 118, 128
Rice, R., 17, 21, 31
Ridley, C., 118, 126
Ristau, C., 120, 128

Ritchie, J. E., 72, 97, 224, 235
Roberts, B., 71, 82, 97
Robertson, J. F., 42, 43, 44, 65, 67
Robins, L. N., 214, 236
Rodes, T., 102, 111, 128
Roff, M., 87, 97
Rogoff, B., 217, 222, 236
Rohlen, T. P., 297, 304
Rohner, R. P., 211, 213, 225, 236
Ronchi, D., 79, 98
Roopnarino, J. L., 81, 95
Rose, A. M., 90, 97
Rosen, B. C., 84, 97
Rosen, L. A., 87, 94
Rosenberg, B. G., 71, 82, 83, 87, 97, 99
Rosenblatt, P. C., 216, 236
Rosenblum, L. A., 293, 304
Rossi, A. S., 15, 31, 288, 304
Rostkowski, J., 160, 179
Rothenberg, B., 77, 78, 87, 97
Rowe, M., 113, 125
Rubenstein, J., 110, 126
Rubin, K. H., 77, 78, 97
Ruble, D. N., 86, 98
Ruddick, W., 28, 30
Ruderman, F., 102, 128
Ruopp, R., 109, 129
Rutter, M., 283, 284
Sale, J., 108, 126
Saltz, E., 78, 98
Saunders, M., 111, 128
Schachter, F. F., 86, 98
Schaffer, H. R., 17, 31
Scheffler, H. W., 214, 236
Schubert, D. S. P., 90, 99
Schubert, H. J. D., 90, 99
Scitovsky, T., 26, 31
Segal, J., 16, 31
Sellers, M. J., 217, 221, 234, 236
Sells, S. B., 87, 97
Sena-Rivera, J., 52, 66
Settles, B., 142, 180
Shanas, E., 34, 66
Shane, H., 121, 122, 128
Shapira, A., 282, 284
Sharpe, R., 59, 62
Shaw, M. E., 84, 93

Shedd, C., 45, 66
Sheehan, A. M., 109, 128
Sherif, C. W., 83, 98
Sherif, M., 83, 98
Sherman, E., 132, 167, 180
Shinn, E., 137, 143, 152, 154, 155, 156, 157, 159, 160, 161, 163, 164, 165, 168, 174, 175, 176, 178
Shoffner, S. M., 48, 66
Shore, F., 86, 98
Shores, R., 88, 98
Shyne, A., 132, 170, 179, 180
Sibbison, V., 102, 128, 132, 136, 137, 139, 140, 151, 154, 162, 163, 164, 174, 180
Silverman, I. W., 77, 98
Siman, M. L., 84, 98
Simpson, R. L., 84, 98
Singer, J. L., 78, 98
Skolnick, A., 4, 20, 31
Skoogberg, E., 216, 236
Slobin, D., 80, 98
Small, W., 120, 128
Smart, R. C., 15, 16, 28, 31
Smart, M. S., 15, 16, 28, 31
Smilansky, S., 78, 98
Smith, A. J., 83, 98
Smith, E. W., 40, 66, 58, 59
Smith, J., 7, 29
Smith, J. W., 52, 66
Smith, R. S., 214, 224, 236
Solnit, A., 148, 178
Solnit, D., 196, 205
Solomon, R. W., 88, 98
Sontag, S., 240, 262
Spanier, G., 20, 56, 63
Spelke, E., 221, 234
Spicer, W. J., 56, 66
Spindler, P., 70
Spiro, M. C., 281, 282, 285
Spiro, M. E., 71, 72, 84, 98
Spitz, R. A., 115, 128, 294, 304
Sprey, J., 46, 66
Srowfe, L. A., 73, 98
Stack, C. B., 50, 66
Staples, R., 40, 52, 54, 66
Steers, R., 118, 128
Stein, T., 147, 180

Steinberg, L., 101, 111, 114, 115, 116, 124, 125, 129,
Steiner, G., 103, 129
Stendler, C. B., 88, 98
Stengel, E., 87, 98
Stern, K., 37, 63
Stone, C. L., 90, 98
Stone, H., 143, 144, 145, 180
Strain, P., 88, 98
Strauss, C. A., 37, 66
Strodtbeck, F. L., 79, 98
Sullivan, H. S., 75, 86, 99
Sullivan, K., 109, 124
Sullivan, M., 132, 178
Sumpter, L., 58
Sumpter, L., 58
Suomi, S. J., 82, 89, 99
Super, C. M., 236
Sussman, M. B., 20, 31
Sutton-Smith, B., 82, 83, 87, 99
Swartz, J. D., 210, 234
Swire, M., 161, 180
Sylva, K., 78, 92
Sywulak, A., 161, 180
Tatsuoka, M. M., 86, 92
Tavormina, J., 136, 145, 157, 180
Textor, R. B., 211, 236
Theis, S., 158, 180
Thomas, A., 7, 31, 267, 285
Thurber, E., 158, 179
Tien, H. Y., 14, 15, 31
Tiger, L., 207, 236
Timm, D., 88, 98
Toffler, A., 10, 23, 24, 25, 27, 28, 31, 120, 121, 122
Toffler, H., 27, 31
Trasler, G., 147, 180
Travers, J., 109, 129
Trivers, R. L., 209, 236
Troll, L. E., 33, 44, 45, 66
Trost, M. A., 87, 93
Tuckman, J. 87, 99
Turiel, E., 85, 99
Turner, M. E., 85, 99
Unco, 48, 66
United States Department of Commerce, 242, 263
United States Department of Labor, 252, 263

U. S. News and World Report, 132, 133, 158, 174, 180
Updegraff, S. G., 40, 67
Urban Institute, 105, 129
Ussery, L., 65
Vandell, D. L., 75, 76, 90, 99
van den Berghe, P. L., 209, 236
VanderVen, K., 123, 124, 129
van de Walle, E., 245, 263
VanName, J., 142, 180
Vaughn, B., 115, 129
Veroff, J., 86, 99
Verway, D. I., 67
Vogel, E. F., 21, 29
Vogelsong, E., 161, 178
Vollmer, H., 37, 66
Von Hentig, H. V., 38, 67
Vygotsky, L., 78, 99
Wagatsuma, H., 290, 304
Wagner, M. E., 90, 99
Wahler, R. G., 88, 98
Walker, A., 101, 114, 115, 116, 125
Walker, K. E., 24, 31
Ward, D., 168, 179
Warnath, C. F., 90, 99
Watson, J. B., 304
Watson, T., 132, 172, 180
Watzawick, P. 17, 31
Webb, M., 58, 67
Weinheimer, S., 78, 99
Weinstein, E., 143, 147, 154, 180
Weinstein, K. K., 39, 41, 43, 65
Weisner, T. S., 70, 72, 99, 217, 224, 236, 265, 283
Werner, E. E., 214, 222, 224, 225, 236, 265
West, P. A., 236
Westinghouse Learning Corporation 110, 113
White, B. J., 83, 98
White, S., 217, 236
Whiting, B. B., 70, 71, 72, 99, 210, 211, 212, 217, 219, 220, 222, 223, 236, 237
Whiting, J. W. M., 70, 71, 72, 99, 208, 210, 211, 212, 217, 219, 222, 223, 224, 226, 227, 232, 233, 235, 236, 237

Williams, J., 20, 31
Williams, M., 84, 95
Williams, T. R., 213
Wilson, E. O., 209, 237
Wilson, S., 88, 95
Wiltse, K., 147, 163, 164, 166,
    167, 168, 174, 178, 180
Winch, R., 33, 34, 67
Winch, R. F., 4, 31
Wineman, D., 189, 206
Winnicott, D. W., 300, 304
Wintermute, W., 150, 172, 174,
    179
Witkin, H. A., 225, 237
Wolf, T. M., 81, 99
Wolfgang, G., 161, 178
Woloshin, G. W., 85, 96
Wood, V., 42, 43, 67
Wooton, B., 205
Worrell, J., 88, 97
Wortis, R. P., 17, 31
Wright, H. F., 69, 91
Yahres, H., 16, 31
Yanagisako, S. J., 218, 237
Young, G., 75, 84, 96
Yawkey, T., 112, 129
Zadny, J., 169, 177, 179
Zajonc, R. B., 80, 100
Zelnik, M., 58, 67
Zykorie, D., 160, 179

Adolescence: sense of hopelessness in, 297; as paradox in post-industrial societies, 298; and strengthening of attachments, 298; individuation in, 298-299; and formation of adult ego-ideal, 299

Adolescent parents: and child-rearing by grandparents, 58; rate of increase of, 58; and outside child care, 58; cognitive development of children of, 59

Adoption: of infants, 137; subsidized, 170

AFDC: families in foster care, 140

Africa: need for child care facilities in, 259. *See also* South Africa

Aggression: peer interaction and expression of, 82; power tactics of siblings, 83

Aggression: effects of day care on, 115-116

Attachment ties: to primary caregiver, 73; to siblings, 74; to family distinguished from those to friends, 74; developmental changes in peer, 74-75; expression of, 75-76; effects of day care on, 115; personality development, 266; primarily to mother, 289, 290, 291

Behavior modification: peers and siblings facilitate, 88

Belgium: trends in births in, 256; trends in number of children in preschool, 256; trends in maternal employment in, 256

British nanny: history of, 218-219

Canada: private day care in, 258

Character disorder children: ex-ternal adversaries of, 189; impulsivity in, 189; little frustration tolerance in, 189; developmental deficiencies of, 190; group living and, 191

Child abuse: parent-child interaction and, 7

Child care institutions: changes in population of, 182; change in nature of, 183; history of, 184; objectives of, 184; pathological defense mechanisms of children in, 185; need for distinct psychotherapy program in, 193

Child caretakers: as common phenomenon, 70; older female siblings, 70; nonsiblings as, 71; conditions producing increased, 71; style of discipline of 72; equity in power with, 70, 72; effects on, 72; and effects on recipient, 72-73; for absent parents, 88-89; synergistic effects with parents, 90; description of societies using, 216, 217; and 5-7 year developmental period, 217; schooling and decreasing age of, 217-218, 231. *See also* Childrearing

Childhood: history of, 292-293; lamentation of discovery of, 292

Childrearing: and family, 3; effect of social changes on family and, 3; as basic family function, 13-14; and socialization, 18; relative importance of socialization and, 18; family mediation with environment and, 21; transfer to nonfamilial institutions, 27; synergistic interactions of systems and, 28; generational changes in, 40; in black families, 50; parental part-time work and, 61; future trends in, 122-123; bias in issues of, 181, 182; universalities in, 210; difficulties in pancultural approach to study of, 210; solution to pancultural approach to study of, 210; effect of economy on goals of, 211; grandparents and, 213; restrictions on individual differences and sibling, 224; sibling, 231; and family alternatives, 291

--supplementary: hands-off policy of grandparents, 42; percent of families using, 48; effects of relative, 48-49; demographics of, 50; rights and duties of kin performing, 51; consequences of, 51; of children of adolescent parents, 58-59; and maternal employment, 60; increasing need for, 60; empty nest and, 61; family characteristics increasing, 61-62; history of, 253-254; widespread use of, 265; and mitigation of parent-child conflicts, 267; effects of, 268; social changes and use of, 268; desirability of, 283. See also Multiple caretakers

Children's mental hospitals: importance of length of stay in, 186

Cognitive development: peer interaction and decrease of egocentrism, 77; effects of peer interactions on, 77-78; interactions with older peers and, 78; fantasy play and, 78; effects of day care on, 114

Communal living: and mother-child attachments, 290-291; childrearing behaviors in, 291

Compensatory masculinity: and paternal salience, 226; and glorification of warfare, 226; and juvenile delinquency, 226

Concern for children in placement project: analysis of, 172

Constancy: in human love, 295

Crowding: and severity of aggression training, 224

Cuba: central control of day care in, 261; stress of academic subjects in day care in, 261

Cultural complexity: and childhood egoism, 229, 231

Day care: ambivalence toward, 101; family inadequacy and history of, 101, 102; family-weakening implications of, 102; in times of emergencies, 102; and family inadequacy, 103; federal policy toward, 103; attitudes impeding acceptance of, 104; as personal service system, 104; types of, 106; auspices of, 106-107; for-profit, 107; not-for-profit, 107; rationales for parent involvement in, 111-113; as a family support system, 113-114; effects on family, 116, 117-118; effects on work, 119; work effects on, 119-120; cultural effects on, 120; effects on culture, 121; as social utility, 123; quality of, 123-124; implications for structuring of, 196

--center-based: advantages of, 108; disadvantages of, 108; emphasis on control in, 108; group size and nurturance in, 109; race differences in desired curricula of, 109; age-integration in, 109-110

--family: most used system, 110; types of, 110; strengths of, 110-111; disadvantages of, 111

Diagnosis: difficulty in children's, 186

Divorce: and living arrangements of children, 55; and

child care involvement of kin, 56-57; remarriage and expansion of kin after, 57

Elderly: in post-industrial societies, 297

Equal rights for women: lacking, 246, 252; gaining, 247

Ethiopia: finding of first family in, 207

Family: and social changes, 3; defined, 4-6 passim, 241, 287; as solution to social problems, 4; critique of definitions, 4-5; systems approach to, 6, 20, 27; cybernetic characteristics of, 6; and economic status, 8; and political system, 8; and complexity of suprasystem, 8; function of and adaptation in, 9; and perceptions of external information, 10; as semi-open system, 11; and environmental feedback, 11-12; and adjustment to stress, 12; and socialization function, 18; mobility, 23; concern about, 23; erosion of power of, 27; within suprasystem, 27-28; myth of extended, 33; current percent of extended, 33-34; and cross-generation help, 34; functions of, 121; types needing foster care, 139-140; time spent in infant care, 213; as an open system, 240; as a human eco-system, 240; and the world future, 241; predicted demise of, 289; passions of life in, 289; social experiments with, 289; as enemy of personal and social progress, 301; and sexual equality, 301; reaffirmation of the future of, 302

--Asian American: characteristics of, 53; extended family patterns in, 53

--black: extensive network in, 49-50; nonmaternal parenting in, 50; swapping in, 50

--fertility: attitudes toward, 14; and family characteristics, 14-15

foster: descriptions of, 138; money to, 142; reasons for attrition of, 143; burnout of, 143; description of, 143; quality of, 143; qualities of successful, 144; single parent, 144; rights of, 144; training of, 144, 145; ambiguous role of, 145; as psychological parents, 174

Italian American: strong kin network of, 54

--Jewish American: close kin ties in, 54; Holocaust generation of, 54-55; childrearing in, 55

--matrilocal: described, 212; Ashanti infants parented by kin in, 213; and feminine identification in males, 227

--Mexican American: characteristics of, 52

--Native American: diversity in, 53; role of extended family in, 53-54

--nuclear: idealized, 4, 22; and adaptation to social change, 22; as most common form, 33; and extensive kin contact, 34; lack of isolated, 41; role of grandparents and autonomy of, 61; alternatives to, 121; proportion of all families, 212; transition to early childhood in, 222; attention-seeking of first borns in, 222; and sex-typing, 223; and aggression training, 224; as product of rapid change, 228; shift in traditional roles of, 287; oppression in, 288; disappointment in, 299

--nurturance: and child development, 15; defined, 16; parental role in, 16-17; outside of family, 17, 28; and family economic condition, 18; as major family function, 28

--patrilocal: described, 212; Arunta infants parented by kin in, 213

--planning: in United States, 243; in Guatemala, 243; acceptance in third world, 244; and infant mortality and morbidity, 245-246; and abortion, 246

--Puerto Rican: characteristics of, 52; migration and changes in, 53

--single-parent: changes in numbers of, 105

Father absence: and compensatory masculinity, 226; in infancy, 226; in matrilocal cultures, 227

Federal Republic of Germany: child care centers in, 255

Field-dependence: characteristics of, 225

Firewood: barren land and the cutting of, 250

France: social utility of preschool in, 255

Foster care: defined, 131, 133; standards for, 131; number of children in, 132; concerns about, 132; as replacement for institutionalized care, 133; normalizing aspect of, 134; distinguished from adoption, 134; classification of children in, 136; numbers of infants in, 137; characteristics of teenagers in, 137; numbers of Native American children in, 138; types of families needing, 139-140; effects of heavy caseloads in, 141-142; age of foster mother and, 147; use of contracts in, 147; preventive services and, 149-153 *passim*; as easy solution, 150; parental visitation and adjustment in, 153-154; parental visitation

and discharge rate from, 154; termination of parental rights and, 155; effects in cognitive development of, 159-160; effects on psychological adjustment of, 160, 161; status changes in, 162; reasons for discharge from, 164; rate of infant discharge from, 165; specific goals for reunion after, 166-167; agency contacts with parents of children in, 167; advocacy for termination from, 167; in-home services during, 172; goal-oriented case management of, 175; advantages of, 183; decline in, 184

--permanent: and rights over child, 135; planning for, 168; value of, 168; The Oregon Project of, 168; and child's well-being, 169; Aggressive Adoption program of, 170; concerns about, 171

--placement: age/sex pattern in, 137; by public agencies, 140; by private agencies, 141; casework factors in successful, 146; criteria for, 147-148; parental inadequacy and, 152-153; numbers of, 155; alternatives in, 164; reasons for, 164; antifamily bias in, 174

--specialized: need for skilled parents in, 135, 157; numbers of teenagers in, 137; as new function of, 175

Foster Care Review: procedures of, 171

Free Home Movement: 134

Ghana: voluntary kin fostering in, 215

Grandmothers: role of, 41, 47; role strain and conflict over childrearing in, 51

Grandparents: current percent of, 35; 19th century functions of, 36; and acculturation, 36,

37; as custodians of family style, 36; 20th century role of, 37, 38; interring, 37; and family stability, 38; grandchildren and familial authority of, 38; typology of roles of, 39-40; generational changes in child-rearing in, 40; child care by, 41; economic aid from, 41; household help from, 41; satis-factions of, 41-42, meaning of role of, 42-43, 46; social class and role of, 44; attitudes toward, 44-45; relationships with grandchildren, 45, 47; visitation rights of, 58; of children of adolescent parents, 58-59; childrearing role of, 213; role in black families, 214; role in Oriental and Poly-nesian families, 214

Group living: advantages and disadvantages of, 190-191; peer support and criticism in, 191; and reactive children, 191; and character disorder children, 191; creativity in, 191

Guardian ad litem: recom-mendations for, 173

Guardianship: and rights over child, 135; agency, 142

Guatemala: family planning in, 243; natural materials used in housing in, 250; failure of housing experts in, 250

Hawaiian-American family: sib-care and resiliance in, 224

Human behavioral environment: defined, 240; helping people and knowledge of, 249

Human constructed environment: defined, 240; economic sector of, 251; schools provided by, 252; group child care evolved from, 253

Human ecological system: de-scription of model of, 240; im-portance of interplay of as-pects of, 249

Individualism: and community welfare, 24; pathology of, 24-25; and marriage, 25; and macroenvironment, 25; as alienation, 25; results of, 26; results of strivings toward, 299, 300

Infancy: long period of human, 208, 265; social order inter-woven with, 296-297

International migration: and brain drain, 251

Italy: museum of humble things started in, 257

Japan: family life and sibling nurturance in, 223-224; pref-erence in day care for working mothers in, 259; maternal domination in, 290; old age in, 297

Kalahari Desert: non-maternal care in societies in the, 216; play groups in societies in the, 216

Kenya: child caretaking in, 71; health care in, 247; women's well in, 250; child care centers in, 259-260

Kibbutz: child caretaking in, 71, 72; structural changes in, 269; definition of, 269; separate children's residence in, 270; diffusion of identification in children of, 275; multigenera-tional units in, 280; con-sistency in, 280; continuity in, 280; and heightened peer at-tachment, 289

--children: negative personality characteristics of, 281; and in-timacy, 281; intellectual growth in, 281; ego develop-ment in, 281, 282; parental identification in, 282; super-ego of, 282; cooperation in, 282; adjustment of, 282; career ambitions of, 282; anx-iety in, 283; psychosomatic

disorders in, 283; response styles of, 283
--classical childrearing: infant house of, 271; toddler house of, 271, 273; stimulation of infants in, 271; parenting in, 272; socialization of child in, 272; parental time with toddlers in, 274; peer group socialization of toddlers in, 274; peer group nurturance of toddlers in, 274; importance of group in, 276; collective superego in, 277, 279, 281; parental contact with school-aged children in, 277; adult influences on adolescents in, 277; relative importance of adults in, 277-278; youth society in, 279; Weltanschauug in, 279
--family: description of, 269-270; sleeping arrangements of, 271
--teacher: functions of kindergarten, 275; modeling of kindergarten, 275; influence in primary school of, 276
Language development: and peer interactions, 80; and family size, 80
Lanham Act: 102-103
Latin America: class distinction in child care in, 260. See also Latin countries
Latin countries: compadrazgo in, 216; godparenthood in, 216
Maternal employment: and family adaptation, 9; and mother-infant bond, 17; historical view of, 23; and Tax Reform Bill, 60; and childcare by relatives, 60; changes in numbers of, 105; day care effects on, 118
Maternal responses: evoked by infant, 293
Metapelet: described, 272; duties of, 272; and socialization

of child, 272, 273; toddler training and, 273; functions in kindergarten, 275; functions in primary school, 276
Mexico: housing in, 249. See also Family
Milieu therapy: defined, 192; and allegiance to reality demands, 193
Mondale-Brademas Act: 102
Moral judgment: and peer interactions, 85
Mother-child relationship: responsibility for adult life in, 296. See also Attachment ties
Multiple caretakers: patterns of caretaker-infant interaction among, 219; sex differences in care patterns among, 220; infant indulgence among, 220; attachment behaviors to, 220; sex differences in attachment behaviors to, 221; and stranger anxiety, 221; and accelerated psychomotor development, 221-222; and transition to early childhood, 222; and attention-seeking, 222; and sex typing, 223; and aggression training, 224; and cognitive style, 225; and social behavior in boys and girls, 231-232. See also Childrearing--supplementary
National Foster Parents Association: 144
Native American: children in foster care, 138. See also Family
Natural environment: defined, 240; as a finite resource, 242; and available for crop production, 242; and energy's effects on families, 243
Netherlands: psychohygienic aims of day care in, 256
Neurotic children: nature of deviance in, 187-188; inner pathology in, 188; pervasive per-

sonality disturbance in, 188; obedience and rebellion in, 188

Nigeria: parental mediation of change in, 227-228

Nurturance: socio-cultural influences on, 287. *See also* Family

Nutritional status: three environments linked to, 247

Open system: defined, 240

Parental goals: universal, 210-211; effect of economy on, 211; variables affecting, 230

Parental rejection: and household composition, 225; and paternal availability, 225

Parental role: defined, 35; and child's development, 69; distinguished from sibling and peer roles, 70; effects of siblings and peers on, 90-91

Parent-child interaction: child's contribution to, 266-267; children's temperament and, 267

Parenting: ethnocentric view of, 265; distinguished from interpersonal interactions, 267; sociological aspects of, 268; psychoanalytic aspects of, 268

Parent-surrogates: in industrialized, urbanized cultures, 214, 230

Peer acceptance: and social skills, 87; and adjustment, 87; and adult mental health, 87

Peer tutoring: and low achievers, 79; benefits to tutors, 79; factors associated with successful, 79

People's Republic of China: grandparents as caretakers in, 214; crop production in, 242-243; family planning in, 244-245; equal rights for women in, 247; health care in, 247; nutrition in, 248; housing in, 249-250; compulsory school attendance in, 253; government responsibility for child care in, 260; docile attitude of children in, 260

Physical development: effects of day care on, 116

Placement: described, 183

Placing Out Program: 134

Play: functions of, 78; and role-taking ability, 78

Poland: nurseries in, 255; kindergartens in, 255

Polynesia: adoptions in, 214-215; fosterage in, 215

Population explosion: severity in less developed countries, 243; and health care, 247

Preindustrial communities: accelerated psychomotor development in, 221-222; constraints on childrearing goals in, 230; continuity in socialization in, 230; population growth in, 245; nutrition in, 248; malnutrition in childbearing-aged women in, 248; aid for food production in, 248-249; schooling in, 252-253; schooling and child labor in, 253; child care centers in, 259

Prosocial behavior: 209; and early nurturant behavior, 223; in children, 231

Psychocultural research: model for, 208

Psychological parent: defined, 148; 174

Psychotherapy: defined, 192. *See also* Child care institutions

Public policy: effects on families, 241; effects on schooling, 252

Rapprochement: 294

Reactive children: no inner pathology in, 187; adaptivity of aggression in, 187; learned acting out in, 187; group living and, 191

Reciprocity: and parent-child interactions, 7; between family and suprasystem, 7-8; and socialization function, 20

Residential treatment center: for problem children, 182-183; purposes of, 183; as substitute for mental hospital, 186; integrated therapeutic program in, 193; importance of all staff levels in, 194; importance of child care person in, 194-195; need for intense adult relationships in, 195; subgrouping in, 196; compactness in, 197; heterogeneity in, 197-198; homogeneous grouping in, 198; nongradual sexual exposure in, 199; competing staffs in, 200; optimal staff goals in, 201; criteria for placement into, 202-203; therapist's role in placement into, 204; crucial period of transition from, 204; rate of recidivism to, 204-205

Role theory: structural-functional stance of, 35; interactional stance of, 35

Russian collectives: child care-taking in, 71

Samoa: child caretaking in, 72

Schooling: provision by public sector, 252; in industrial countries, 252; sexism and racism in, 252; in developing work, 253

Self-concept: and chumships, 86; in siblings, 86

Sex-role development: peers as role models of, 81; peers responses to, 81; modeling and contrast effects on, 82

Sexual behavior: peers as role models of, 81; with peers, 81

Sexual equality: possible effects of, 232

Single child-care worker: and self-identity seeking, 196

Social Security Act: day care amendments to, 103

Socialization: social class and

strategies of, 19; and locus of control, 19; positive promotion of, 19; child's role in, 20; and family as a system, 20; and rapid social change, 24; defined, 266

Sociobiology: and child care, 209; altruistic behavior and, 209

South Africa: family life of blacks in, 251

Soviet Union: government authority over preschools, 257; preschool curriculum in, 258; experiment in sexual permissiveness and serial monogamy in, 290

Stranger wariness: 293-294

Sweden: government-operated child care programs in, 256; objectives of child centres in, 256

Trigenerational enmeshment: 59

United Kingdom: government operated day care in, 258. See also British nanny

United States: child care in, 207; egoism in children in, 229; agriculture in, 242; family planning in, 243; European industrial system adapted in, 252

Urbanization: and disorganized child care, 228; and maternal assertion of power, 229

U.S. Children's Bureau: funding of research by, 177

Value acquisition in peer groups, 83-84; in adolescence, 84; concordance of adult and peer values, 84

Women's workload: responsibility training and, 211; altruistic behavior and, 211-212; egoistic behavior and, 212

Work Incentive Program: provisions for child care, 104

World citizens: duties of, 239-240, 262

WPA: administration of day
care, 102
Yugoslavia: preference for
problem families in day care
in, 258